AS LAW FOR OCR

The Elliott & Quinn Series
for the best start in law

This renowned author team draw on their extensive experience to bring an unbeatable selection of texts that provide total clarity on the core areas of law.

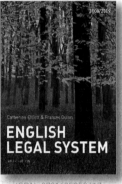

ISBN: 9781405859417

ISBN: 9781405858717

ISBN: 9781405846714

ISBN: 9781405846721

Sourcebooks of carefully selected cases, commentary and articles are also available to accompany books in the series.

The Elliott & Quinn Series is supported by extended companion websites that include regular updates to the law and a range of resources from interactive questions, exam advice and weblinks, for students to use throughout their course.

For further information or to order these books, please visit:
www.pearsoned.co.uk/law

PEARSON
Longman

AS LAW FOR OCR

Catherine Elliott and
Frances Quinn

PEARSON
Longman

Harlow, England • London • New York • Boston • San Francisco • Toronto
Sydney • Tokyo • Singapore • Hong Kong • Seoul • Taipei • New Delhi
Cape Town • Madrid • Mexico City • Amsterdam • Munich • Paris • Milan

Pearson Education Limited

Edinburgh Gate
Harlow
Essex CM20 2JE
England

and Associated Companies throughout the world

Visit us on the World Wide Web at:
www.pearsoned.co.uk

_____

First published 2008

ISBN: 978-1-4058-5884-7

British Library Cataloguing-in-Publication Data
A catalogue record for this book is available from the British Library

Library of Congress Cataloging-in-Publication Data
Elliott, Catherine, 1966–
    As law for OCR / Catherine Illiott and Frances Quinn.
        p.   cm.
    Includes bibliographical references and index.
    ISBN 978-1-4058-5884-7 (pbk.)
    1. Justice, Administration of—Great Britain—Problems, exercises, etc.
2. Law—Great Britain—Sources—Problems, exercises, etc.   3. Law—Great
Britain—Examinations—Study guides.   I. Quinn, Frances.   II. Title.
    KD663.E448 2008
    347.42–dc22
                                                2008009683

10 9 8 7 6 5 4 3 2 1
11 10 09 08

Typeset in 9.5/12.5pt Stone Serif by 35
Printed and bound by Ashford Colour Press Ltd. in Gosport

The publisher's policy is to use paper manufactured from sustainable forests.

Brief contents

Detailed contents

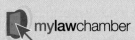 mylawchamber

Visit the *AS Law for OCR* mylawchamber site at
www.mylawchamber.co.uk/elliottocr to access valuable learning material.

FOR STUDENTS

Do you want to give yourself a head start come exam time?

Companion website support
■ Use the multiple choice questions, quizzes and activities to test yourself on each topic.
■ Use our weblinks and further reading suggestions to help you read more widely around the
  subject, and really impress your lecturers.

For more information please contact your local Pearson Education sales representative
or visit **www.mylawchamber.co.uk/elliottocr**

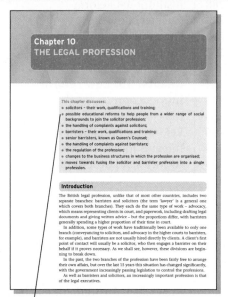

Chapter Outlines at the start of each chapter introduces the content of each chapter.

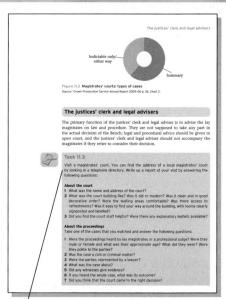

Task boxes provide activities that can be carried out to help you to explore the subject

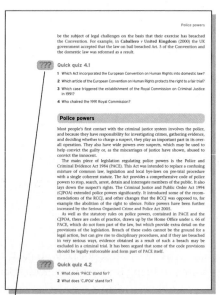

Quick quizzes allow you to test your knowledge and understanding of the law.

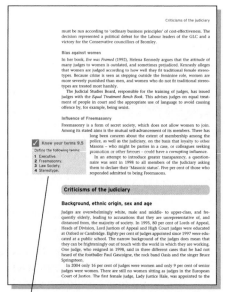

Know your terms boxes will help you to understand and remember technical legal terms.

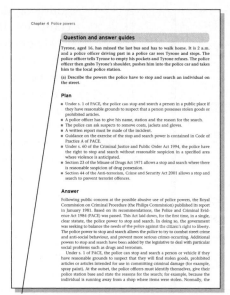

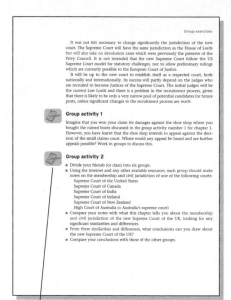

Exam questions and answer guides placed at the end of each chapter aid your exam preparations and provide useful advice on answering exam questions.

Group Activities give you the opportunity to compare notes with your fellow students on key issues.

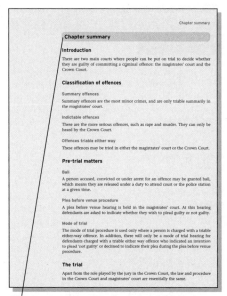

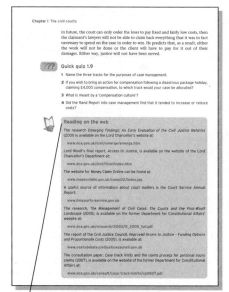

Chapter summaries provide you with an outline of the main topic areas covered in the chapter to ensure that you have covered all the essential points.

Reading on the web sections direct you to interesting further reading which is available on the internet.

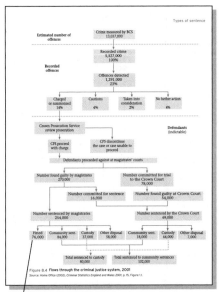

Tables and diagrams are used to highlight complicated legal processes

Sourcebook icons indicate when a case or document is included in *the English Legal System Sourcebook*, and direct you to the relevant page.

Accompanied by a Companion Website, including links to valuable web resources, an online glossary to explain key terms and extra quizzes and exercises

Preface

This book aims to be both interesting and enjoyable to read while at the same time providing excellent preparation for the AS examinations. It follows very closely the AS specifications for the OCR examination board, so that students can rely on this book to help them to be fully prepared for their AS examinations. In every subject there is sufficient depth of coverage, followed by OCR exam questions (or, where these are not available, OCR-style exam questions) and answer guidelines to help students get top grades in their examinations. The book builds on the strengths of previous books written by the authors by offering a clear explanation of the law in plain English. It includes certain features to provide extra help and stimulation for the student, including:

- **Chapter outlines** at the start of each chapter, introducing the student to the content of each chapter.
- **Know your terms** boxes to help students understand and remember some of the technical legal vocabulary that they need to know. There is also a detailed glossary at the back of the book.
- **Tasks** providing possible activities that can be carried out easily to help the student explore the subject further.
- **Quick quizzes** at key stages in each chapter, to give students an opportunity to test their knowledge and understanding of the law.
- **Reading on the web** sections at the end of each chapter. These provide references to interesting material that has been referred to in the chapter and which is available free on the internet.
- **Exam questions and answer guidelines** at the end of each chapter to assist students in preparing for their assessments.
- **Chapter summaries** at the end of each chapter, providing a quick and easy outline of the material covered.

All the chapters are structured so that the material is in a systematic order for the purposes of both learning and revision, and clear subheadings make specific points easy to locate. There is also an appendix at the end of the book which gives useful general advice on answering exam questions in law.

We would like to thank Peter Blood and Elaine Williams for their invaluable assitance in the preparation of the group exercises and exam question and answers in this book. Peter Blood is a barrister and part-time tutor. He has extensive experience of teaching law and is a regular contributor to student law journals. Elaine Williams is a law lecturer with considerable experience in teaching and examining law.

This book is part of a series that has been written by the same authors. The other books in the series which will be of use to students when they progress to A2 level law and the study of law at university are *Criminal Law*, *Contract Law* and *Tort Law*.

We have endeavoured to state the law as at 1 March 2008.

Catherine Elliott
Frances Quinn
London, 2008

Acknowledgements

We are grateful to the following for permission to reproduce copyright material:

Figure 1.1 County Court claims issued by amount of claim, 2004 (with footnote); Figure 1.2 A claim form; Figure 1.3 Small claims – average time from issue to hearing; Figure 1.4 County court claims; Figure 1.5 Claims in the Queen's Division of the High Court; Figure 1.6 Comparison of disposal of 'fast track' cases; Figure 1.7 Trials – average time from issue to trial by claim value; Figure 4.2 Rating of the local police by type of contact; Figure 4.3 Offenders cautioned for indictable offences by offence group. 1991–2001; Figure 6.2 Appellate Courts: Appeals entered, 1995–2004; Figure 6.3 An outline of the court structure in England and Wales; Figure 6.4 The value of Criminal Cases Review Commission; Figure 8.2 Persons sentence to immediate custody, 1950–2001; Figure 8.3 Proportion of persons sentenced to immediate custody for indictable offences by type of court, 1991–2001; Figure 8.4 Flows through the criminal justice system, 2001; Figure 9.1 Court of Appeal: days sat, 2004; Figure 11.1 Justices of the Peace 1995–2004 reproduced with permission of the Controller of HMSO; Figure 3.1 Logo from ABTA – the Travel Association, reproduced with permission; Figure 4.1 The Birmingham Six outside the Old Bailey after their convictions were quashed; Figure 8.1 Wormwood Scrubs, an example of a Victorian prison; Figure 12.1 The Old Bailey Central Criminal Court in London; Figure 12.2 Tracie Andrews, the defendant in R v Andrews (1998), arrives at the High Court in London to find if her Court Appeal bid for freedom has succeeded, after being jailed for life for murdering her fiancé, Lee Harvey, who she claimed was killed by a mystery motorist in a road rage attack; Figure 19.3 Scene outside the Lawrence inquiry, Elephant and castle, London, Copyright PA Archive/PA Photos; Teachers' Guide 2001/2 © Fareen Mahar; Figure 15.1 Criminal Defence Service (Advice and Assistance) Act 2001; Crown copyright reproduced with permission of the Controller of HMSO; Figure 3.1 Logo from ABTA – the Travel Association, reproduced with permission; Figure 4.1 The Birmingham Six outside the Old Bailey after their convictions were quashed; Figure 5.2 Crown Court caseload; Figure 11.3 Magistrate's Courts – type of cases from Crown Prosecution Service Annual Report 2005/6; Figure 6.1 The Criminal Cases Review Commission's offices in Alpha Tower, Birmingham © Roy Peters Photography, reproduced with permission; Figure 8.1 Wormwood Scrubs, an example of a Victorian prison; Figure 12.1 The Old Bailey, the Central Criminal Court in London; Figure 12.2 Tracie Andrews, the defendant in R v Andrews (1998), arrives at the High Court in London to find if her Court Appeal bid for freedom has succeeded, after being jailed for life for murdering her fiancé, Lee Harvey, who she claimed was killed by a mystery motorist in a road rage attack; Figure 19.3 Scene outside the Lawrence inquiry, Elephant and Castle, London,

Copyright PA Archive/Pa Photos; Figure 10.1 Growth in the numbers of solicitors with practising certificates, 1950–2003; Figure 10.2 My Hero, My Solicitor, © The Law Society; Figure 10.3 One of the dining rooms of the Inns of Court, Masters of the Bench of the Honourable Society of Grays Inn, with permission Figure 11.2 from F. Mahar and M. J. Duffy, AQA General Certificate of Education Law Teachers' Guide 2001/2 © Fareen Mahar; Figure 13.1 The logo of the Community Legal Service from Legal Services Commission. Community Legal Advice; Figure 15.2 Houses of Parliament, © Education Service, Houses of Parliament; Figure 19.1 from Remember When, The Newspaper Archive. The News of the World, 23 July, 2000. © NI Syndication, London, 2008; Figure 19.2 Victoria Climbie from Rex Features Ltd, with permission;

In some instances we have been unable to trace the owners of copyright material, and we would appreciate any information that would enable us to do so.

List of figures

Table of cases

Table of legislation

Table of statutory instruments

Unit 1

THE ENGLISH LEGAL SYSTEM

This Unit looks at core aspects of the English legal system. It starts by exploring the civil court system and the alternatives to using that court system for people in civil disputes. It then considers the criminal system, starting with police powers and then moving on to the criminal court system and the sentencing powers of the courts. The Unit then examines the key players in the English legal system: the judges, barristers, solicitors, magistrates and jurors. It concludes by looking at how people pay for these legal services, either through private funding or with the help of state funding.

Chapter 1
THE CIVIL COURTS

This chapter discusses:

- the division between civil and criminal courts;
- an introduction to the civil justice system;
- the civil courts;
- the requirement that the courts deal with cases 'justly';
- civil procedure;
- problems with the civil court system.

Civil or criminal?

The laws that have developed in the English legal system can be divided between civil and criminal laws and often separate courts are responsible for civil and criminal matters. A crime is a wrong which is punished by the state; in most cases, the parties in the case are the wrongdoer and the state (called the Crown for these purposes), and the primary aim is to punish the wrongdoer. By contrast, a civil action is between the wrongdoer and a potential victim and the aim is to compensate the victim for the harm done. There are cases in which the same incident may give rise to both criminal and civil proceedings. An example would be a car accident, in which the driver might be prosecuted by the state for dangerous driving, and sued by the victim for the injuries caused.

This chapter looks at the civil courts which are responsible for dealing with civil legal issues. Chapter 5 looks at the criminal courts.

The civil justice system

The civil justice system is designed to sort out disputes between individuals or organisations. One party, known as the claimant, sues the other, called the defendant, usually for money they claim is owed or for compensation for a harm to their interests. Typical examples might be the victim of a car accident suing the driver of the car for compensation, or one business suing another for payment due on goods supplied. The burden of proof is usually on the claimant, who must prove his or her case on a balance of probabilities – that it is more likely than not. This is a lower standard of proof than the 'beyond reasonable doubt' test used by the criminal courts and, for this reason, it is possible to be acquitted of a criminal charge yet still be found to have breached the civil law. This happened to the celebrity O. J. Simpson in America who, having been acquitted by the criminal courts of murdering his ex-wife and her friend, was successfully sued in the civil courts for damages by the victim's family.

Major changes have been made to the civil justice system in recent years. After the Civil Justice Review of 1988, reforms were made by the Courts and Legal Services Act 1990. Following continued criticism of the civil justice system, the previous Conservative government ten years later appointed Lord Woolf to carry out an in-depth review of the civil justice system. Lord Woolf's inquiry was the sixty-third such review in a hundred years. Lord Woolf made far-reaching recom-

sourcebook p. 271 → mendations in his report, *Access to Justice*, which was published in 1996. As with the Civil Justice Review, his aim was to reduce the cost, delay and complexity of the system and increase access to justice. Most of his recommendations were implemented in April 1999.

The civil courts

There are two main civil courts which hear civil cases at first instance. These are the county courts and the High Court. The county courts hear the cases where less money is involved, whereas the High Court hears the bigger financial cases. Thus, most civil cases start in the county court. They start in the High Court only if the claimant expects to recover more than £15,000, or £50,000 if it is a personal injury case.

There are currently around 300 county courts. The High Court is divided into three divisions: the Queen's Bench Division, the Family Division and the Chancery Division. The Family Division hears cases concerning marriage, children and the family, such as divorce, adoption and wills. The Chancery Division deals with matters of finance and property, such as tax and bankruptcy. The Queen's Bench Division is the biggest of the three, with the most varied jurisdiction. The major part of its work is handling those contract and tort cases which are unsuitable for the county courts. Sitting as the Divisional Court of the Queen's Bench, its judges also hear certain criminal appeals and applications for judicial review. High Court judges usually sit alone, but the Divisional Court is so important that two or three judges sit together.

Trials in the High Court are heard either in London or in one of the 26 provincial trial centres. In theory, they are all presided over by High Court judges, but in fact there are not enough High Court judges to cope with the case load. Some cases, therefore, have to be dealt with by circuit judges and others by barristers sitting as part-time, temporary, deputy judges.

Although most civil cases are dealt with by either the county courts or the High Court, magistrates' courts have a limited civil jurisdiction, and some types of cases are tried by tribunals.

Quick quiz 1.1

1 What is the burden of proof in civil cases?

2 What major piece of legislation followed the Civil Justice Review of 1988?

3 What is the name of Lord Woolf's final report on the civil justice system?

4 Name the three divisions of the High Court.

Dealing with cases 'justly'

On 26 April 1999 new Civil Procedure Rules and accompanying Practice Directions came into force. These rules constitute the most fundamental reform of the civil justice system in the twentieth century, introducing the main recommendations of Lord Woolf in his final report, *Access to Justice*. He described his proposals as providing 'a new landscape for civil justice for the twenty-first century'. The general approach of Lord Woolf is reflected in his statement: 'If "time and money are no object" was the right approach in the past, then it certainly is not today. Both lawyers and judges, in making decisions as to the conduct of litigation, must take into account more than they do at present, questions of cost and time and the means of the parties.' Lord Woolf has said that the reforms should lead to a reduction in legal bills by as much as 75 per cent, though it might also mean that some lawyers would lose their livelihoods.

The ultimate goal is to change the litigation culture fundamentally. Thus, the first rule of the new Civil Procedure Rules lays down an overriding objective which is to underpin the whole system. This is that the rules should enable the courts to deal with cases 'justly'. This objective prevails over all other rules in case of a conflict. The parties and their legal representatives are expected to assist the judges in achieving this objective. The Woolf Report heavily criticised practitioners, who were accused of manipulating the old system for their own convenience and causing delay and expense to both their clients and the users of the system as a whole. Lord Woolf felt that a change in attitude among the lawyers was vital for the new rules to succeed. According to r. 1.1(2):

> *'Dealing with a case justly includes, so far as is practicable –*
> *a. ensuring that the parties are on an equal footing;*
> *b. saving expense;*
> *c. dealing with the case in ways which are proportionate –*
>   *i.   to the amount of money involved;*
>   *ii. to the importance of the case;*
>   *iii. to the complexity of the issues; and*
>   *iv. to the financial position of each party;*
> *d. ensuring that it is dealt with expeditiously and fairly; and*
> *e. allotting to it an appropriate share of the Court's resources, while taking into account the need to allot resources to other cases.'*

The emphasis of the new rules is on avoiding litigation through pre-trial settlements. Litigation is to be viewed as a last resort, with the court having a continuing obligation to encourage and facilitate settlement. Lord Woolf had observed that it was strange that, although the majority of disputes ended in settlement, the old rules had been directed mainly towards preparation for trial. Thus, the new rules put a greater emphasis on preparing cases for settlement rather than a trial.

The new approach to civil procedure will now be examined in more detail.

Quick quiz 1.2

1 Do the new rules of procedure prioritise preparation for a settlement or for a trial?

2 When did the new Civil Procedure Rules come into force?

3 What is the overriding objective contained in the first rule of the new Civil Procedure Rules?

4 Is the cost of bringing legal proceedings relevant in deciding how to deal with a case justly?

Civil procedure

Before proceedings are commenced, claimants should send a letter to the defendants warning them that they are considering bringing legal proceedings. Almost all proceedings then start with the same document, called a claim form. The claim form informs the defendant that an action is being brought against them. When claimants are making a claim for money, they must provide a statement as to the value of the claim in the claim form.

For non-personal injury actions, a claim may be started in the High Court where the claimant expects to recover more than £15,000 (this limit is expected to be raised to £50,000 in the near future). For personal injury actions, a claim can be started in the High Court only where the claimant expects to recover at least £50,000 for pain, suffering and loss of amenity.

The claim form is served on the defendant to a case. The methods of service have been liberalised to reflect modern modes of communication, including the use of fax and emails. Service will normally be carried out by the court through postage by first class post, unless a party notifies the court that they will serve the documents. Defendants must acknowledge service. The claimant (known before 1999 as the plaintiff) must then serve on the defendant the particulars of claim.

The defendant should respond within 14 days by filing either an acknowledgement of service or a defence with the court. If the defendant fails to do either of these within that period of time, the claimant can enter judgment in default against the defendant.

If the defendant files a defence, the court will serve an allocation questionnaire on each party. This is designed to enable the court to allocate each claim to one of the three tracks discussed at p. 9.

The disclosure procedures are then followed, under which the parties are required to disclose the documents on which they intend to rely and also the documents which go against their case. Either party may seek more details from the other, through a 'request for information'. If the case is not settled out of court, the case proceeds to trial.

The different formal documents are described as the statement of case. All statements of case must be verified by a statement of truth. This is a statement signed by the claimant (or his/her legal representative) in the following words: 'I believe that the facts stated in these particulars of claim are true.' The purpose of the statement of case is to prevent parties from putting in facts for purely tactical purposes which they have no intention of relying upon. If a party makes a false statement in a statement of case verified by a statement of truth, the party will be guilty of contempt of court.

Either party can apply for a summary judgment on the ground that the claim or defence has no real prospect of success. The court can also reach this conclusion on its own initiative. At any stage of the proceedings the parties can enter into 'without prejudice' negotiations to try and settle the dispute out of court. The without prejudice rule makes all negotiations genuinely aimed at settlement, whether oral or in writing, inadmissible in evidence at any subsequent trial. The rule lets litigants make whatever concessions or admissions are necessary to achieve a compromise, without fear of these being held against them if negotiations break down and the case goes to court. It is hoped that this will help and encourage the parties to settle their disputes early.

Task 1.3

Look at the diagram and answer the questions that follow.

Questions

1 In 2004, which types of cases were the most likely to be heard by the county court?

2 Which types of cases were least likely to be heard by the county court?

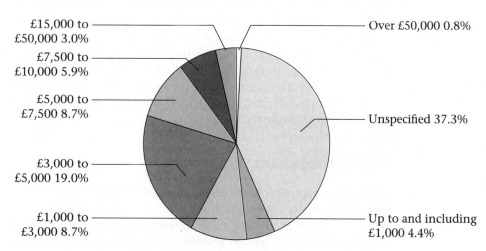

Figure 1.1 **County Court claims issued by amount of claim, 2004**[1]

1. Figures are based on three months' sample data from selected county courts

Source: K. Dibdin, A. Sealy and S. Aktar, *Judicial Statistics Annual Report 2004*, p. 48.

Pre-action protocols

The pre-trial procedure is perhaps the most important area of the civil process, since few civil cases actually come to trial. To push the parties into behaving reasonably during the pre-trial stage, Lord Woolf recommended the development of pre-action protocols to lay down a code of conduct for this stage of the proceedings. The pre-action protocols aim to encourage:

- more pre-action contact between the parties;
- an earlier and fuller exchange of information;
- improved pre-action investigation;
- a settlement before proceedings have commenced.

They strive to achieve this through establishing a timetable for the exchange of information, by setting standards for the content of correspondence and by providing schedules of documents that should be disclosed, along with a mechanism for agreeing a single joint expert. The pre-action protocols seek to encourage a culture of openness between the parties. This should lead to the parties being better informed as to the merits of their case so that they will be in a position to settle cases fairly, and thereby reduce the need for litigation. Compliance with a pre-action protocol is not compulsory, but if a party unreasonably refuses to comply, then this can be taken into account when the court makes orders for costs.

Alternative dispute resolution

At various stages in a dispute's history, the court will actively promote settlement by alternative dispute resolution (ADR). For a detailed discussion of ADR in the English legal system, see Chapter 3. There is a general statement in the new rules that the court's duty to further the overriding objective by active case management includes both encouraging the parties to use an alternative dispute resolution procedure (if the court considers that appropriate) and facilitating the use of that procedure. Also, when filling in the allocation questionnaire, the parties can request a one-month stay of proceedings while they try to settle the case by ADR or other means. The parties will have to show that they genuinely attempted to resolve their dispute through ADR and have not just paid lip-service to the idea, as has been the tendency in the past.

Case management

This is the most significant innovation of the 1999 reforms. Case management means that the court will be the active manager of the litigation. The main aim of this approach is to bring cases to trial quickly and efficiently. Traditionally, it has been left to the parties and their lawyers to manage the cases. The current rules firmly place the management of a case in the hands of the judges, with r. 1.4 emphasising that the court's duty is to take a proactive role in the management of each case.

Once proceedings have commenced, the court's powers of case management will be triggered by the filing of a defence. When the defence has been filed and case management has started, the parties are on a moving train, trial dates will be fixed and will be difficult to postpone, and litigants will not normally be able to slow down or stop the case unless they settle. The court first needs to allocate the case to one of the three tracks – the small claims track, the fast track or the multi-track – which will determine the future conduct of the proceedings. To determine which is the appropriate track, the court will serve an allocation questionnaire on each party. The answers to this questionnaire will form the basis for deciding the appropriate track.

Quick quiz 1.4

1 Before 1999, a person bringing an action was called a plaintiff. What is such a person called now?

2 What is the name of the document used to commence civil proceedings?

3 If a person wishes to bring an action for £26,000 compensation for a head injury, which court will normally hear the case?

4 What happens if a party does not comply with a pre-action protocol?

5 Under the system of case management, who controls the progress of a case through the civil justice system?

The three tracks

The court allocates the case to the most appropriate track, depending primarily on the financial value of the claim, but other factors that can be taken into account include the case's importance and complexity. Normally:

- small claims track cases deal with actions with a value of less than £5,000 (or £1,000 for personal injury cases);
- fast-track cases deal with actions of a value between £5,000 and £15,000;
- multi-track cases deal with actions with a value higher than £15,000.

The three tracks will now be considered in turn.

The small claims track

The handling of small claims was largely unchanged by the Woolf reforms. In the small claims track, directions will be issued for each case providing a date for the hearing and an estimate of the hearing time, unless the case requires a preliminary hearing appointment to assist the parties in the conduct of the case. This track was previously known as the small claims court, though it was never actually a separate court, but a procedure used by county courts to deal with relatively small claims. It was introduced in response to a report from the Consumers' Association in 1967 which claimed that county courts were being used primarily as a debt-collection agency for businesses: 89.2 per cent of the summonses were taken out by businesses and only 9 per cent by individuals, who were put off by costs and complexity.

Established in 1973, this special procedure aims to provide a cheap, simple mechanism for resolving small-scale consumer disputes. Disclosure is dispensed with and, if the litigation continues to trial, it is usually held in private rather than in open court. The hearing is simple and informal, with few rules about the admissibility or presentation of evidence. No experts may be used without leave.

It is usually a very quick process, with 60 per cent of hearings taking less than 30 minutes. Costs are limited except where, by consent, a case with a financial value such that it would normally be allocated to the fast track was allocated to the small claims track. The procedure is designed to make it easy for parties to represent themselves without the aid of a lawyer, and state funding for representation is not available. A party can choose to be represented by a lay person, though the party must also attend.

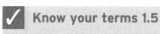

Know your terms 1.5

Define the following terms:

1 Queen's Bench Division.
2 The Woolf Report.
3 Pre-action protocol.
4 Case management.

The fast track

Fast-track cases will normally be dealt with by the county court. Upon allocation to the fast track, the court gives directions for the management of the case, and sets a timetable for the disclosure of documents, the exchange of witness statements, the exchange (and number) of expert reports, and the trial date or a period within which the trial will take place, which will be no more than 30 weeks later (compared to an average of 80 weeks before 1999).

A typical timetable that a court may give under this track is:

- disclosure: 4 weeks;
- exchange of witness statements: 10 weeks;
- exchange of experts' reports: 14 weeks;
- hearing: 30 weeks.

Although the parties can vary certain matters by agreement, such as disclosure or the exchange of witness statements, the rules are quite clear that an application must be made to court if a party wishes to vary the date for the trial.

Under this track the maximum length of the trial is normally one day. The relevant Practice Direction states that the judge will normally have read the papers in the trial bundle and may dispense with an opening address. Witness statements will usually stand as evidence-in-chief. Oral expert evidence will be limited to one expert per party in relation to any expert field and expert evidence will be limited to two expert fields.

In an attempt to keep lawyers' bills down, fixed costs for fast-track trials have been introduced, but the introduction of pre-trial fixed costs has been delayed until additional information is available to inform the development of the revised costs regime. Lord Woolf had recommended that there should be a £2,500 limit on costs for fast-track cases (though clients could enter a written agreement to pay more to their solicitors). Apart from the trial itself, litigants are still committing themselves to open-ended payment by the hour, which Lord Woolf described as being equivalent to handing out a blank cheque. He observed: 'If you and I are having our house repaired, we don't do it on a time and materials basis, because we know it will be a disaster. There is no incentive for the builder to do it in the least time and do it with the most economical materials.'

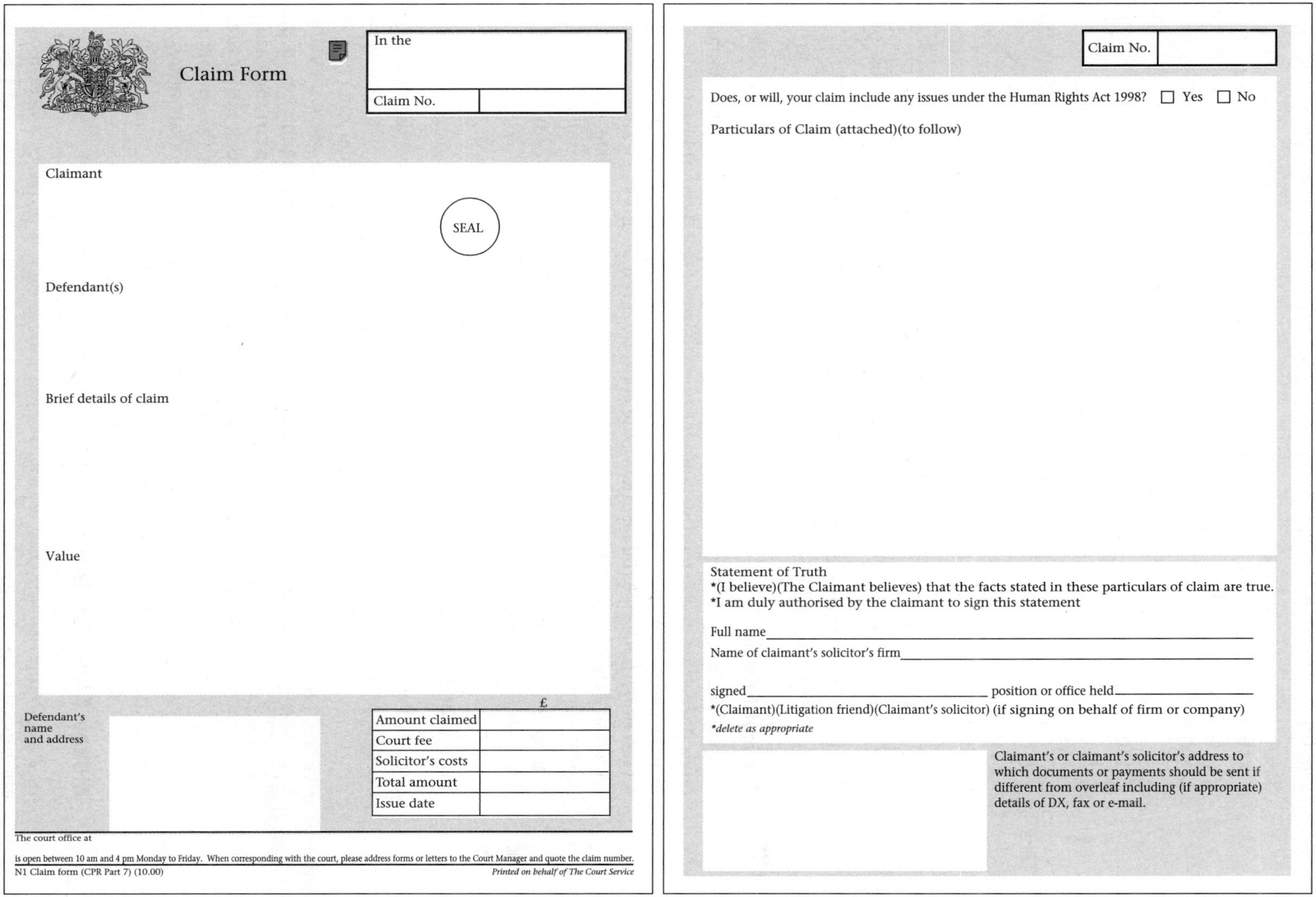

Claim Form

In the

Claim No.

Claimant

Defendant(s)

Brief details of claim

Value

SEAL

	£
Amount claimed	
Court fee	
Solicitor's costs	
Total amount	
Issue date	

Defendant's
name
and address

The court office at

Is open between 10 am and 4 pm Monday to Friday. When corresponding with the court, please address forms or letters to the Court Manager and quote the claim number.

N1 Claim form (CPR Part 7) (10.00)   *Printed on behalf of The Court Service*

Claim No.

Does, or will, your claim include any issues under the Human Rights Act 1998?   ☐ Yes   ☐ No

Particulars of Claim (attached)(to follow)

Statement of Truth

*(I believe)(The Claimant believes) that the facts stated in these particulars of claim are true.

*I am duly authorised by the claimant to sign this statement

Full name _____

Name of claimant's solicitor's firm _____

signed _____   position or office held _____

*(Claimant)(Litigation friend)(Claimant's solicitor) (if signing on behalf of firm or company)

*delete as appropriate

Claimant's or claimant's solicitor's address to
which documents or payments should be sent if
different from overleaf including (if appropriate)
details of DX, fax or e-mail.

Figure 1.2 A claim form

Source: Court Service website at www.mcsi.gov.uk.

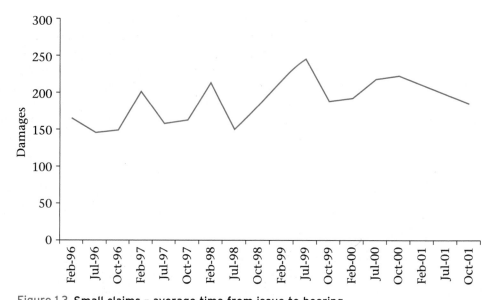

Figure 1.3 Small claims – average time from issue to hearing

Source: Department for Constitutional Affairs (2002), *Civil Justice Reform Evaluation Further Findings*, Figure 12.

The multi-track

Upon allocation to the multi-track, the court can give directions for the management of the case and set a timetable for those steps to be taken. Alternatively, for heavier cases, the court may fix a case management conference or a pre-trial review or both. Unlike the fast track, the court does not at this stage automatically set a trial date or a period within which the trial will take place. Instead, it will fix this as soon as it is practicable to do so. Thus, this track offers individual case management with tailor-made directions according to the needs of the case. Only the High Court hears multi-track cases.

Sanctions

Tough rules on sanctions give the courts stringent powers to enforce the new rules on civil procedure to ensure that litigation is pursued diligently. The two main sanctions are an adverse award of costs, and an order for a case or part of a case to be struck out. These sanctions were available under the old rules, but the novelty of the new regime lies in the commitment to enforce strict compliance. There is an increasing willingness of the courts to manage cases with a stick rather than a carrot. The courts can treat the standards set in the pre-action protocols as the normal approach to pre-action conduct and have the power to penalise parties for non-compliance.

> ✓ **Know your terms 1.6**
>
> Define the following terms:
> 1 Multi-track.
> 2 Fast track.
> 3 Disclosure.
> 4 Sanction.

Money Claim Online

In 2002, Money Claim Online (MCOL) was established. It provides a debt recovery service over the Internet for sums up to £100,000. The debts might be for unpaid goods or services, or rent arrears, for example. Claimants can issue money claims via the internet at **www.moneyclaim.gov.uk**. Fees are paid electronically by debit or credit card. The defence can use the online service to acknowledge service and file a defence. Most debt claims are undefended and if no defence is filed then the claimant can apply online for a judgment and enforcement. The parties can use the website to check the progress of their case, such as whether a defence has been filed. The service is available 24 hours a day, seven days a week. The new service has proved very popular with creditors, who have issued thousands of claims to date using the new service.

Task 1.7

Read the following extract from Lord Woolf's Report, *Access to Justice*, and answer the questions that follow.

The principles

I have identified a number of principles which the civil justice system should meet in order to ensure access to justice. The system should:

(a) be *just* in the results it delivers;
(b) be *fair* in the way it treats litigants;
(c) offer appropriate procedures at a reasonable cost;
(d) deal with cases with reasonable *speed*;
(e) be *understandable* to those who use it;
(f) be *responsive* to the needs of those who use it;
(g) provide as much *certainty* as the nature of particular cases allows; and
(h) be *effective*, adequately resourced and organised.

The basic reforms

The **interim report** set out a blueprint for reform based on a system where the courts with the assistance of litigants would be responsible for the management of cases. I recommended that the courts should have the final responsibility for determining what procedures were suitable for each case; setting realistic timetables; and ensuring that procedures and timetables were complied with.

The recommendations in my final report, together with the new code of rules, form a comprehensive and coherent package for the reform of civil justice. Each contributes to and underpins the others. Their overall effectiveness could be seriously undermined by piecemeal implementation. My overriding concern is to ensure that we have a civil justice system which will meet the needs of the public in the twenty first century.

(Adapted from Lord Woolf's report, *Access to Justice*)

Questions

1 What is the goal that Lord Woolf hopes his reforms will achieve?
2 One of the principles on which Lord Woolf thinks a civil justice system should be based is that it offers 'appropriate procedures at a reasonable cost'. How far do you think the issue of cost should be taken into account when trying to achieve justice?
3 What is meant by an 'interim report'?
4 Lord Woolf was anxious that his reforms should not be undermined by piecemeal implementation. Has this proved to be a problem?

Problems with the civil court system

Out-of-court settlements

The use of pre-action protocols and claimant offers to encourage pre-trial settlements has diverted cases from being litigated in the courts. As a result only 8 per cent of cases listed for trial settle at the trial, while 70 per cent settle much earlier. The reforms put considerable emphasis on the use of out-of-court settlements which can have the advantage of providing a quick end to the dispute, and a reduction in costs. For the claimant, a settlement means they are sure of getting something, and do not have to risk losing the case altogether and probably having to pay the other side's costs as well as their own. But they must weigh this up against the chances of being awarded a better settlement if the case goes to trial and they win. The defendant risks the possibility that they might have won and therefore had to pay nothing, or that they may be paying more than the judge would have awarded had the claimant won the case, against the chance that the claimant wins and is awarded more than the settlement would have cost.

The high number of out-of-court settlements creates injustice, because the parties usually hold very unequal bargaining positions. In the first place, one party might be in a better financial position than the other, and therefore under less pressure to keep costs down by settling quickly.

Secondly, as Galanter's 1984 study revealed, litigants can often be divided into 'one-shotters' and 'repeat players'. One-shotters are individuals involved in litigation for probably the only time in their life, for whom the procedure is unfamiliar and traumatic; the case is very important to them and tends to occupy most of their thoughts while it continues. Repeat players, on the other hand, include companies and businesses (particularly insurance companies), for whom litigation is routine. They are used to working with the law and lawyers and, while they obviously want to win the case for financial reasons, they do not have the same emotional investment in it as the individual one-shotter. Where a repeat player and a one-shotter are on opposing sides – as is often the case in personal injury litigation, where an individual is fighting an insurance company – the repeat player is likely to have the upper hand in out-of-court bargaining.

A third factor was highlighted by Hazel Genn's 1987 study of negotiated settlements of accident claims. She found that having a non-specialist lawyer could seriously prejudice a client's interests when an out-of-court settlement is made. A non-specialist may be unfamiliar with court procedure and reluctant to fight the case in court. They may, therefore, not encourage their client to hold out against an unsatisfactory settlement. Specialist lawyers on the other side may take advantage of this inexperience, putting on pressure for the acceptance of a low settlement. Repeat players are more likely to have access to their own specialist lawyers, whereas, for the one-shotter, finding a suitable lawyer can be something of a lottery, since they have little information on which to base their choice.

Clearly, these factors affect the fairness of out-of-court settlements. In court, the judge can treat the parties as equals, but for out-of-court negotiations one party often has a very obvious advantage.

The government's first evaluation of the new Civil Procedure Rules has found that overall the reforms have been beneficial: *Emerging Findings: an early evaluation of the Civil Justice Reforms* (2001). It seems that cases are settling earlier, rather than at the door of the court. Lawyers and clients are now regarding litigation as a last resort, and making more use of alternative methods of dispute resolution. The pre-action protocols have been a success. Their effect has been to concentrate the minds of defendants and make them deal properly with a claim at the early stages rather than months after the issue of proceedings (conditional fee agreements could also be an explanation for this). While generally cases are being heard more quickly after the issue of the claim, small claims are taking longer. But the picture is not quite as straightforward as it looks. Lawyers know that as soon as they issue the claim form they will lose control of the pace of the negotiations and are going to be locked into timetables and procedures which they may find burdensome as well as costly. There is evidence that lawyers are therefore delaying issuing the claim. It is not yet clear whether litigation has become cheaper. The report quotes practitioners who believe the front-end loading of costs caused by the pre-action protocols means that overall costs have actually gone up.

In their research paper, *More Civil Justice: the impact of the Woolf reforms on pre-action behaviour* (2002), the Law Society and the Civil Justice Council assessed the success of the new pre-action procedures. Most of the respondents were positive about their introduction. In particular, personal injury practitioners and insurers have welcomed the additional information that the protocol requires to be disclosed during the early stages of proceedings, as it facilitates early settlement.

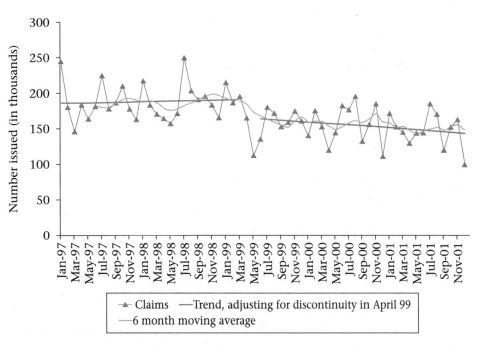

Figure 1.4 **County court claims**

Source: Department for Constitutional Affairs (2002), *Civil Justice Reform Evaluation Further Findings*, Figure 1.

The latest research into the civil justice system, *The Management of Civil Cases: The Courts and the Post-Woolf Landscape* (2005), concludes that the reforms have led to a better litigation culture. They have significantly reduced the amount of litigation going to court from 2.2 million cases in 1997 to 1.5 million cases in 2003. However, costs have increased, they have become front loaded (in other words, more costs are incurred at the earlier stages of the litigation process) and the cost of each case is higher overall.

Small claims track

The small claims procedure is an important part of the civil procedure system, involving around 80,000 actions each year. The procedure is quicker, simpler and cheaper than the full county court process, which is helpful to both litigants and the overworked court system. It gives individuals and small businesses a useful lever against creditors or for consumer complaints. Without it, threats to sue over small amounts would be ignored on the basis that going to court would cost more than the value of the debt or compensation claimed. Public confidence is also increased, by proving that the legal system is not only accessible to the rich and powerful. The academic, John Baldwin, has carried out research into the small claims track, *Lay and Judicial Perspectives on the Expansion of the Small Claims Regime* (2002). He noted that the official statistics show that the recent rises in the small claims limit have not led, as many feared, to the county courts being inundated with new cases. There has been only a slight increase in the number of small claims cases. Most small claims litigants involved in relatively high-value

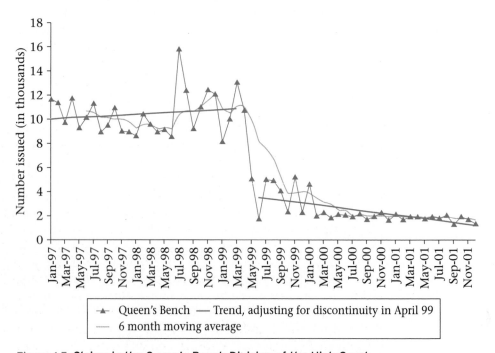

Figure 1.5 Claims in the Queen's Bench Division of the High Court

Source: Department for Constitutional Affairs (2002), *Civil Justice Reform Evaluation Further Findings*, Figure 2.

claims are satisfied with the experience. However, there are long-standing concerns about the small claims procedure, which have not been tackled by the 1999 reforms. Small claims are not necessarily simple claims; they may involve complex and unusual points of law. Is the small claimant entitled to be judged by the law of the land or by speedier, more rough-and-ready concepts of fairness?

The Consumers' Association magazine is of the view that the small claims procedure is not simple enough. It reported in 1986 that the process was still 'quite an ordeal', and the level of formality varied widely. The submissions of both the National Consumer Council and the National Association of Citizens' Advice Bureaux to the Civil Justice Review echoed this feeling. The Civil Justice Review recommended that court forms and leaflets should be simplified. The system is still largely used by small businesses chasing debtors, rather than by the individual consumer for whom it was set up. A consultation paper was issued in 1995 suggesting that, in limited cases, the judge might be given the power to award an additional sum of up to £135 to cover the cost of legal advice and assistance in the preparation of the case. If this reform were to be introduced, it might assist individual consumers to bring their cases.

There are also problems with enforcement. A survey by the old Lord Chancellor's Department in 1986 found that 25 per cent of parties were failing to get the payment owed to them from the defendant following a successful application. A report by the Consumers' Association (November 1997) suggests that many people using the small claims procedure are being denied justice because of slow and inefficient enforcement procedures. The court is not responsible for enforcement, which is left to the winning party to secure. The report found that only a minority of defendants paid up on time and that after six months a substantial minority of people still had not paid their debts. The report's author, Professor John Baldwin, concluded that the enforcement problem was so serious that it threatened to undermine the small claims procedure itself by deterring people from using it.

The government considered raising the financial level of personal injury cases that can be considered by the small claims procedures from £1,000 to £5,000. The Better Regulation Taskforce (an independent advisory body established in sourcebook p. 281 → 1997) published a report *Better Routes to Redress* (2004). This suggested that the government should consider raising the limits for personal injury cases to bring them into line with most other civil claims, which can already be considered by the small claims court when they involve claims of up to £5,000. The Taskforce suggested that the reform would 'increase access to justice for many as it will be less expensive, less adversarial and less stressful'. The government is concerned that procedures and costs should be proportionate to the size of the claim.

At the moment, most personal injury cases are heard under the fast track procedure which means costs can be recovered and lawyers can represent clients on a no-win, no-fee basis. If the financial limits were changed about 70 per cent of personal injury cases would be heard by the small claims procedure. On the small claims track, court costs cannot be recovered and lawyers are not able to represent clients on a no-win, no-fee basis. Litigants would therefore frequently be forced to represent themselves. The Association of Personal Injury Lawyers has argued that personal injury cases are complex and people want and need the help of a lawyer to prepare their case. The person being sued is likely to have been insured and will benefit from the specialist help of the insurers' lawyers.

Baldwin's research (2002) concluded that the informal small claims procedures inevitably involve a sacrifice in the standards of judicial decision making. He questioned whether this could be justified in claims involving more than the existing financial limits.

The Civil Justice Council spent three years looking at the funding of civil claims and how to keep costs in proportion. In 2005 it published its report, *Improved Access to Justice – Funding Options and Proportionate Costs* (2005). It recommends that the small claims track limit for personal injury cases should be retained at £1,000. It considers that the fast track limit for personal injury cases should be increased from £15,000 to £25,000 though parties could opt to have their cases dealt with on this track for claims up to £50,000.

In 2007 the government announced that it no longer intended to raise the small claims limit to £5,000 because this would not be in the interests of consumers. It is, however, considering increasing the fast track limit to £25,000. It is also looking at introducing a streamlined claims process for personal injury claims under £25,000. A consultation paper has been issued on the subject, entitled *Case track limits and the claims process for personal injury claims* (2007).

Compensation culture

There has been some concern that the UK might be developing a compensation culture, which has historically been associated with the US. A compensation culture implies that people with frivolous and unwarranted claims bring cases to court with a view to making easy money. The phenomenon of a more litigious society can be interpreted in two very different ways. It can be seen as a good thing because more people are asserting their rights and obtaining stronger legal protection. At the same time, it can be seen as a bad thing because the law is pushing people into relationships which lack trust and creating confrontational communities.

The government has concluded that the UK does not have an unhealthy compensation culture (accident claims actually fell by 10 per cent in 2004), but the increased number of threats to sue and the resulting fear of being sued is having a negative effect on people's work and behaviour, and this trend needs to be reversed. In 2004 the Lord Chancellor commented:

> 'If you have a genuine claim – where someone else is to blame – you should be able to get compensation from those at fault. This is only fair. The victim or taxpayer shouldn't have to pay out where someone else is to blame. But there is not always someone else to blame. Genuine accidents do happen. People should not be encouraged to always "have a go" however meritless the claim. The perception that there is easy money just waiting to be had – the so-called "compensation culture" – creates very real problems. People become scared of being sued; organizations avoid taking risks and stop perfectly sensible activities. It creates burdens for those handling claims and critically it also undermines genuine claims.'

sourcebook p. 109 → The Compensation Act 2006 contains provisions to encourage the courts to consider whether a successful negligence claim in a particular case might prevent a desirable activity, such as a school trip, from taking place in future.

The government is concerned that the problems relating to a compensation culture are being aggravated by the unscrupulous sales tactics of some claims management companies, which encourage people who have suffered minor personal injuries to bring litigation. Advertisements are frequently broadcast on television asking the viewers if they have suffered an accident in the last three years. A report on the issue, *Better Routes to Redress*, was published in 2004. This recommended that stronger guidelines regarding appropriate advertisements needed to be issued, and that the claims management companies needed to be more carefully regulated. However, it did feel that these companies and advertisements should be allowed to continue, as they helped improve access to legal services by spreading information about the services available and the ways that these could be paid for. Claims management companies are now regulated following the passing of the Compensation Act 2006.

The insurers, Norwich Union, have suggested a radical solution to the compensation culture, of abolishing all claims for under £1,000 (*A Modern Compensation System: moving from concept to reality* (2004)). The Law Society has rejected this suggestion, pointing out that denying people their right to seek compensation for claims under £1,000 would prevent the courts from getting to the root cause of injuries and falsely assumes that a loss of £1,000 is a trivial matter.

The Bar Council is concerned that plans to allow private companies to own law firms (see p. 176) would fuel the move towards a compensation culture, because such companies would seek to stimulate demand for legal services to increase profits. The legal sector could as a result become more commercialised, with franchising, national brand-building and more television advertising.

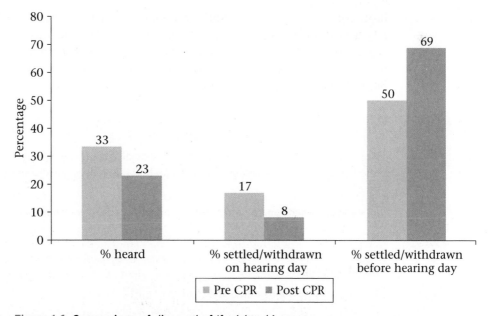

Figure 1.6 Comparison of disposal of 'fast track' cases

Source: Department for Constitutional Affairs (2002), *Civil Justice Reform Evaluation Further Findings*, Figure 6.

Open to the public

There has been some controversy over whether the family courts are too secretive. This debate stems from the concern of fathers who feel that they have been treated unfairly by the courts. They have argued that the courts have been biased in favour of mothers when determining such issues as access to their children. Some fathers managed to get support for their cause in the media, but there were suggestions that, actually, the public were not able to get a full picture of the case because many of the court proceedings took place in private, so journalists might not be aware of good reasons why access to the father's children was being restricted, such as that he had been violent in the past. These issues raised the question of whether the public would have a better understanding of the court proceedings if they were open to the public. A balance needs to be achieved between the public's interest and the interests of the children in a case. This balance has been highlighted where children have been taken into care by social services when there has been a suspicion of abuse and the family have claimed their innocence. While the family are free to speak to the media and put their side of the case, the social services have an obligation to respect the privacy of the children and fear that the public are getting a very one-sided perspective of the case.

In the light of these debates, the government issued a consultation paper on whether the court privacy rules should be reformed. The paper is entitled *Confidence and Confidentiality: Improving Transparency and Privacy in Family Courts* (2006) and looks at how to find the delicate balance between the need for a transparent and open justice system while maintaining an individual's right to privacy.

Professor Zander's concern

Professor Zander (1998), a leading academic, felt that the reforms were fundamentally flawed, rather than prone to temporary hiccups, and was very vociferous in expressing his opposition to the reforms prior to their implementation. He is reported to have said that they amounted to taking a sledgehammer to crack a nut. Below is an analysis of the main concerns he has expressed.

Task 1.8

Visit a county court. You can find the address of a local county court by looking in a telephone directory. Alternatively, you can find the addresses of county courts on the court service website at:

www.courtservice.gov.uk/notices/county/ccadd/circuits.htm

Write up a report of your visit by answering the following questions:

About the court

1 What was the name and address of the court?
2 What was the court building like? Was it old or modern? Was it clean and in good decorative order? Were the waiting areas comfortable? Was there access to

refreshments? Was it easy to find your way around the building, with rooms clearly signposted and labelled?

3 Did you find the court staff helpful? Were there any explanatory leaflets available?

About the proceedings

Take one of the cases that you watched and answer the following questions:

1 Was the judge male or female and what was their approximate age? What did the judge wear? Was he or she polite to the parties?

2 Were the parties represented by a lawyer?

3 What was the case about?

4 Did any witnesses give evidence?

5 If you heard the whole case, what was its outcome?

6 Did you think that the court came to the right decision?

Use the material you have gathered to prepare an oral presentation about your visit for your fellow students.

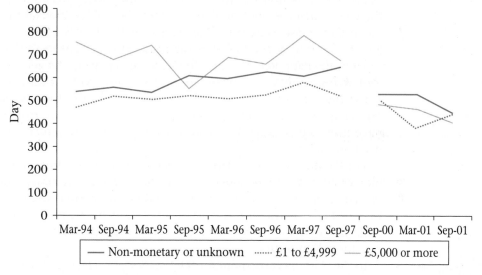

Figure 1.7 **Trials – average time from issue to trial by claim value**

Source: Department for Constitutional Affairs (2002), *Civil Justice Reform Evaluation Further Findings*, Figure 10.

Case management

Zander feels that court management is appropriate in only a minority of cases and that the key is to identify these. He has remarked that judges do not have the time, skills or inclination to undertake the task of case management. The court does not know enough about the workings of a solicitor's office to be able to set appropriate timetables. In addition, litigants on the fast track may feel that the brisk way in which a three-hour hearing deals with the dispute is inadequate. Most will feel that justice has not been done by a short, sharp trial with restricted oral evidence and an interventionist judge chivvying the parties to a resolution of their dispute.

A move towards judicial management has already been seen in America, Australia and Canada. A major official study was published by the Institute of Civil Justice at the Rand Corporation in California (Kakalite, 1996). This research was not available to Lord Woolf while he was compiling his report. The study was based on a five-year survey of 10,000 cases looking at the effect of the US Civil Justice Reform Act 1990. This Act required certain federal courts to practise case management. Judicial case management has been part of the American system for many years, so that, compared with this country, the procedural innovations being studied operated from a different starting point.

The study found that judicial case management did lead to a reduced time to disposition. Its early use yielded a reduction of one and a half or two months to resolution for cases that lasted at least nine months. Also, having a discovery timetable and reducing the time within which discovery took place significantly reduced both the time to disposition and the number of hours spent on the case by a lawyer. These benefits were achieved without any substantial change in the lawyers' or litigants' satisfaction or views of fairness.

On the other hand, case management led to an approximate 20-hour increase in lawyers' work hours overall. Their work increased with the need to respond to the court's management directions. In addition, once judicial case management had begun, a disclosure cut-off date had usually been established and lawyers felt an obligation to begin disclosure on a case which might be settled.

Thus, the Rand Report found that case management, by generating more work for lawyers, tended to increase rather than reduce costs. If the fixed costs did not reflect the extra cost, then this would be unjust to the lawyers and their clients. The danger is that case management will front-load costs on to cases which would have been settled anyway before reaching court, and which therefore did not need judicial management.

The Rand Report noted that the effectiveness of implementation depended on judicial attitudes. Some judges viewed these procedural innovations as an attack on judicial independence and felt that they emphasised speed and efficiency at the possible expense of justice. The report concluded, among other things, that judicial management should wait a month after the defence has been entered in case the action settles.

In the research carried out for the Law Society, *The Woolf Network Questionnaire* (2002), 84 per cent of solicitors questioned said they thought the new procedures were quicker and 70 per cent said they were more efficient than the old ones. Greater use of telephone case management conferences was cited as leading to greater efficiency.

Sanctions

Procedural timetables for the fast track are, according to Professor Zander, doomed to failure because a huge proportion of solicitors, for a range of reasons, will fail to keep to the prescribed timetables. This will necessitate enforcement procedures and sanctions on a vast scale which, in turn, will lead to innumerable appeals. Sanctions will be imposed that are disproportionate and therefore unjust, and will cause injustice to clients for the failings of the lawyers. Furthermore, if the judges did impose severe sanctions when lawyers failed to comply with timetable deadlines, it would usually be the litigants rather than the lawyers who would be penalised.

Professor Zander has pointed to the courts' experience of Order 17 under the old County Court Rules as evidence that lawyers are not good at time limits, and sanctions were unlikely to change that. Under that order, an action would be automatically struck out if the claimant failed to take certain steps within the time limits set by the rule. From its introduction in 1990 until 1998, roughly 20,000 cases had been struck out on this basis leaving 20,000 people either to sue their lawyers for negligence or to start all over again. In relation to Order 17, the Court of Appeal stated in **Bannister** *v* **SGB plc** (1997):

> *'This rule has given rise to great difficulties and has generated an immense amount of litigation devoted to the question whether a particular action has been struck out and if so, whether it should be reinstated. In short, the rule has in a large number of cases achieved the opposite of its object, which was to speed up the litigation process in the county courts.'*

There is the danger that, if a court does not exercise its power temperately and judiciously, then in its eagerness to dispose of litigation it will actually generate more litigation. This danger is particularly acute where a court exercises powers on its own initiative. If, for example, a court moves to strike out a statement of case on its own initiative, the likely result is that the party affected will apply to have its case reinstated; and if, in fact, it was not a suitable case for striking out, unnecessary cost and delay will be the result.

There is a risk that unrealistic trial dates and timetables will be set, particularly in heavy litigation, at an early stage, and of the judges insisting on their being adhered to thereafter, regardless of the consequences.

In research carried out for the Law Society, *The Woolf Network Questionnaire* (2002), some solicitors said they were reluctant to apply for sanctions against those who did not stick to the pre-action protocols. This was because they felt that the courts were unwilling to impose sanctions for non-compliance in all but the most serious cases, judges were inconsistent in their approach to sanctions and an application for sanctions was likely to cause more delays and additional costs.

Costs

Litigation can be very costly and state funding is often not available (see Chapter 13). Research carried out for the Law Society, *The Woolf Network Questionnaire* (2002), suggests that the cost of engaging in civil litigation has not been reduced by the civil justice reforms. In many cases, especially those involving personal injury, the defendant's costs, and sometimes those of the claimant, will be paid by an insurance company – for example, the parties in a car accident are likely to have been insured and professionals such as doctors are insured against negligence claims. As Hazel Genn's 1987 study showed, where only one party is insured, this can place great pressure on the other, unless the other has been granted state funding. The insured side may try to drag out the proceedings for as long as possible, in the hope of exhausting the other party's financial reserves and forcing a low settlement.

Professor Zander has argued that in many civil cases the claimant wins and the defendant is an insurance company, which currently pays the claimant's costs. If, in future, the court can only order the loser to pay fixed and fairly low costs, then the claimant's lawyers will not be able to claim back everything that it was in fact necessary to spend on the case in order to win. He predicts that, as a result, either the work will not be done or the client will have to pay for it out of their damages. Either way, justice will not have been served.

Quick quiz 1.9

1 Name the three tracks for the purposes of case management.

2 If you wish to bring an action for compensation following a disastrous package holiday, claiming £4,000 compensation, to which track would your case be allocated?

3 What is meant by a 'compensation culture'?

4 Did the Rand Report into case management find that it tended to increase or reduce costs?

Reading on the web

The research *Emerging Findings: An Early Evaluation of the Civil Justice Reforms* (2001) is available on the Lord Chancellor's website at:

www.dca.gov.uk/civil/emerge/emerge.htm

Lord Woolf's final report, *Access to Justice*, is available on the website of the Lord Chancellor's Department at:

www.dca.gov.uk/civil/final/index.htm

The website for Money Claim Online can be found at:

www.moneyclaim.gov.uk/csmc02/index.jsp

A useful source of information about court matters is the Court Service Annual Report:

www.hmcourts-service.gov.uk

The research, *The Management of Civil Cases: The Courts and the Post-Woolf Landscape (2005)*, is available on the former Department for Constitutional Affairs' website at:

www.dca.gov.uk/research/2005/9_2005_full.pdf

The report of the Civil Justice Council, *Improved Access to Justice - Funding Options and Proportionate Costs* (2005), is available at:

www.costsdebate.civiljusticecouncil.gov.uk

The consultation paper, *Case track limits and the claims process for personal injury claims* (2007), is available on the website of the former Department for Constitutional Affairs at:

www.dca.gov.uk/consult/case-track-limits/cp0807.pdf

The consultation paper, *Confidence and Confidentiality: Improving Transparency and Privacy in Family Courts* (2006), is available on the website of the former Department for Constitutional Affairs at:

www.dca.gov.uk/consult/courttransparencey1106/consultation1106.pdf

Chapter summary

Civil or criminal?

The laws that have developed in the English legal system can be divided between civil and criminal laws and often separate courts are responsible for civil and criminal matters.

The civil justice system

The civil justice system is designed to sort out disputes between individuals or organisations. The burden of proof is usually on the claimant, who must prove his or her case on a balance of probabilities. Major reforms were introduced following Lord Woolf's report, *Access to Justice*, which was published in 1996.

The civil courts

There are two main civil courts which hear civil cases at first instance. These are the county courts and the High Court. The county courts hear the cases where less money is involved, whereas the High Court hears the bigger financial cases.

Dealing with cases 'justly'

The first rule of the new Civil Procedure Rules lays down an overriding objective which is to underpin the whole system. This overriding objective is that the rules should enable the courts to deal with cases 'justly'.

Civil procedure

Almost all proceedings start with the same document, called a claim form. If the defendant files a defence, the court will serve an allocation questionnaire on each party. This is designed to enable the court to allocate each claim to one of the three tracks. For non-personal injury actions, a claim may be started in the High Court where the claimant expects to recover more than £15,000. For personal injury actions a claim can be started in the High Court only where the claimant expects to recover at least £50,000.

Pre-action protocols

To push the parties into behaving reasonably during the pre-trial stage pre-action protocols have been developed. These lay down a code of conduct for this stage of proceedings.

Alternative dispute resolution

At various stages in a dispute's history, the court will actively promote settlement by alternative dispute resolution (ADR).

Case management

Case management has been introduced, whereby the court plays an active role in managing the litigation. To determine the level and form of case management cases have been divided into three types:

- small claims track;
- fast track; and
- multi-track.

Sanctions

The courts now have tough powers to enforce the new rules on civil procedure to ensure that litigation is pursued diligently.

Money Claim Online

In 2002 Money Claim Online (MCOL) was established. It provides a debt recovery service over the internet for sums up to £100,000.

Problems with the civil court system

The high number of out-of-court settlements creates injustice, because the parties usually hold very unequal bargaining positions. The small claims procedure is quicker, simpler and cheaper than the full county court process, but the Consumers' Association is of the view that the small claims procedure is not simple enough. In 2007 the government announced that it no longer intended to raise the small claims limit to £5,000 because this would not be in the interests of consumers. There has been some concern that the UK might be developing a compensation culture, which has historically been associated with the US.

Professor Zander has been a vociferous critic of Lord Woolf's reforms, suggesting that they would not succeed in reducing delays and expense.

Question and answer guides

1. Briefly explain the three track system of civil justice.

(OCR Specimen Paper 2007, English Legal System Unit)

Plan

Here is a possible outline plan of what you should include in a good answer to this question. You may want to try making your own plan first, and then compare your plan with this one. Don't worry if you don't get all the points; seeing what you have missed out will help you to remember the topic and tell you what you need to look at again.

(Please note that this advice will not be repeated in the following chapters but will apply to all outline plans in the book.)

- Two main civil trial courts: the county court and the High Court.
- Under the rules of civil procedure following the Woolf reforms, judges exercise a case management role, which varies depending on which track a case is allocated to following the completion of an allocation questionnaire.
- Small claims track in the county court for damages of up to £5,000 or £1,000 for personal injury.
- Fast track in the county court for cases between £5,000 and £15,000.
- Multi-track for cases over £15,000 or those involving complex points of law. Multi-track cases are heard in the county court or High Court, depending on the value and complexity of the case. The county court has unlimited jurisdiction in contract and tort claims, while the High Court's jurisdiction is now limited to claims over £15,000, personal injury over £50,000, and specialist claims required to be heard in the High Court.

The aims of the three track system are to:

- Save expense by making litigation cheaper.
- Handle cases in a way which is proportionate to the amount involved, the importance of the case and the complexity of the issues.

Answer

Here is a good, potentially A-grade answer to this question. Please note that this is not the only answer that could be written to this question and you are unlikely to get exactly the same question in your exam. So you need to practise developing your own skills in answering questions, in consultation with your teacher. You may want to attempt the question first, and then compare your answer with this one.

(Please note that this advice will not be repeated in the following chapters but will apply to all answers to exam questions in the book.)

Civil court cases arise where an individual or a business believe their rights have been infringed in some way. Following the Woolf reforms and the Access to

Justice Act 1999, the procedure for making a claim was streamlined and simplified so that cases should always be dealt with in the most appropriate court, taking into account the amount involved and the complexity of the law at issue, to avoid unnecessary legal expenses. Judges are now more responsible for managing cases as they progress to trial and all parties are sent an allocation questionnaire once a defence has been filed. They have to list the salient factors of their case and are asked for an estimate of the time required for the presentation of their evidence. The case is then allocated to one of the three tracks, based on the answers to this questionnaire and the value, complexity, remedies sought and specialist nature of the case at hand. The court may 'upgrade' a case to a higher track if cases are especially complex or there is a large body of evidence to be presented.

The small claims track in the county court is for cases involving financially small claims for damages. In practice, it is an important part of the civil procedure system, with around 80,000 actions a year being brought in this way. Legal representation is not necessary and individuals should feel comfortable presenting their case in person. The judge will assist unrepresented litigants to present their case and hearings are generally informal. The small claims track is used for remedies sought of up to £5,000, or £1,000 for personal injury. Any legal costs awarded are strictly limited to discourage wealthier parties with deeper pockets from overwhelming their poorer opponents. This is a cheap, simple form of resolving small scale disputes such as consumer disputes.

The academic, John Baldwin, has carried out research into the small claims track, *Lay and Judicial Perspectives on the Expansion of the Small Claims Regime* (2002). He noted that most litigants using the small claims system were satisfied with the experience. However, the Consumers' Association magazine is of the view that the small claims procedure is not simple enough. It reported in 1986 that the process was still 'quite an ordeal', and the level of formality varied widely. The system is still largely used by small businesses chasing debtors, rather than by the individual consumer for whom it was set up. The government considered raising the financial level of personal injury cases that can be considered by the small claims procedures from £1,000 to £5,000 but concluded that this would not be in the interests of justice.

The fast track is for cases worth between £5,000 and £15,000, which are not expected to need a trial lasting more than one day. This procedure was introduced as part of Lord Woolf's reforms, and is designed to produce more affordable justice for mid-range claims. Fast track cases are heard in the county court. As soon as the case is allocated to the fast track, the district judge responsible for the case gives directions for its management. These include a timetable, a trial date or trial period no more than 30 weeks away, provision for the disclosure of documents and the exchange of witness statements. The court will want to keep the trial as short as possible, while still allowing justice to be done. This should all ensure that litigation costs are minimised.

The multi-track is for cases involving large sums of money or raising complex points of law. Once the case is allocated to this track, the court gives directions for management, including a timetable. In the past, the time between the start of formal proceedings and the start of the trial has been about 15 months in the county court or three years in the High Court, but the new Civil Procedure Rules (which transfer responsibility for ensuring progress from the lawyers to the judge as case managers) have sought to reduce this delay. Claims with an expected quantum of more than £50,000 for personal injury and £15,000 for other civil claims are dealt with in the High Court by more senior judges.

Most civil cases, on any of the three tracks, are tried by a judge sitting alone, who decides both questions of fact and questions of law and assesses quantum of damages. A jury may exceptionally be used particularly for cases of libel. The introduction of the three-track system has not caused many problems in practice and the judges seem to have adapted well to their role as case managers.

Group activity 1

Imagine you bought a pair of boots for £100, which fell apart the second time you wore them. You took them back to the shop and were told you should not have worn them in the rain, so there is no possibility of refund or repair.

Having received no response to your letter of complaint to the shop, you have decided to make a legal claim for the ruined boots on the grounds that they were 'not fit for purpose' under the Sale of Goods Act 1979. Working in groups, look at how you could go about making a small claim in a civil court. Print off a claim form and complete it with details of your claim. You will find the form you need on the following website:

www.hmcourts-service.gov.uk/courtfinder/forms/n1_0102.pdf32+/76

Group activity 2

■ Divide your friends (or class) into groups of two or three people.
■ Each group should choose a claims management firm (CMF) operating in England and Wales. If you do not already know of one, look in the telephone directory or on the internet. (A complete list of all authorised CMFs can be found on the website **www.claimsregulation.gov.uk**, which is maintained by the Ministry of Justice.)
■ Starting from the firm's website, prepare a profile of your chosen CMF, focusing on its size and location, the services that it offers and its terms of business. Ask yourself, 'Is it clear to me how this CMF makes its money?'
■ Once you have prepared your profile, meet with the other groups to compare notes, looking for any common themes.

Visit **www.mylawchamber.co.uk/elliottocr** to access questions, quizzes and activities to test yourself on this chapter.
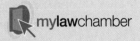

Chapter 2
CIVIL APPEALS

This chapter discusses:

- appeals from the county court;
- appeals from the High Court;
- the House of Lords;
- criticism and reform of the civil appeal system.

Introduction

Civil appeals may be made by either party to a dispute. Permission to appeal must be obtained for almost all appeals. This permission can be obtained either from the court of first instance or from the appellate court itself. Permission will be given where the appeal has a realistic prospect of success or where there is some other compelling reason why the appeal should be heard. The general rule is that appeal lies to the next level of judge in the court hierarchy.

The Access to Justice Act 1999 provides that in normal circumstances there will be only one level of appeal to the courts. Where the county court or High Court has already reached a decision in a case brought on appeal, there will be no further possibility for the case to be considered by the Court of Appeal, unless it considers that the appeal would raise an important point of principle or practice, or there is some other compelling reason for the Court of Appeal to hear it. Thus, in future, second appeals will become a rarity. Only the Court of Appeal can grant permission for this second appeal.

In the Court of Appeal cases are normally heard by three judges but, following the Access to Justice Act 1999, some smaller cases can be heard by a single judge.

Civil appeals will normally simply be a review of the decision of the lower court relying on the notes made by the earlier judge(s) and other documentary evidence of the proceedings, rather than a full rehearing, calling witnesses etc., unless the appeal court considers that it is in the interests of justice to hold a rehearing. Written skeleton arguments should normally be provided to the court so that oral submissions can be kept brief to save time and costs. The appeal will only be allowed where the decision of the lower court was wrong, or where it was unjust because of a serious procedural or other irregularity in the proceedings of the lower court.

Appeals from the county court

Appeals from the county court based on alleged errors of law or fact are made to the Civil Division of the Court of Appeal. Appeals from a district judge's decision normally have to go first to a circuit judge and then to the High Court.

The Court of Appeal may affirm, vary (for example, by altering the amount of damages) or reverse the judgment of the county court. It is generally reluctant to overturn the trial judge's finding of fact because it does not hold a complete rehearing. As the trial judge will have had the advantage of observing the demeanour of witnesses giving their evidence, the Court of Appeal will hardly ever question his or her findings about their veracity and reliability as witnesses. From the Court of Appeal, there may be a further appeal to the House of Lords, for which leave must be granted.

Judicial review by the High Court is also possible.

Appeals from the High Court

Cases started in the High Court may be appealed to the Civil Division of the Court of Appeal. From there, a further appeal on questions of law or fact may be made, with permission, to the House of Lords.

The exception to this process is the 'leap-frog' procedure, provided for in the Administration of Justice Act 1969. Under this procedure, an appeal can go directly from the High Court to the House of Lords, missing out the Court of Appeal. The underlying rationale is that the Court of Appeal may be bound by a decision of the House of Lords, so that money and time would be wasted by going to the Court of Appeal when the only court that could look at the issue afresh is the House of Lords. In order to use this procedure, all the parties must consent to it and the High Court judge who heard the original trial must certify that the appeal is on a point of law that either:

(a) relates wholly or mainly to the construction of an enactment or of a statutory instrument, and has been fully argued in the proceedings and fully considered in the judgment of the judge in the proceedings; or

(b) is one in respect of which the judge is bound by a decision of the Court of Appeal or of the House of Lords in previous proceedings, and was fully considered in the judgments given by the Court of Appeal or the House of Lords (as the case may be) in those previous proceedings (s. 12(3)).

The trial judge has a discretion whether or not to grant this certificate, and there is no right of appeal against this decision. If a certificate is granted, leave will still need to be obtained from the House of Lords. Even if that leave is obtained, the appellant might decide that it has been given on such restrictive terms that it would prefer to follow the ordinary appeal procedure rather than go ahead with a leap-frog appeal: **R(Jones) v Ceredigion County Council** (2007).

Quick quiz 2.1

1 Which court(s) can give permission to appeal for civil cases?

2 How many judges normally sit in the Court of Appeal?

3 Which court hears civil appeals from the High Court?

4 Why is the Court of Appeal reluctant to overturn a trial judge's ruling on the facts of a case?

The House of Lords

sourcebook
p. 326

Apart from cases concerning European law, this is the highest appeal court on civil matters, and all other English courts are bound by it. The government intends to abolish the House of Lords and replace it with a Supreme Court. This reform is contained in the Constitutional Reform Act 2005 and is discussed below.

Criticism and reform of the appeal system

A Supreme Court

sourcebook
p. 293

Rather unexpectedly, the government announced in June 2003 that it was going to abolish the House of Lords and replace it with a Supreme Court. It subsequently issued a consultation paper, *Constitutional Reform: a Supreme Court for the United Kingdom* (2004), which considered the shape that this reform should take. The Constitutional Reform Act 2005 has now been passed, which contains provisions for the creation of the new court. It is expected to start hearing cases in October 2009.

The government was undoubtedly wrong to announce a decision, then consult afterwards merely on the detail, but the decision itself was probably right. There is a natural inclination towards the saying, 'If it isn't broke, don't mend it'. But, with the highest court in the land, one cannot afford to wait until it is broken before one starts to mend. It is now important that the new Supreme Court gets some quality accommodation that matches its status. The judges need space, computer support, research facilities and research assistants. The new court will have to work hard in its early years to establish its reputation nationally and internationally. It must be given all the resources necessary in order to be able to achieve this.

Reasons for abolishing the House of Lords

sourcebook
p. 153

The consultation paper stated that this reform was necessary to enhance the independence of the judiciary from both the legislature and the executive. It pointed to the growth of judicial review cases and the passing of the Human Rights Act 1998 as two key reasons why this reform was becoming urgent. Article 6 of the European

Convention on Human Rights requires not only that the judges should be independent, but also that they should be seen to be independent. The fact that the Law Lords are currently a Committee of the House of Lords can raise issues about the appearance of independence from the legislature.

The government is, however, anxious to point out that the reform does not imply any dissatisfaction with the performance of the House of Lords as the country's highest court of law:

> *'On the contrary its judges have conducted themselves with the utmost integrity and independence. They are widely and rightly admired, nationally and internationally. The Government believes, however, that the time has come to establish a new court regulated by statute as a body separate from Parliament.'*

Six of the current Law Lords are opposed to the reform, considering the change unnecessary and harmful.

Separation from Parliament

The new Supreme Court will be completely separate from Parliament. Its judges will have no right to sit and vote in the upper House. Only the current Law Lords will have the right to sit and vote in the House of Lords after their retirement from the judiciary.

One advantage of this change will be that the court will no longer sit in the Palace of Westminster, where there is a shortage of space, and could be given more spacious accommodation elsewhere. It will be based in a refurbished gothic building opposite Parliament in Parliament Square.

Jurisdiction

The proposed court will be the Supreme Court for the whole of the UK. Its jurisdiction will remain the same as that of the House of Lords, but with the addition of jurisdiction in relation to devolution cases. At the moment, the Privy Council has the jurisdiction to hear cases concerning the devolution of Scotland, Wales and Northern Ireland. This jurisdiction will be transferred to the new Supreme Court. The reason for the transfer is to remove any perceived conflict of interest in which the UK Parliament, with an obvious interest in a dispute about devolution, appears to be sitting in judgment over the case.

There is no proposal to create a Supreme Court on the US model, with the power to overturn legislation. Nor is there any proposal to create a specific constitutional court. The new court will not have the power to give preliminary rulings on difficult points of law. It has been pointed out that English courts do not traditionally consider issues in the abstract, so giving such a power to the Supreme Court would sit very uneasily with our judicial traditions. This is despite the fact that we have become accustomed to this procedure for the European Court of Justice.

The Government realised that there were already various entities in the United Kingdom which were known as supreme courts. In particular, the Court of Appeal, the High Court and the Crown Court were together known as the supreme court for the purposes of allocating jurisdictions to judges and routing work between the courts. But this title was not in common usage and now the title of Supreme Court is reserved for the new court to be created as a result of this legislation.

Membership

The existing 12 full-time Law Lords will form the initial members of the new court. The government wants to keep the same number of full-time judges, but to continue to allow the court to call on the help of other judges on a part-time basis. The Lord Chancellor was a member of the Appellate Committee of the House of Lords, but does not have a right to sit in the Supreme Court. A President of the Court will be appointed.

The judges will no longer automatically become Lords. Members of the Supreme Court will be called 'Justices of the Supreme Court'.

Qualifications for membership will remain the same. The government has rejected the idea that changes should be made to make it easier for distinguished academics to be appointed in order to enhance the diversity of the court. This is disappointing, as the government itself acknowledges that the current pool of candidates for the post is very narrow, and the government's statistics themselves show that the current senior judiciary are not representative of society.

Candidates will not be subjected to confirmation hearings before Parliament as these would risk politicising the appointments process.

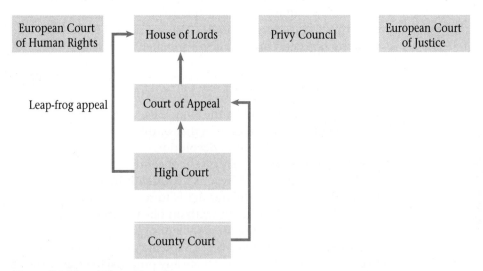

Figure 2.1 **The civil court system**

Reading on the web

Any developments in the establishment of a Supreme Court are likely to be signalled on the website of the Ministry of Justice:

www.justice.gov.uk/

Chapter summary

Appeals in civil law cases

Civil appeals may be made by either party to a dispute. Permission to appeal must be obtained for almost all appeals. The Access to Justice Act 1999 provides that in normal circumstances there will be only one level of appeal to the courts. Civil appeals will normally simply be a review of the decision of the lower court.

Appeals from the county court

Appeals from the county court based on alleged errors of law or fact are made to the Civil Division of the Court of Appeal. The Court of Appeal may affirm, vary or reverse the judgment of the county court. From the Court of Appeal, there may be a further appeal to the House of Lords, for which leave must be granted.

Appeal from the High Court

Cases started in the High Court may be appealed to the Civil Division of the Court of Appeal. From there, a further appeal on questions of law or fact may be made, with permission, to the House of Lords. The exception to this process is the 'leap-frog' procedure.

The House of Lords

Apart from cases concerning European law, this is the highest appeal court on civil matters, and all other English courts are bound by it.

Criticism and reform of the appeal system

The government intends to abolish the House of Lords and replace it with a new, independent Supreme Court. The provisions for this reform are contained in the Constitutional Reform Act 2005.

Question and answer guides

1. The government intends to replace the House of Lords with a Supreme Court. Discuss why the government wants to reform the appeals system in this way.

Plan

- Plans contained in the Constitutional Reform Act 2005.
- The new court will have the same jurisdiction as the old court, plus devolution cases.
- Reform reinforces the separation of powers as the new court ensures total separation and independence of the judiciary.
- Future appointments to the Supreme Court will not sit in the House of Lords.
- Growth in judicial review applications means that the courts are often being asked to examine decisions of the executive, so it is important that the judges are seen to be independent of the executive.
- It is not intended to follow the US Supreme Court model or to allow preliminary rulings, as in the Article 234 referrals to the European Court of Justice.
- Still only a narrow pool from which to draw potential judges to the Supreme Court.

Answer

Traditionally, the highest appellate court in the UK has been the House of Lords. The Law Lords have sat in judgment in that court while also sitting in the House of Lords in its legislative capacity. In plans contained in the Constitutional Reform Act 2005, the government will abolish the House of Lords and a new Supreme Court will be established. This reform was necessary to reinforce the separation of powers. The new Supreme Court will respect the principle of the separation of powers and thereby help to reinforce the independence of the judiciary. While the Law Lords are currently housed at Westminster, there is a risk that they could be subjected to undue influence by the legislature, as this is based in the same building. The planned separation will add to the costs of running the court – the estimated running costs for the new Supreme Court are in the region of £10 million a year – but any additional expenses are considered to be necessary to achieve this desirable reform.

In recent years, there has been a growth in judicial review applications, partly because of the passing of the Human Rights Act 1998, increasing citizens' rights. The courts are therefore often being asked to examine decisions of the executive and, where appropriate, overturn these decisions. It is, as a result, particularly important that all the judges are seen to be independent of the executive in their decision-making procedures. Historically, the Lord Chancellor was a member of the executive, the legislative and sat as a judge in the House of Lords. In recent years, the Lord Chancellor has chosen not to sit as a judge and he or she will have no right to sit in the new Supreme Court.

It was not felt necessary to change significantly the jurisdiction of the new court. The Supreme Court will have the same jurisdiction as the House of Lords but will also take on devolution cases which were previously the preserve of the Privy Council. It is not intended that the new Supreme Court follow the US Supreme Court model for statutory challenges, nor to allow preliminary rulings which are currently possible to the European Court of Justice.

It will be up to the new court to establish itself as a respected court, both nationally and internationally. Its success will partly depend on the judges who are recruited to become Justices of the Supreme Court. The initial judges will be the current Law Lords and there is a problem in the recruitment process, given that there is likely to be only a very narrow pool of potential candidates for future posts, unless significant changes to the recruitment process are made.

Group activity 1

Imagine that you won your claim for damages against the shoe shop where you bought the ruined boots discussed in the group activity number 1 for chapter 1. However, you have learnt that the shoe shop intends to appeal against the decision of the small claims court. Where would any appeal be heard and are further appeals possible? Work in groups to discuss this.

Group activity 2

- Divide your friends (or class) into six groups.
- Using the internet and any other available resources, each group should make notes on the membership and civil jurisdiction of one of the following courts:
     Supreme Court of the United States
     Supreme Court of Canada
     Supreme Court of India
     Supreme Court of Ireland
     Supreme Court of New Zealand
     High Court of Australia (= Australia's supreme court)
- Compare your notes with what this chapter tells you about the membership and civil jurisdiction of the new Supreme Court of the UK, looking for any significant similarities and differences.
- From these similarities and differences, what conclusions can you draw about the new Supreme Court of the UK?
- Compare your conclusions with those of the other groups.

Visit **www.mylawchamber.co.uk/elliottocr** to access questions, quizzes and activities to test yourself on this chapter.

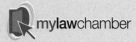

Chapter 3
ALTERNATIVE METHODS OF
DISPUTE RESOLUTION

Chapter outline

This chapter considers the alternatives to courts. In particular, it looks at:

● the problems with court hearings;

● the four main alternative dispute resolution (ADR) mechanisms;

● examples of ADR;

● the advantages and disadvantages of using ADR.

Introduction

Court hearings are not always the best method of resolving a dispute, and their disadvantages mean that, for some types of problem, alternative mechanisms may be more suitable. Under the rules of civil procedure, the courts are required to encourage and facilitate the use of alternative methods of dispute resolution (ADR) and help the parties to settle a case out of court.

In **Halsey** *v* **Milton Keynes General NHS Trust** (2004) the Court of Appeal held that the courts do not, however, have the power to force parties to try ADR, as this might amount to a breach of a person's right to a fair trial under Art. 6 of the European Convention on Human Rights.

Problems with court hearings

Alternative methods of dispute resolution have become increasingly popular because of the difficulties of trying to resolve disputes through court hearings. Below are some of the specific problems posed by court hearings.

The adversarial process

A trial necessarily involves a winner and a loser, and the adversarial procedure, combined with the often aggressive atmosphere of court proceedings divides the parties, making them end up enemies even where they did not start out that way. This can be a disadvantage where there is some reason for the parties to sustain a relationship after the problem under discussion is sorted out – child custody cases are the obvious example, but in business, too, there may be advantages in resolving a dispute in a way which does not make enemies of the parties. The court system is often said to be best suited to areas where the parties are strangers and happy to remain so – it is interesting to note that in small-scale societies with close kinship links, court-type procedures are rarely used, and disputes are usually settled by negotiation processes that aim to satisfy both parties, and thus maintain the harmony of the group.

Technical cases

Some types of dispute rest on detailed technical points, such as the way in which a machine should be made, or the details of a medical problem, rather than on points of law. The significance of such technical details may not be readily understandable by an ordinary judge. Expert witnesses or advisers may be brought in to advise on these points, but this takes time, and so raises costs. Where detailed technical evidence is at issue, alternative methods of dispute resolution can employ experts in a particular field to take the place of a judge.

Inflexible

In a court hearing, the rules of procedure lay down a fixed framework for the way in which problems are addressed. This may be inappropriate in areas which are of largely private concern to the parties involved. Alternative methods can allow the parties themselves to take more control of the process.

Imposed solutions

Court hearings impose a solution on the parties, which, since it does not involve their consent, may need to be enforced. If the parties are able to negotiate a settlement between them, to which they both agree, this should be less of a problem.

Publicity

The majority of court hearings are public. This may be undesirable in some business disputes, where one or both of the parties may prefer not to make public the details of their financial situation or business practices because of competition.

Alternative dispute resolution mechanisms

Where, for one or more of the reasons explained above, court action is not the best way of solving a dispute, a wide range of alternative methods of dispute resolution (ADR) may be used. Four main forms of ADR can be identified: arbitration, mediation, conciliation and negotiation.

Arbitration is a procedure whereby both sides to a dispute agree to let a third party, the arbitrator, decide. The arbitrator may be a lawyer, or may be an expert in the field of the dispute. He or she will make a decision according to the law and the decision is legally binding.

Mediation involves the appointment of a mediator to help the parties to a dispute reach an agreement which each considers acceptable. Mediation can be 'evaluative', where the mediator gives an assessment of the legal strength of a case, or 'facilitative', where the mediator concentrates on assisting the parties to define the issues. When a mediation is successful and an agreement is reached, it is written down and forms a legally binding contract unless the parties state otherwise.

Conciliation is similar to mediation but the conciliator takes a more interventionist role than the mediator in bringing the two parties together and in suggesting possible solutions to help achieve an agreed settlement. The term conciliation is gradually falling into disuse and the process is regarded as a form of mediation.

Negotiation is one of the simplest forms of ADR involving discussions between the parties with or without the help of lawyers to try to resolve the dispute – the high numbers of civil cases settled out of court are examples of this.

Formal ADR schemes include the Advisory, Conciliation and Arbitration Service (ACAS), which mediates in many industrial disputes and unfair dismissal cases; the role of ombudsmen in dealing with disputes in the fields of insurance and banking, and in complaints against central and local government and public services; the work done by trade organisations such as ABTA – The Travel Association in settling consumer complaints; inquiries into such areas as objections concerning compulsory purchase or town and country planning; the conciliation schemes offered by courts and voluntary organisations to divorcing couples; and the arbitration schemes run by the Institute of Arbitrators for business disputes. We will look at some of these in more detail below. Though procedural details vary widely, what they all have in common is that they are attempting to provide a method of settling disagreements that avoids some or all of the disadvantages of the court system listed above.

The Travel Association

Figure 3.1 **The ABTA logo**
Source: ABTA - The Travel Association

Examples of ADR

Below are some examples of ADR being used in practice.

Conciliation in unfair dismissal cases

A statutory conciliation scheme administered by ACAS operates before cases of unfair dismissal can be taken to an employment tribunal. ACAS conciliation officers talk to both sides, with the aim of settling the dispute without a tribunal hearing; they are supposed to procure reinstatement of the employee where possible, but in practice most settlements are only for damages.

A conciliation officer contacts each party or their representatives to discuss the case and advise each side on the strength or weakness of their position. They may tell each side what the other has said, but if the case does eventually go to a tribunal, none of this information is admissible without the consent of the party who gave it.

Evaluation

The success of the scheme is sometimes measured by the fact that two-thirds of cases are either withdrawn or settled by the conciliation process. However, this ignores the imbalance in power between the employer and the employee, especially where the employee has no legal representation – the fact that there has been a settlement does not necessarily mean it is a fair one, when one party is under far more pressure to agree than the other. Dickens's 1985 study of unfair dismissal cases found that awards after a hearing were generally higher than those achieved by conciliation, implying that employees may feel under pressure to agree to any settlement. The study suggested that the scheme would be more effective in promoting fair settlements – rather than settlement at any price – if conciliation officers had a less neutral stance and instead tried to help enforce the worker's rights.

> ✓ **Know your terms 3.1**
>
> Define the following terms:
>
> 1 Adversarial process.
> 2 Arbitrator.
> 3 ADR.
> 4 ACAS.

Mediation in divorce cases

In many ways, the court system is an undesirable forum for divorce and its attendant disputes over property and children, since the adversarial nature of the system can aggravate the differences between the parties. This makes the whole process more traumatic for those involved, and clearly is especially harmful where there are children. Consequently, conciliation has for some time been made available to divorcing couples, not necessarily to get them back together (though this can happen), but to try to ensure that any arrangements between them can be made as amicably as possible, reducing the strain on the parties themselves as well as their children.

The Family Law Act 1996 makes changes to the divorce laws and places a greater emphasis on mediation. The Act requires those seeking public funding for representation in family proceedings to attend a meeting with a mediator to consider whether mediation might be suitable in their case.

Evaluation

In divorce cases generally, success depends on the parties themselves and their willingness to cooperate. The parties may find that meeting in a neutral environment, with the help of an experienced, impartial professional helps them communicate calmly, and can make the process of divorce less painful for the couple and their children, by avoiding the need for a court battle in which each feels obliged to accuse the other of being unfit to look after their children – a battle which can be as expensive as it is unpleasant, at a time when one or both parties may be under considerable financial strain.

A three-year study undertaken as a pilot scheme for the new reforms found that eight out of ten couples reached agreement on some issues through mediation, and four in ten reached a complete settlement. However, the Solicitors' Family Law Association (SFLA) points out that because men are usually the main earners in a family, and women's earning abilities may be limited by the demands of childcare, women may need lawyers to get a fair deal financially; in fact, the SFLA says the reforms may well turn out to be 'a rogue's charter for unscrupulous husbands'.

Commercial arbitration

Many commercial contracts contain an arbitration agreement, requiring any dispute to be referred to arbitration before court proceedings are undertaken – the aim being to do away with the need for going to court. Arbitrators usually have some expertise in the relevant field, and lists of suitable individuals are kept by the Institute of Arbitration. The parties themselves choose their arbitrator, ensuring that the person has the necessary expertise in their area and is not connected to either of them. Once appointed, the arbitrator is required to act in an impartial, judicial manner just as a judge would, but the difference is that they will not usually need to have technical points explained to them, so there is less need for expert witnesses.

Disputes may involve disagreement over the quality of goods supplied, interpretation of a trade clause or point of law, or a mixture of the two. Where points of law are involved the arbitrator may be a lawyer.

The Arbitration Act 1996 aims to promote commercial arbitration, by providing a clear framework for its use. It sets out the powers of the parties to shape the process according to their needs, and provides that they must each do everything necessary to allow the arbitration to proceed properly and without delay. It also spells out the powers of arbitrators, which include limiting the costs to be recoverable by either party and making orders which are equivalent to High Court injunctions if the parties agree. Arbitrators are also authorised to play an inquisitorial role, investigating the facts of the case – many of them are, after all, experts in the relevant fields.

Arbitration hearings must be conducted in a judicial manner, in accordance with the rules of natural justice, but proceedings are informal and held in private, with the time and place decided by the parties. The arbitrator's decision, known as the award, is often delivered immediately, and is as binding on the parties as a High Court judgment would be, and if necessary can be enforced as one.

The award is usually to be considered as final, but appeal may be made to the High Court on a question of law, with the consent of all the parties, or with the permission of court. Permission will only be given if the case could substantially affect the rights of one of the parties, and provided (with some exceptions) that they had not initially agreed to restrict rights of appeal. The High Court may confirm, vary or reverse the award, or send it back to the arbitrator for reconsideration.

Evaluation

Arbitration fees can be high, but for companies this may be outweighed by the money they save through being able to get the problem solved as soon as it arises, rather than having to wait months for a court hearing. The arbitration hearing itself tends to be quicker than a court case, because of the expertise of the arbitrator – in a court hearing time, and therefore money, can be wasted in explanation of technical points to the judge.

The ability of the parties to choose their arbitrator promotes mutual trust in and respect for the decision, and arbitration is conducted with a view to compromise rather than combat, which avoids destroying the business relationship between the parties. Privacy ensures that business secrets are not made known to competitors. Around 10,000 commercial cases a year go to arbitration, which tends to suggest that business people are fairly happy with the system and the more detailed framework set out by the 1996 Act is thought likely to increase use even further.

Quick quiz 3.2

1 Which body administers the statutory conciliation scheme in cases of unfair dismissal?

2 Which Act introduced a greater emphasis on mediation in divorce proceedings?

3 If you had a disastrous holiday in Spain which you think is the fault of your travel agent, which body will arrange conciliation and arbitration of any subsequent dispute?

4 What is the name of the Act which lays down the main laws governing the use of arbitration procedures?

Advantages of ADR

Cost

Many procedures try to work without any need for legal representation, and even those that do involve lawyers may be quicker and therefore cheaper than going to court.

In 1998, Professor Genn carried out research into a mediation scheme at Central London County Court. The scheme's objective was to offer virtually cost-free court-annexed mediation to disputing parties at an early stage in litigation. This involved a three-hour session with a trained mediator assisting parties to reach a settlement, with or without legal representation. The scheme's purpose was to promote swift dispute settlement and a reduction in legal costs through an informal process that parties might prefer to court proceedings. Hazel Genn's research did not find clear evidence that mediation saved costs. The overall cost of cases which were settled through mediation was significantly less than those which were litigated; but where mediation was used and the parties failed to reach an agreement, and then went on to litigate, it was possible for costs to be increased.

Accessibility

Alternative methods tend to be more informal than court procedures, without complicated rules of evidence. The process can therefore be less intimidating and less stressful than court proceedings.

Speed

The delays in the civil court system are well known, and waiting for a case to come to court may, especially in commercial cases, add considerably to the overall cost, and adversely affect business.

The research carried out by Professor Genn (1998) found that mediation was able to promote and speed up settlement. The majority (62 per cent) of mediated cases were settled at the mediation appointment.

Expertise

Those who run alternative dispute resolution schemes often have specialist knowledge of the relevant areas, which can promote a fairer as well as a quicker settlement.

Conciliation of the parties

Most alternative methods of dispute resolution aim to avoid irrevocably dividing the parties, so enabling business or family relationships to be maintained.

Customer satisfaction

Research by Hazel Genn (2002) found that ADR generally results in a high level of customer satisfaction.

Problems with ADR

Imbalances of power

As the unfair dismissal conciliation scheme shows, the benefits of voluntarily negotiating agreement may be undermined where there is a serious imbalance of power between the parties – in effect, one party is acting less voluntarily than the other.

Lack of legal expertise

Where a dispute hinges on difficult points of law, an arbitrator may not have the required legal expertise to judge.

No system of precedent

There is no doctrine of precedent, and each case is judged on its merits, providing no real guidelines for future cases.

Enforcement

Decisions not made by courts may be difficult to enforce.

Low take-up rate

There is a low take-up rate for ADR, and the numbers have not increased as much as expected following the introduction of the Woolf reforms. Research carried out for the government, *Further Findings: a continuing evaluation of the civil justice reforms* (2002), has found that after a substantial rise in the first year following the introduction of the Civil Procedure Rules 1998, there has been a levelling off in the number of cases in which alternative dispute resolution is used.

Hazel Genn's research (2002) found that, outside commercial practice: 'the profession remains very cautious about the use of ADR. Positive experience of ADR does not appear to be producing armies of converts.' She looked at the reasons why parties choose not to use ADR. For the Commercial Court ADR scheme, the most common reasons given for refusal to mediate were:

- a judgment was required for policy reasons;
- the appeal turned on a point of law;
- the past history or behaviour of the opponent.

The most common reasons given for not trying ADR following an ADR order in the Court of Appeal were:

- the case was not appropriate for ADR;
- the parties did not want to try ADR;
- the timing of the order was wrong (too early or too late); or
- there was no faith in ADR as a process in general.

In addition, Professor Hazel Genn has suggested that, following the Woolf reforms, the increased number of pre-trial settlements might mean that fewer people feel the need for ADR in 'run of the mill' cases. The research concluded that an individualised approach to the directing of cases towards ADR is likely to be more effective than general invitations at an early stage in the litigation process. This would require the development of clearly articulated selection principles. The timing of invitations or directions to mediate is crucial. The early stages of proceedings may not be the best time, and should not be the only opportunity to consider using ADR.

The future for ADR

Although ADR appears to meet many of the principles for effective civil justice, the proportion of people with legal problems who choose to use ADR has remained very low, even when there are convenient and free schemes available. It is not altogether clear why this is so. Hazel Genn's research (1998) found that in only 5 per cent of cases did the parties agree to try mediation, despite vigorous attempts to stimulate demand. It was least likely to be used where both parties had legal representation.

At present, many of those contemplating litigation will go first to a solicitor and Professor Genn's research shows widespread misunderstanding about mediation processes amongst solicitors. Many did not know what was involved and were therefore not able to advise clients on whether their case was suitable for any form of ADR, or the benefits that might flow from seeking to use it. Solicitors were apprehensive about showing weakness through accepting mediation in the context of traditional adversarial litigation. Litigants were also hostile to the idea of compromise, particularly in the early stages of litigation.

It is likely that, in the future, ADR will play an increasingly important role in the resolution of disputes. It is already widely used in the US, where the law frequently requires parties to try mediation before their case can be set down for trial. It is generally accepted that the UK will see a similar expansion in the use of ADR, as both the courts and the legal profession begin to take ADR more seriously than they once did. Following Lord Woolf's reforms of the civil justice system, the new rules of procedure in the civil courts impose on the judges a duty to encourage parties in appropriate cases to use ADR and to facilitate its use. Parties can request that court proceedings be postponed while they try ADR and the court can also order a postponement for this reason. Backing up this position is the fact that the government has said, in the explanatory notes to the Access to Justice Act 1999, that in time it hopes to extend public funding increasingly to cover the use of ADR.

Reading on the web

The research carried out by Professor Genn in 1998 on the mediation scheme at Central London County Court is available on the former Department for Constitutional Affairs' website:

www.dca.gov.uk/research/1998/598esfr.htm

Chapter summary

Introduction

Following Lord Woolf's reforms of the civil justice system, ADR should play a more important role in solving all types of civil disputes. ADR has become increasingly popular because of problems resolving disputes through court hearings.

Alternative dispute resolution mechanisms

Four main forms of ADR can be identified:

- arbitration;
- mediation;
- conciliation; and
- negotiation.

Conciliation in unfair dismissal cases

A statutory conciliation scheme administered by the Advisory, Conciliation and Arbitration Service (ACAS) operates before cases of unfair dismissal can be taken to an employment tribunal.

Mediation in divorce cases

The Family Law Act 1996 has made changes to the divorce laws and places a greater emphasis on mediation.

Commercial arbitration

Many commercial contracts contain an arbitration agreement, requiring any dispute to be referred to arbitration before court proceedings are undertaken.

Advantages of ADR

The advantages of ADR include:

- cost;
- accessibility;
- speed;
- expertise;
- conciliation of the parties; and
- customer satisfaction.

Problems with ADR

The problems with ADR are that:

- there may be a serious imbalance of power between the parties;
- an arbitrator may lack legal expertise;
- there is no system of precedent;
- enforcement may be difficult; and
- there is a low take-up rate.

The future of ADR

It is likely that in the future ADR will play an increasingly important role in the resolution of disputes.

Question and answer guides

1 (a) Describe the different methods of alternative dispute resolution available to deal with civil disputes.

(OCR Specimen Paper 2007, English Legal System Unit)

Plan

(a) Alternative dispute resolution (ADR) is a term for describing the process of resolving disputes outside the courts and includes mediation, conciliation, arbitration and negotiation. It has become a more established part of the civil justice system since the introduction of the Woolf reforms. Cost penalties can be levied against parties that unreasonably refuse to mediate. Litigation should be a last resort: **Dunnett** *v* **Railtrack** (2002).

- **Mediation** – a neutral person helps the parties reach a compromise solution. The mediator does not offer an opinion, but will liaise between the parties. It is particularly useful for family disputes.
- **Conciliation** – conciliators go beyond mediation, as they can suggest grounds for compromise or a settlement. This process is often used by ACAS for employer/ employee negotiations.
- **Arbitration** – both parties voluntarily agree to let their dispute be left to the judgment of an arbitrator (or a panel of arbitrators) who is neutral and is often a member of a professional body, such as an architect or an engineer. Agreements to arbitration are governed by the Arbitration Act 1996. The procedure can amount to a 'paper' arbitration or a formal court-like hearing. Arbitration decisions are binding on the parties and can be enforced by the courts if necessary.
- **Negotiation** – the parties hold talks between themselves to solve a dispute. The process can be formal or informal. The negotiated agreement is not in itself enforceable in law but allows the continuance of business relationships.

Answer

Alternative dispute resolution (ADR) is a term for describing the process of resolving disputes in place of litigation and includes mediation, conciliation, arbitration and negotiation. It is promoted as an attempt to limit litigation costs while providing a quick resolution to disputes. It has become more established since the introduction of the Woolf reforms and, under the rules of civil procedure, courts will usually expect ADR to have been tried before litigation. ADR is required in publicly funded family cases and many judges will limit costs awards if ADR has been unreasonably refused. Litigation should only be pursued to trial as a last resort – **Dunnett** *v* **Railtrack** (2002) – and judges can stay proceedings pending the completion of ADR.

Mediation involves the appointment of a neutral person who tries to help the parties reach an acceptable compromise solution by liaising between them without being judgmental, though they can give evaluations of the proposals if asked. This process can be particularly useful for domestic or family disputes. If a warring family is involved, the presence of a mediator can often work, as the parties do not have to be brought face to face. If agreement is reached and is formally recorded, this can be used as the basis for a legally binding contract.

Conciliators go beyond mediation in that they are more interventional and have the power to suggest grounds for compromise, solution or settlement. They are often used to try to resolve public employer/employee wage disputes and dispute resolution organisations such as ACAS are mentioned in the media where industrial disputes are reported.

Mediation and conciliation both allow the parties to have a lot of control over the resolution process as the parties can withdraw at any time and a resolution to the dispute cannot be imposed on them as they must agree to it.

With arbitration, both parties voluntarily agree to let their dispute be left to the judgment of an independent third party – an arbitrator (or a panel of arbitrators) – who is often a member of a professional body, such as an architect or engineer. Arbitrators charge a professional fee for their services. Arbitration can consist of a 'paper' procedure or involve a more formal court-like hearing. Agreements to arbitration are governed by the Arbitration Act 1996 and are often included as a term in the trading conditions or original contract between the parties. Travel agents frequently choose to join the Association of British Travel Agents (ABTA), which provides an industry-run arbitration scheme. Under this scheme, disgruntled holidaymakers, once the internal complaints procedure of the travel agency has been exhausted, can have their dispute dealt with by an arbitrator free of charge. An arbitrator's award is legally binding.

Negotiation is popular with businesses anxious to maintain a working relationship whilst trying to find a solution to a particular issue in private. The parties will hold talks between themselves to solve a dispute, and this can be a formal or informal procedure. The agreement reached is not enforceable but enables the parties to continue doing business together. Many business disputes are settled by negotiation without court proceedings.

(b) Discuss the advantages and disadvantages of using Alternative Dispute Resolution.

(OCR Specimen Paper 2007, English Legal System Unit)

Plan

Discuss the advantages

- Cheap, informal and simple procedures.
- Many trade associations run their own schemes, e.g. ABTA.
- Quick.
- The parties keep control over the dispute resolution process.
- Avoids aggravating bad relations between the parties.
- Allows business relations to continue unhindered.
- Privacy – unflattering media coverage should be avoided, which can be important if household brand names are involved.
- Use of experts in arbitration. Judges tend not to be so specialist.

Discuss disadvantages

- Increased risk that a party might settle for less than their claim is worth.
- Professional arbitrators can be expensive.
- There can be an imbalance of bargaining power between the parties.
- More sophisticated clients prefer court formality.
- Some clients want a public declaration of being right 'in law' rather than a private process.

Group activity 1

Working in groups, look at the booking conditions of any ABTA member holiday tour operator, either on a travel agent's website or in a holiday brochure. Find the clause dealing with 'disputes' or 'complaints'. Imagine that you had booked a cruise with this travel agent and had suffered severe food poisoning after eating from the ship's buffet. How will your subsequent complaint be handled by the travel agent? Look at the ABTA code of conduct on its website:

www.abta.com/download/codeofconduct.pdf

Looking at the ABTA code of conduct, do you think an alternative method of dispute resolution might be used to try and resolve your complaint?

Group activity 2

- Divide your friends (or class) into groups of two or three people.
- Using the internet and any other available resources, each group should make notes on the membership and jurisdiction of any one type of tribunal. Make your choice from the list of tribunals on the Tribunals Service website: **www.tribunals.gov.uk/tribunalatoz.htm**.
- Compare notes with the other groups, looking for any common themes.
- What conclusions can your draw about the membership and jurisdiction of tribunals generally?

Group activity 3

- Divide your friends (or class) into groups of two or three people.
- Using the internet and any other available resources, prepare a short profile of one of the organisations listed as 'Accredited Mediation Providers' on the website of the Civil Mediation Council: **www.civilmediation.org/provider-organisations.php**.
- Your profile should concentrate on the type of ADR services the organisation offers and the type of people (qualifications, training, etc) they employ to deliver those services. Try also to find out what the organisation charges for its services, though this may be difficult!
- Compare your profile with those of the other groups, looking for any common themes.

Chapter 4
POLICE POWERS

This chapter discusses:

- the miscarriages of justice, where an appropriate balance has not been achieved between an individual's rights and police powers so that an innocent person has been convicted of a criminal offence they did not commit;
- the Human Rights Act 1998 protecting an individual's rights against excessive police powers;
- the police powers of stop and search, arrest and detention;
- the treatment of suspects at the police station;
- the safeguards of the suspect;
- problems with the police.

Introduction

The criminal justice system is one of the most important tools available to society for the control of anti-social behaviour. It is also the area of the English legal system which has most potential for controversy, given that through the criminal justice system the state has the means to interfere with individual freedom in the strongest way: by sending people to prison.

An effective criminal justice system needs to strike a balance between punishing the guilty and protecting the innocent; our systems of investigating crime need safeguards which prevent the innocent being found guilty, but those safeguards must not make it impossible to convict those who are guilty. This balance has been the subject of much debate in recent years: a large number of miscarriages of justice, where innocent people were sent to prison, suggested the system was weighted too heavily towards proving guilt, yet shortly after these cases had been uncovered, there were claims, particularly from the police, that the balance had tipped too far in the other direction. It may be that the incorporation of the European Convention on Human Rights into British law will lead to a further shift in the balance, as the British courts interpret such rights as the right to a 'fair trial' contained in Art. 6 of the Convention.

Miscarriages of justice

In recent years, confidence in the criminal justice system has been seriously dented by the revelation that innocent people had been wrongly convicted and sentenced to long periods in prison. High-profile cases have included the Guildford Four, the Birmingham Six and the Tottenham Three. We will look closely at just one of these cases to see where the system went wrong, before examining in detail the rules that govern the criminal justice system.

The Birmingham Six

In November 1974, 21 people died and 162 were injured when IRA bombs exploded in two crowded pubs in the centre of Birmingham. The bombs caused outrage in Britain, and led to a wave of anti-Irish feeling.

The six Irishmen, who became known as the Birmingham Six, were arrested after police kept a watch on ports immediately after the bombings. The police asked them to undergo forensic tests in order to eliminate them from their enquiries. The men had told the police that they were travelling to Northern Ireland to see relatives; this was partly true, but their main reason for travelling was to attend the funeral of James McDade, an IRA man. Although some of the six may well have had Republican sympathies, none was actually a member of the IRA. They were unaware, until McDade was killed, that he was involved in terrorism. Nevertheless, they all knew his family, and intended to go to the funeral as a

Figure 4.1 The Birmingham Six outside the Old Bailey after their convictions were quashed

Source: © EMPICS.

mark of respect, a normal practice in Northern Ireland, which would not necessarily suggest support for the dead person's political views.

Perhaps not surprisingly, given the situation at the time, the men did not mention the funeral when the police asked why they were travelling and, equally unsurprisingly, when the police searched their luggage and found evidence of the real reason for their journey, they became extremely suspicious. When the forensic tests, conducted by a Dr Skuse, indicated that the men had been handling explosives, the police were convinced their suspicions were right.

At their trial, the case rested on two main pieces of evidence: the forensic tests and confessions which the men had made to the police. The six claimed that, while at the police station, they had been beaten, kicked and threatened with death; they were also told that their families were in danger and would only be protected if the men confessed. There was clear evidence that the six were beaten up; photos taken three days after their admission on remand to Winston Green prison show serious scars. However, the men were also beaten up by prison officers once they were remanded in custody, and the prosecution used this beating to explain the photographic evidence, stating that there had been no physical abuse by the police and that, therefore, the confessions were valid. Yet a close examination of the confessions would have made it obvious that they were made by people who knew nothing about the bombings: they contradicted each other, none of them revealed anything that the police did not know already about the way the terrorist attacks were carried out, and some of the 'revelations' proved to be untrue – for example, three of the men said the bombs were left in carrier bags, when forensic evidence later showed them to have been in holdalls. The men were never put on identity parades, even though at least one person who had been present in one of the bombed pubs felt he could have identified the bombers. Nevertheless, the six were convicted and sentenced to life imprisonment, the judge commenting: 'You have been convicted on the clearest and most overwhelming evidence I have ever heard in a case of murder.' On appeal, the judges reprimanded the trial judge for aspects of his summing up and a character attack on a defence witness; they acknowledged the weaknesses in the forensic evidence, yet concluded that this evidence would have played a small part in the jury's decision; and as far as the confession evidence was concerned, a judge mentioned the black eye on one of the defendants, 'the origin of which I have forgotten', but said: 'I do not think it matters much anyway.' The appeal was dismissed.

Fourteen prison officers were subsequently tried for assaulting the six men; their victims were not allowed to appear as witnesses, and they were all acquitted. Evidence given suggested that the men had already been injured when they arrived at the prison. The six then brought a civil action for assault against the police force. This claim was struck out. Lord Denning's judgment summed up the legal system's attitude to the case, pointing out that if the six won, and proved they had been assaulted in order to secure their confessions, this would mean the police had lied, used violence and threats, and that the convictions were false; the Home Secretary would have to recommend a pardon or send the case back to the Court of Appeal. The general feeling seemed to be that such serious miscarriages of justice were simply unthinkable, and so the system for a long time turned its back on the growing claims that the unthinkable had actually happened.

In January 1987, the Home Secretary referred the case back to the Court of Appeal. The appeal took a year; the convictions were upheld. The Lord Chief Justice, Lord Lane, ended the court's judgment with remarks which were to become notorious: 'The longer this hearing has gone on, the more convinced this court has become that the verdict of the jury was correct. We have no doubt that these convictions were both safe and satisfactory.'

In the end, it took 16 years for the six to get their convictions quashed. In 1990, another Home Secretary referred the case back to the Court of Appeal. A new technique had been developed, known as electrostatic document analysis (ESDA), which could examine the indentations made on paper by writing on the sheets above. The test suggested that notes of a police interview with one of the six had not been recorded contemporaneously, as West Midlands detectives had claimed in court. The scientific findings in the Maguire case also meant that the nitroglycerine tests could no longer be relied on. The prosecution decided not to seek to sustain the convictions and the six were finally freed in 1991.

The response to the miscarriages of justice

The miscarriages of justice described above, and others, showed that there was something seriously wrong with the criminal justice system and that the right balance was not being achieved between individual rights and the need for the police to have investigative powers. On 14 March 1991, when the Court of Appeal quashed the convictions of the Birmingham Six, the Home Secretary announced that a Royal Commission on Criminal Justice (RCCJ) would be set up to examine the penal process from start to finish – from the time the police first investigate to the final appeal. The RCCJ (sometimes called the Runciman Commission, after its chairperson) considered these issues for two years, during which they received evidence from over 600 organisations and asked academics to carry out 22 research studies on how the system works in practice. In July 1993 they published their final report. In examining the criminal justice system, we will consider some of the research presented to the RCCJ, its recommendations and some changes that have subsequently been made.

The Human Rights Act 1998

The passing of the Human Rights Act 1998, incorporating the European Convention on Human Rights into domestic law, will have a significant impact on all stages of the criminal justice system. The provisions of the European Convention could potentially provide an important safeguard against abuses and excesses within the system, most notably in protecting individual rights from being abused when the police exercise their investigative powers. Of particular relevance in this field are Art. 3 prohibiting torture and inhuman or degrading treatment; Art. 5 protecting the right to liberty including the right not to be arrested or detained by the police without lawful authority; Art. 6 guaranteeing a fair trial; and Art. 8 which recognises the right to respect of an individual's right to private and family life. The powers of arrest, stop and search and the refusal of bail are all likely to be the subject of legal challenges on the basis that their exercise has breached the Convention. For example, in **Caballero** *v* **United Kingdom** (2000) the UK government accepted that the law on bail breached Art. 5 of the Convention and the domestic law was reformed as a result.

 ## Quick quiz 4.1

1 Which Act incorporated the European Convention on Human Rights into domestic law?

2 Which article of the European Convention on Human Rights protects the right to a fair trial?

3 Which case triggered the establishment of the Royal Commission on Criminal Justice in 1991?

4 Who chaired the 1991 Royal Commission?

Police powers

Most people's first contact with the criminal justice system involves the police, and because they have responsibility for investigating crimes, gathering evidence, and deciding whether to charge a suspect, they play an important part in its overall operation. They also have wide powers over suspects, which may be used to help convict the guilty or, as the miscarriages of justice have shown, abused to convict the innocent.

The main piece of legislation regulating police powers is the Police and Criminal Evidence Act 1984 (PACE). This Act was intended to replace a confusing mixture of common law, legislation and local bye-laws on pre-trial procedure with a single coherent statute. The Act provides a comprehensive code of police powers to stop, search, arrest, detain and interrogate members of the public. It also lays down the suspect's rights. The Criminal Justice and Public Order Act 1994 (CJPOA) extended police powers significantly. It introduced some of the recommendations of the RCCJ, and other changes that the RCCJ was opposed to, for example the abolition of the right to silence. Police powers have been further increased by the Serious Organised Crime and Police Act 2005.

As well as the statutory rules on police powers, contained in PACE and the CJPOA, there are codes of practice, drawn up by the Home Office under s. 66 of PACE, which do not form part of the law, but which provide extra detail on the provisions of the legislation. Breach of these codes cannot be the ground for a legal action, but can give rise to disciplinary procedures, and if they are breached in very serious ways, evidence obtained as a result of such a breach may be excluded in a criminal trial. It has been argued that some of the code provisions should be legally enforceable and form part of PACE itself.

 ## Quick quiz 4.2

1 What does 'PACE' stand for?

2 What does 'CJPOA' stand for?

3 What is the legal status of the codes of practice drawn up by the Home Office under s. 66 of PACE?

4 Which government ministry draws up the police codes of practice?

Stop and search before arrest

PACE repealed a variety of often obscure and unsatisfactory statutory provisions on stop and search; the main powers in this area are now contained in s. 1 of PACE. Under s. 1, a police officer may search a person or vehicle in public, for stolen or prohibited articles (defined as offensive weapons, articles used for the purpose of burglary or related crimes and professional display fireworks). This power can only be used where the police have 'reasonable grounds for suspecting that they will find stolen or prohibited articles' (s. 1(3)). The Criminal Justice Act 2003 extended the power to stop and search to cover searches for articles intended to cause criminal damage. This reform is aimed at people suspected of causing graffiti and who might be carrying cans of spray paint in their pockets.

The exercise of the power to stop and search is also governed by Code of Practice A. This Code starts by stating:

> *'1.1. Powers to stop and search must be used fairly, responsibly, with respect for people being searched and without unlawful discrimination. The Race Relations (Amendment) Act 2000 makes it unlawful for police officers to discriminate on the grounds of race, colour, ethnic origin, nationality or national origins when using their powers.'*

The requirement of reasonable suspicion is intended to protect individuals from being subject to stop and search on a random basis, or on grounds that the law rightly finds unacceptable, such as age or racial background. Code of Practice A provides guidance on the meaning of 'reasonable grounds for suspecting'.

> *'2.2 Reasonable grounds for suspicion depend on the circumstances in each case. There must be an objective basis for that suspicion based on facts, information, and/or intelligence which are relevant to the likelihood of finding an article of a certain kind or, in the case of searches under section 43 of the Terrorism Act 2000, to the likelihood that the person is a terrorist. Reasonable suspicion can never be supported on the basis of personal factors alone without reliable supporting intelligence or information or some specific behaviour by the person concerned. For example, a person's race, age, appearance, or the fact that the person is known to have a previous conviction, cannot be used alone or in combination with each other as the reason for searching that person. Reasonable suspicion cannot be based on generalizations or stereotypical images of certain groups or categories of people as more likely to be involved in criminal activity. A person's religion cannot be considered as reasonable grounds for suspicion and should never be considered as a reason to stop or stop and search an individual.*
>
> *2.3 Reasonable suspicion can sometimes exist without specific information or intelligence and on the basis of some level of generalization stemming from the behaviour of a person. For example, if an officer encounters someone on the street at night who is obviously trying to hide something, the officer may (depending on the other surrounding circumstances) base such suspicion on the fact that this kind of behaviour is often linked to stolen or prohibited articles being carried. Similarly, for the purposes of section 43 of the Terrorism Act 2000, suspicion that a person is a terrorist may arise from the person's behaviour at or near a location which has been identified as a potential target for terrorists.'*

Before searching under these powers, police officers must, among other things, identify themselves and the station where they are based, and tell the person to be searched the grounds for the search. If not in uniform, police officers must provide documentary identification (s. 2(3)). Reasonable force may be used (s. 117), but the suspect cannot be required to remove any clothing in public, except for an outer coat, jacket or gloves (s. 2(9)). Police officers must ask anyone stopped to give their name and address and to define their ethnicity.

Any stolen or prohibited articles discovered by the police during the search may be seized (s. 1(6)). A written record of the search must be made at the time of the search, unless there are exceptional circumstances which would make this wholly impracticable. The record should state why the person was stopped and what the outcome was. The person searched must be given a copy of this immediately.

In the past the police could, and frequently did, carry out a search where there was no statutory power to search but with the consent of the member of the public. These searches could then take place without any of the legislative safeguards. In practice some people would 'consent' to a search in that they would offer no resistance to it, because they did not know their legal rights. Since 2003 voluntary searches are no longer allowed.

Other powers to stop and search

Various statutes give specific stop and search powers regarding particular offences. For example, the Misuse of Drugs Act 1971, s. 23, allows the police to stop and search anyone who is suspected on reasonable grounds to be in unlawful possession of a controlled drug.

Following the 11 September 2001 attacks on the US, the Anti-terrorism, Crime and Security Act 2001 was passed. Section 44 of that Act allows the Home Secretary secretly to authorise the police to carry out random stop and searches in the fight against terrorism. There is no requirement that the police have reasonable suspicion against the person being searched. These powers have, in practice, been used extensively and controversially by the police.

There are clearly potential dangers in granting wide stop and search powers to the police if there is a possibility that the powers will be abused, with harassment of ethnic minority groups being a particular concern.

Powers of arrest

Powers of arrest allow people to be detained against their will. Such detention is only lawful if the arrest is carried out in accordance with the law. An arrest can take place either with or without a warrant. As well as the relevant legislative provisions, guidance for the police on the use of their power of arrest is provided in Code of Practice G.

Arrest with a warrant

Under s. 1 of the Magistrates' Courts Act 1980, criminal proceedings may be initiated either by the issue of a summons requiring the accused to attend court on a

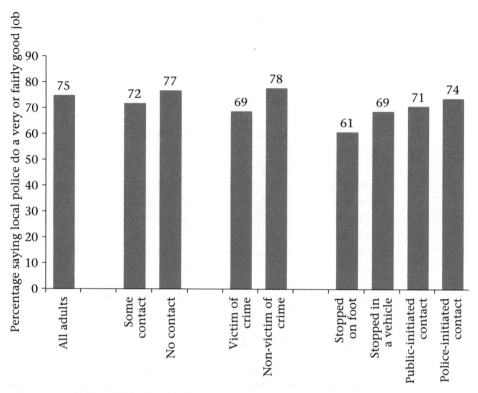

Figure 4.2 Rating of the local police by type of contact

Source: S. Nicholas and A. Walker (2004), *Crime in England and Wales 2002/2003: Supplementary Vol. 2: Crime, disorder and the criminal justice system and public attitudes and perceptions*, p. 11, Figure 2.1.

particular day or, in more serious cases, by a warrant of arrest issued by the magistrates' court. The police obtain a warrant by applying in writing to a magistrate, and backing up the application with an oral statement made on oath. The warrant issued must specify the name of the person to be arrested and general particulars of the offence. When an arrest warrant has been granted, a constable may enter and search premises to make the arrest, using such reasonable force as is necessary (PACE, s. 117).

Arrest without a warrant

The powers of the police to arrest without a warrant were increased by the Serious Organised Crime and Police Act 2005. The extension of police arrest powers were considered in the consultation paper, *Modernising Police Powers to Meet Community Needs* (2004). The reforms have simplified the police powers of arrest, but at the same time they have given the police more powers than they need, and are open to abuse.

In the past, s. 24 of PACE allowed a person to be arrested only for quite serious offences, known as arrestable offences, unless certain additional requirements were satisfied when an arrest would also be possible for a minor offence. The 2005 Act amended PACE, so that now a police officer can arrest a person for committing any offence if this is necessary. Police officers must reasonably suspect that a person has committed, is committing, or is about to commit an offence and have reasonable grounds for believing that it is necessary to arrest that person. It will be necessary to carry out an arrest if:

■ the person will not give their name and address, or the police officer reasonably suspects that the name or address given is false; or

■ the arrest will prevent the person from causing physical injury to him or herself or another person; suffering physical injury; causing loss or damage to property; committing an offence against public decency; or obstructing the highway;

■ to protect a child or other vulnerable person;

■ to allow the prompt and effective investigation of the offence or of the conduct of the person in question; or

■ to prevent the person disappearing.

These last two reasons are likely to justify an arrest in most cases. Further guidance on the issue is contained in a Code of Practice. In **G v DPP** (1989) it was held that a belief of the police officer concerned that suspects generally give false names was not sufficient to satisfy the general arrest conditions.

The same rules apply to the concept of reasonable suspicion for arrest as were discussed for stop and search powers. Its meaning in the context of an arrest was considered by the House of Lords in **O'Hara v Chief Constable of the Royal Ulster Constabulary** (1997). A two-stage test was identified. First, there must be actual suspicion on the part of the arresting officer (the subjective test) and, secondly, there must be reasonable grounds for that suspicion (the objective test). This approach was upheld by the European Court of Human Rights in **O'Hara v United Kingdom** (2002).

Citizen's arrest

A member of the public is entitled to arrest a person in certain circumstances. This power to carry out a citizen's arrest is contained in s. 24A of PACE. The exercise of the citizen's power of arrest is limited to indictable offences. The person must have reasonable grounds for believing that an arrest is necessary and that it is not reasonably practicable for a police officer to carry out the arrest instead. If the citizen has made a mistake, and an offence has not actually been committed by anyone, the citizen may be liable for damages (**Walters v WH Smith & Son Ltd** (1914)). For example, if a man hears somebody shout 'Stop thief' and, seeing a woman running away with a handbag, wrongly assumes she is the thief, he can be sued for damages by that woman if he tries to grab her.

Manner of arrest

PACE requires that, at the time of the arrest, or as soon as practicable after the arrest, the person arrested must be informed that they are under arrest, and given the grounds for that arrest, even if it is perfectly obvious that they are being arrested and why (s. 28). This is in line with the pre-existing case law, where in **Christie v Leachinsky** (1947) Viscount Simon said: 'No one, I think, would approve a situation in which when the person arrested asked for the reason, the policeman replied "that has nothing to do with you: come along with me" . . . '

There is no set form of words that must be used, and colloquial language such as 'You're nicked for mugging' may be acceptable.

Quick quiz 4.3

1 What is the main statutory provision allowing the police to stop and search a member of the public?

2 Which code of practice provides guidance on the meaning of 'reasonable suspicion'?

3 When do the police have a power to arrest without a warrant under s. 24 of PACE?

4 What is meant by a 'citizen's arrest'?

Detention at the police station

Under PACE, suspects can be detained without charge for up to four days, although there are some safeguards designed to prevent abuse of this power. PACE provides that an arrested person must be brought to a police station as soon as practicable after the arrest, though this may be delayed if their presence elsewhere is necessary for an immediate investigation (s. 30). On arrival at the police station, the arrested person should usually be taken to the custody officer, who has to decide whether sufficient evidence exists to charge the person. If, on arrest, there is already sufficient evidence to charge the suspect, he or she must be charged and then released on bail unless there are reasons why this is not appropriate. Such reasons include the fact that the defendant's name and address are not known, that there are reasonable grounds for believing that the address given is false, or that the suspect may commit an offence while on bail (s. 38(1)). A person who has been charged and is being held in custody must be brought before magistrates as soon as practicable, and in any event not later than the first sitting after being charged with the offence (s. 46).

If there is not sufficient evidence to charge the suspect, then the person can be detained for the purpose of securing or obtaining such evidence – often through questioning (s. 37). Where a person is being detained and has not been charged, a review officer should assess whether there are grounds for continued detention after the first six hours and then at intervals of not more than nine hours (s. 40). These reviews can sometimes be carried out by telephone. As a basic rule, the police can detain a person for up to 36 hours from the time of arrival at the police station (this was increased from 24 hours by the Criminal Justice Act 2003). After this time, the suspect should generally be either released or charged (s. 41). However, there are major exceptions to this. Continued detention for a further 12 hours can be authorised by the police themselves, if the detention is necessary to secure or preserve evidence and the offence is an indictable offence (meaning an offence which can be tried in the Crown Court rather than the magistrates' court).

Further periods of continued detention, up to 96 hours, are possible with approval from the magistrates' court. After 96 hours the suspect must be charged or released. In fact, prolonged detention is rare, with only 5 per cent of suspects detained for more than 18 hours, and 1 per cent for more than 24 hours. In terrorist cases, under the Terrorism Act 2006, a person can be detained for up to 28 days and some politicians have been pushing for this to be increased to 90 days.

The custody officer is responsible for keeping the custody record (which records the various stages of detention) and checks that the provisions of PACE in relation to the detention are complied with. These theoretical safeguards for the suspect have proved weak in practice. PACE seems to contemplate that custody officers will be quasi-judicial figures, who can distance themselves from the needs of the investigation and put the rights of the suspect first. In practice, this has never been realistic; custody officers are ordinary members of the station staff, and likely to share their view of the investigation. In addition, they will often be of a more junior rank than the investigating officer. They are therefore highly unlikely to refuse to allow the detention of a suspect, or to prevent breaches of PACE and its codes during the detention.

Once a person has been charged, they cannot normally be subject to further questioning by the police. In a consultation paper, *Modernising Police Powers: Review of the Police and Criminal Evidence Act 1984* (2007), the Home Office is considering whether this ban on further questioning should be lifted in the future.

Treatment of suspects at the police station

Search of the person after arrest

The police have the power to search arrested persons on arrival at the police station, and to seize anything which they reasonably believe the suspect might use to injure anyone, or use to make an escape, or that is evidence of an offence or has been obtained as the result of an offence (s. 54).

Intimate searches and fingerprinting

Section 55 of PACE gives police the power to conduct intimate searches of a suspect, which means searches of the body's orifices. Such a search must be authorised by a superintendent, who must have reasonable grounds for believing that a weapon or drug is concealed, and must be carried out by a qualified doctor or nurse.

The safeguards on the use of this power caused problems for the police when confronted with drug dealers. The dealers frequently stored drugs in their mouths, knowing that search of the mouth was regarded as an intimate search that needed to be carried out by a member of the medical profession with special authorisation. To address this problem, s. 65 of PACE, as amended by the CJPOA 1994, now provides that a search of the mouth is not an intimate search.

The police are permitted to take fingerprints from a suspect under s. 61 of PACE. Section 62 of PACE states that intimate samples, including blood, saliva or semen, can be taken from a suspect, but in some cases the suspect's written consent is required, though this is becoming increasingly rare following the Criminal Evidence (Amendment) Act 1997. Non-intimate samples, such as hair or nail clippings, can be taken from a suspect without their consent, under s. 63, although this procedure must be authorised by an officer at the level of inspector or above. The authorisation must be in writing and recorded on the custody record.

These powers have been extended by the Criminal Justice and Police Act 2001, which allows what the Act calls 'speculative searches', whereby fingerprints, samples or information drawn from them can be checked against other similar data available to the police. These changes broadly reflect the recommendations of the RCCJ. The powers of the police to take and retain DNA samples are also contained in the 2001 Act.

The Criminal Justice and Court Services Act 2000 allows the compulsory drug testing of alleged offenders.

Non-intimate samples

Urine and other non-intimate samples can be taken after arrest for a trigger offence, such as theft and burglary, to test for the presence of Class A drugs.

Police interrogation

The usual reason for detaining suspects is so that the police can question them, in the hope of securing a confession. This has come to be a very important invest-igative tool, since it is cheap (compared, for example, to scientific evidence) and the end result, a confession, is seen as reliable and convincing evidence by judges and juries alike. Research by Mitchell (1983) suggests that a high proportion of suspects do make either partial or complete confessions.

Unfortunately, as the miscarriages of justice show, relying too much on confes-sion evidence can have severe drawbacks. Instances of police completely falsify-ing confessions, or threatening or beating suspects so that they confess even when they are innocent, may be rare, but the miscarriages show that police have been willing to use these techniques where they think they can get away with it. In addition, there are less dramatic, but probably more widespread problems. The 1993 Royal Commission raised questions about the poor standard of police inter-viewing; research by John Baldwin (*Video Taping Police Interviews with Suspects: an Evaluation*, 1992) suggested that police officers went into the interview situation not with the aim of finding out whether the person was guilty, but on the assumption of guilt and with the intention of securing a confession to that effect. Interviews were often rambling and repetitious; police officers dismissed suspects' explanations and asked the same questions over and over again until they were given the answer they wanted. In some cases the researchers felt this treatment amounted to bullying or harassment, and in several cases the 'admissions' were one-word answers given in response to leading questions. Suspects were also offered inducements to confess, such as lighter sentences.

Obviously, the implication here is that, under this kind of pressure, suspects might confess to crimes they did not commit – as many of the miscarriage of justice victims did. But such false confessions do not only occur where the sus-pects are physically threatened. A study by psychologist G. H. Gudjonsson (*The Psychology of Interrogations, Confessions and Testimony*, 1992) found that there were four situations in which people were likely to confess to crimes they did not commit. First, a minority may make confessions quite voluntarily, out of a disturbed desire for publicity, to relieve general feelings of guilt or because they cannot distinguish between reality and fantasy – it has been suggested that this was partly the case with Judith Ward. Secondly, they may want to protect someone else, perhaps a friend or relative, from interrogation and prosecution. Thirdly, they may be unable to see further than a desire to put an end to the questioning and get away from the police station, which can, after all, be a frightening place for those who are not accustomed to it. A psychologist giving evidence to the 1993 Royal Commission commented that: 'Some children are brought up in such a way that confession always seems to produce forgiveness, in which case a false confession may be one way of bringing an unpleasant situation [the interrogation] to an end.' Among this group there may also be a feeling that, once they get out of the police station, they will be able to make everyone see sense, and realise their innocence. Unfortunately, this does not always happen.

Finally, the pressure of questioning, and the fact that the police seem convinced of their case, may temporarily persuade the suspect that they must have done the act in question. Obviously, the young and the mentally ill are likely to be particularly vulnerable to this last situation, but Gudjonsson's research found that its effects were not confined to those who might be considered abnormally suggestible. Their subjects included people of reasonable intelligence who scored highly in tests on suggestibility, showing that they were particularly prepared to go along with what someone in authority was saying. Under hostile interrogation in the psychologically intimidating environment of a police station, even non-vulnerable people are likely to make admissions which are not true, failing to realise that, once a statement has been made, it will be extremely difficult to retract.

Safeguards for the suspect

Certain safeguards are contained in PACE to try to protect the suspect in the police station. Some of these – the custody officer, the custody record, and the time limits for detention – have already been mentioned, and we will now look at the rest. It has been claimed that these safeguards would prevent miscarriages of justice in the future, yet the police station where Winston Silcott was questioned was meant to be following the PACE guidelines on a pilot basis. PACE officially came into force in January 1986 and Mark Braithwaite was arrested in February of that year, yet he was denied access to the legal advice guaranteed by the Act.

The caution

Under Code C, a person must normally be cautioned on arrest, and a person whom there are grounds to suspect of an offence must be cautioned before being asked any questions regarding involvement, or suspected involvement, in that offence. Until recently, the caution was: 'You do not have to say anything unless you wish to do so but what you say may be given in evidence.' Since the abolition of the right to silence (see p. 66), the correct wording is: 'You do not have to say anything, but it may harm your defence if you do not mention when questioned anything which you later rely on in court. Anything that you do say may be given in evidence.'

Tape-recording

Section 60 of PACE states that interviews must be tape-recorded. This measure was designed to ensure that oppressive treatment and threats could not be used, nor confessions made up by the police. Sadly, it has proved a weaker safeguard than it might seem. In the first place, research presented to the RCCJ showed that police routinely got round the provision by beginning their questioning outside the interview room – in the car on the way to the police station, for example. In addition, they appeared quite willing to use oppressive questioning methods even once the tape-recorder was running – the RCCJ listened to tapes of interviews with the 'Cardiff Three', victims of another miscarriage of justice whose convictions were quashed in December 1992, and expressed concern at the continuous repetitive questioning that the tapes revealed. The Home Office is carrying out pilot schemes for the use of video recordings in interviews. However, video recording is unlikely to be introduced at a national level in the near future as the cost of establishing such a scheme would be about £100 million.

The right to inform someone of the detention

Section 56 of PACE provides that, on arrival at a police station, a suspect is entitled to have someone, such as a relative, informed of their arrest. The person whom the suspect chooses must be told of the arrest, and where the suspect is being held, without delay.

This right may be suspended for up to 36 hours if the detention is in connection with an indictable offence, and the authorising officer reasonably believes that informing the person chosen by the suspect would lead to interference with, or harm to, evidence connected with a serious arrestable offence; the alerting of other suspects; interference with or injury to others; hindrance in recovering any property gained as a result of a serious arrestable offence; or in drug-trafficking offences, hindrance in recovering the profits of that offence.

The right to consult a legal adviser

Under s. 58 of PACE, a person held in custody is entitled to consult a legal adviser privately and free of charge. The House of Lords ruled in **R** *v* **Chief Constable of the Royal Ulster Constabulary, ex parte Begley** (1997) that there was no equivalent right under common law. The right to see a legal adviser may be suspended for up to 36 hours on the same grounds as the right to have another person informed. The legal adviser will either be a solicitor or, since 1995, an 'accredited representative'. To become an accredited representative a person must register with the Legal Services Commission with a signed undertaking from a solicitor that he or she is 'suitable' for this work. Once registered, representatives can attend police stations on behalf of their solicitor and deal with summary or either-way offences, but not indictable-only offences. Within six months the representative must complete and submit a portfolio of work undertaken. This will include two police station visits where the representative observed his/her instructing solicitor, two visits where the solicitor observed the representative and five visits which the representative completed on his/her own. If representatives pass the portfolio stage, they then have to take and pass a written and an oral examination, at which point they are fully qualified to represent clients in the police station for any criminal matters. The right to see a legal adviser may be suspended for up to 36 hours on the same grounds as the right to have another person informed.

An 'appropriate adult'

PACE and Code C provide that young people and adults with a mental disorder or mental disability must have an 'appropriate adult' with them during a police interview, as well as having the usual right to legal advice. This may be a parent, but is often a social worker. Surprisingly, Evans's 1993 research for the RCCJ found that parents were not necessarily a protection for the suspect, since they often took the side of the police and helped them to produce a confession.

Physical comfort

PACE codes stipulate that interview rooms must be adequately lit, heated and ventilated, that suspects must be allowed to sit during questioning, and that adequate breaks for meals, refreshments and sleep must be given.

Record of the interview

After the interview is over, the police must make a record of it, which is kept on file. Baldwin's 1992 research checked a sample of such records against the taped recordings, and concluded that even those police forces considered to be more progressive were often failing to produce good quality records of interviews. Half the records were faulty or misleading, and the longer the interview, the more likely the record was to be inaccurate. These findings were backed up by a separate study carried out by Roger Evans (1993). He found that in some summaries the police stated that suspects had confessed during the interview, but, on listening to the tape recordings, the researchers could find no evidence of this, and felt that the suspects were in fact denying the offence.

Exclusion of evidence

One of the most important safeguards in PACE (ss. 76 and 78) is the possibility for the courts to refuse to admit evidence which has been improperly obtained. Given that the reason why police officers bend or break the rules is to secure a conviction, preventing them from using the evidence obtained in this way is likely to constitute an effective deterrent. The House of Lords in **A** *v* **Secretary of State for the Home Department** (2005) held that, if it was established that evidence had been obtained by torture abroad, such as from detainees of Guantanamo Bay, this evidence would not be admissible in proceedings in English courts.

Article 8 of the European Convention on Human Rights protects the right to privacy. Article 8(2) adds that interference with that right is permitted if it is in accordance with the law and necessary in a democratic society for the prevention of crime. A careful balance has to be drawn by the law where surveillance techniques are used, for example, by bugging a private home. Breach of Art. 8 can give rise to a right to damages, but there is no guarantee that the evidence will be excluded at trial as the ordinary rules in ss. 76 and 78 of PACE apply.

The right to silence

Until 1994, the law provided a further safeguard for those suspected of criminal conduct, in the form of the traditional 'right to silence'. This essentially meant that suspects were free to say nothing at all in response to police questioning, and the prosecution could not suggest in court that this silence implied guilt (with some very limited exceptions).

Once PACE was introduced, the police argued that its safeguards, especially the right of access to legal advice, had tipped the balance too far in favour of suspects, so that the right to silence was no longer needed. Despite the fact that the Royal Commission on Criminal Justice (1993) opposed this view, the government agreed with the police, and the right to silence was abolished by the Criminal Justice and Public Order Act 1994. This does not mean that suspects can be forced to speak, but it provides four situations in which, if the suspect chooses not to speak, the court will be entitled to draw such inferences from that silence as appear proper. The four situations are where suspects:

- when questioned under caution or charge, fail to mention facts which they later rely on as part of their defence and which it is reasonable to expect them to have mentioned (s. 34);
- are silent during the trial, including choosing not to give evidence or to answer any question without good cause (s. 35);
- following arrest, fail to account for objects, substances or marks on clothing when requested to do so (s. 36);
- following arrest, fail to account for their presence at a particular place when requested to do so (s. 37).

No inferences from silence can be drawn where a suspect was at a police station and has been denied access to legal advice (s. 34(2)(A)).

Interviews outside the police station

PACE states that, where practicable, interviews with arrested suspects should always take place at a police station. However, evidence obtained by questioning or voluntary statements outside the police station may still be admissible. Since such interviews are not subject to most of the safeguards explained above, the obvious danger is that police may evade PACE requirements by conducting 'unofficial' interviews – such as the practice known as taking the 'scenic route' to the station, in which suspects are questioned in the police car. The RCCJ found that about 30 per cent of suspects report being questioned prior to arrest.

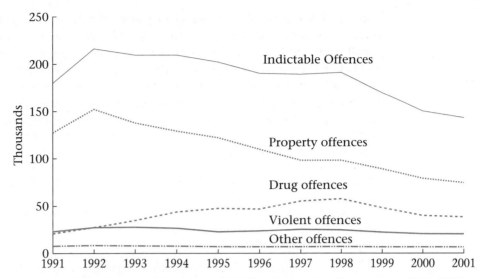

Figure 4.3 Offenders cautioned for indictable offences by offence group, 1991-2001
Source: Home Office (2002), *Criminal Statistics England and Wales 2001*, p. 34, Figure 5.7.

Problems with the police

Criticisms and suggestions for reform have been made throughout this chapter, but the following have been the subject of particular debate and highlight the problem of balancing an individual's rights with the need for the police to have effective investigative powers.

A graduate profession

The work of a police officer requires a wide range of skills, both intellectual and personal. At the moment, a candidate does not need any formal qualifications to join the police force. Now that increasing numbers of young people are going to university, it is time to transform the police force into a graduate profession. Only then would the UK have an efficient police force with the skills to combat crime effectively. The police force currently struggles with the paperwork that their job requires because they have an inadequate education. Without better preparation for their career, the police will continue to be perceived by many in the public as slow, lazy and inefficient. With the creation of community support officers, the higher pay and status of the police can only be justified if they actually have better qualifications and skills.

sourcebook p. 201 →

Review of PACE

The Home Office issued a consultation paper in 2007, *Modernising Police Powers: Review of the Police and Criminal Evidence Act 1984*. The paper covers a wide variety of topics and seems to be looking at ways to reduce unnecessary paperwork to help the police to work more efficiently and effectively and spend more time on front-line duty. It considers whether the codes could be simplified and shorter to make them more accessible. To save police time, short-term holding facilities could be established in shopping centres. People arrested for minor crimes, such as shoplifting, could be taken there instead of to the police station. The cells could hold suspects for up to four hours to enable finger-printing, photographing and DNA sampling. The rules relating to the taking and storing of identification samples could be relaxed, so that DNA samples and finger-prints could be taken from those suspected of minor crimes. The pressure group, Liberty, has commented that: 'Six years ago, DNA sampling was about combatting serious crime. Today, dropping litter is proposed as a lame excuse for an ever-growing national DNA database.'

Racism and the police

Britain is a multicultural and ethnically diverse community. Three per cent of the population aged 10 and over is of black ethnic origin, 5 per cent of Asian origin. Successful policing requires that all members of British society must have confidence in the police force. Following the fatal stabbing of Stephen Lawrence, a black teenager who was an A-level student from south London, by a group of racist youths in 1993, defects in several aspects of the English legal system failed to bring his killers to justice. Following concern at the handling of the police

sourcebook
p. 202 → investigation into the killing, a judicial inquiry headed by a former High Court judge, Sir William Macpherson, was set up by the government in 1997 and its report was published in February 1999. It found that the Metropolitan Police suffered from institutional racism. This is defined as existing where there is:

> '[a] collective failure of an organisation to provide an appropriate and professional service to people because of their colour, culture and ethnic origin. It can be seen or detected in processes, attitudes and behaviour which amount to discrimination through unwitting prejudice, ignorance, thoughtlessness and racist stereotypical behaviour.'

The presence of institutional racism was reflected in the fact that the first senior officer at the scene of the crime assumed that what had occurred had been a fight; it was also expressed in the absence of adequate family liaison and the 'patronising and thoughtless approach' of some officers to Mr and Mrs Lawrence; and it could be seen in the side-lining of Stephen Lawrence's friend, the surviving victim of the attack. There was, furthermore, a refusal to accept, by at least five officers involved in the case, that this was a racist murder. Finally, there was the use of inappropriate and offensive language by police officers, including, on occasion, during their appearance before the inquiry itself. It found that racism awareness training was 'almost non-existent at every level', and concluded that institutional racism could only be tackled effectively if there was an 'unequivocal acceptance that the problem actually exists'.

The inquiry concluded, however, that institutional racism was not 'universally the cause of the failure of this investigation'. The investigation by the Metropolitan Police was 'marred by a combination of professional incompetence, institutional racism and a failure of leadership by senior officers'.

The report contained 20 recommendations for reform. In March 1999, the government issued its Action Plan in response to the Macpherson Report. A steering group, chaired by the Home Secretary, has been established to oversee the programme of reform. In the past, the Race Relations Act 1976 did not apply to the police, so that there was no legal remedy if a black person thought they had been stopped by the police because of racial prejudice. Now the Race Relations (Amendment) Act 2000 has been passed. This Act amends the 1976 Act, making it unlawful for a public authority, including the police, to discriminate in carrying out any of their functions. Police forces have reviewed their provision of racism awareness training. Targets have been set for the recruitment and retention of ethnic minority police officers. Currently 2.6 per cent of police officers are from an ethnic minority. The recommendation that the use of racist language in private should be criminalised has been rejected.

While the Macpherson Report is one step towards tackling institutional racism in the police, it is worrying that Lord Scarman's report into the Brixton riots of 1981 had already identified this problem and, though some progress was subsequently made, this has clearly not been sufficient. In 1999/2000 the British Crime Survey suggested that there were 143,000 racially motivated crimes committed and yet only 1,832 defendants were prosecuted for such offences.

sourcebook
p. 226 →

A particularly sensitive area of policing is the power to stop and search. A police operation against street robberies in Lambeth (South London) in 1981, code-named SWAMP 81, involved 943 stops, mostly of young black men, over a period of two weeks. Of these, only 118 led to arrests and 75 to charges, one of which was for robbery. The operation, which had no noticeable effect on the crime figures, shattered relations between the police and the ethnic community, and was one of the triggers of the Brixton riots that occurred soon afterwards. Nevertheless, in his report on the Brixton disorders, Lord Scarman thought such powers necessary to combat street crime, provided that the safeguard of 'reasonable suspicion' was properly and objectively applied. But in 1999 the Macpherson Report concluded that the 'perception and experience of the minority communities that discrimination is a major element in the stop and search problem is correct'.

In accordance with recommendations made by Macpherson, the police are now required to monitor the use of stop and search powers, and 'consider in particular whether there is any evidence that they are being exercised on the basis of stereotyped images or inappropriate generalisations'. Regrettably, these statistics show that an increasing proportion of those stopped and searched by the police are black. Home Office statistics (*Statistics on Race and the Criminal Justice System 2003*) show that, while black people make up only 3 per cent of the population, 14 per cent of stop and searches were carried out on black people, an increase of more than a third on the previous year. The Commission for Racial Equality (2004) has concluded that stop and search has been used disproportionately against black and Asian people. This has:

'led to the perception among some communities that stop and search is being used in a discriminatory way – affecting confidence levels in the police and in some cases reducing the willingness of people to assist with the investigation of crime.'

An increasing worry is the number of black murder victims and the failure of the police to bring the offenders to court. Between 2000 and 2003, 10 per cent of homicide victims were black. The police were statistically less likely to identify suspects for homicides involving black and Asian victims than for white victims, though this can partly be explained by the method of killing used.

Police corruption

The police exercise an extremely delicate role in society and, as criminals are able to generate large sums of money from their criminal conduct, the danger of corruption is real. High risk areas include the handling of informers and positions within drug, vice and crime squads where constant vigilance is required. Where corruption is rife, one can no longer fall back on the idea of a few rotten apples and accept that the system itself must be corrupting its members.

Sir Paul Condon made anti-corruption a touchstone of his tenure as Commissioner of the Metropolitan Police. He has estimated that there may be as many as 250 corrupt officers in his force, some of whom are directly involved in very serious criminal activity, and has dedicated resources to their detection. A more proactive approach can be expected at a national level, as New Scotland Yard has established a special squad concentrating on corruption in the police and the Association of Chief Police Officers established in 1998 a Taskforce on Corruption. During the course of that year, 28 police officers were convicted of corruption-related offences, and at the end of the year, 153 police officers were suspended for alleged corruption and similar matters.

Armed officers

There is an on-going debate as to whether our police officers should carry guns. The majority of police in other countries do carry guns. In the UK, the tradition is that police do not carry guns, and only 5 per cent have carried out special training to be authorised to carry them. They work, for example, in armed response vehicles, so that they can provide swift support to their colleagues where necessary. Following the fatal shooting in Bradford of a 28-year-old police officer, Sharon Beshenivsky, who was investigating a robbery at a travel agents, the Police Federation and the Association of Chief Police Officers called for more police in the UK to be armed. On the other hand, the fatal shooting of Jean Charles de Menezes at Stockwell tube station in the summer of 2005 highlighted the risks of police officers being armed, as the police are only human and can make mistakes.

Police conduct

During 1997, well over 6,000 complaints of alleged rudeness and incivility by police officers were recorded. Her Majesty's Inspectorate of Constabulary undertook a wide-ranging exploration of the level of integrity in the police because it was recognised that 'public confidence was becoming seriously affected by the bad behaviour of a small minority of police'. In *Police Integrity: Securing and Maintaining Public Confidence* (1999), Her Majesty's Inspectorate reported that: 'Numerous examples were found in all forces visited of poor behaviour towards members of the public and colleagues alike, including rudeness, arrogance and discriminatory comment.' In the Inspectorate's view, one consequence of tolerating bullying, rudeness and racist or sexist behaviour is that 'corruption and other wrongdoing will flourish'.

The right to silence

The abolition of the right to silence has been one of the most severely criticised changes to the criminal justice system in recent years. As the academic John Fitzpatrick has written, the basis of the right to silence is the presumption of innocence, which places the burden of proof on the prosecution: 'this burden begins to shift, and the presumption of innocence to dwindle, as soon as we are obliged to explain or justify our actions in any way' (*Legal Action*, May 1994).

Those who objected to the right to silence claimed that only the guilty would have anything to hide and that the innocent should therefore have no objection to answering questions. It was suggested that the calculated use of this right by professional criminals was leading to serious cases being dropped for lack of evidence, and that 'ambush' defences (in which defendants remain silent till the last moment and then produce an unexpected defence) were leading to acquittals because the prosecution had no time to prepare for the defence.

These arguments were put to the RCCJ, by a Home Office Working Group among others, but, after commissioning its own research into the subject the RCCJ rejected the idea of abolishing the right to silence. This research, by Leng (1993), and McConville and Hodgson (1993), showed that in fact only 5 per cent of suspects exercised their right to silence, and there was no evidence of an unacceptable acquittal rate for these defendants. Nor was there any serious problem with ambush defences.

As we have seen, the Conservative government decided to ignore the RCCJ recommendations and abolish the right to silence – a somewhat strange decision considering that it was the same government which set up the Commission in the first place. The law reform body, Justice, has claimed that this decision will lead to increased pressure on suspects and, in turn, to more miscarriages of justice. It studied the effects of removing the right to silence in Northern Ireland (which took place five years before removal of the right in England and Wales). Apparently, suspects frequently failed to understand the new caution and were put under unfair pressure to speak, while lawyers found it difficult to advise suspects when they did not know the full case against them. Most importantly, Justice claims that, while at first trial judges were cautious about drawing inferences of guilt from a suspect's silence, five years on they were giving such silence considerable weight, and in some cases treating it almost as a presumption of guilt.

Deaths in police custody

Almost 700 people have died in police custody or in contact with the police since 1990. Very few police officers have been prosecuted following a death in custody, and none has been convicted. A report on the subject by Vogt and Wadham (2003),

Deaths in Custody: Redress and Remedies, for the pressure group Liberty, concluded that these deaths were not being adequately investigated. The police, the Police

sourcebook p. 176 → Complaints Authority (now the Independent Police Complaints Commission) and the coroner could all be involved. These investigations were ineffective, secretive, slow and insufficiently independent.

Reading on the web

The revised Code A for PACE can be found on the Home Office website at:

www.policehomeoffice.gov.uk/news-and-publications/publication/operational-policing/PACE_Chapter_A.pdf

www.liberty-human-rights.org.uk

Information on the criminal justice system is available at:

www.cjsonline.org/index.html

Chapter summary

Introduction

The criminal justice system needs to strike a balance between punishing the guilty and protecting the innocent. Recent miscarriages of justice have raised concerns as to whether this balance is being achieved.

Stop and search

Under s. 1 of PACE, a police officer may search a person or vehicle in public, for stolen or prohibited articles where the police have 'reasonable grounds for suspecting that they will find stolen or prohibited articles'.

Powers of arrest

An arrest can take place either with or without a warrant. The powers of the police to arrest without a warrant were increased by the Serious Organised Crime and Police Act 2005.

Citizen's arrest

A member of the public is entitled to arrest a person in certain circumstances. This power to carry out a citizen's arrest is contained in s. 24A of PACE.

Police detention

Under PACE, the police can detain a suspect for up to four days without charge.

Police interrogation

The usual reason for detaining suspects is so that the police can question them, in the hope of securing a confession. Certain safeguards exist to protect people while they are being detained and questioned. These include the tape-recording of police interviews in the police station and the right to inform someone of the detention. Since 1994 the right to silence has been effectively abolished.

Problems with the police

A range of criticisms and reform proposals have been put forward relating to the police:

A graduate profession

Now that increasing numbers of young people are going to university, it is time to transform the police force into a graduate profession. Only then would the UK have an efficient police force with the skills to combat crime effectively.

Review of PACE

The Home Office issued a consultation paper in 2007, *Modernising Police Powers: Review of the Police and Criminal Evidence Act 1984*. The paper covers a wide variety of topics and seems to be looking at ways to reduce unnecessary paperwork to help the police to work more efficiently.

Racism and the police

Following the unsuccessful police investigation into the murder of the black teenager Stephen Lawrence, Sir William Macpherson found that the Metropolitan Police suffered from 'institutional racism'. A particularly sensitive area of policing is the power to stop and search, and the targeting of black people can have a detrimental effect on the relationship of the police with black people generally.

Police corruption

The police exercise an extremely delicate role in society and, as criminals are able to generate large sums of money from their criminal conduct, the danger of corruption is real.

The right to silence

The abolition of the right to silence has been one of the most severely criticised changes to the criminal justice system in recent years.

Deaths in police custody

Almost 700 people have died in police custody or in contact with the police since 1990. Very few police officers have been prosecuted following a death in custody, and none has been convicted.

Question and answer guides

Tyrone, aged 16, has missed the last bus and has to walk home. It is 2 a.m. and a police officer driving past in a police car sees Tyrone and stops. The police officer tells Tyrone to empty his pockets and Tyrone refuses. The police officer then grabs Tyrone's shoulder, pushes him into the police car and takes him to the local police station.

(a) Describe the powers the police have to stop and search an individual on the street.

Plan

- Under s. 1 of PACE, the police can stop and search a person in a public place if they have reasonable grounds to suspect that a person possesses stolen goods or prohibited articles.
- A police officer has to give his name, station and the reason for the search.
- The police can ask suspects to remove coats, jackets and gloves.
- A written report must be made of the incident.
- Guidance on the exercise of the stop and search power is contained in Code of Practice A of PACE.
- Under s. 60 of the Criminal Justice and Public Order Act 1994, the police have the right to stop and search without reasonable suspicion in a specified area where violence is anticipated.
- Section 23 of the Misuse of Drugs Act 1971 allows a stop and search where there is reasonable suspicion of drug possession.
- Section 44 of the Anti-terrorism, Crime and Security Act 2001 allows a stop and search to prevent terrorist offences.

Answer

Following public concern at the possible abusive use of police powers, the Royal Commission on Criminal Procedure (the Philips Commission) published its report in January 1981. Based on its recommendations, the Police and Criminal Evidence Act 1984 (PACE) was passed. This Act laid down, for the first time, in a single, clear statute, the police power to stop and search. In doing so, the government was seeking to balance the needs of the police against the citizen's right to liberty. The police power to stop and search allows the police to try to combat street crime and anti-social behaviour, and prevent more serious crimes occurring. Additional powers to stop and search have been added by the legislative to deal with particular social problems such as drugs and terrorism.

Under s. 1 of PACE, the police can stop and search a person or vehicle if they have reasonable grounds to suspect that they will find stolen goods, prohibited articles or articles intended for use in committing criminal damage (for example, spray paint). At the outset, the police officers must identify themselves, give their police station base and state the reasons for the search; for example, because the individual is running away from a shop where items were stolen. Normally, the police officer will be in uniform, but plain-clothed police officers can also carry out this search if they show the person their identity card. They can use reasonable force to carry out the search.

Code of Practice A contains guidance on how and when a search can be carried out. This code provides that the police must not stop an individual because of their age, race, gender, sexual orientation, disability, religion or faith, the way they look or dress, the language they speak, or because they may have committed a crime in the past. Whilst in a public place they cannot compel a suspect to remove anything other than outside clothing such as a coat, hat and gloves. They must take the suspect somewhere private if they want any other clothing to be removed. They must ask the suspect for their name, address and ethnicity and written documentary evidence of the search must be provided to the suspect immediately after the search is completed unless this is impossible.

Additional legislation has been passed to allow the police to carry out stop and searches in particular situations. Under s. 60 of the Criminal Justice and Public Order Act 1994, the police have the right to stop and search without reasonable suspicion in a specified area where violence is anticipated, if express authorisation has been given for this in the relevant geographical area. Section 23 of the Misuse of Drugs Act 1971 allows a stop and search where there is reasonable suspicion that an individual possesses controlled drugs. Finally, under s. 44 of the Anti-terrorism, Crime and Security Act 2001, random stop and searches are possible to try to prevent the commission of a terrorist offence.

(b) Advise Tyrone on whether the police officer acted lawfully with regard to stop and search and the arrest. [12]

(OCR Specimen Paper 2007, English Legal System Unit)

Plan

- It appears that Tyrone has been stopped only because he is young and it is 2 a.m.
- The police officer is therefore unlikely to have reasonable suspicion under s. 1 of PACE, taking into account the Code of Practice.
- The police officer failed to give a reason for the search and it is therefore likely to be considered unlawful.
- The police officer did not have valid grounds for carrying out an arrest under s. 24 of PACE.
- Again, the police must inform a person that they are under arrest and the police officer appears to have failed to do so.
- Only reasonable force can be used to carry out an arrest. Pushing a person into a car may not be an unreasonable amount of force.
- In conclusion, the police officer's actions were probably unlawful.

Group activity 1

Take a look at the police recruitment website:

www.policecouldyou.co.uk

On this website you will see that the police are recruiting for a number of different ancillary positions as well as the regular police service. In groups, look at the positions on offer on the site. Compare the pay that is being offered and the qualifications that are being required. If you had to apply for a position, which job would you choose and why?

Visit **www.mylawchamber.co.uk/elliottocr** to access questions, quizzes and activities to test yourself on this chapter.

Chapter 5
CRIMINAL COURTS

This chapter discusses:

- the two criminal trial courts: the magistrates' court and the Crown Court;
- the classification of offences as summary, indictable or either-way offences;
- pre-trial procedures: bail, plea before venue and mode of trial hearings;
- the criminal trial process for adults and young people.

Introduction

There are two main courts where people can be put on trial to decide whether they are guilty of committing a criminal offence: the magistrates' court and the Crown Court. In general terms, magistrates' courts hear the less serious cases (such as minor driving offences), while the Crown Court hears the more serious offences (such as murder and rape). In most magistrates' courts, three 'lay magistrates' (in other words, they are not qualified lawyers) hear the case. In the Crown Court, a jury hears the case with a professional judge presiding over the proceedings. When a person has committed a criminal offence, the classification of that offence determines which court will hear the case.

Classification of offences

There are three different categories of criminal offence: summary, indictable and triable either way.

Summary offences

Summary offences are the most minor crimes, and are only triable summarily in the magistrates' court. 'Summary' refers to the process of ordering the defendant to attend the court by summons, a written order usually delivered by post, which is the most frequent procedure adopted in the magistrates' courts. There has been some criticism of the fact that more and more offences have been made summary only, reducing the right to trial by jury in the Crown Court.

Indictable offences

These are the more serious offences, such as rape and murder. They can only be heard by the Crown Court. The indictment is a formal document containing the alleged offences against the accused, supported by brief facts.

Offences triable either way

These offences may be tried in either the magistrates' court or the Crown Court. Common examples are theft and burglary.

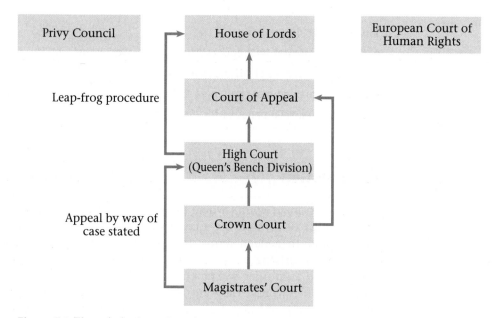

Figure 5.1 **The criminal court system**

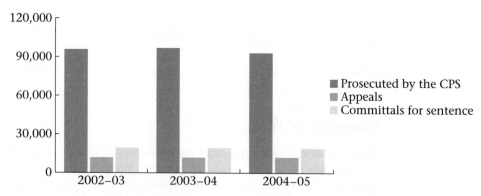

Figure 5.2 **Crown Court case load**

Source: *Crown Prosecution Service Annual Report 2004-2005*, p. 38, Chart 5.

Pre-trial matters

Bail

A person accused, convicted or under arrest for an offence may be granted bail, which means they are released under a duty to attend court or the police station at a given time. The right to bail has been reduced in recent years amid concern that individuals on bail reoffend and fail to turn up at court for their trial. Fourteen per cent of those bailed to appear at court fail to do so (*Criminal Justice Statistics 2003*) and nearly 25 per cent of defendants commit at least one offence while on bail (Brown (1998) *Offending While on Bail*, Home Office, Report No. 72). The criteria for granting or refusing bail are contained in the Bail Act 1976 and the Bail (Amendment) Act 1993. There is a general presumption in favour of bail for unconvicted defendants, but there are some important exceptions. Bail need not be granted where there are substantial grounds for believing that, unless kept in custody, the accused would fail to surrender to bail, or would commit an offence, interfere with witnesses or otherwise obstruct the course of justice. In assessing these risks, the court may take account of the nature and seriousness of the offence and the probable sentence, along with the character, antecedents, associations and community ties of the defendant. Following the Criminal Justice and Court Services Act 2000, a court considering the question of bail must take into account any drug misuse by the defendant. The Criminal Justice Act 2003 has created a presumption against bail for a person charged with an imprisonable offence, who tests positive for a specified Class A drug and refuses treatment, unless there are exceptional circumstances. This provision may breach Art. 5 of the European Convention on Human Rights, which guarantees the right to freedom of the person.

The courts need not grant bail when the accused should be kept in custody for their own protection, where the accused is already serving a prison sentence or where there has been insufficient time to obtain information as to the criteria for bail. If the court does choose to grant bail in such cases, its reasons for doing so must be included in the bail record. The presumption in favour of bail is reversed where someone is charged with a further indictable offence which appears to have been committed while on bail.

Following concern at offences being committed by accused persons while on bail, the Criminal Justice and Public Order Act 1994 provided that a person charged or convicted of murder, manslaughter, rape, attempted murder or attempted rape could never be granted bail if they had a previous conviction for such an offence. This complete ban breached the European Convention on Human Rights. The law has now been reformed by the Crime and Disorder Act 1998, under which such a person may be granted bail only where there are exceptional circumstances which justify doing so. Thus, Sion Jenkins, who was convicted of the murder of his foster-daughter Billy-Jo, was on bail throughout most of the proceedings.

When bail is refused for any of the stated reasons, other than insufficient information, the accused will usually be allowed only one further bail application;

the court does not have to hear further applications unless there has been a change in circumstances. Where the remand in custody is on the basis of insufficient information, this is not technically a refusal of bail, so the accused may still make two applications.

Bail can be granted subject to conditions, such as that the accused obtain legal advice before their next court appearance or that the accused or a third party give a security (which is a payment into court that will be forfeited if the accused fails to attend a court hearing). The Police and Justice Act 2006 increased the range of conditions that can be imposed when granting bail. When a defendant fails to attend court, any money held by the court is immediately forfeited and it is up to the person who paid that money to show why it should not be forfeited. A defendant refused bail, or who objects to the conditions under which it is offered, must be told the reasons for the decision, and informed of their right to appeal. The prosecution also has increasing rights to appeal against a decision to grant bail.

The Criminal Justice Act 2003 has given the police the power to grant bail at the place of arrest. This is called 'street bail'. It means that the police do not have to take suspects to the police station and undertake lengthy paperwork. A form is completed on the street and later entered in police records. The power has not been used much by the police and is unlikely to be used much until compulsory ID cards have been introduced.

In 1992 the average proportion of unconvicted and unsentenced prisoners was 22 per cent of the average prison population. Many of these remand prisoners, who have not been convicted of any offence, are kept in prison for between six months and a year before being tried, despite the fact that 60 per cent of them go on to be acquitted or given a non-custodial sentence.

Plea before venue procedure

The plea before venue procedure was introduced in 1997 to try to reduce the number of cases that were sent to the Crown Court and then the defendant subsequently pleaded guilty, as this was felt to incur unnecessary delay and expense. A plea before venue hearing is held in the magistrates' court. At this hearing defendants are asked to indicate whether they wish to plead guilty or not guilty. They are not obliged to answer this question and if they choose not to do so then the court will proceed to a full mode of trial hearing (discussed below). If they plead guilty, the court will then hear some more detail about the case and either sentence the defendant themselves there and then (or after they have adjourned until they have received a pre-sentence report); or altern-atively commit for sentence to the Crown Court if the magistrates consider their powers of punishment insufficient. If defendants enter a plea of guilty, they have themselves no right to demand that the case be sent up to the Crown Court for sentencing, only the magistrates can decide to do this. The advant-age for the defendant of pleading guilty at this stage is that they can expect to benefit from a reduced sentence because they pleaded guilty at the earliest opportunity.

If the accused pleads not guilty then the case will proceed to a full trial.

Mode of trial

The mode of trial procedure is used only where a person is charged with a triable either-way offence. In addition, there will be a mode of trial hearing only for defendants charged with such an offence who indicated an intention to plead 'not guilty' or declined to indicate their plea during the plea before venue procedure. A person charged with an offence triable either way can insist on a trial by jury. If the person states that they wish to be tried in the magistrates' court, the magistrates can still decide that they think the Crown Court would be the more appropriate venue and send the case to be heard in a Crown Court, despite the person's preference to be tried by a magistrates' court. In reaching this decision, the magistrates will take into account the seriousness of the case and whether they are likely to have sufficient sentencing powers to deal with it. Since 1996, the magistrates are also able to take into account the defendant's plea of guilty or not guilty, which will be given, for triable either-way offences, before the mode of trial decision.

The Criminal Justice Act 2003, Sch. 3, has made certain changes to the mode of trial procedures. When deciding whether the case should stay in the magistrates' court, the magistrates will be informed of the defendant's prior convictions. If the magistrates decide summary trial is appropriate, defendants will have the right to ask for an indication of sentence on plea of guilty before deciding which court to choose. Committal for sentence has been abolished for less serious either-way cases. Magistrates' sentencing powers have been increased from six to twelve months' custody, in the hope that magistrates will send fewer cases to the Crown Court for sentencing.

Dr Andrew Herbert (2003) has carried out research into the magistrates' decision to send cases to the Crown Court. He has concluded that the reforms in the Criminal Justice Act 2003 are doomed to fail in reducing the number of cases referred to the Crown Court. The main Home Office reason for the recent reform attempts has been to reduce costs and increase efficiency. The chief finding of the research is that the magistrates overwhelmingly reject this reason for changing the court venue:

> 'There was a virtual consensus among those interviewed that there was no need for any significant change in the division of business between the higher and the lower courts.'

Magistrates felt that the existing law produced a fair and realistic choice of court. They resented reforms being made for economic or political reasons. Some of the magistrates interviewed pointed to the importance of their judicial independence, so that government policy would not persuade them to keep more cases. One of the magistrates said:

> 'I would never agree to retaining cases on economic grounds. I am fed up with political speak. There should not be pressure put on us. We are trained to do a job and should be left to do it.'

The lawyers interviewed thought that lay magistrates were already being asked to handle cases at the extreme of their ability and were not capable of dealing with more serious cases.

Task 5.1

Complete the following table.

Type of offence	Trial court
Summary	
Triable either way	
Indictable offence	

The trial

Apart from the role played by the jury in the Crown Court, the law and procedure in the Crown Court and magistrates' court are essentially the same. Defendants should normally be present at the trial, though the trial can proceed without them if they have chosen to abscond. A lawyer should usually represent them in their absence (**R** v **Jones** (2002)).

The trial begins with the prosecution outlining the case against the accused, and then producing evidence to prove its case. The prosecution calls its witnesses, who will give their evidence in response to questions from the prosecution (called examination-in-chief). These witnesses can be questioned by the defence (called cross-examination), and then if required, re-examined by the prosecution to address any points brought up in cross-examination.

When the prosecution has presented all its evidence, the defence can submit that there is no case to answer, which means that on the prosecution evidence, no reasonable jury (or Bench of magistrates) could convict. If the submission is successful, a verdict of not guilty will be given straight away. If no such submission is made, or if the submission is unsuccessful, the defence then puts forward its case, using the same procedure for examining witnesses as the prosecution did. The accused is the only witness who cannot be forced to give evidence.

Once the defence has presented all its evidence, each side makes a closing speech, outlining their case and seeking to persuade the magistrates or jury of it. In the Crown Court, this is followed by the judge's summing up to the jury. The judge should review the evidence, draw the jury's attention to the important points of the case, and direct the jury on the law if necessary, but must not trespass on the jury's function of deciding the true facts of the case. At the end of the summing up, the judge reminds the jury that the prosecution must prove its case beyond reasonable doubt, and tries to explain in simple terms what this means.

Trial of young offenders

Young offenders are usually tried in youth courts, which are a branch of the magistrates' court. Other than those involved in the proceedings, the parents and the press, nobody may be present unless authorised by the court. Parents or guardians of children under 16 must attend court at all stages of the proceedings, and the court has the power to order parents of older children to attend.

In limited circumstances, young persons can be tried in a Crown Court; for example, if the offence charged is murder, manslaughter or causing death by dangerous driving. They may sometimes be tried in an adult magistrates' court or the Crown Court if there is a co-defendant in the case who is an adult. Following a Practice Direction discussed below, a separate trial should be ordered unless it is in the interests of justice to do otherwise. If a joint trial is ordered, the ordinary procedures apply 'subject to such modifications (if any) as the court might see fit to order'.

The trial procedures for young offenders have been reformed in the light of a recent ruling of the European Court of Human Rights. This found that Jon Venables and Robert Thompson, who were convicted by a Crown Court of murdering the two-year-old James Bulger in 1993, did not have a fair trial in accordance with Art. 6 of the European Convention on Human Rights. It concluded that the criminal procedures adopted in the trial prevented their participation:

> 'The public trial process in an adult court with attendant publicity was a severely intimidating procedure for 11-year-old children . . . The way in which the trial placed the accused in a raised dock as the focus of intense public attention over a period of three weeks, had impinged on their ability to participate in the proceedings in any meaningful manner.'

Following this decision, a Practice Direction was issued by the Lord Chief Justice, laying down guidance on how young offenders should be tried when their case is to be heard in the Crown Court. The language used by the Practice Direction follows closely that used in the European decision. It does not lay down fixed rules but states that the individual trial judge must decide what special measures are required by the particular case, taking into account 'the age, maturity and development (intellectual and emotional) of the young defendant on trial'. The trial process should not expose that defendant to avoidable intimidation, humiliation or distress. All possible steps should be taken to assist the defendant to understand and participate in the proceedings. It recommends that young defendants should be brought into the court out of hours in order to become accustomed to its layout. Jon Venables and Robert Thompson had both benefited from these familiarisation visits. The police should make every effort to avoid exposure of the defendant to intimidation, vilification or abuse.

As regards the trial, it is recommended that wigs and gowns should not be worn and public access should be limited. The courtroom should be adapted so that, ordinarily, everyone sits on the same level. In the Bulger trial, the two defendants sat in a specially raised dock. The decision to raise the dock had been done so that the defendants could view the proceedings, but the European Court of Human Rights noted that, while it did accomplish this, it also made the defendants aware that everyone was looking at them. Placing everyone on the same level should alleviate this problem. In addition, the Practice Direction states that young defendants should sit next to their families or an appropriate adult and near their lawyers.

The Practice Direction suggests that only those with a direct interest in the outcome of the trial should be permitted within the court. Where the press is restricted, provision should be made for the trial to be viewed through a CCTV link to another court area.

Task 5.2

In 2003 the Youth Justice Board published its annual report, *Gaining Ground in the Community*. This report examined the types of crime being committed by young offenders and the experience of young people as victims of crime. The report states:

Types of offence
Both the annual MORI Youth Survey and the data from Young Offending Teams provide information on the types of crimes being committed by young people. The most common offences committed by young people brought into contact with the youth justice system fall into the following categories:

- Motoring offences (23%).
- Theft and handling (17.8%).
- Violence against the person (13%).
- Criminal damage (10.2%).
- Public order offences (6.7%).

Victimisation and fears of young people
There are continuing high levels of fear among young people, according to the MORI Youth Survey, with a third of respondents saying that they felt unsafe in their local area after dark. Over half of young people in school are worried about being physically assaulted or being the victim of theft. A third worry about bullying and racism.

Some 46% of young people in school and 61% of excluded young people say that they have been a victim of crime in the last 12 months. Two-thirds of young people who have been victims of crime say that the perpetrator of the offence is another young person aged under 18.

Questions

1 What type of crime is a young person most likely to commit?
2 Are you frightened to go out in your local area after dark?
3 What percentage of young people have been the victim of a crime in the last 12 months?
4 Have you been the victim of a crime?

Reading on the web

The Youth Justice Board has a website that can be found at:

www.yjb.gov.uk/en-gb

Chapter summary

Introduction

There are two main courts where people can be put on trial to decide whether they are guilty of committing a criminal offence: the magistrates' court and the Crown Court.

Classification of offences

Summary offences

Summary offences are the most minor crimes, and are only triable summarily in the magistrates' court.

Indictable offences

These are the more serious offences, such as rape and murder. They can only be heard by the Crown Court.

Offences triable either way

These offences may be tried in either the magistrates' court or the Crown Court.

Pre-trial matters

Bail

A person accused, convicted or under arrest for an offence may be granted bail, which means they are released under a duty to attend court or the police station at a given time.

Plea before venue procedure

A plea before venue hearing is held in the magistrates' court. At this hearing defendants are asked to indicate whether they wish to plead guilty or not guilty.

Mode of trial

The mode of trial procedure is used only where a person is charged with a triable either-way offence. In addition, there will only be a mode of trial hearing for defendants charged with a triable either way offence who indicated an intention to plead 'not guilty' or declined to indicate their plea during the plea before venue procedure.

The trial

Apart from the role played by the jury in the Crown Court, the law and procedure in the Crown Court and magistrates' court are essentially the same.

Trial of young offenders

Young offenders are usually tried in youth courts, which are a branch of the magistrates' court. In limited circumstances young persons can be tried in a Crown Court. The trial procedures for young offenders have been reformed in the light of a recent ruling of the European Court of Human Rights.

Question and answer guides

1. (a) Describe the current system for granting or refusing bail.

(OCR Specimen Paper 2007, English Legal System Unit)

Plan

- The granting of bail allows a defendant to remain at liberty until the next stage of their case.
- The key legislation on the subject is the Bail Act 1976, the Bail (Amendment) Act 1993, the Crime and Disorder Act 1998 and the Drugs Act 2005.
- Both the police and magistrates can grant bail.
- Defendants have a general right to bail.
- In determining whether to grant bail, the courts will take into account such issues as the seriousness of the offence, the defendant's criminal record, earlier breaches of bail and the strength of the evidence against the defendant.
- Bail can be refused for a number or reasons, including a failure to surrender to custody, the likelihood that further offences will be committed and the risk of interference with justice (for example, an attempt to threaten a prosecution witness).
- Either unconditional or conditional bail can be granted.
- Bail will only be granted in exceptional circumstances for murder, attempted murder, manslaughter, rape or attempted rape if the defendant has already served a custodial sentence for such a crime.

Answer

The award of bail allows a defendant to remain at liberty until the next stage of their case. Bail can be granted before, during and even after the trial while the court determines the appropriate sentence. Generally, bail allows defendants to remain at liberty under the condition that they report to a police station or court at a required time and day. Unfortunately, 14 per cent of those granted bail fail to appear at court when required to do so, despite the fact that it is a criminal offence to abscond on bail.

The criteria for bail decisions is contained in the Bail Act 1976 and the Bail (Amendment) Act 1993. The starting point is that there is a general presumption in favour of bail for the defendant at court under s. 4 of the 1976 Act. There is no such presumption in favour of suspects at police stations. Bail may be refused if the defendant is on trial for an imprisonable offence and the court is satisfied that there are reasons for believing the defendant, if released on bail, would either fail to surrender to custody, commit an offence while on bail, interfere with witnesses or otherwise obstruct the course of justice. If the court is satisfied that defendants should be kept in custody for their own protection, or they are already in custody for an unrelated conviction, or the court needs more time in which to make a decision, bail can be refused. A defendant who tests positive for a class A drug is subject to a presumption against bail under the Criminal Justice Act 2003. In making their bail decision the court must consider the antecedents, previous bail record, family and community ties of the defendant, as well as the nature and seriousness of the offence.

Bail is only granted in exceptional circumstances for murder, attempted murder, manslaughter, rape or attempted rape if the defendant has already served a custodial sentence for such a crime. In such cases the court must give reasons for granting bail. If bail is refused after two applications or granted with conditions in the magistrates' court, the defence may appeal against the refusal or for a variation of conditions to the High Court. The prosecution may appeal against a grant of bail.

Bail may be conditional or unconditional. Conditions will be imposed on the award of bail where this appears necessary to ensure that the defendant surrenders to custody at the time appointed, does not commit an offence while on bail, does not interfere with any witnesses or obstruct the criminal trial process, attends the court as required and the court services where reports need to be prepared. A range of conditions can be imposed, which include the requirement for someone to pay a surety into court of a sum of money which will be kept by the state if the defendant breaches their bail conditions. Other conditions might be that the defendant has to report regularly to a police station or reside at a certain address. The Criminal Justice Act 2003 gives the police power to grant 'street bail', whereby the police can grant bail at the place of arrest to avoid having to take suspects to the police station and to reduce the amount of time-consuming paperwork that needs to be completed. In practice, the power to issue street bail has not been used much by the police.

(b) Discuss whether the criteria used by the police or the courts when granting or refusing bail are satisfactory.

(OCR Specimen Paper 2007, English Legal System Unit)

Plan

- In granting or refusing bail, the police and the courts are striving to balance the rights of the individual to remain at liberty prior to their trial (who should be treated as innocent until proven guilty) and the right of the public to be protected from offenders.
- The general right to bail should be understood in the context of the presumption of innocence which is protected by the European Convention on Human Rights.
- The reasons for refusing bail, such as the risk that the defendant might fail to surrender to custody or commit offences while on bail, are logical and justifiable.
- The factors taken into account in deciding the award of bail, including a past criminal record and the strength of the evidence against the defendant, are logical and relevant.

■ The restrictions on the presumption to bail for murder, manslaughter and rape were controversial amendments to the Bail Act 1976. These restrictions can be criticised as ignoring the risks posed by an individual offender, but can be justified given the gravity of the offences concerned. If the offender has already served a custodial sentence for their prior offending behaviour, is it right that they should be indirectly punished again by withholding bail?

Group activity 1

■ Divide your friends (or class) into groups of two or three people.

■ In your groups, visit the website **www.cjsonline.gov.uk**, which is maintained by the Ministry of Justice, and take the virtual tour in the site's 'Defendant' section. You can take either the interactive version of the tour or, if your computer will not run this, the text version.

■ As you are watching the tour, imagine that you are a person who has been charged with a crime, that you have never had any involvement with the law before and that you strongly deny any wrongdoing. In that role, make notes on what you think you would want to know and how well the tour answers your questions.

■ Meet with the other groups and compare notes, looking for any common themes.

Visit **www.mylawchamber.co.uk/elliottocr** to access questions, quizzes and activities to test yourself on this chapter.

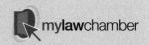

Chapter 6
CRIMINAL APPEALS

This chapter discusses:

- appeals from the magistrates' court and the Crown Court;
- the powers of the prosecution to appeal following the acquittal of a defendant;
- the criticisms and reform plans for the appeal system.

Introduction

The appeal process is supposed to spot cases where there have been wrongful convictions at an early stage so that the injustice can be promptly remedied. A wrongful conviction could arise because of police or prosecution malpractice, a misdirection by a judge, judicial bias, or because expert evidence, such as forensic evidence, was misleading. Sadly, the Court of Appeal in particular failed in the past to detect such problems and this led to demands for reform. The Criminal Appeal Act 1995 was therefore passed to make major amendments to the criminal appeal procedure.

From the magistrates' court

There are four routes of appeal from a magistrates' court:

Rectification

The magistrates can rectify an error they have made under s. 142 of the Magistrates' Courts Act 1980. The case is retried before a different bench where it would be in the interests of justice to do so and the sentence can be varied.

Right to appeal to the Crown Court

A defendant who has pleaded not guilty may appeal as of right to the Crown Court on the grounds of being wrongly convicted or too harshly sentenced. Only appeals against sentence are allowed if the defendant pleaded guilty. The appeal has to be made within 28 days of the conviction. These appeals are normally heard by a circuit judge sitting with between two and four magistrates (not those who heard the original trial). Each person's vote has the same weight, except where the court is equally divided; in such a case the circuit judge has the casting vote.

The court will rehear the facts of the case and either confirm the verdict and/or sentence of the original magistrates, or substitute its own decision for that of the lower court. It can impose any sentence that the magistrates might have imposed – which can occasionally result in the accused's sentence being increased.

Appeals by way of case stated

Alternatively, either the prosecution or the accused may appeal on the grounds that the magistrates have made an error of law, or acted outside their jurisdiction. The magistrates are asked to 'state the case' for their decision to be considered by the High Court. This is, therefore, known as an appeal by way of case stated.

Appeals by way of case stated are heard by up to three judges of the Queen's Bench Division and the sitting is known as a Divisional Court. The court can confirm, reverse or vary the decision; give the magistrates its opinion on the relevant point of law; or make such other order as it sees fit, which may include ordering a rehearing before a different Bench.

sourcebook
p. 340 → ## Referral by the Criminal Cases Review Commission

The Criminal Cases Review Commission can refer appeals from the magistrates' court to the Crown Court. This body is discussed in more detail on p. 92 onwards.

Figure 6.1 The Criminal Cases Review Commission's offices in Alpha Tower, Birmingham
Source: The Criminal Cases Review Commission.

In fact, only 5 per cent of new cases received by the Commission since 1997 have been against convictions by the magistrates.

Further Appeals

If an appeal has been made to the Crown Court, either side may then appeal against the Crown Court's decision by way of case stated. If a party has already appealed to the High Court by way of case stated, the party may not afterwards appeal to the Crown Court.

From the Divisional Court there may be a further appeal, by either party, to the House of Lords, but only if the Divisional Court certifies that the question of law is one of public importance and the House of Lords or the Divisional Court gives permission for the appeal to be heard.

Criminal cases tried by magistrates are also subject to judicial review.

In practice, appeals from the decisions of magistrates are taken in only 1 per cent of cases. This may be because most accused plead guilty, and since the offences are relatively minor and the punishment usually a fine, many of those who pleaded not guilty may prefer just to pay up and put the case behind them, avoiding the expense, publicity and embarrassment involved in an appeal.

From the Crown Court

There are three types of appeal for cases tried in the Crown Court.

To the Court of Appeal with judicial permission

An appeal on grounds that involve the facts, the law or the length of the sentence can be made to the Court of Appeal. The accused must get permission to appeal from the trial judge or the Court of Appeal. A sentence cannot be imposed that is more severe than that ordered by the Crown Court. An appeal against sentence will only be successful where the sentence is wrong in principle or manifestly severe; the court will not interfere merely because it might have passed a different sanction.

Task 6.1

Look at Figure 6.2 on page 92 and answer the following questions.

Questions

1 Which appellate court hears the fewest cases?
2 Which division of the Court of Appeal is the busiest?
3 Did the High Court's workload increase or decrease in 2003-04?
4 What is the trend in the workload of the House of Lords?

While only the accused can appeal to the Court of Appeal, from there either the accused or the prosecution may appeal on a point of law to the House of Lords, provided that either the Court of Appeal or the House of Lords grants permission for the appeal and that the Court of Appeal certifies that the case involves a matter of law of general public importance.

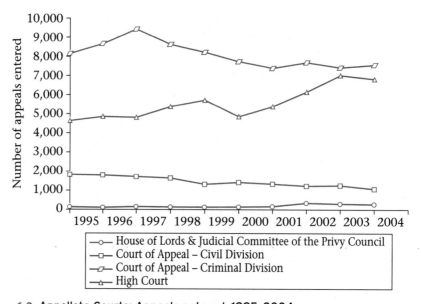

Figure 6.2 Appellate Courts: Appeals entered, 1995-2004

Source: K. Dibdin, A. Sealy and S. Aktar, *Judicial Statistics Annual Report 2004*, p. 6.

Referral by the Criminal Cases Review Commission

The Criminal Appeal Act 1995 established the Criminal Cases Review Commission (CCRC), following a proposal made by the Royal Commission on Criminal Justice 1993 (RCCJ). This body is not a court that decides appeals; rather it is responsible for bringing cases, where there may have been a miscarriage of justice, to the attention of the Court of Appeal if the case was originally heard by the Crown Court (or the Crown Court if the case was originally heard by a magistrates' court). Either a person can apply to the Commission to consider his/her case or the Commission can consider it on its own initiative if an ordinary appeal is time barred. The Commission can carry out an investigation into the case, which may involve asking the police to reinvestigate a crime.

The decision as to whether or not to refer a case will be taken by a committee consisting of at least three members of the Commission. It can make such a refer-ence in relation to a conviction where it appears to them that any argument or evidence, which was not raised in any relevant court proceedings, gives rise to a real possibility that the conviction would not be upheld were the reference to be made. A reference in relation to a sentence will be possible if 'any argument on a point of law, or any information' was not so raised and, again, there is a real possibility that the conviction might not be upheld. Where the Commission refers a conviction or sentence to the Court of Appeal, it is treated as a fresh appeal and the Commission has no further involvement in the case.

One of the first referrals made by the CCRC concerned Derek Bentley. He had been involved with a friend in an unsuccessful burglary. This had resulted in a police chase, during which his friend had pointed a gun at a police officer and

Derek Bentley had said 'let him have it', at which point the friend shot and killed the officer. Derek Bentley was convicted as an accomplice to the murder. He appealed but his appeal was rejected and he was hanged in January 1953.

The circumstances of his conviction gave rise to a long campaign by his family, and numerous representations were made to the Home Office. He was given a royal pardon in 1993 but this was in respect of the sentence only. The family continued its campaign for the conviction itself to be quashed and, in 1998, the CCRC referred the case to the Court of Appeal, which quashed the conviction, stating that the conviction was unsafe because of a defective summing-up by the trial judge to the jury, which had included such prejudicial comments about the defence case that Bentley had been denied a fair trial. This was a notable high-profile success for the CCRC, but it remains to be seen whether the Commission will have success with lower-profile referrals.

Case stated

Following the Access to Justice Act 1999, appeals by way of case stated have been introduced from the Crown Court to the High Court. Previously, these were available only from the magistrates' court.

Second appeal to the Court of Appeal

In exceptional circumstances the Court of Appeal will be prepared to hear an appeal twice; in other words, an appeal from its own earlier decision in the same case. This was decided in the landmark case of **Taylor** *v* **Lawrence** (2002). The Court of Appeal had dismissed the first appeal which had been based on the fact that the judge at first instance had been a client of the claimants. After that first appeal, the appellant then discovered that the judge had not been asked to pay for work carried out the night before the case went to court. When this came to light, the Court of Appeal ruled that it would hear a second appeal. The Court of Appeal laid down guidelines for future cases on when it would be prepared to hear a second appeal in the same case. It must be clearly established that a significant injustice has probably been done, the circumstances are exceptional and there is no alternative effective remedy. There is no effective remedy if leave would not be available for an appeal to the House of Lords. Leave to appeal would not have been given by the House of Lords in **Taylor** *v* **Lawrence** because the case was not of sufficient general importance and merit.

Procedure before the Court of Appeal

Whichever appeal route is taken to reach the Court of Appeal, once the case is before the court, it is dealt with under the same procedure, which will now be considered. The Court of Appeal in criminal cases does not rehear the whole case with all its evidence. Instead, it aims merely to review the lower court's decision.

This is at least partly because the Court of Appeal is reluctant to overturn the verdict of a jury, apparently fearing that to do so might undermine the public's respect for juries in general. The Court of Appeal can admit fresh evidence 'if they think it necessary or expedient in the interests of justice' (Criminal Appeal Act 1968, s. 23(1)).

The appellate court can allow the appeal, dismiss it or order a new trial. Under s. 2 of the Criminal Appeal Act 1968 (as amended by the 1995 Act), an appeal should be allowed if the court thinks that the conviction is 'unsafe'. There is conflicting case law as to whether, if a person is found to have had an unfair trial under Art. 6 of the European Convention on Human Rights, this will automatically mean that the conviction is unsafe and should be quashed. Some English judges prefer the view that if the defendant is clearly guilty their conviction should be upheld as safe even if the trial was unfair. This seems to conflict with the view of the European Court of Human Rights, which suggested in **Condron** v **United Kingdom** (1999) that the conviction should always be quashed if there has been an unfair trial. The Court of Appeal may order a retrial where it feels this is required in the interests of justice. It will only do so if it accepts that the additional evidence is true but is not convinced that it is conclusive – in other words, that it would have led to a different verdict.

Appeal to the House of Lords

A small number of criminal appeals are heard each year by the House of Lords. Planned reforms to the House of Lords are discussed at p. 32.

Powers of the prosecution following acquittal

sourcebook
p. 202 →

In the past, there was a general rule that once a person had been tried and acquitted they could not be retried for the same offence, under the principle of double jeopardy. The rule aimed to prevent the oppressive use of the criminal justice system by public authorities. Following the unsuccessful private prosecution of three men suspected of killing Stephen Lawrence, the judicial inquiry into the affair recommended that the principle of double jeopardy should be abolished. It proposed that the Court of Appeal should have the power to permit prosecution after acquittal 'where fresh and viable evidence is presented'.

The Criminal Justice Act 2003, s. 75 has now abolished the double jeopardy rule. The Act introduces an interlocutory prosecution right of appeal against a ruling by a Crown Court judge that there is no case to answer or any other ruling made before or during the trial that has the effect of terminating the trial. A retrial is permitted in cases of serious offences where there has been an acquittal in court, but compelling new evidence subsequently comes to light against the acquitted person. Twenty-nine serious offences are listed in Sch. 5 to the Act, and are most of the offences which carry a maximum sentence of life imprisonment. This is wider than the recommendations of the Law Commission and Sir Robin Auld.

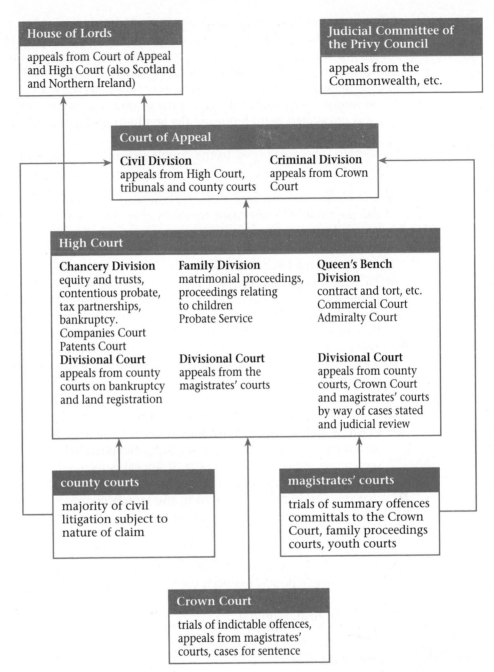

Figure 6.3 An outline of the court structure in England and Wales[1]

1. This diagram is, of necessity, much simplified and should not be taken as a comprehensive statement on the jurisdiction of any specific court.

Source: K. Dibdin, A. Sealy and S. Aktar, *Judicial Statistics Annual Report 2004*, p. 3.

The consent of the Director of Public Prosecutions is required to reopen investigations and to apply to the Court of Appeal. The first person in 800 years to be tried and convicted for a crime he was previously cleared of was a man called William Dunlop. He had been tried twice for the murder of Julie Hogg in 1989, but at these two earlier trials the jury were unable to reach a verdict and he had been formally acquitted at the end of the second trial. When new evidence arose, he was prosecuted again following the abolition of the double jeopardy rule and he pleaded guilty.

Certain other exceptions to the double jeopardy rule also existed prior to the 2003 Act:

- The prosecution can state a case for consideration of the High Court following the acquittal of a defendant by the magistrates' court. This is restricted to a point of law or a dispute on jurisdiction.
- The prosecution can also, with leave, appeal to the House of Lords against a decision of the Court of Appeal.
- The Criminal Justice Act 1972 gives the Attorney-General powers to refer any point of law which has arisen in a case for the opinion of the Court of Appeal, even where the defendant was acquitted. Defendants are not identified (though they may be represented) and their acquittal remains unaffected even if the point of law goes against them – so this procedure is not, strictly speaking, an appeal. The purpose of this power is to enable the Court of Appeal to review a potentially incorrect legal ruling before it gains too wide a circulation in the trial courts.
- The Criminal Justice Act 1988 enables the Attorney-General to refer to the Court of Appeal cases of apparently too lenient sentencing for certain offences, including cases where it appears the judge has erred in law as to their powers of sentencing. Leave from the Court of Appeal is required. The Court of Appeal may quash the sentence and pass a more appropriate one. This is the first time that the prosecution is involved in the sentencing process. The provision was enacted in response to the government's view that public confidence in the criminal justice system was being undermined by unduly lenient sentences, which had been given much publicity by the tabloid press.
- The Criminal Procedure and Investigations Act 1996 created a power to order a retrial where a person has been convicted of an offence involving interference with, or intimidation of, a juror, witness or potential witness, in any proceedings which led to an acquittal.

 Quick quiz 6.2

1 Which court hears appeals by way of case stated from the magistrates' court?

2 Which court hears appeals from the Divisional Court?

3 What percentage of magistrates' cases are the subject of an appeal?

4 When can the Court of Appeal admit new evidence that was not heard in the original trial?

Criticism and reform of the appeal system

The criminal appeal system has been the subject of a range of criticism over the years. Some reforms have already been introduced and others are likely in the near future. For a discussion of the planned abolition of the House of Lords and its replacement by a Supreme Court see p. 32.

Procedural irregularities

In his *Review of the Criminal Courts* (2001), Sir Robin Auld highlighted the difference between a conviction which was unsafe, in the sense that it was incorrect (or lacked supporting evidence), and one which was unsatisfactory because something had gone wrong in the trial process. He queried whether in the latter situation the conviction should be quashed. In September 2006, the government issued a consultation paper, *Quashing convictions – report of a Review by the Home Secretary, Lord Chancellor and Attorney General*. This paper reviewed the legal test used by the Court of Appeal to quash criminal convictions. The Criminal Justice and Immigration Bill effectively accepts Sir Robin Auld's recommendations on this subject. Clause 26 of the Bill provides that 'a conviction is not unsafe if the Court of Appeal are satisfied that the appellant is guilty of the offence'. Clause 27 adds that the Court of Appeal can allow the appeal against conviction 'where they think that it would be incompatible with the appellant's Convention Rights to dismiss the appeal'. Thus, if passed, the Bill would alter the test applied by the Court of Appeal when considering appeals against conviction. A conviction would not be unsafe if the Court of Appeal is satisfied that the appellant is guilty of the offence. If it appears to the Court of Appeal, in determining an appeal, that there has been serious misconduct by any person involved in the investigation or prosecution of the offence, the court may refer the matter to the Attorney-General.

In support of this reform, the government has argued that to acquit defendants where the Court of Appeal considers that they are guilty is itself an injustice to the victim and the public, because the guilty are being allowed to walk free without punishment; their conviction is being quashed 'on a technicality'. In its consultation paper, the government observes: 'if the system or those who operate it are at fault it is they and not the public who should be punished or required to learn lessons, if appropriate.'

This proposed reform has proved highly controversial. Critics, such as the academic Ian Dennis (2006), have argued that it would remove an important safeguard in the criminal justice system, which effectively discourages abuse of procedural rules by representatives of the state, such as the police or prosecution. They have argued that a conviction is fundamentally unsatisfactory if it is gained in breach of the rule of law and to uphold such a conviction undermines the rule of law. Will the public be happy to see the criminal courts appear to sanction a flagrant illegality by an agent of the state? The Court of Appeal does not rehear the evidence of a case and is not therefore in a strong position to reach a view on whether a person is innocent or guilty. Alternative sanctions of, for example, the police for procedural irregularities have not always proved effective. Alarmingly, in

R (Mullen) *v* **Secretary of State for the Home Department** (2004), the government seems to view unlawful rendition – when a person is removed from a country without following the lawful procedures – as a mere technicality, yet this constitutes a major violation of an individual's human rights.

 sourcebook p. 340 → ## The Criminal Cases Review Commission

The Criminal Cases Review Commission (CCRC) was established in 1995 with the hope that it would detect miscarriages of justice more rapidly than the old procedures followed by the Home Office. But the CCRC has itself been the subject of some criticism. One weakness in the new arrangements is that the CCRC does not itself hear the appeals. Cases such as the Birmingham Six (where six Irishmen were wrongly convicted in the 1970s for planting bombs in Birmingham as part of an IRA bombing campaign, see p. 52 above) had to be repeatedly referred back to the Court of Appeal before the court would eventually overturn the original conviction. The establishment of the CCRC will not end this obstacle.

The pressure group, Justice, has criticised the fact that the CCRC has no power to assign in-house staff as investigating officers. It has argued that, without this power, the Commission could not guarantee the independence of an inquiry. The CCRC has no independent powers to carry out searches of premises, to check criminal records, to use police computers or to make an arrest. To do this it would have to appoint someone who had these powers, usually a police officer. The fact that investigations carried out on behalf of the CCRC will be by the police has caused concern. Many allegations of a miscarriage of justice involve accusations of malpractice by the police. Experience of police investigations into the high-profile miscarriages of justice suggests that these are not always effective, and there is a tendency for the police to close ranks and try to protect each other. Justice has also questioned the independence of the organisation, as its members are government appointees.

Task 6.3

The Chairman of the Criminal Cases Review Commission wrote in its third annual report an open letter to the then Home Secretary, David Blunkett. This stated:

'Although early stakeholder concerns regarding the Commission's likely independence, and ability to investigate miscarriages of justice thoroughly, are now only rarely repeated, there has been persistent, well-founded criticism of the Commission's accumulation of cases awaiting review. That accumulation derives directly from the fact that the Commission's initial funding and corresponding scale of operations were inadequate to cope with the case intake that materialised. The Commission can satisfy the legitimate expectations of Parliament and its other stakeholders only if the resources allocated to it are sufficient for it to minimise its case accumulation.

Projections made in February 1998 suggested that some 50 Case Review Managers (CRMs) would be needed for a few years to enable expeditious progress to be made towards that minimisation. Subsequent funding increases allowed that complement of CRMs to be reached just before 31 March 2002...

There has been an unexpected 12% increase in applications to the Commission, combined with fast CRM turnover and slower recruitment than expected. These factors have retarded progress towards minimisation of the case accumulation.'

Questions

1 What is meant by 'stakeholders'?
2 What is meant by the term 'case accumulation'?
3 What problems have the CCRC encountered in reducing the backlog of cases?

 Know your terms 6.4

Define the following terms:

1 The 'leap-frog' procedure.
2 Divisional Court.
3 Double jeopardy.
4 Criminal Cases Review Commission.

The Criminal Cases Review Commission states that its values are:

- Independence
- Integrity
- Impartiality
- Professionalism
- Accountability
- Transparency

Figure 6.4 **The value of the Criminal Cases Review Commission**
Source: Criminal Cases Review Commission Annual Report and Accounts 2004–5.

 Quick quiz 6.5

1 When was the Criminal Appeals Review Commission created?

2 What is the single test that the Court of Appeal applies in deciding whether to allow a criminal appeal?

3 Explain the case involving Derek Bentley.

4 Which court hears cases involving judicial review?

 Reading on the web

The annual report of the Criminal Cases Review Commission is published on the Commission's website at:

www.ccrc.gov.uk/publications/publications_get.asp

Chapter summary

Appeals in criminal cases

From the magistrates' court

There are four routes of appeal:

- the magistrates can rectify an error they have made;
- a defendant who has pleaded not guilty may appeal as of right to the Crown Court on the grounds of being wrongly convicted or too harshly sentenced;
- either the prosecution or the accused may appeal to the High Court on the grounds that the magistrates have made an error of law or acted outside their jurisdiction; and
- the Criminal Cases Review Commission can refer appeals from the magistrates' court to the Crown Court.

From the Crown Court

There are three types of appeal from the Crown Court:

- an appeal to the Court of Appeal;
- an application to the Criminal Cases Review Commission; and
- an appeal by way of case stated from the Crown Court to the High Court.

Powers of the prosecution following acquittal

The general rule is that, once a person has been tried and acquitted, he or she cannot be retried for the same offence, under the principle of double jeopardy. Major exceptions have now been developed.

Criticism and reform of the appeal system

The appeal system has been the subject of considerable criticism. The government intends to abolish the House of Lords and replace it with a new, independent Supreme Court. The government plans to restrict when a conviction can be quashed 'on a technicality'. There has been concern over the working of the Criminal Cases Review Commission.

Question and answer guides

1. Describe the rights of both the prosecution and the defence to appeal from the magistrates' court. Include further appeals to the House of Lords. (OCR, January 2007)

Plan

Appeals to the Crown Court:

- Defendants have an automatic right of appeal against conviction, sentence or both to the Crown Court if they pleaded not guilty at their trial.
- The case is completely reheard by a judge and two magistrates.
- The conviction may be confirmed, varied (with the defendant convicted of a different offence) or reversed (with the defendant acquitted).
- If the defendants' original plea was guilty they only have a right to appeal against their sentence.
- The sentence may be confirmed, increased (only to the magistrates' maximum) or decreased.

Appeals by way of case stated to the High Court:

- Either side can appeal to the High Court on a point of law.
- The defence can only appeal following a conviction and the prosecution following an acquittal.
- This appeal can either be directly from the magistrates' court or, after an appeal, to the Crown Court.
- The High Court may confirm, vary or reverse the decision or send the case back to the magistrates' court to apply the corrected interpretation of the law.

Appeals to the House of Lords:

- Both the prosecution and the defence can seek permission to appeal from the High Court to the House of Lords. The High Court has to certify that the case involves a point of law of public importance and either the High Court or the House of Lords must give permission to appeal.
- In practice, only a small number of criminal cases reach the House of Lords each year.

Group activity 1

On 15 February 1997, Billie-Jo Jenkins, aged 13, was battered to death on the patio at her home in Hastings, East Sussex. Sion Jenkins was prosecuted for the murder of his foster daughter. His case was the subject of two appeals and three trials but ended with no verdict from the final jury. Working in groups, investigate the appeals process in this murder case. You could start by looking at *The Times* website:

www.timesonline.co.uk/tol/news/uk/article728984.ece

- What is the Criminal Cases Review Commission?

Group activity 2

- Divide your friends (or class) into groups of two or three people.
- Each group should visit the 'Cases We Have Referred' page of the website of the Criminal Cases Review Commission: **www.ccrc.gov.uk/cases/case_referred.asp**.
- Half of the groups should choose a case in which the original conviction was quashed by the Court of Appeal and the other half should choose a case in which the original conviction was upheld.
- Each group should read the judgment of the Court of Appeal (accessible via the CCRC website) in its chosen case and make notes summarising the reasons it gave for its decision to quash or uphold. (If you find that the judgment in your chosen case has not been posted on the CCRC website yet, pick another case.)
- The groups should then meet to compare notes, looking to see what conclusions they can draw about how the Court of Appeal deals with CCRC references.

Visit **www.mylawchamber.co.uk/elliottocr** to access questions, quizzes and activities to test yourself on this chapter.

Chapter 7
PRINCIPLES OF SENTENCING

This chapter discusses:

● government reforms to the sentencing process;

● the main aims of sentencing which are the punishment of offenders; the reduction of crime; the reform and rehabilitation of offenders; the protection of the public; and the making of reparation by offenders to persons affected by their offences.

The Criminal Justice Act 2003

The Home Office undertook a review of sentencing that was carried out by John Halliday and published in 2001. A wide range of recommendations were contained in his report, *Making Punishment Work, Report of the Review of the Sentencing Framework for England and Wales*. Central to the approach of the Halliday Review is that the courts should have a greater role in the implementation of sentences and that offenders should spend more time under supervision after their release from custody. He also wanted to see a greater predictability in sentencing so that the sentencing practice would have a stronger deterrent effect on potential offenders. He was particularly concerned by the approach of the courts to persistent offenders, whom he thought committed a disproportionate amount of crime.

The government accepted many of the report's recommendations and introduced significant reforms to the sentencing system in the Criminal Justice Act 2003. Politicians are continually tinkering with the sentencing system and the process of consultation and reform is on-going. The latest consultation paper on the topic is called *Making Sentencing Clearer* (2006) and considers, among other things, giving back some sentencing discretion to judges.

Purposes of sentencing

This chapter is concerned with the sentencing of those convicted of crimes, looking at why people are punished at all – what is the punishment supposed to achieve? Section 142 of the Criminal Justice Act 2003 states that:

> *'Any court dealing with an [adult] offender in respect of his offence must have regard to*
> *the following purposes of sentencing –*
> *(a) the punishment of offenders;*
> *(b) the reduction of crime (including its reduction by deterrence);*
> *(c) the reform and rehabilitation of offenders;*
> *(d) the protection of the public; and*
> *(e) the making of reparation by offenders to persons affected by their offences.'*

Each of these purposes of sentencing will now be examined in turn.

Punishment of offenders

Punishment is concerned with recognising that the criminal has done something wrong and taking revenge on behalf of both the victim and society as a whole. This can also be described as retribution. Making punishments achieve retribution was a high priority during the last years of the Conservative government with Michael Howard as the Home Secretary. In the White Paper of 1990, *Crime, Justice and Protecting the Public*, reference was made to the need for sentences to achieve 'just deserts', stating that punishments should match the harm done, and show society's disapproval of that harm. The problem with this is that other factors all too often intervene: for example, those from stable homes, with jobs, are more likely to get non-custodial sentences than those without, who may be sent to prison even though their crime more properly fits a non-custodial sentence.

The reduction of crime

Crime is a harm which society wishes to eradicate. One way of reducing crime is through using a sentence as a deterrent. Deterrence is concerned with preventing the commission of future crimes; the idea is that the prospect of an unpleasant punishment will put people who might otherwise commit crime off the idea. Punishments may aim at individual deterrence (dissuading the offender in question from committing crime again), or general deterrence (showing other people what is likely to happen to them if they commit crime).

One problem with the use of punishment as a deterrent is that its effectiveness depends on the chances of detection: a serious punishment for a particular crime will not deter people from committing that offence if there is very little chance of being caught and prosecuted for it. This was shown when Denmark was occupied during the Second World War. All the Danish police were interned, drastically cutting the risk for ordinary criminals of being arrested. Despite increases in punishment, the number of property offences soared.

Linked with this problem is the fact that a deterrent effect requires the offender to stop and think about the consequences of what they are about to do, and, as the previous government's 1990 White Paper pointed out, this is often unrealistic:

> *'Deterrence is a principle with much immediate appeal . . . But much crime is committed*
> *on impulse, given the opportunity presented by an open window or unlocked door, and it*

is committed by offenders who live from moment to moment; their crimes are as impulsive as the rest of their feckless, sad or pathetic lives. It is unrealistic to construct sentencing arrangements on the assumption that most offenders will weigh up the possibilities in advance and base their conduct on rational calculation. Often they do not.'

The deterrent effect of punishment on individuals becomes weaker each time they are punished. The more deeply a person becomes involved with a criminal way of life, the harder it is to reform and, at the same time, the fear of punishment becomes less because they have been through it all before.

It has been argued that, to deal with this problem, offenders should be given a severe sentence at an early stage – which politicians like to call a 'short, sharp, shock' – rather than having gradually increased sentences which are counter-balanced by the progressive hardening of the offender to the effects of punishment. Successive attempts at the 'short, sharp, shock' treatment have, however, shown it to have no meaningful effect on reconviction rates. The approach was introduced under the Detention Centre Order, created by the Criminal Justice Act 1982; it was abolished in the Criminal Justice Act 1988.

Where a specific crime is thought to be on the increase, the courts will some-times try to stem this increase by passing what is called an exemplary sentence. This is a sentence higher than that which would normally be imposed, to show people that the problem is being treated seriously, and make potential offenders aware that they may be severely punished. There is some debate as to whether exemplary sentences actually work; their effectiveness depends on publicity, yet British newspapers tend to highlight only those sentences which seem too low for an offence which concerns society, or which seem too high for a trivial offence. In addition, even where there is publicity, the results may be negligible – Smith and Hogan (2002) point to an exemplary sentence passed for street robbery at a time when mugging was the subject of great social concern. The sentence was publicised by newspapers and television, yet there was no apparent effect on rates of street robbery even in the area where the case in question took place. We should also question whether exemplary sentences are in the interests of justice, which demands that like cases be treated alike; the person who mugs someone in the street when there has not been a public outcry about that offence is no better than one who mugs when there has.

Reform and rehabilitation

The aim of rehabilitation is to reform offenders, so that they are less likely to commit offences in the future – either because they learn to see the harm they are causing, or because, through education, training and other help, they find other ways to make a living or spend their leisure time. During the 1960s, a great deal of emphasis was placed on the need for rehabilitation, but the results were felt by many to be disappointing. By 1974 the American researcher Robert Martinson was denouncing rehabilitation programmes for prisoners in his paper *What Works*, in which he came to the conclusion that 'nothing works'.

Although rehabilitation sounds like a sensible aim, Bottoms and Preston argue, in *The Coming Penal Crisis* (1980), that rehabilitative sentences are fundamentally flawed. First, such sentences assume that all crime is the result of some deficiency or fault in the individual offender; Marxist academics argue that crime is actually a result of the way society is organised. Secondly, they discriminate against the less advantaged in society, who are seen as in need of reform, whereas when an offender comes from a more privileged background, their offence tends to be seen as a one-off, temporary slip. This means that punishment is dictated not by the harm caused, but by the background of the offender. Thirdly, in some cases the pursuit of reform can encourage inexcusable interference with the dignity and privacy of individuals. This has included, in some countries, implanting electrodes in the brain, and in the UK in the 1970s experiments were carried out involving hormone drug treatment for sex offenders.

In light of the fact that there is a growing prison population, there seems to be a renewed interest in the idea of rehabilitation. Over the past five years, offending behaviour programmes have been developed in many of the prisons of England and Wales. From an initial fragmented range of courses on such matters as anger management, alcohol and drug abuse, domestic violence and victim awareness, the emphasis is now on programmes aimed at changing the way the prisoners think, such as 'Reasoning and Rehabilitation' and 'Enhanced Thinking Skills'. 'Reasoning and Rehabilitation' courses do not look directly at the prisoners' offending; instead, over a 35-session course, run by prison probation officers and psychologists, they focus on six key areas – impulse control, flexible thinking (learning from experience), means-end testing (predicting probable outcomes of behaviour), perspective taking (seeing other people's points of view), problem solving and social skills. 'Enhanced Thinking Skills' courses follow a similar pattern, but over 20 sessions. Attendance on the courses is voluntary – but a long-term prisoner is unlikely to be released early without having completed one.

In 1998–99, 3,000 prisoners successfully completed one of these programmes, but this still represents only a very small proportion of the prison population. The number completing a programme is expected to increase significantly over the next few years. Whether a prisoner has the opportunity to undertake a course depends on the establishment in which he or she is being held. Not all prisons run these courses and, in most of the ones that do, priority is given to prisoners serving four years or more – in other words, those who have to apply for early release. Yet many persistent offenders are in prison for less than four years. It is common to find people who have had a series of successive two- and three-year sentences, separated by mere weeks and often only days of freedom before they have reoffended and returned to prison. The senior judge, Lord Bingham, would like to see offending behaviour programmes made a legal requirement for all prisoners.

But how far will efforts to change the way a prisoner thinks reduce reoffending? One of the main problems faced by prisoners on release is a lack of work and consequent lack of an honest income or legitimate ways to spend their time. Many prisoners come out with the best of intentions but faced with empty days and even emptier pockets, they soon succumb to their old temptations. There is a danger that prisoners released into their old environment without having acquired any practical or vocational skills to help them on their way will fall back into a life of crime.

A report of the Parliamentary Penal Affairs Group, *Changing Offending Behaviour – Some Things Work* (1999), found that 'cognitive behavioural' programmes did work. But, in addition, they argued that there is increasing evidence that programmes focused directly on the needs of the offender in relation to the offending behaviour are successful in reducing the risk of reoffending. The types of needs that can be tackled include the need for employment, education, improved social skills and a break from negative peer groups. The need to tackle alcohol and drug problems was also highlighted.

Protection of the public

By placing an offender in custody, he or she is prevented from committing further offences and the public are thereby protected. While this has its merits where highly dangerous offenders are concerned, it is an extremely expensive way of dealing with crime prevention and, since prison is often the place where criminals pick up new ideas and techniques, may be ultimately counter-productive.

Reparation

sourcebook
p. 264 →

The government has been developing ways in which offenders can provide remedies to their victims or the community at large. This is known sometimes as **restorative justice**, and has been pioneered for young offenders. So far, it seems to have been surprisingly successful in reducing reoffending and increasing victim satisfaction with the criminal justice system. Offenders can be required, for example, to write letters of apology to their victims, help to repair damage they have caused or take part in other community work.

Research has been carried out into the effectiveness of restorative justice which was published in a report, *Restorative Justice: the Evidence* (Sherman 2007). This concluded that many violent criminals are less likely to commit further offences after participating in a restorative justice programme. The victim's symptoms of post-traumatic stress disorder are reduced, partly because meeting their offender demystifies the offence. Restorative justice was also cheaper than traditional criminal sentences.

Quick quiz 7.1

1 What are the five purposes of sentencing identified by the Criminal Justice Act 2003?

2 The White Paper, *Crime, Justice and Protecting the Public* (1990), identified one reason why a sentence might not act as a deterrent in practice. What reason was this?

3 What problems are identified by Bottoms and Preston in the use of rehabilitative sentences?

4 Is a sentence that includes restorative justice beneficial to the victim?

Reading on the web

The guide entitled *Restorative Justice: helping to meet local need* (2004), published by the Office for Criminal Justice Reform, is available on the Home Office website at:

www.crimereduction.gov.uk/criminaljusticesystem12.htm

The report by L. Sherman and H. Strang, *Restorative Justice: The Evidence* (2007), is available on the website of the Esmée Fairbairn Foundation at:

www.esmeefairbairn.org.uk/docs/RJ_full_report.pdf

Chapter summary

The Home Office undertook a review of sentencing that was carried out by John Halliday and published in 2001. The government accepted many of Halliday's recommendations and introduced significant reforms to the sentencing system in the Criminal Justice Act 2003.

Purposes of sentencing

Section 142 of the Criminal Justice Act 2003 states that:

'any court dealing with an [adult] offender in respect of his offence must have regard to the following purposes of sentencing –
(a) the punishment of offenders;
(b) the reduction of crime (including its reduction by deterrence);
(c) the reform and rehabilitation of offenders;
(d) the protection of the public; and
(e) the making of reparation by offenders to persons affected by their offences.'

Question and answer guides

1. **Explain the main aims of sentencing as set out in the Criminal Justice Act 2003.**
(OCR Specimen Paper 2007)

Plan

- **Punishment**: often called retribution. Society wants revenge for the offender's criminal behaviour. The sentence should be proportionate to the crime so that criminals receive their 'just desserts'.
- **Reduction of crime**: particularly through deterrence. The sentence can deter the particular individual from reoffending (individual deterrence) and the general public (general deterrence).

- **Rehabilitation**: the aim is to reform the offender to stop reoffending. Custodial sentences only have a very limited rehabilitative effect.
- **Protection of the public**: by preventing the offender from reoffending. This is most easily achieved in the short-term by locking the offender up.
- **Reparation**: the sentence looks at how offenders can make reparation to the victim and society for the crimes they have committed.

Group activity 1

The *Adult Court Bench Book* is a substantial book prepared by the Judicial Studies Board to assist magistrates in carrying out their work. The aim of the *Bench Book* is to support the judicial process and promote national consistency of approach to increase the confidence the public have in the administration of justice. It is available on line at:

www.jsboard.co.uk/downloads/acbb_complete_07.pdf

Working in groups, take a look at this book. See if you can find out the procedure the magistrates must follow before they impose a custodial sentence – look at pp. 201–3 for some useful guidance on this subject. When you visited a magistrates' court, did the magistrates follow that procedure?

Visit **www.mylawchamber.co.uk/elliottocr** to access questions, quizzes and activities to test yourself on this chapter.

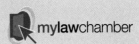

Chapter 8
COURT SENTENCING POWERS

This chapter discusses:

- sentencing practice in the courts;
- fines;
- custodial sentences;
- community sentences;
- some problems with sentencing.

Sentencing practice

When an offender is convicted in the Crown Court, it is the trial judge alone (without the help of the jury) who determines the appropriate sentence. On conviction in the magistrates' court, the magistrates can determine the sentence themselves or, under s. 3 of the Powers of Criminal Courts (Sentencing) Act 2000 (PCC(S)A), the defendant can be committed to the Crown Court for sentence. If sentenced by the magistrates' court, the maximum sentence that can be imposed for a summary offence has been increased from six months to 12 months by the Criminal Justice Act 2003, s. 154. The minimum is five days (s. 132 of the Magistrates' Courts Act 1980).

Once the defendant has been found guilty, it must be decided first what category of sentence is appropriate and then the amount, duration and form of that sentence.

In recent years there has been a considerable amount of legislation trying to control and regulate the sentencing practices of the judges. The legislature has increasingly sought to reduce the discretion available to the judiciary in selecting the sentence.

Types of sentence

There are four main categories of sentence: custodial sentences; community sentences; fines; and other miscellaneous sentences. The death penalty has been abolished. We will now look in detail at the different types of sentences that can be imposed on an offender.

Fines

A fine may be imposed for almost any offence other than murder. Offences tried in the magistrates' court carry a set maximum, depending on the offence; the highest is £5,000. There is no maximum in the Crown Court. The courts must ensure that the amount of the fine reflects the seriousness of the offence, and also takes account of the offender's means, reducing or increasing it as a result (Criminal Justice Act 2003, s. 167). Magistrates' courts can arrange for the automatic deduction of a fine from the offender's earnings, known as an 'attachment of earnings order', when imposing the fine or following a failure to pay. Under ss. 300 and 301 of the Criminal Justice Act 2003 the court has the power to impose unpaid work or curfew requirements on a fine defaulter or to disqualify them from driving, rather than sending them to prison.

The Courts Act 2003 seeks to improve the information available to magistrates on offenders' means prior to sentence, and to ensure that enforcement action is taken promptly. The Act has introduced a new framework for fine enforcement. When a collection order is issued by the court, fine officers manage and collect fines instead of the court. Discounts of up to 50 per cent are given to those who pay promptly. If the offender fails to pay promptly, the fine can be increased by the fines officer by up to 50 per cent without the case being referred back to the courts. The fines officer may also issue a 'further steps notice'. This can, for example, require payments to be deducted automatically from an offender's pay, for their property to be seized and sold, or their car clamped. Once clamped the car can be removed for sale or other disposal and any proceeds are used to discharge or reduce the offender's outstanding fine.

The fine is the most common sentence issued by the court, with three-quarters of all offenders sentenced at magistrates' courts in 2000 being issued with a fine. The number of fines issued has decreased in recent years and the researchers Flood-Page and Mackie (1998) concluded that 'there seems to have been a general disenchantment with financial penalties'.

Since 2007, alongside every fine issued by the magistrates, the defendant also has to pay an additional £15 towards services for victims and witnesses. Some magistrates have been unhappy with this requirement, as they feel like unofficial tax collectors and the amount collected cannot be adapted to reflect the financial means of the convicted person.

Advantages

Evidence suggests that people are less likely to reoffend after being sentenced to a fine than following other sentences, though this can be partly explained by the type of offenders that are given fines in the first place. Fines also bring income into the system, and they do not have the long-term disruptive effects of imprisonment.

Disadvantages

There have been high rates of non-payment, a problem which the Courts Act 2003 is intended to tackle. A third of fines are never paid, so that in 2000–01, according to the National Audit Office, £74 million of fines were written off (mainly because the offender could not be traced). Not only does this make the sentence ineffective, but repeated non-payment of a fine can lead to a custodial sentence, with the result that some inmates of English prisons are there for very minor offences, such as failure to pay for a television licence.

Research carried out for the Home Office, *Enforcing Financial Penalties* (Whittaker 1997), found that the majority of fine defaulters were out of work (only 22 per cent of the men and 11 per cent of the women had any paid employment, even part time). Predominant among reasons for non-payment were changes in circumstances through illness or job loss, and financial difficulties brought on by other debts.

A wide range of enforcement methods are available to the courts, including attachment of earnings orders and the automatic deduction of fines from social security benefits. In practice, these enforcement methods are only rarely used. The 1997 Home Office study highlighted practical difficulties in trying to arrange the deduction of fines from social security benefits. Some magistrates felt that attachment of earnings orders removed the responsibility from the defaulter for ensuring that the fine was paid, which was seen as part of the punishment. The government is now planning to establish a National Enforcement Service, which should be fully operational in 2008. This will employ 4,000 enforcement officers who will wear a uniform and be responsible for ensuring fines are paid and other court orders obeyed.

Fines can be unfair, since the same fine may be a very severe punishment to a poor defendant, but make little impact on one who is well off. In an attempt to address this problem, the Criminal Justice Act 1991 originally laid down a system of unit fines for the magistrates' courts. A maximum number of units was allocated to each offence, up to a total of 50. Within that maximum, the court had to determine the number of units which was commensurate with the seriousness of the case. The value of the unit depended on the offender's disposable weekly income (their income after having deducted any regular household expenses), with the minimum value of a unit being £4, and the maximum £100. The unit fines system aimed to even out the effects of fines so that, although the sums to be paid were different, the impact on the offender would be similar. The pilot schemes for the unit fines suggested that fines were paid more quickly and there was a drop in debtors ending up in prison, because of the more realistic assessment of the fines.

Unfortunately, the idea aroused huge public opposition after press coverage of what seemed to be high fines for relatively minor offences and very low fines for the unemployed – despite the fact that even if some of these were unfair, they were less unfair than the previous system. There was public uproar when a man received a £1,200 fine for dropping a crisp packet. As a result, unit fines were abolished, and the courts reverted to their previous practice, except that they are now required to take into account ability to pay when setting fines.

The government has been considering the reintroduction of the unit fine scheme. The relevant legislative provisions were contained in the Management of Offenders and Sentencing Bill, but this part of the Bill was subsequently dropped.

Figure 8.1 **Wormwood Scrubs, an example of a Victorian prison**
Source: © EMPICS.

Fixed-penalty fines

In order to clamp down on loutish behaviour, the police have been given the power to impose fixed-penalty fines by the Criminal Justice and Police Act 2001. These fines can be imposed for such offences as being drunk in a public place and being drunk and disorderly. A police officer may give a person aged 16 and over a penalty notice if there is reason to believe that the person has committed a penalty offence (s. 2). The fine for each offence is fixed by the Home Secretary and can be for up to a quarter of the maximum fine applicable to the offence. Recipients must either pay the fine within 21 days or opt for trial (they will not be marched off to the cash machine by the police officer, as was originally suggested). If they fail to do either, then a sum which is one and a half times the penalty will be registered against them for enforcement as a fine. If the person pays the fixed-penalty fine, there is no criminal conviction or admission of guilt associated with the payment of the penalty.

The system of fixed-penalty fines is currently being piloted, and if these pilot schemes are successful they will be extended nationwide. The pilots have been criticised by the police. Fifty per cent of the fines have not been paid, and there is a problem with people giving false names and addresses.

Advantages

In the past, much minor offending escaped sanction because of the need to focus police and court resources on more important matters. It is hoped that fixed-penalty fines will provide a quick and efficient way of dealing with low-level, but disruptive criminal behaviour.

Disadvantages

Fixed-penalty fines take place outside the protective framework of the court system, and there is therefore a danger of abuse and corruption.

Custodial sentences

For adult defendants, a custodial sentence means prison; for young offenders, it usually means being detained in a young offenders' institution. A court should not pass a custodial sentence unless it considers that the crime was so serious that only a custodial sentence is justified (s. 152, Criminal Justice Act 2003). Section 153 of the Criminal Justice Act 2003 directs the court to impose the shortest custodial term that is commensurate with the seriousness of the offence(s), subject to certain exceptions. Section 143 of the 2003 Act states that:

> 'In considering the seriousness of any offence, the court must consider the offender's culpability in committing the offence and any harm which the offence caused, was intended to cause or might foreseeably have caused.'

The court also has to take into account previous convictions, failure to respond to previous sentences and the commission of an offence while on bail (Criminal Justice Act 2003, s. 143).

Where a judge intends to impose a custodial sentence (unless the sentence is fixed by law), a pre-sentence report must normally be prepared by the probation service, containing background information about the defendant. This will assist the judge in selecting the appropriate sentence.

Most of those given custodial sentences do not serve the full sentence in custody, but are released early on licence. If they breach the terms of that licence, then they can be recalled to prison.

The Criminal Justice Act 2003 has introduced a new scheme for the sentencing of dangerous adults. The scheme applies to offenders who have committed a specified sexual or violent offence and have been assessed as dangerous. Such offenders can receive an extended sentence and their release is at the discretion of the Parole Board. The most dangerous offenders who continue to pose a risk to the public may be kept in prison for an indeterminate period. These measures will allow the state to hold offenders in prison for longer than is required by the gravity of their offence in order to protect the public. In practice, the heavy use of indeterminate sentences has increased the problem of prison overcrowding.

Task 8.1

Read the following extract and answer the questions that follow:

Tagging is harder than prison because I have to make an effort every day
'I don't like tagging. It's harder than prison because I have to make an effort every day', Mark, 27, who has a long list of drug-related burglaries on his record, says. But it imposed a strict, disciplined framework on his life for the first time in years. This would not, on its own, keep him out of trouble – but it would give Mark and his probation officer the chance to start other longer-term programmes that might.

Tagging's intrusion into family life has produced mixed results. Some women, in particular, found the enforced presence of their partner added to both tension in their relationship and the risk of violence. Others welcomed a period in which the partner learnt to see more of his children.

'He really resented our home being his prison', one wife said, 'and when I went out to work part time and left him to put the children to bed it was – well, he thought it was the end of the world. But after a bit, when he saw how they responded, he was really proud. It won't change everything, but it has done a lot of good.'

Not everyone agrees and research in Scotland revealed that some parents of tagged young adults were resentful about the role of unpaid jailers which they felt had been forced upon them.

Extensive Home Office research has concluded that tagging is 'offence neutral' – that is, it has no real impact on longer-term reoffending rates. But electronic monitoring can be positively used. Politicians have capitalised on its usefulness in terms of crisis management of prison numbers.

In technology terms, electronic tagging schemes are basic – much more sophisticated technology, using satellites to track offenders rather than simply enforcing a curfew, is already in use in the US and could soon be available here.

If all tagging can do is provide a short-term fix, the enormous investment already made will simply have been wasted. Using technology in ways that make a real impact on crime figures and on reoffending rates must be the aim.

(Adapted from an article by Dick Whitfield which was published in *The Times*, 11 March 2003.)

Questions

1 Why did some parents in Scotland resent the tagging of their children?
2 Does tagging currently reduce the longer-term reoffending rates?
3 What does the author consider should be the aim of using technology?
4 Do you think that tagging is a good idea?

Custody plus

John Halliday's report on sentencing (discussed at p. 103) argued that prison sentences of less than 12 months had little meaningful impact on criminal behaviour, because only half of the sentence time was actually served in prison, and the person was then released without conditions. The Prison Service had little opportunity to tackle criminal behaviour as the period served in custody was so short. In addition, such sentences could have long-term adverse effects on family cohesion, employment and training prospects – all of which are key to the rehabilitation of offenders. This was particularly regrettable, as these sentences are used for large numbers of persistent offenders who are likely to reoffend.

Halliday recommended that, to tackle this weakness in short prison sentences, there should be a new sentence which he described as 'custody plus'. The government has adopted this reform in the Criminal Justice Act 2003. Under s. 181, all sentences for less than 12 months' custody are replaced by custody plus (or intermittent custody, discussed below). After spending a maximum of three months in custody, the offender will be released and subjected to at least six months' post-release supervision in the community. The court can attach specific requirements to the sentence, based upon those available under a community sentence. If an offender fails to comply with the terms of the community part of the sentence, he or she will be returned to custody.

Sentences for more than 12 months require the offender to spend half their time in custody (unless they obtain early release on home detention curfew), and the remainder of their sentence under supervision in the community. It is hoped that these reforms will provide a more effective framework within which to address the needs of offenders. Following negative media coverage, this automatic reduction of a custodial sentence by half is currently being reconsidered by the Home Office with regard to the most serious offenders and may be removed in the near future.

Suspended sentence

Under ss. 189–194 of the Criminal Justice Act 2003, a custodial sentence can be suspended. A court is able to suspend a short custodial sentence for between six months and two years. The offender can be required to undertake certain activities in the community.

If the offender breaches the terms of the suspension, the suspended sentence will be activated. The commission of a further offence during the entire length of suspension will also count as breach, and the offender's existing suspended sentence will be dealt with at the time the court sentences him or her for the new offence. Courts have a discretion to review an offender's progress under a suspended sentence.

Suspended sentences were created in 1967 and were intended to be used as an alternative to a custodial sentence. In practice, they have sometimes been used where a community sentence would have been adequate. If the offender then commits another offence, the suspended sentence is activated, so that the offender ends up in prison. The Criminal Justice and Immigration Bill contains a provision to abolish suspended sentences for summary only offences to reduce this problem.

Home detention curfew

Home detention curfews were introduced by the Crime and Disorder Act 1998. Prisoners sentenced to between three months' and four years' imprisonment can be released early (usually 60 days early) on a licence that includes a curfew condition. This requires the released prisoners to remain at a certain address at set times, during which period they will be subjected to electronic monitoring. Most curfews are set for 12 hours between 7 p.m. and 7 a.m. The person can be recalled to prison if there is a failure to comply with the conditions of the curfew condition or in order to protect the public from serious harm. Private contractors fit the electronic tag to a person's ankle, install monitoring equipment which plugs into the telephone system in their home and connects with a central computer system, and notify breaches of curfew to the Prison Service.

Research has been carried out by Dodgson (2001) and others into the first 16 months' experience of home detention curfew. It found that only 5 per cent were recalled to prison. The main reasons for recall were breach of the curfew conditions (68 per cent) or a change of circumstances (25 per cent). The use of home detention curfew appeared to have eased the transition from prison to the community. Offenders were very positive about the scheme, with only 2 per cent saying that they would have preferred to have spent their time in prison. Prior to release, over a third of prisoners said that the prospect of being granted home detention curfew influenced their behaviour in prison. Other household members were also very positive about the scheme.

Sentences for murder

An area that has caused considerable controversy and litigation in recent years is the question of the release of prisoners sentenced to life imprisonment, and in particular the Home Secretary's involvement in this decision. In the recent past, the final decision as to when murderers should be released on licence lay with a politician, the Home Secretary. This was found to be in breach of the European Convention on Human Rights in the case of **R (Anderson)** v **Secretary of State for the Home Department** (2002). The danger was that Home Secretaries might be influenced by issues of political popularity rather than the justice in the particular case. The matter was highlighted in the case of Myra Hindley, who was convicted for life in 1966 for the murder of two children and for her involvement in the killing of a third.

The Home Secretary, however, seems anxious to retain some control in this area. Provisions have been added to the Criminal Justice Act 2003 which aim to promote consistency in the sentencing of murderers. Under these provisions, judges are required to slot offenders into one of three categories according to the severity of their crime. For the first category, actual life will be served by those convicted of the most serious and heinous crimes: multiple murderers, child killers and terrorist murderers. For the second category, there is a starting point of 30 years. This category includes murders of police and prison officers and murders with sexual, racial or religious motives. For the third category, the starting point is 15 years. In addition, there are 14 mitigating and aggravating factors which will affect the sentence imposed. Judges are able to ignore these guidelines, provided they explain why. Once the minimum term has expired, the Parole Board will consider the person's suitability for release. If the Parole Board considers that the person no longer poses a significant risk of reoffending, it can order their release. They are released on licence for the rest of their lives, and are supervised by the probation service until they are assessed as being fully reintegrated into the community. If they reoffend, while under supervision, or if they fail to cooperate, or to keep in contact with the probation service, the licence is revoked by the Lifer Review and Recall Section at the Home Office; a warrant of arrest is issued by Scotland Yard and they are classed as unlawfully at large until arrested and returned to prison.

There are at present 22 people serving whole-life tariffs in England and Wales, none in Europe and 25,000 in the US (along with 3,500 people under sentence of death).

Quick quiz 8.2

1 Does the jury, the judge or both together select the offender's sentence in the Crown Court?

2 What is the automatic sentence for murder?

3 What is a fixed-penalty fine?

4 What happens if a convicted murderer commits theft after they have been released from prison on licence?

Advantages of custodial sentences

The previous Conservative government claimed that prison 'works', in the sense that offenders cannot commit crime while they are in prison, and so the public is protected. The current government claims that prison can be made to work both by protecting the public and by making use of the opportunity for rehabilitation.

Disadvantages of custodial sentences

Fifty-nine per cent of prisoners are reconvicted within two years of being released. In her book, *Bricks of Shame* (1987), Vivienne Stern highlights several reasons why imprisonment lacks any great reformative power, and may even make people more, rather than less, likely to reoffend. Prisoners spend time with other criminals, from whom they frequently acquire new ideas for criminal enterprises; budget cuts have meant there is now little effective training and education in prisons, while the stigma of having been in prison means their opportunities for employment are fewer when they are released; and families often break down, so that the ex-prisoner may become homeless. The result, says Stern, is that 'going straight

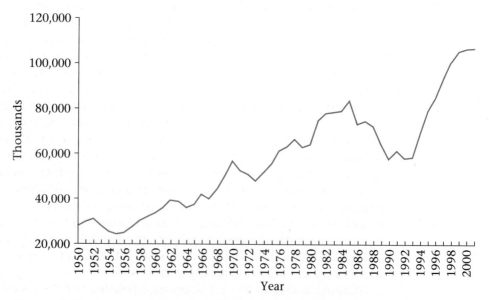

Figure 8.2 Persons sentenced to immediate custody, 1950-2001

Source: Home Office (2002), *Criminal Statistics England and Wales 2001*, p. 18, Figure 1.3.

can present the quite unattractive option of a boring, lonely existence in a hostel or rented room, eking out the Income Support'. All this can also mean that prison punishes the innocent as well as the guilty, with the prisoner's family suffering stigma, financial difficulties, the misery of being parted from the prisoner and often family breakdown in the end. The research, *Poverty and Disadvantage Among Prisoners' Families* (Smith 2007), noted that about 4 per cent of children experience the imprisonment of their father during their school years. It found that this frequently caused them to suffer emotional and economic hardship, with a negative effect on their personal development.

Stern rejects the idea that prison works because it protects the public. She points out that although it may prevent the individual offending for a while, the percentage of crime that is actually detected and prosecuted is so small that imprisonment has little effect on the crime rate.

Prisons are also extremely expensive – at £36,000 a year per prisoner, three weeks in prison costs as much as a lengthy community sentence. To this must be added the costs associated with the family breakdown and unemployment that imprisonment frequently causes. As well as those who find themselves in prison through non-payment of fines, many of those actually sentenced to prison have committed relatively minor offences and could be dealt with just as effectively, and far more cheaply, in the community.

The conditions within prisons continue to cause concern. While all prisoners are now supposed to have 24-hour access to toilet facilities, the practice of 'slopping out' having ended in 1996, other problems remain. A continuing area of concern that has been highlighted in the Prison Ombudsman's report for 1998 is the failure of the Prison Service's internal complaints system to investigate complaints adequately. Lord Woolf, in his inquiry into the prison disturbances that took place in 1990, found that one of the root causes of the riots was that prisoners believed they had no other effective method of airing their grievances.

Where prison conditions are poor, there is an increased risk of suicide. Between 1999 and 2003 a total of 434 people committed suicide in prison. There were over 16,000 incidents of self-harm recorded in 2003. A report of the Joint Committee on deaths in custody in 2004 found that the young, the mentally unstable and women are most at risk.

The number of people in prison has been growing at an alarming rate over recent years. In 2004 the UK was holding over 75,000 prisoners, an increase of more than 50 per cent in the previous ten years. This figure is expected to reach 80,000 by 2009. Seventy per cent of sentenced prisoners are serving 12 months or less. This increase in the prison population is not due to an increase in criminal activity, but simply that heavier sentences are being imposed. A Home Office bulletin issued in 2000 showed the courts in England and Wales to be among the toughest in western Europe in terms of numbers imprisoned, while a Council of Europe study revealed that defendants in English courts get longer sentences for assault, robbery or theft than they do elsewhere in Europe. Average prison populations in Europe are approximately one-third lower as a proportion of the population to that of the UK. A report carried out by the businessman Patrick Carter in 2003 estimated that the increased use of custody had only reduced crime by 5 per cent at the most.

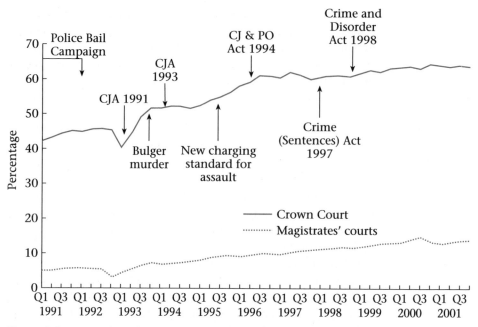

Figure 8.3 **Proportion of persons sentenced to immediate custody for indictable offences by type of court, 1991–2001**

Source: Home Office (2002), *Criminal Statistics England and Wales 2001*, p. 81, Figure 7.4.

The Chief Inspector of Prisons claimed, in an interview for *The Guardian* in 2001, that the prison population could be cut to 40,000 if 'the kids, the elderly, the mentally ill, the asylum seekers, those inside for trivial shoplifting or drug offences' were taken away. The inevitable result of a growing prison population is prison overcrowding. In 1996 matters reached crisis point and this led to a controversial scheme whereby a converted ship was used as a floating prison. In *Prison Sardines* (1996), a Howard League report, it was noted that, at the end of February 1996, 46 prisons were overcrowded, with Usk Prison in Gwent being 75 per cent overcrowded. By 2007 the prison population had increased further and the government decided to put some prisoners in police cells. This was an unsatisfactory solution to prison overcrowding because it is more expensive than prisons, while providing no facilities for education and rehabilitation.

The Home Office has issued a five-year strategic plan (*Cutting Crime – Delivering Justice: Strategic Plan for Criminal Justice 2004–08*). This states that the government wishes to stop the drift towards longer custodial sentences. In fact, the prison population has continued to rise rapidly.

In recent years there has been concern that dangerous offenders have been released on licence, and have subsequently reoffended. There have been suggestions that the Parole Board has been wrong to agree the release of certain individuals and, when they have been released, they have not been adequately supervised by the probation service. Such concerns were expressed in the media following the murder of the wealthy banker, John Monckton, at his home in Chelsea by Damien Hanson when he was on probation. The Parole Board may be giving undue weight to the human rights of the offender rather than the rights of potential victims, but they may also not have sufficient information to make a fully informed decision. Some of the criticism of the probation service may reflect an unrealistic expectation of the level of supervision that can be provided with the level of funding available.

Quick quiz 8.3

1 Do you think that 'prison works'?

2 How much does it cost to keep a person in prison for a year?

3 In 2004 how many people were in prison in the UK?

4 Does the UK imprison more or fewer people than most other European countries?

Community sentence

Section 148 of the Criminal Justice Act 2003 states that a community sentence can only be imposed if the offence was 'serious enough to warrant such a sentence'. Where a court passes a community sentence, the particular requirements of the sentence must be the most suitable for the offender. The restrictions on liberty imposed by the order must be 'commensurate with the seriousness of the offence, or the combination of the offence and one or more offences associated with it'.

Recent governments have been anxious to emphasise that community sentences impose substantial restrictions on the offender's freedom and should not be seen as 'soft options'. Home Office statistics show that 56 per cent of offenders given community sentences reoffend within two years.

The Criminal Justice Act 2003 has established a single community order which can be applied to an offender aged 16 or over. This order can contain a range of possible requirements. These are:

- an unpaid work requirement;
- an activity requirement;
- a programme requirement;
- a prohibited activity requirement;
- a curfew requirement;
- an exclusion requirement;
- a residence requirement;
- a mental health treatment requirement;
- a drug rehabilitation requirement;
- an alcohol treatment requirement;
- a supervision requirement;
- an attendance centre requirement (where the offender is aged under 25).

Each of these requirements will now be considered in turn.

Unpaid work requirement

The offender can be required to perform, over a period of 12 months, a specified number of hours of unpaid work for the benefit of the community. The number of hours must be between 40 and 300. The kind of work done includes tasks on conservation projects, archaeological sites and canal clearance. This requirement allows useful community work to be done, and may give offenders a sense of achievement which helps them stay out of trouble afterwards. There is a recurring discussion as to whether people carrying out work as part of a community sentence should be required to wear uniforms so that they can be recognised as offenders contributing to the community by the public, or whether this is unnecessarily humiliating to the offender.

Activity requirement

Under an activity requirement, offenders must present themselves to a specified person, at a specified place, for a maximum of 60 days, and/or take part in specified activities for a certain number of days. An activity requirement may include such tasks as receiving help with employment, group work on social problems and providing reparation to the victim.

Programme requirement

A programme requirement obliges the offender to participate in an accredited programme on a certain number of days. Programmes are courses which address offending behaviour, such as anger management, sex offending and drug abuse.

Prohibited activity requirement

The court can instruct an offender to refrain from participating in certain activities. For example, it might forbid an offender from contacting a certain person, or from participating in specified activities during a period of time. The court can make a prohibited activity requirement which prohibits a defendant from possessing, using or carrying a firearm.

Curfew requirement

An offender can be ordered to remain in a specified place or places for periods of not less than two hours or more than 12 hours in any one day for up to six months. The court should avoid imposing conditions which would interfere with the offender's work or education, or cause conflict with their religious beliefs. A specified person must be made responsible for monitoring the offender's whereabouts. Courts can require offenders to wear electronic tags, in order to monitor that they are conforming to their curfew order.

Advantages

Tagging costs about £4,000 a year, compared with £24,000 for a prison place. Curfew orders have the potential to keep offenders out of trouble and protect the public, without the disruptive effects of imprisonment. In the US city of Atlanta, a night curfew has been imposed on anyone under 16. This was introduced to protect children, but has also had the effect of considerably reducing juvenile crime. While such use of curfew orders on those who have not been convicted of crimes intrudes on the right to freedom of movement, the results show that, as a sentence, it could prove very useful.

At the moment, electronic tags are used that set off an alarm if a curfew is breached, but cannot identify where the criminal has then gone. The government is now considering a more technologically advanced system which can track the precise movements of the offender. This could have the advantage, for example, of making sure that a convicted paedophile does not enter a school building.

Disadvantages

The Penal Affairs Consortium have argued that the money spent on electronic tagging would be better spent on constructive options such as supervision requirements, which work to change offenders' long-term attitudes towards offending. Opponents of electronic tagging claim it is degrading to the person concerned, but its supporters – including one or two well-known former prisoners – point out that it is far less degrading than imprisonment. This argument applies only where tagging is used as an alternative to imprisonment: its opponents claim that it is likely to be used in practice to replace other non-custodial measures. Existing research suggests, however, that curfew orders with tagging are being seen as a genuine alternative to custody (Nuttall *et al.* (1998)).

Exclusion requirement

An offender can be required to stay away from a certain place or places at set times. Electronic tags can be used to monitor compliance with this requirement. It is aimed at people, such as stalkers, who present a particular danger or nuisance to a victim. An exclusion requirement is similar in many respects to a curfew requirement. However, whereas under a curfew requirement an offender has to remain at a specified place, an exclusion requirement prohibits an offender from entering a specific place.

Residence requirement

A residence requirement obliges the offender to reside at a place specified in the order for a specified period.

Mental health treatment requirement

A court can direct an offender to undergo mental health treatment for a certain period(s) as part of a community sentence or suspended sentence order, under the treatment of a registered medical practitioner or chartered psychologist. Before including a mental health treatment requirement, the court must be satisfied that the mental condition of the offender requires treatment and may be helped by treatment, but is not such that it warrants making a hospital or guardianship order (within the meaning of the Mental Health Act 1983). The offender's consent must be obtained before the requirement is imposed.

Drug rehabilitation requirement

As part of a community sentence or suspended sentence, the court may impose a drug rehabilitation requirement, which includes drug treatment and testing. In order to impose such a requirement, the court must be satisfied that the offender is dependent on or has a propensity to misuse any controlled drug and therefore requires and would benefit from treatment. In addition, the court must be satisfied that the necessary arrangements are or can be made for the treatment and that the offender has expressed a willingness to comply with the drug rehabilitation requirement. The treatment provided must be for a minimum of six months.

A court may provide for the review of this requirement, and such reviews must take place if the order is for more than 12 months. Review hearings provide the court with information about the offender's progress, including the results of any drug tests.

Alcohol treatment requirement

A court can require an offender to undergo alcohol treatment to reduce or eliminate the offender's dependency on alcohol. The offender's consent is required. This requirement must last at least six months.

Supervision requirement

The offender can be placed under the supervision of a probation officer for a fixed period of between six months and three years. Home Office research into the probation service (Mair and May, *Offenders on Probation* (1997)) found that 90 per cent of the people supervised thought that their supervision had been useful. The most common reason given for this view was that it offered them someone independent to talk to about their problems. A third mentioned getting practical help or advice with specific problems and about 20 per cent mentioned being helped to keep out of trouble and avoid reoffending. The research concluded:

> 'The message contained in this report is a good one for the probation service; it is viewed favourably by most of those it supervises, and seems to work hard at trying to achieve its formal aims and objectives as stated in the National Standards. However, this should not lead to any sense of complacency. It is arguable that any agency which provided similar help to that provided by the probation service to the poor and unemployed would be seen in an equally positive light.'

Due to staff shortages, particularly in London, some offenders who are subject to a supervision requirement, are merely being required to turn up and have their names ticked off.

Attendance centre requirement

This requirement tends to be imposed on young offenders.

Miscellaneous sentences

A range of other sentences are also available to the court. These include the following:

Compensation orders

Where an offence causes personal injury, loss or damage (unless it arises from a road accident), the courts may order the offender to pay compensation. This may be up to £1,000 in a magistrates' court and is unlimited in the Crown Court. Orders

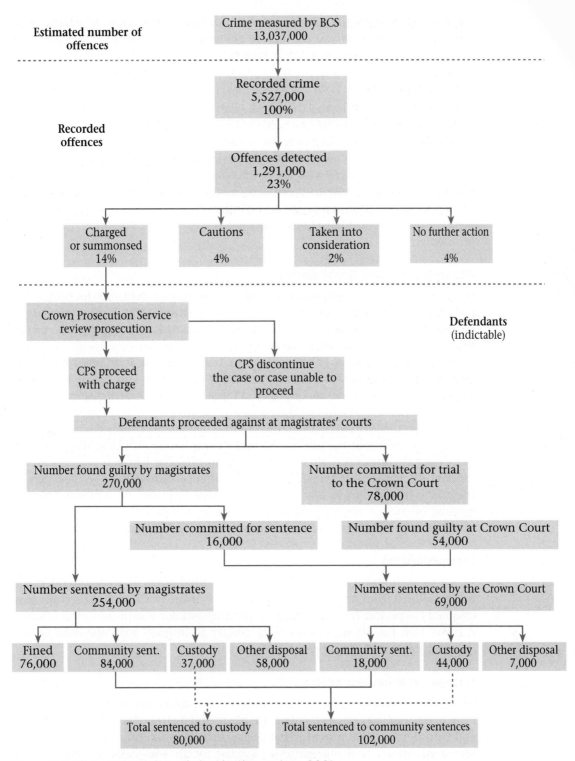

Figure 8.4 **Flows through the criminal justice system, 2001**

Source: Home Office (2002), *Criminal Statistics England and Wales 2001*, p. 15, Figure 1.1.

an also be made for the return of stolen property to its owner, or, where stolen operty has been disposed of, for compensation to be paid to the victim from v money taken from the offender when arrested.

Binding over to be of good behaviour

This order dates back to the thirteenth century and the relevant legislative provisions can be found in the Justices of the Peace Act 1361 and the Magistrates' Courts Act 1980. A binding over order can be made against any person who is before a court and has 'breached the peace' – not just the defendant, but also any witness or victim. People who are bound over have to put up a sum of money and/or find someone else to do so, which will be forfeited if the undertaking is broken. A person who refuses to be bound over can be imprisoned, despite the fact that they may not have been convicted of any offence. The order usually lasts for a year.

Absolute and conditional discharges

If the court finds an offender guilty of any offence (except one for which the penalty is fixed by law), but believes that in the circumstances it is unnecessary to punish the person and a community rehabilitation order is inappropriate, it may discharge the defendant either absolutely or conditionally.

An absolute discharge effectively means that no action is taken at all, and is generally made where the defendant's conduct is wrong in law, but no reasonable person would blame them for doing what they did. A conditional discharge means that no further action will be taken unless the offender commits another offence within a specified period of up to three years. This order is commonly made where the court accepts that the offender's conduct was wrong as well as illegal but the mitigating circumstances are very strong. If an offender who has received a conditional discharge is convicted of another offence during the specified period, they may, in addition to any other punishment imposed, be sentenced for the original offence. A discharge does not count as a conviction unless it is conditional and the offender reoffends within the specified period.

Disqualification

This is most common as a punishment for motoring offences, when offenders can be disqualified from driving. Under ss. 146–147 of the PCC(S)A 2000, a court may disqualify a person from driving as a punishment for a non-motoring offence. A conviction for offences concerning cruelty to animals may also lead to disqualification from keeping pets or livestock.

Anti-social behaviour orders

Anti-social behaviour orders are civil orders issued by a court to protect the public from behaviour that causes harassment, alarm and distress. Section 1 of the Crime and Disorder Act 1998 provides that bodies such as local authorities or the police may apply under civil procedures to a court for an anti-social behaviour order (ASBO). An ASBO can also be ordered as part of a criminal sentence. The order will be made against a person aged 10 or over who has acted in an anti-social manner, that is, a manner which is likely to cause harassment, alarm or distress to someone not in the same household as the person described in the order, and who is likely to do so again. Guidance on the legislation provided by the Home Office suggests that typical behaviour which might fall within this provision includes 'serious vandalism or persistent intimidation of elderly people'. The court has power to prohibit that person from doing anything described in the order for a period of not less than two years. For example, a person could be prohibited from entering a certain geographical area. Thus, in 2002, a woman was banned from going near her local police station for three years, as she had been harassing police officers. While the ASBO is obtained using civil procedures, breach of the ASBO can give rise to the criminal sanctions of a fine or five years' imprisonment.

There has been much controversy over the way ASBOs have been used in practice. The pressure groups Liberty, the National Association of Probation Officers (NAPO) and the Howard League for Penal Reform have together formed a campaign group, ASBO Concern, calling for a public review of the way anti-social behaviour orders are used. Initially, ASBOs were intended to deal primarily with anti-social behaviour by neighbours and young people, but they are increasingly being used for a wider range of problems. For example, an anti-social behaviour order was issued in 2004 against Sony Music Entertainment (UK) Ltd, to stop flyposting around the country.

A survey published by the probation officers' union, NAPO, has revealed that ASBOs are being inappropriately used against the mentally ill (*Anti-Social Behaviour Orders: analysis of the first six years* (2004)). As a result, people who are unable to control their behaviour owing to mental ill-health are being sanctioned, when treatment would actually be more effective and humane. NAPO give an example of a man who had been standing on a windowsill and moaning while pretending to dance with a Christmas tree. An ASBO was issued against him banning him from shouting, swearing and banging windows. He breached the order in August 2004, and was imprisoned for two months for continuing to moan in public. He breached the order again and was imprisoned for four months.

By the end of 2003, 42 per cent of all ASBOs were breached and 55 per cent of the breaches resulted in custody. Forty-five per cent of ASBOs have been issued against children. Nearly half of children subject to such an order have breached it, with ten young people each week being placed in custody for breaching an ASBO. Custodial sentences are being handed down for breach of an ASBO where the triggering anti-social conduct was not actually criminal.

The local authorities and police feel that it is necessary for photographs of people sanctioned with an ASBO to be made public in order for the ASBO to be effectively enforced. Photographs have been posted on council websites, leaflets distributed and local newspapers informed. There is concern that such publicity simply stigmatises families, could lead to a surge in vigilantism and does nothing to tackle the underlying causes of a person's anti-social behaviour. In **R (Stanley, Marshall and Kelly)** *v* **Metropolitan Police Commissioner** (2004) the High Court held that the authorities were entitled to 'name and shame' people who have been subjected to an ASBO, and it did not amount to a breach of their right to a private and family life which are guaranteed by Art. 8 of the European Convention.

Task 8.4

Try to visit a Crown Court. This will give you an opportunity both to see a jury at work and to see defendants being sentenced. You can find the address of your local Crown Court by looking in a telephone directory. Alternatively, Crown Court addresses are available on the Court Service's website at: **www.courtservice.gov.uk/ HMCSCourtFinder.**

You are unlikely to be able to see a whole case from beginning to end, as they tend to spread over several days. Near the entrance to the court will be a list of cases that are going to be heard and employees at the reception will also be able to help advise you on suitable cases to watch. Some cases will merely be concerned with sentencing an offender, who has been convicted at an earlier stage. Try to see at least one sentencing hearing, as well as trying to see a case where a jury is sitting. Note that the jury are never involved in the sentencing decision. Write up a report of your visit by answering the following questions:

About the court
1 What was the name and address of the court?
2 What was the court building like? Was it old or modern? Was it clean and in good decorative order? Were the waiting areas comfortable? Was there access to refreshments? Was it easy to find your way around the building, with rooms clearly signposted and labelled?
3 Did you find the court staff helpful? Were there any explanatory leaflets available?

About the proceedings involving a jury
Choose one hearing involving a jury and answer the following questions:

1 How many men and how many women were sitting on the jury?
2 Were there any black jurors?
3 How did the jurors behave during the case?
4 Did the jurors take notes?
5 Did the jurors ask any questions?
6 Did the jurors appear to be paying attention?
7 Was the professional judge male or female?
8 What was the ethnic origin of the judge?
9 What did you think of the way the judge behaved during the case?

About the sentencing process
Choose one hearing where the offender was sentenced and answer the following questions:

1 What offence had the offender committed?
2 Was the offender male or female?
3 Approximately how old do you think the offender was?
4 Was the offender represented by a lawyer?
5 Did the court refer to a pre-sentence report?
6 Did the defence lawyer present any arguments in mitigation in favour of a lighter sentence?

7 What sentence did the offender receive?

8 How did the offender react to his or her sentence?

9 Did the judge explain the choice of sentence?

10 Do you think that the court gave the right sentence?

Write up a short oral presentation about your visit to present to the other students with whom you are studying.

Problems with sentencing

The role of the judge

We have seen that the sentence in England is traditionally a decision for the judge, which can lead to inconsistent punishments, especially among magistrates' courts. This situation clearly offends against the principle of justice that requires like cases to be treated alike.

The government has tried to restrict judicial discretion through legislative guidelines and has also set up a Sentencing Advisory Panel, a Sentencing Guidelines Council and a Judicial Studies Board. Overseen by the Ministry of Justice, the Judicial Studies Board has functions that include running seminars on sentencing, which seek to reduce inconsistencies; courses for newly appointed judges; and refresher courses for more experienced members of the judiciary. The Board also publishes a regular bulletin, summarising recent legislation, sentencing decisions, research findings and developments in other countries, while the Magistrates' Association issues a *Sentencing Guide for Criminal Offences* to its members.

Other jurisdictions generally allow judges less discretion in sentencing. In the US, for example, many states use 'indeterminate' sentencing by which a conviction automatically means a punishment of, say, one to five years' imprisonment, and the exact length of the sentence is decided by the prison authorities. However, in this country, control of sentencing is seen as an important aspect of judicial independence, and the introduction of more legislative controls has been criticised as interfering with the judiciary's constitutional position.

Racism

Critics of sentencing practice in England have frequently alleged that members of ethnic minorities are treated more harshly than white defendants. For example, in 2001, 21 per cent of the prison population was from an ethnic minority, which is significantly higher than their representation in the general population. This difference becomes much less if only UK nationals are considered, because one in four black people in prison is a foreign national, often imprisoned for illegally importing drugs. Whether these figures actually point to racial discrimination in sentencing is the subject of much debate.

What is clear from recent research is that some members of the ethnic minorities perceive the sentencing process as racist. Research undertaken in 2003 by

Roger Hood and others (*Ethnic Minorities in the Criminal Courts: Perceptions of Fairness and Equality of Treatment*) investigated how far black and Asian defendants considered that they had been treated unfairly by the courts because of their race. Most complaints about racial bias concerned sentences perceived to be more severe than those imposed on a similar white defendant.

In addition to any racism in the system, the legal and procedural factors which affect sentencing may account for some of the differences in the punishment of black and white offenders. More black offenders elect for Crown Court trial and plead not guilty, which means that, if convicted, they would probably receive harsher sentences, because the sentences in the Crown Court are higher than those in the magistrates' court and they would not benefit from a discount for a guilty plea. Research by Flood-Page and Mackie in 1998 found that there was no evidence that black or Asian offenders were more likely than white offenders to receive a custodial sentence when all relevant factors were taken into account.

The experience of black people when in the prison system has also given rise to concern. An internal report commissioned by the Prison Service in 2000 found a blatantly racist regime at Brixton prison, where black staff as well as inmates suffered from bullying and harassment. The head of the Prison Service acknowledged that the service is 'institutionally racist' and that 'pockets of malicious racism exist'. He promised to sack all prison officers found to be members of extreme right-wing groups such as the British National Party. Prison officers' training now includes classes on race relations.

Sexism

sourcebook p. 245 →

There is enormous controversy over the treatment of women by sentencers. On the one hand, many claim that women are treated more leniently than men. In 2001, 19 per cent of known offenders were women. In 2003, women made up only 6 per cent of the prison population, but their numbers are growing. A Home Office study carried out by Hedderman and Hough in 1994 reported that, regardless of their previous records, women were far less likely than men to receive a custodial sentence for virtually all indictable offences except those concerning drugs, and that, when they do receive prison sentences, these tend to be shorter than those imposed on men. Flood-Page and Mackie also found in 1998 that women were less likely to receive a prison sentence or be fined when all relevant factors were taken into account. This has been variously attributed to the fact that women are less likely to be tried in the Crown Court; chivalry on the part of sentencers; assumptions that women are not really bad, but offend only as a result of mental illness or medical problems; and reluctance to harm children by sending their mothers to prison.

On the other hand, some surveys have suggested that women are actually treated less leniently than men. A 1990 study by the National Association for the Care and Resettlement of Offenders (NACRO) found that one-third of sentenced female prisoners had no previous convictions, compared with 11 per cent of men, and most of them were in prison for minor, non-violent offences. Because they are usually on lower incomes than men, women are thought more likely to end up in prison for non-payment of fines.

Several critics have suggested that women who step outside traditional female roles are treated more harshly than both men and other women. Sociologist Pat Carlen (1983) studied the sentencing of a large group of women, and found that judges were more likely to imprison those who were seen as failing in their female role as wife and mother – those who were single or divorced, or had children in care. This was reflected in the comments made by sentencers, including, 'It may not be necessary to send her to prison if she has a husband. He may tell her to stop it', and 'If she's a good mother we don't want to take her away. If she's not, it doesn't really matter'.

Today, women represent the fastest-growing sector of the prison population; their numbers nearly trebled in the space of nine years from 1,300 in 1992 to 4,300 in 2002. About one-fifth of the total female prison population have been sentenced as drugs couriers and, of these, some seven out of every ten are foreign nationals (Penny Green, *Drug Couriers: A New Perspective* (1996)). HM Chief Inspector of Prisons, Sir David Ramsbotham, has commented: 'There is considerable doubt whether all the women in custody [at Holloway] really needed to be there in order for the public to be protected' (*Report on Holloway Prison* (1997)). Helen Edwards, the Chief Executive of NACRO, has observed that: 'the vast majority of women in prison do not commit violent offences and much of their offending relates to addiction and poverty. Prison is not an appropriate, necessary or cost-effective way of dealing with these problems.'

The needs of women prisoners have wrongly been assumed to be the same as those of men. The Chief Inspector of Prisons has emphasised that female prisoners have different social and criminal profiles, as well as different health care, dietary and other needs. The Home Office published a study of women in prison: *Women in Prison: A Thematic Review* (Ramsbotham, 1997). Their survey revealed that the great majority of women in prison come from deprived backgrounds. Over half had spent time in local authority care, had attended a special school or had been in an institution as a child. A third had had a period of being homeless, half had run away from home, half reported having suffered violence at home (from a parent or a partner) and a third had been sexually abused. Forty per cent of sentenced women prisoners had a drug dependency, and alcohol problems were also found to be very common. Almost 20 per cent had spent time in a psychiatric hospital prior to being imprisoned and 40 per cent reported receiving help or treatment for a psychiatric, nervous or emotional problem in the year before coming into prison. Nearly two in five reported having attempted suicide.

The government has established a three-year plan, called 'The Women's Offending Reduction Programme'. This aims to increase the opportunities for tackling women's offending in the community. Each year about 17,000 children are separated from their mother when she is put into prison.

> ✓ **Know your terms 8.5**
>
> Define the following terms:
>
> 1 Retribution.
> 2 Absolute discharge.
> 3 An anti-social behaviour order.
> 4 Sexism.

Privatisation

Criminal justice has, historically, been regarded as a matter for the state. Recently, however, first under the Conservative government in the early 1990s, and now under Labour, various parts of the system have been privatised, including ten prisons. The Home Secretary said in 1998 that all new prisons would be privately built and run. Such moves have not generally been seen as runaway successes. Privatized prison escort services have come in for severe criticism, with prisoners managing to escape or not being brought to the court on time.

Reading on the web

The report of the National Association of Probation Officers, entitled *Anti-Social Behaviour Orders: analysis of the first six years*, is available on their website at:

www.napo.org.uk

The report of John Halliday on sentencing is available at:

www.homeoffice.gov.uk/documents/halliday-report-sppu

Information about the confiscation powers can be found at:

www.assetsrecovery.gov.uk

The consultation paper, *Making Sentencing Clearer* (2006), is available on the website of the National Offender Management Service:

www.noms.homeoffice.gov.uk

The report by R. Smith *et al.*, *Poverty and Disadvantage Among Prisoners' Families* (2007), is available on the website of the Joseph Rowntree Foundation at:

www.jrf.org.uk/knowledge/findings/socialpolicy/2065.asp

Chapter summary

Sentencing practice

In recent years there has been a considerable amount of legislation trying to control and regulate the sentencing practices of the judges.

Types of sentence

The judge has the power to impose a wide range of sentences:

Fines

The fine is the most common sentence issued by the court, but there is a major problem with fines not being paid.

Custodial sentences

Adult offenders can be sent to prison. Some offenders will be released early on home detention curfew. The Criminal Justice Act 2003 has introduced 'custody plus'.

Community sentence

The Criminal Justice Act 2003 has established a single community order that can be applied to an offender aged 16 or over. This order can contain a range of possible requirements. These are:

- an unpaid work requirement;
- an activity requirement;
- a programme requirement;
- a prohibited activity requirement;
- a curfew requirement;
- an exclusion requirement;
- a residence requirement;
- a mental health treatment requirement;
- a drug rehabilitation requirement;
- an alcohol treatment requirement;
- a supervision requirement; and
- an attendance centre requirement (where the offender is aged under 25).

Miscellaneous sentences

A range of other sentences is also available to the court. These include:

- compensation orders;
- binding over to be of good behaviour;
- absolute and conditional discharges;
- disqualification;
- anti-social behaviour orders.

Problems with sentencing

The role of the judge

There has been concern that there is inconsistency in sentencing.

Racism

Critics of sentencing practice in England have frequently alleged that members of ethnic minorities are treated more harshly than white defendants.

Sexism

There is enormous controversy over the treatment of women by sentencers.

Privatisation

Criminal justice has, historically, been regarded as a matter for the state. Recently, however, various parts of the system have been privatised, including ten prisons.

Question and answer guides

1 (a) Describe the sentences available for adult offenders.

Plan

- The key legislation on this subject is the Powers of Criminal Courts (Sentencing) Act 2000 and the Criminal Justice Act 2003.
- Some sentences are mandatory, most are discretionary.
- In practice, the most common sentence is a fine.
- Custodial sentences can be for life or for a limited period. Indeterminate sentences and extended sentences can be given to dangerous offenders for public protection.
- Community orders can include a range of different requirements, such as unpaid work, supervision by a probation officer, drug treatment and testing and a curfew.
- Conditional discharge.
- Absolute discharge.

(b) Discuss the advantages and disadvantages of custodial sentences.

(OCR Specimen Paper 2007, English Legal System Unit)

Plan

Advantages of custodial sentences:

- Protection of the public, as offenders cannot commit crimes against members of the general public while they are in prison.
- Opportunity for rehabilitation. Various courses are offered to educate offenders and to try to teach them to deal with their offending behaviour.
- An effective punishment which satisfies the principle of retribution.

Disadvantages of custodial sentences:

- Most offenders are eventually released from prison and they frequently reoffend.
- Prison overcrowding and poor conditions can be inhumane, increasing the risk of suicide and restricting the opportunities for rehabilitation.
- Expensive, particularly as the prison population is growing rapidly.
- Many people in prison would be better dealt with elsewhere, such as children, the mentally ill and minor offenders (including shoplifters).
- Prison does not just punish the offender, but also the offender's family, particularly their children, who can suffer from the social stigma of having a parent in prison and may find themselves in local authority care because there is no parent at home to look after them. It can lead to social breakdown, divorce, unemployment and poverty.

Answer

There is constant academic, political and media interest in the use of custodial sentences – do they work or are they merely a school for crime? The aims of a custodial sentence are clear: deterrence, protection of the public, retribution, rehabilitation and denunciation. But it is questionable whether all of these aims are actually attained when a custodial sentence is handed down.

There are certain advantages of imposing custodial sentences on convicted criminals. First, it physically removes them from society and thereby provides some protection to the public. Burglaries in an area might drop while a convicted burglar is in custody. However, most offenders are in prison only for a limited period, so this protection is offered only while the person is detained. Media reporting of prison sentences imposed may deter others from potential criminal behaviour and express society's denunciation of such conduct.

Rehabilitation is one of the aims of a prison sentence and this aim is supported in some prisons where educative programmes are available. Particularly popular at the moment are offending behaviour programmes aimed at changing the way prisoners think. But such courses are frequently short and available only to a minority of prisoners owing to a lack of funds. Prisoners wishing to take university degrees have to seek permission for this, and authorisation is dependent on funds being available and only likely to be given if the offender is serving a long sentence, since an Open University degree often takes six years to complete.

The Criminal Justice Act 2003 states that prison should only be used where it is really necessary, but in practice many of those in prison would be better dealt with elsewhere, particularly the mentally ill, children and those who have committed relatively minor offences, such as shoplifting. There have been high-profile media campaigns where an elderly person is imprisoned for failing to pay trivial amounts for their council tax – this does not create a good impression on the developed world stage and provides a poor image of the criminal justice system.

It costs approximately £36,000 per year to hold a prisoner and, in addition to the direct financial cost to the taxpayer, there are also social costs which are incurred. A prison sentence stops an offender from being able to work and contribute to the tax budget, welfare benefits might be needed to support their family financially, the separation in prison can lead to divorce and a person will usually lose their job.

A prison sentence punishes not only the offender, but also innocent members of their family, particularly their children, who can suffer from the social stigma of having a parent in prison, as well as the complications of poverty and perhaps the need to go into care if their main carer is no longer at home.

The prison population has been growing rapidly in the last 15 years and is much higher than any other European country. This growth has put considerable strain on the prison system, leading to unsatisfactory conditions of detention and increased risks of suicide – between 1999 and 2003 a total of 434 people committed suicide in prison. There were also over 16,000 incidents of self-harm recorded in 2003. Politicians are frightened of seeming to be soft on crime, so they have encouraged the use of prisons, but the reconviction rates following a prison sentence do not suggest that this is the best solution. Perhaps there are lessons that we could learn from continental Europe, rather than taking our lead from the US, which has for some time spent considerably more on its prison system than on education.

Group activity 1

Look at recent copies of your local newspaper. There will be reports about criminal cases heard in the local courts. List the variety of sentences passed on those convicted. Repeat the exercise using a national paper. Contrast and compare the sentences handed down and consider the reasons for any differences that you note.

Group activity 2

■ Divide your friends (or class) into groups of two or three people.
■ In your groups, visit the website **www.crimeinfo.org.uk**, which is maintained by the Centre for Crime and Justice Studies at King's College London.
■ Click on 'Judge for Yourself' and you will find an interactive exercise on sentencing.
■ Work through this exercise in your group, making notes as you go along that record the sentencing decisions you made and why you made them. At the end of the exercise, ask yourself: 'What has this exercise taught me about the sentencing process?'
■ Meet with the other groups and compare notes, looking for any common themes.

Visit **www.mylawchamber.co.uk/elliottocr** to access questions, quizzes and activities to test yourself on this chapter.

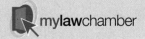

Chapter 9
THE JUDICIARY

This chapter discusses:

- the role of the judges;
- the different types of judges, known as the 'judicial hierarchy';
- how judges are appointed and trained;
- the five ways that a judge may cease to be a judge;
- the independence of the judiciary;
- criticisms of the judiciary.

The role of the judges

The judges play a central role under the British constitution. A basic principle of our constitution is known as the 'rule of law'. Under the rule of law, judges are expected to deliver judgments in a completely impartial manner, applying the law strictly, without allowing any personal preferences to affect their decision-making.

sourcebook p. 153 → The judges play a vital but sensitive role in controlling the exercise of power by the state. They do this, in particular, through the procedure of judicial review. The passing of the Human Rights Act 1998 significantly increased the powers of the judges to control the work of Parliament and the executive. A controversial judicial decision which highlights the tension between the roles of the judges, sourcebook p. 163 → Parliament and the executive is **A and others *v* Secretary of State for the Home Department (2004)**. Following fear over the increased risks of terrorism, Parliament had passed the Anti-terrorism, Crime and Security Act 2001. This allowed the government to detain in prison suspected terrorists without trial. The subsequent detention of nine foreign nationals was challenged through the courts and the House of Lords ruled that their detention was unlawful because it violated the Human Rights Act. As a result, the legislation was repealed and replaced by the Prevention of Terrorism Act 2005. This established control orders, which can potentially amount to house arrest – the first time we have seen this measure in the UK.

Judicial hierarchy

 sourcebook p. 81 → The judges are at the centre of any legal system, as they sit in court and decide the cases. At the head of the judiciary is the President of the Courts of England and Wales. This position was created by the Constitutional Reform Act 2005. Before that Act was passed, the Lord Chancellor had been the head of the judiciary. The new President of the Courts of England and Wales (in practice the Lord Chief Justice, discussed below) is now the head of the judiciary, being officially the president of the Court of Appeal, the High Court, the Crown Court, the county courts and the magistrates' courts. He or she is technically allowed to hear cases in any of these courts, though in practice he or she is only likely to choose to sit in the Court of Appeal. Under s. 7 of the Act, the President's role is to represent the views of the judiciary to Parliament and to government ministers. He or she is also responsible for the maintenance of appropriate arrangements for the welfare, training and guidance of the judiciary and for arranging where judges work and their workload.

The most senior judges are the 12 Lords of Appeal in Ordinary, more commonly known as the Law Lords. They currently sit in the House of Lords and the Privy Council. Their role will soon change, as the government has decided to abolish the House of Lords and replace it with a Supreme Court. The Constitutional Reform Act 2005 contains this reform and the new court is likely to be established in 2009. It is discussed in detail at p. 32.

At the next level down, sitting in the Court of Appeal, are 37 judges known as Lord Justices of Appeal and Lady Justices of Appeal. The Criminal Division of the Court of Appeal is presided over by the Lord Chief Justice who, following the Constitutional Reform Act 2005, is also known as the President of the Courts of England and Wales (discussed above). He or she can at the same time act as the Head of Criminal Justice or appoint another Court of Appeal judge to take this role.

The Civil Division of the Court of Appeal is presided over by the Master of the Rolls. There is also a head of civil justice and a head of family justice.

In the High Court, there are 107 full-time judges. As well as sitting in the High Court itself, they hear the most serious criminal cases in the Crown Court. Although – like judges in the Court of Appeal and the House of Lords – High Court judges receive a knighthood, they are referred to as Mr or Mrs Justice Smith (or whatever their surname is), which is written as Smith J.

The next rank down concerns the circuit judge, who travels around the country, sitting in the county courts and also hearing the middle-ranking Crown Court cases. The Criminal Justice and Public Order Act 1994 added a further role, allowing them occasionally to sit in the Criminal Division of the Court of Appeal.

The slightly less serious Crown Court criminal cases are heard by district judges, and then there are recorders, who are part-time judges dealing with the least serious Crown Court criminal cases. Recorders are usually still working as barristers or solicitors, and the role is often used as a kind of apprenticeship before becoming a circuit judge. Because of the number of minor cases coming before

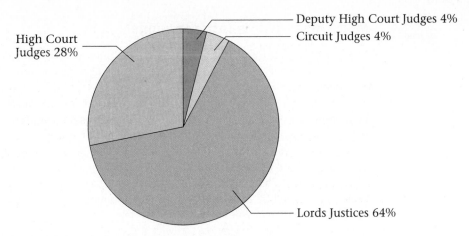

High Court
Judges 28%

Deputy High Court Judges 4%

Circuit Judges 4%

Lords Justices 64%

Figure 9.1 **Court of Appeal: days sat, 2004**

Source: K. Dibdin, A. Sealy and S. Aktar, *Judicial Statistics Annual Report 2004*, p. 131.

the Crown Court, there are now assistant recorders as well, and at times retired circuit judges have been called upon to help out. Finally, in larger cities there are district judges (magistrates' courts), who were previously known as stipendiary magistrates, and are full-time, legally qualified judges working in the magistrates' courts.

In practice, there is some flexibility between the courts, so that judges sometimes sit in more senior courts than their status would suggest. This practice is illustrated in Table 9.1.

Table 9.1 **The hierarchy of the judiciary**

Judge	*Usual court*
Lord of Appeal in Ordinary	House of Lords and Privy Council
Lord Chief Justice	Criminal Division of the Court of Appeal
Master of the Rolls	Civil Division of the Court of Appeal
Lord Justice of Appeal	Court of Appeal
High Court judge	High Court and Crown Court
Circuit judge	County court and Crown Court
District judge	County court and Crown Court
District judge (magistrates' court)	Magistrates' court
Recorder	Crown Court

Moderniser swims into top judge's post

A brainy moderniser who keeps fit by swimming outdoors all year round is to become the new top judge in England and Wales when Lord Woolf retires at the end of September 2005.

Lord Phillips will take over as Lord Chief Justice for England and Wales from 1 October 2005. He will move from the number two post in the judiciary, Master of the Rolls, to the top job. Like Lord Woolf, he is seen as a liberal, while the other candidate who had been tipped for the job, the deputy Chief Justice, Lord Justice Judge, is regarded as more conservative.

The new Lord Chief Justice is less at ease with the media than Lord Woolf, but his friends say he will be equally effective in the top judge's most difficult role, standing up to the executive in defence of the rule of law.

'He's quite a shy, internal person with a very great sense of duty and obligation', said one judge who knows him well. 'He's very jolly with his friends, but finds it quite difficult to have a public persona.'

Source: Adapted from Claire Dyer, *The Guardian*, 18 June 2005.

Appointments to the judiciary

The way in which judges are appointed has been radically reformed by provisions in the Constitutional Reform Act 2005. In order to evaluate the new appointment procedures, it is useful to understand how judges were appointed before these reforms were introduced. We will therefore look first at the old procedures before looking at the new ones.

The old appointment procedures

Prior to the 2005 Act, the Lord Chancellor (who is the government minister at the head of the Ministry of Justice) played a central role in the appointment of judges. The Lords of Appeal in Ordinary and the Lord Justices of Appeal were appointed by the Queen on the advice of the Prime Minister, who in turn was advised by the Lord Chancellor. High Court judges, circuit judges and recorders were appointed by the Queen on the advice of the Lord Chancellor.

Over the years there had been considerable criticism of the way in which judges were appointed and, as a result, changes had been made even before the more radical reforms of the 2005 Act. In the past only barristers could become senior judges. The Courts and Legal Services Act 1990 widened entry to the judiciary, reflecting the changes in rights of audience (see p. 161), and (at least in theory) opening up the higher reaches of the profession to solicitors as well as barristers. The selection process for judges in the High Court involved the old Department for Constitutional Affairs gathering information about potential candidates over a period of time by making informal inquiries (known as 'secret soundings') from leading barristers and judges.

The normal procedure for recruiting for a job is to place an advertisement in a newspaper and to allow people to apply. By contrast, until recently, there were no advertisements for judicial office, one simply waited to be invited to the post. Advertisements have more recently been placed for junior and High Court judges, but still not for positions in the Court of Appeal and the House of Lords.

In the past, the final selection process consisted of a traditional job interview. For the appointment of most judges, this was replaced, in 2003, with the attendance at an assessment centre for a whole day. The centres require judicial applicants to sit through an interview, participate in role-play and pass a written examination and are meant to offer applicants a fairer opportunity to demonstrate their knowledge and skills and thereby reduce the danger of subjective judgments and resulting discrimination. Research carried out for the government has found that these assessment centres are, indeed, a fairer method of judicial selection than one relying solely on an interview process.

The Law Society, the professional body representing solicitors, considered the limited reforms made following Sir Leonard Peach's report in 1999 'inadequate', particularly as the new Commissioner was merely responsible for monitoring the existing system, rather than having any direct involvement in the appointments process itself.

The three main criticisms of the old system of selecting judges were that it was dominated by politicians and was secretive and discriminatory. On the first issue, the Lord Chancellor and the Prime Minister played central roles in this process but they were politicians and could be swayed by political factors in the selection of judges. The Lord Chancellor presented the Prime Minister with a shortlist of two or three names, listing them in the order of his or her own preference. Mrs Thatcher is known to have selected Lord Hailsham's second choice on one occasion.

On the second issue, the constitutional reform organisation Charter 88, among others, criticised the old selection process for being secretive and lacking clearly defined selection criteria. The process was handled by a small group of civil servants who, although they consulted widely with judges and senior barristers, nevertheless wielded a great deal of power. This process was considered to be unfair because it favoured people who had a good network of contacts, perhaps because of their education or family, rather than focusing on the individual's strength as a future judge. There was also a danger that too much reliance was placed on a collection of anecdotal reports from fellow lawyers, with candidates given no opportunity to challenge damning things said about them.

Since 1999 the Law Society had refused to participate in the secret soundings process. The president of the Law Society described the system as having 'all the elements of an old boys' network', and being inconsistent with an open and objective recruitment process: 'We suspect we were being used to legitimise a system where other peoples' views were more important than ours. It didn't really matter what we thought, it was the views of the senior judiciary and the Bar which counted.' The highest ranking solicitor among the judiciary is a single High Court judge.

As regards the third criticism, that the old appointments process was discriminatory, a 1997 study commissioned by the Association of Women Barristers is of interest. It found that there was a strong tendency for judges to recommend candidates from their own former chambers. The study looked at appointments to the High Court over a ten-year period (1986–96) and found that of the 104 judges appointed, 70 (67.3 per cent) came from a set of chambers which had at least one ex-member among the judges likely to be consulted. In addition, a strikingly high percentage of appointments came from the same handful of chambers: 28.8 per cent of new judges from chambers which represented 1.8 per cent of the total number of chambers in England and Wales. The fact that those who advised on appointments were already well established within the system could make it unlikely that they would encourage appointment from a wider base: Lord Bridge, the retired Law Lord, commented in a 1992 television programme that they tend to look for 'chaps like ourselves'. As Helena Kennedy QC has put it, 'the potential for cloning is overwhelming', and the outlook for potential female judges and those from the ethnic minorities not promising.

The process of 'secret soundings' gave real scope for discrimination, with lawyers instinctively falling back on gender and racial stereotypes in concluding whether someone was appropriate for judicial office. For example, individuals were asked whether they thought candidates showed 'decisiveness' and 'authority'. But these are very subjective concepts and Kamlesh Bahl has argued (*The Guardian*, 10 April 1995) that, as the judiciary is seen as a male profession, perceptions of judicial characteristics, such as 'authority', are also seen as male characteristics. 'Authority' is dependent more on what others think than on the person's own qualities. Indeed, research published by the Bar Council in 1992 concluded:

> 'It is unlikely that the judicial appointment system offers equal access to women or fair access to promotion to women judges . . . The system depends on patronage, being noticed and being known.' (Holland (1992) Without Prejudice? Sex Equality at the Bar and in the Judiciary, *para. 48(1)*)

However, in his book, *The Judge*, Lord Devlin (1979) says that, while it would be good to open up the legal profession, so that it could get the very best candidates from all walks of life, the nature of the job means that judges will still be the same type of people whether they come from public schools and Oxbridge or not, namely those 'who do not seriously question the status quo'.

In its second annual report published in 2003, the Commission for Judicial Appointments concluded that there was systemic bias in the way that the judiciary and the legal profession operated. This bias prevented women, ethnic minorities and solicitors from applying successfully for judicial office. The Commission was fundamentally unhappy with the appointment process for High Court judges and recommended that it should be stopped immediately because it was 'opaque, out-dated and not demonstrably based on merit'.

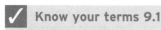 **Know your terms 9.1**

Define the following terms:

1 Secret soundings.
2 Law Lord.
3 Master of the Rolls.
4 Lord Chief Justice.

The new appointment procedures

The government published a consultation paper, *Constitutional Reform: a new way of appointing judges* (2003). While some improvements had been made in recent years to the appointment procedures, the government concluded that:

> 'The most fundamental features of the system . . . remain rooted in the past. Incremental changes to the system can only achieve limited results, because the fundamental problem with the current system is that a Government minister, the Lord Chancellor, has sole responsibility for the appointments process and for making or recommending those appointments.

However well this has worked in practice, this system no longer commands public confidence, and is increasingly hard to reconcile with the demands of the Human Rights Act.'

Following a limited consultation process, the Constitutional Reform Act 2005 was passed, containing provisions for the establishment of a new Judicial Appointments Commission responsible for a new judicial appointments process. This Commission started working in 2007. It is hoped that the creation of this body will help to put an end to the breaches of the principle of the separation of powers and reinforce judicial independence.

Under Sch. 12 to the Act, the Commission has 14 members: five lay members (including the chair), five judges, two legal professionals, a tribunal member and a lay magistrate. The members are appointed by the Queen on the recommendation of the Lord Chancellor. Candidates must be selected on the basis of merit and be of good character. Part 2 of the Tribunals, Courts and Enforcement Act 2007 contains provisions to try and widen the pool of lawyers eligible to become judges. In the past, to be eligible for appointment as a judge, a person needed to have experience as a judge in a more junior court or rights of audience in a court (which effectively limited judicial appointments to barristers and solicitors). If these professions were dominated by white men from an upper-middle class background, then the judiciary would inevitably share this profile. Under the 2007 Act, eligibility is no longer based on the number of years candidates have had rights of audience before a court, but instead on their number of years' post-qualification experience. The latter is a much broader concept but equally reflects a person's experience of the law. The required number of years' experience has been reduced from seven to five years and ten to seven years depending on the seniority of the judicial office. In order to be considered for judicial office, a person must have a relevant qualification. Following the 2007 Act, the Lord Chancellor can provide that the qualification of a legal executive, for example, will be sufficient for judicial appointment in certain courts. Sixty per cent of legal executives are women, so this should help to increase the number of female judges.

In performing its functions, the Commission must have regard to the need to encourage diversity in the range of persons available for selection (s. 64). It is allowed to encourage people it believes should apply for judicial posts to apply. The minister is able to issue guidance which the Commission must have regard to. This guidance can include directions on increasing diversity in the judiciary.

The Judicial Appointments Commission evaluates candidates and recommends, on the basis of merit only, one individual for each vacancy. The minister is not able to choose someone who has not been recommended to him or her by the Commission. He or she is, however, able to ask for a candidate who is not initially recommended by the Commission to be reconsidered, and can refuse the appointment of someone recommended and ask for a new name to be put forward. The minister has the ability to reject a candidate once, and to ask the Commission to reconsider once. Having rejected once, the minister must accept whichever subsequent candidate is selected.

There is special provision for the appointment of the Lord Chief Justice, the heads of Division and the Lord Justices of Appeal. The Commission establishes a selection panel of four members, consisting of two senior judges (normally including the Lord Chief Justice) and two lay members of the Commission.

Appointments of Lords Justices and above will continue to be made formally by the Queen on the advice of the Prime Minister, after the Commission has made a recommendation to the minister.

The new Appointments Commission will not be involved in the appointment of judges to the future Supreme Court. Instead, when there is a vacancy, the minister will appoint a temporary Commission. This Commission will include the President and Deputy President of the Supreme Court, as well as one member of each of the three judicial appointing bodies of England and Wales, Scotland and Northern Ireland. The temporary Commission will put forward between two and five recommended candidates to the minister, according to prescribed criteria. The minister must then consult with the senior judges, the First Minister in Scotland, the National Assembly for Wales, and the First Minister and deputy First Minister in Northern Ireland. The minister will afterwards notify the name of the selected candidate to the Prime Minister, who must recommend this candidate to the Queen for appointment.

The Law Society thinks that a choice of up to five gives too much scope for political interference, and thinks that only one name should be put forward for each job vacancy.

A Judicial Appointments and Conduct Ombudsman now oversees the recruitment process and has the power to investigate individual complaints about judicial appointments. The Commission for Judicial Appointments has been abolished.

The judicial appointment process has undoubtedly been improved by the reforms introduced by the Constitutional Reform Act 2005. However, there are some weaknesses in those reforms and the government could have gone much further in removing itself from the appointment process. The pressure group, Civil Liberties, is concerned that the Act only creates an advisory panel for judicial appointments, as the ultimate decision to appoint will still be made by the government minister (or effectively the Prime Minister for Court of Appeal and Supreme Court judges).

The government's consultation paper, *Constitutional Reform: a new way of appointing judges* (2003), considered the creation of three possible types of commission:

- An Appointing Commission.
- A Recommending Commission.
- A Hybrid Commission.

An Appointing Commission would itself make the decision whom to appoint with no involvement of a minister at any stage. This is similar to the arrangements that exist in some continental European countries.

A Recommending Commission would make recommendations to a minister as to whom he or she should appoint (or recommend that the Queen appoints). The final decision on who to appoint would rest with the minister.

A Hybrid Commission would act as an Appointing Commission in relation to the more junior appointments and as a Recommending Commission for the more senior appointments.

Ultimately, the government favoured the creation of a Recommending Commission, but an Appointing Commission would have more effectively removed government interference in the judicial appointment process.

Wigs and gowns

Traditionally, judges have been required to wear a wig made of horse hair and a gown when sitting in court. The government became concerned that this tradition could make the judges appear old-fashioned to court users. Following a consultation process, it has been decided that judges hearing civil court cases are no longer required to wear a wig. Judges hearing criminal cases will continue to wear a wig. This is because the wig provides a degree of anonymity for judges so that they are less likely to be recognised by defendants or their associates outside court, and also an important element of dignity to the court proceedings.

Training

Although new judges have the benefit of many years' experience as barristers or solicitors, they have traditionally received a surprisingly small amount of training for their new role, limited until recently to a brief training period, organised by the Judicial Studies Board. In the last few years, this has been supplemented in several ways: the advent of the Children Act 1989 has meant that social workers, psychiatrists and paediatricians have shared their expertise with new judges, while concern about the perception of judges as racist, or at best racially unaware, has led to the introduction of training on race issues. The reforms to the civil justice system and the passing of the Human Rights Act 1998 have led to the provision of special training to prepare for these legal reforms.

Pay

Judges are paid large salaries – £162,000 at High Court level – which are not subject to an annual vote in Parliament. The official justification for this is the need to attract an adequate supply of candidates of sufficient calibre for appointment to judicial office, and in fact some top barristers can earn more by staying in practice. One of the attractions for a barrister of becoming a judge is the security of a pensionable position after years of self-employment.

Table 9.2 **Judicial salaries**

Judge	Pay
Lord of Appeal in Ordinary (Law Lord)	£194,000
Lord Chief Justice	£225,000
Master of the Rolls	£200,800
Lord Justice of Appeal	£184,000
High Court judge	£162,000
Circuit judge	£120,300
District judge	£96,300
District judge (magistrates' court)	£96,300

Task 9.2

Read the following newspaper article and answer the questions below.

Wigs in court – it's time for this horseplay to stop

There are more important issues about the future of the legal system than whether lawyers and judges should continue to wear wigs and gowns. But the Lord Chancellor issued a consultation paper inviting us all to express our views. The legal bigwigs should be told by as many people as possible that fancy dress for lawyers is a non-sense that should have been mothballed long ago.

There is no positive case for retaining legal costume. As the consultation paper observes, tradition is no justification since 'our courts are not a tourist attraction'. The suggestion that the wearing of wigs and gowns symbolises the authority of office holders, instils respect for the law, and emphasises the impersonal and disinterested approach of the judge is impossible to sustain.

We are mature enough to understand that legal authority depends on the quality of the justice on offer, not on whether the judge and the lawyers have some horse hair on their head and a piece of cloth on their back. Indeed, it would be a sad reflection on the quality of the legal profession if its ability to command respect really did depend on its clothing.

Many courts of law perform their functions very satisfactorily without imposing a dress code. Neither the magistrates' courts nor employment tribunals require judges and lawyers to dress up for the occasion. The law lords sitting in the highest court of the land wear ordinary business suits. Without any noticeable effect on the quality of the product, judges of the High Court frequently make orders unrobed, indeed occasionally undressed (vice-chancellor Sadwell is said to have granted an injunction during the 1840s while bathing in the Thames).

Those judges and lawyers who argue that the wig and gown provide a welcome measure of anonymity which protects them from the antipathy of defendants and witnesses who may meet them out of court have no right to impose their lack of self-confidence on the rest of us. Anyone who insists on maintaining a disguise is free to wear fake spectacles, a false nose and an imitation moustache during court proceedings.

It is not simply that legal dress has no justification. It is positively damaging to the health of the legal system. The legal profession cannot convince its customers that it understands contemporary concerns and can provide a service for today's community when it looks as if it is still living in the eighteenth century.

Legal workers of the world unite. We have nothing to lose but our manes.

(Adapted from an article by David Pannick, published in *The Times* on 27 May 2003.)

Questions

1 Does the author of this article favour the wearing of wigs and gowns in court?
2 What are judges' wigs made out of?
3 Do the Law Lords wear wigs and gowns in the House of Lords?
4 Do you think judges should wear wigs and gowns in court?

Termination of appointment

There are five ways in which a judge may leave office:

Dismissal

Judges of the High Court and above are covered by the Act of Settlement 1700, which provides that they may only be removed from office by the Queen on the petition of both Houses of Parliament. The machinery for dismissal has been used successfully only once and no judge has been removed by petition of Parliament during the twentieth or twenty-first centuries.

Under the Courts Act 1971, circuit judges and district judges can be dismissed by the Lord Chancellor, if the Lord Chief Justice agrees, for 'inability or misbehaviour'. In fact, this has occurred only once since the passing of the Act: Judge Bruce Campbell (a circuit judge) was sacked in 1983 after being convicted of smuggling spirits, cigarettes and tobacco into England in his yacht. 'Misbehaviour' can include a conviction for drink-driving or any offence involving violence, dishonesty or moral turpitude. It would also include any behaviour likely to cause offence, particularly on religious or racial grounds or behaviour that amounted to sexual harassment.

In dismissing a judge, s. 108(1) of the Constitutional Reform Act 2005 provides that the Lord Chancellor will have to comply with any procedures that have been laid down to regulate this process.

In addition to dismissal there is, of course, also the power not to re-appoint those who have been appointed for a limited period only.

Discipline

In practice, the mechanisms for disciplining judges who misbehave are more significant than those for dismissal, which is generally a last resort. There was concern in the past that there were no formal disciplinary procedures for judges. Over the years there had been a few judges whose conduct had been frequently criticised, but who had nevertheless remained on the Bench, and the lack of a formal machinery for complaints was seen as protecting incompetent judges. The pressure group Justice had recommended the establishment of a formal disciplinary procedure in its report on the judiciary in 1972. The Constitutional Reform Act 2005 contains provision for the establishment of such procedures. The Act gives the Lord Chancellor and the Lord Chief Justice joint responsibility for judicial discipline. Section 108(3) states:

> 'The Lord Chief Justice may give a judicial office holder formal advice, or a formal warning or reprimand, for disciplinary purposes (but this section does not restrict what he may do informally or for other purposes or where any advice or warning is not addressed to a particular office holder).'

A person can be suspended from judicial office for any period when they are subject to criminal proceedings, have been convicted, are serving a criminal sentence, are subject to disciplinary procedures or where it has been determined under prescribed procedures that a person should not be removed from office, but it appears to the Lord Chief Justice, with the agreement of the Lord Chancellor, that the suspension is necessary for maintaining public confidence in the judiciary. The Judicial Appointments and Conduct Ombudsman will consider complaints about disciplinary cases.

The Judicial Appointments and Conduct Ombudsman will be able to review the handling of complaints about judicial conduct.

As well as the formal procedures discussed above, judges may be criticised in Parliament, or rebuked in the appellate courts, and are often censured in the press. There may be complaints from barristers, solicitors or litigants, made either in court or in private to the judge personally. 'Scurrilous abuse' of a judge may, however, be punished as contempt of court.

Resignation

Serious misbehaviour has on occasion been dealt with not by dismissal, but by the Lord Chancellor suggesting to the judge that he or she should resign.

Retirement

Judges usually retire at 70.

Removal due to infirmity

The Lord Chancellor has the power to remove judges who are disabled by permanent infirmity from the performance of their duties and who are incapacitated from resigning their post.

Independence of the judiciary

In our legal system great importance is attached to the idea that judges should be independent and be seen to be independent. In addition to the common sense view that they should be independent of pressure from the government and political groups, and in order to decide cases impartially, judicial independence is required by the constitutional doctrine known as the separation of powers. Under this doctrine, the power of the state has to be divided between three separate and independent arms: the judiciary (comprising the judges), the legislature (Parliament in the UK); and the executive (the government of the day). The idea is that the separate arms of the state should operate independently, so that each one is checked and balanced by the other two, and none becomes all powerful. The doctrine of the separation of powers was first put forward in the eighteenth century by the French political theorist Montesquieu. Montesquieu argued that if all the powers were concentrated in the hands of one group, the result would be tyranny. Therefore, the doctrine requires that individuals should not occupy a position in more than one of the three arms of the state – judiciary, legislature and executive; each should exercise its functions independently of any control or interference from the others; and one arm of the state should not exercise the functions of either of the others.

In the past, the broad role of the Lord Chancellor was seen as both a threat to judicial independence and as the protector of judicial independence. He was a threat because he breached the doctrine of the separation of powers, but at the same time as the head of the judiciary, he was responsible for defending judges from government influence. When the government announced in 2003 that it planned to introduce major constitutional changes, including the abolition of the position of Lord Chancellor, this caused some concern among the judges. They were worried that, without the Lord Chancellor, there would be nobody with responsibility for protecting their independence, and that as a result their independence could be threatened. In response to these concerns, the Lord Chancellor signed an agreement with the senior judge, the Lord Chief Justice, known as the Concordat. This agreement provided that some of the key judicial functions of the Lord Chancellor would be handed to the Lord Chief Justice when the constitutional reforms were introduced and that key aspects of this agreement would be incorporated into the legislation which was subsequently done. Following political negotiations, the post of Lord Chancellor was not actually abolished, though the role of the Lord Chancellor has significantly changed. With the changes in the role of the Lord Chancellor introduced by the Constitutional Reform Act 2005, the government sought to reassure judges that their independence would still be guaranteed, by introducing a statutory guarantee of the independence of the judiciary. Section 3 states:

'The Lord Chancellor, other Ministers of the Crown and all with responsibility for matters relating to the judiciary or otherwise to the administration of justice must uphold the continued independence of the judiciary.'

It also provides that:

'The Lord Chancellor and other Ministers for the Crown must not seek to influence a particular judicial decision through any special access to the judiciary.'

Other safeguards of judicial independence include the security of tenure given to judges, which ensures they cannot be removed at the whim of one of the other branches of power (see p. 147); the fact that they are well paid and their salaries are not subject to a parliamentary vote; and the rule that they cannot be sued for anything done while acting in their judicial capacity. Independence in decision-making is provided through the fact that judges are accountable only to higher judges in appellate courts.

The importance of the independence of the judiciary can be seen, for example, in judicial review, where the courts can scrutinise the behaviour of the executive, and in some cases declare it illegal. If the judges were not independent from the executive, the judges might always make decisions on judicial review that favoured the executive, rather than decisions that were fair and impartial.

Quick quiz 9.3

1 In which court does the Lord Chief Justice sit?

2 What is the Judicial Appointments Commission?

3 Which body is responsible for providing judicial training?

4 What is the doctrine of the separation of powers?

Problems with judicial independence

While the Constitutional Reform Act 2005 has now given statutory recognition to the independence of the judiciary, there remain a number of threats to judicial independence.

Supremacy of Parliament

Apart from where European law is involved, it is never possible for the courts to question the validity of existing Acts of Parliament. In the UK all Acts of Parliament are treated by the courts as absolutely binding, until such time as any particular Act is repealed or altered by Parliament itself in another statute or by a minister under the special fast-track procedure provided for under the Human Rights Act 1998. The judiciary is therefore ultimately subordinate to the will of Parliament.

The House of Lords

Lords of Appeal in Ordinary are also members of more than one arm of the state, since they take part in the legislative business in the House of Lords. However, they tend not to get involved in political controversy or ally themselves with a particular party, confining their contributions to technical questions of a legal nature. The Royal Commission on the House of Lords recommended in 2000 that the basic conventions restricting the role of the Law Lords should be put down in writing. The government announced in 2003 that it intended to replace the House of Lords with a Supreme Court and the Constitutional Reform Act 2005 contains provisions for the creation of this new court (see p. 32).

Non-judicial work

sourcebook p. 202 →

Judges also get involved in non-judicial areas with political implications, for example, chairing inquiries into Bloody Sunday in Northern Ireland, the Brixton riots or the Zeebrugge ferry disaster. Thus, Sir William Macpherson headed the inquiry into the handling of the police investigation of the death of the black teenager Stephen Lawrence, who was murdered in South London. This function can often be seen to undermine the political neutrality of the judiciary. The Hutton Inquiry, following the war against Iraq and Dr David Kelly's death, raised questions about the future role of judges in public inquiries. There was wide public dissatisfaction with the Hutton Report (2003), and a general unease as to how independent the judge and chair, Lord Hutton, had been. As a result the Lord Chief Justice, Lord Woolf, wrote a memo to the House of Commons Public Administration Select Committee expressing concern that Lord Hutton had been used as a political tool by the government.

Cases with political implications

Although judges generally refrain from airing their political views, they are sometimes forced to make decisions that have political ramifications. Concerns have been expressed that too often such decisions defend the interests of the government of the day, sometimes at the expense of individual liberties.

Certain cases have borne out this concern. In **McIlkenny v Chief Constable of the West Midlands** (1981) Lord Denning dismissed allegations of police brutality against the six men accused of the Birmingham pub bombings with the words:

> *'Just consider the course of events if this action were to go to trial . . . If the six men fail, it will mean that much time and money and worry will have been expended by many people for no good purpose. If the six men win, it will mean that the police were guilty of perjury, that they were guilty of violence and threats, that the confessions were involuntary and were improperly admitted in evidence: and that the convictions were erroneous. That would mean that the Home Secretary would have either to recommend they be pardoned or he would have to remit the case to the Court of Appeal under section 17 of the Criminal Appeal Act 1968. This is such an appalling vista that every sensible person in the land would say: it cannot be right that these actions should go any further. They should be struck out.'*

In other words, Lord Denning was saying that the allegations should not be addressed, because if proved true, the result would be to bring the legal system into disrepute.

The danger of political bias has been increased with the passing of the Human Rights Act 1998. While judges already decide some politically sensitive cases, their number is likely to increase, with litigation directly accusing government actions and legislation of breaching fundamental human rights. Over time the changing role of the judiciary is most likely to be visible in the House of Lords (or the Supreme Court when this is established in 2009 – see p. 32). These judges currently decide about 100 cases a year, which are usually on technical commercial and tax matters. With the implementation of the Human Rights Act 1998, the House of Lords has moved closer to the US Supreme Court, deciding fundamental issues on the rights of the individual against the state.

At the moment there appear to be the greatest tensions between the judges and the government with regard to the application of the terrorist legislation and the judges' approach to sentencing. In 2006, the Attorney-General published a list of more than 200 judges who have given 'unduly lenient' sentences to criminals. The list was drawn up by looking at successful appeals against lenient sentences made by the Attorney-General to the Court of Appeal. In response, a spokesperson from the Judicial Communications Office stated:

> *'Figures on successful appeals against a judge's sentencing can only begin to have relevance if they are set against the total number of sentencing decisions made by the judge in question, and those where there has been no appeal or an appeal has been rejected. It should also be borne in mind that some judges have caseloads involving more complex and serious cases, so they might be more likely to feature in appeal cases. In any event, there are many cases where the Court of Appeal reduces sentences without implying any criticism of the sentencing judges, sometimes indeed because of changes of circumstances – such as new evidence – after the original sentencing decision.'*

At the same time, the then Constitutional Affairs Minister, Vera Baird, criticised the judiciary during an appearance on BBC Radio 4's *Any Questions* programme. Baird attacked a trial judge for giving a convicted paedophile, Craig Sweeney, a sentence which potentially allowed him to be released after six years' imprisonment. The Lord Chancellor came to the defence of the trial judge and pointed out that he had simply applied the relevant sentencing guidelines to the case. Vera Baird subsequently apologised, in a letter to the Lord Chancellor, for her remarks.

The pressure group, Justice, has issued a *Manifesto for the rule of law*. This document seeks to remind politicians that there is a constitutional convention that the government should refrain from criticising the judiciary in any manner that would diminish public confidence. This convention was repeatedly breached by the former Home Secretaries John Reid and David Blunkett. Under their own rules of professional conduct, judges are not usually allowed to publicly respond to criticisms, so such remarks do not lead to a constructive debate. In addition, it is in everyone's interests that the judges who enforce the law are respected in society.

Quick quiz 9.4

1 What are the five ways in which a judge may leave office?

2 Who developed the doctrine of the separation of powers?

3 What is the average age of the Law Lords?

4 Can judges question the validity of an Act of Parliament?

Right-wing bias

In addition to its alleged readiness to support the government of the day, the judiciary has been accused of being particularly biased towards the interests traditionally represented by the right wing of the political spectrum. In his influential book, *The Politics of the Judiciary* (1985), Griffith states that: 'in every major social issue which has come before the courts in the last thirty years – concerning industrial relations, political protest, race relations, government secrecy, police powers, moral behaviour – the judges have supported the conventional, settled and established interests'.

Among the cases he cites in support of this theory is **Bromley London Borough Council *v* Greater London Council** (1983). In this case the Labour-run GLC had won an election on a promise to cut bus and tube fares by 25 per cent. The move necessitated an increase in the rates levied on the London boroughs, and one of those boroughs, Conservative-controlled Bromley, challenged the GLC's right to do this. The challenge failed in the High Court, but succeeded on appeal. The Court of Appeal judges condemned the fare reduction as 'a crude abuse of power', and quashed the supplementary rate that the GLC had levied on the London boroughs to pay for it. The House of Lords agreed, the Law Lords holding unanimously that the GLC was bound by a statute requiring it to 'promote the provision of integrated, efficient and economic transport facilities and services in Greater London', which they interpreted to mean that the bus and tube system must be run according to 'ordinary business principles' of cost-effectiveness. The decision represented a political defeat for the Labour leaders of the GLC and a victory for the Conservative councillors of Bromley.

Bias against women

In her book, *Eve was Framed* (1992), Helena Kennedy argues that the attitude of many judges to women is outdated, and sometimes prejudiced. Kennedy alleges that women are judged according to how well they fit traditional female stereotypes. Because crime is seen as stepping outside the feminine role, women are more severely punished than men, and women who do not fit traditional stereotypes are treated most harshly.

The Judicial Studies Board, responsible for the training of judges, has issued judges with the *Equal Treatment Bench Book*. This advises judges on equal treatment of people in court and the appropriate use of language to avoid causing offence by, for example, being sexist.

Influence of Freemasonry

Freemasonry is a form of secret society, which does not allow women to join. Among its stated aims is the mutual self-advancement of its members. There has long been concern about the extent of membership among the police, as well as the judiciary, on the basis that loyalty to other Masons – who might be parties in a case, or colleagues seeking promotion or other favours – could have a corrupting influence.

In an attempt to introduce greater transparency, a questionnaire was sent in 1998 to all members of the judiciary asking them to declare their 'Masonic status'. Five per cent of those who responded admitted to being Freemasons.

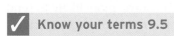 **Know your terms 9.5**

Define the following terms:

1 Executive.
2 Freemasonry.
3 Law Society.
4 Stereotype.

Criticisms of the judiciary

Background, ethnic origin, sex and age

Judges are overwhelmingly white, male and middle- to upper-class, and frequently elderly, leading to accusations that they are unrepresentative of, and distanced from, the majority of society. In 1995, 80 per cent of Lords of Appeal, Heads of Division, Lord Justices of Appeal and High Court judges were educated at Oxford or Cambridge. Eighty per cent of judges appointed since 1997 were educated at a public school. The narrow background of the judges does mean that they can be frighteningly out of touch with the world in which they are working. One judge, who resigned in 1998, said in three different cases that he had not heard of the footballer Paul Gascoigne, the rock band Oasis and the singer Bruce Springsteen.

In 2004 only 16 per cent of judges were women and only 9 per cent of senior judges were women. There are still no women sitting as judges in the European Court of Justice. The first female judge, Lady Justice Hale, was appointed to the

sourcebook
p. 72 → House of Lords in 2004. There are only two female judges in the Court of Appeal and ten female High Court judges. In 2006, the Equal Opportunities Commission warned that at the current rate, it will take 40 years for women to achieve equality in the senior judiciary. Just 3 per cent of court judges in 2004 came from an ethnic minority, with one member of the Court of Appeal coming from an ethnic minority and one High Court judge. By comparison, 8 per cent of the population of England and Wales come from an ethnic minority. Lord Lane, the former Lord Chief Justice, said after his retirement that his regret at being forced off the bench was due, at least partly, to the fact that his colleagues were 'a jolly nice bunch of chaps'. This remark reinforces the view of many that the judiciary is actually a sort of rarefied gentlemen's club.

The age of the full-time judiciary has remained constant over many years with the average age of a judge being 58. With a retirement age of 70, judges are allowed to retire five years later than most other professions. David Pannick has written in his book, *Judges*, that 'a judiciary composed predominantly of senior citizens cannot hope to apply contemporary standards or to understand contemporary concerns'.

Before the Courts and Legal Services Act 1990, judges were almost exclusively selected from practising barristers. Since it is difficult for anyone without a private income to survive the first years of practice, successful barristers have tended to come from reasonably well-to-do families, who are, of course, more likely to send their sons or daughters to public schools and then to Oxford or Cambridge. Although the background of the Bar is gradually changing, the age at which judges are appointed means that it will be some years before this is reflected in the ranks of the judiciary.

The new opportunities provided for solicitors to join the judiciary, provided by the Courts and Legal Services Act 1990 and the new right of government lawyers to become junior judges may in time help to alter the traditional judicial background, since there are larger numbers of women, members of the ethnic minorities and those from less privileged backgrounds working as solicitors and government lawyers than in the barrister profession. Since April 2005, judges below High Court level are able to sit part-time, which may prove attractive to women combining work with childcare responsibilities.

sourcebook
p. 81 → Section 64 of the Constitutional Reform Act 2005 provides that the Judicial Appointments Commission 'must have regard to the need to encourage diversity in the range of persons available for selection for appointments'. The Lord Chancellor can issue guidance for the Commission in order to encourage a range of persons to be available for selection (s. 65). The government issued a consultation paper, *Increasing Diversity in the Judiciary* (2004). At the launch of this paper, the Government Minister stated:

> 'It is a matter of great concern that the judiciary in England and Wales – while held in high regard for its ability, independence and probity, is not representative of the diverse society it serves. A more diverse judiciary is essential if the public's confidence in its judges is to be maintained and strengthened.
>
> We need to find out why people from diverse backgrounds and with disabilities are not applying for judicial appointment in the numbers we might expect and, once we have identified the barriers, we need to do something about removing them. Judicial appointments will

continue to be made on merit. But I do not believe that there is any conflict between merit and diversity.'

sourcebook
p. 84 →

A diversity strategy was launched by the Lord Chancellor in 2006 which aims to increase the number of women and black and ethnic minority judges. The strategy seeks to achieve this by promoting fair and open selection processes based solely on merit and by ensuring that the culture and working environment for judicial office-holders encourages and supports a diverse judiciary. The Lord Chancellor is considering introducing flexible working hours for judges, career breaks, a work-shadowing programme and changes to age limits in order to try to attract a more diverse range of people to a judicial career. Part 2 of the Tribunals, Courts and Enforcement Act 2007 aims to widen the pool of lawyers eligible to become judges (see p. 143).

Training

Considering the importance of their work, judges receive very little training, even with recent changes. They may be experienced as lawyers, but the skills needed by a good lawyer are not identical to those required by a good judge.

Reading on the web

The website of the Judicial Appointments Commission is available at:

   www.judicialappointments.gov.uk/index.htm

The consultation paper, *Constitutional Reform: A New Way of Appointing Judges*, is available on the website for the former Department for Constitutional Affairs at:

   www.dca.gov.uk/consult/jacommission/index.htm

The consultation paper, *Court Working Dress in England and Wales*, is available on the website for the former Department for Constitutional Affairs at:

   www.dca.gov.uk/consult/courtdress

Sir Leonard Peach's report into judicial appointments is available on the former Department for Constitutional Affairs' website:

   www.dca.gov.uk/judicial/peach/indexfr.htm

General information on the judiciary is available on:

   www.judiciary.gov.uk

The website of the Judicial Studies Board can be found at:

   www.jsboard.co.uk

The booklet, *Judicial Appointments in England and Wales: Policies and Procedure*, is available on the former Department for Constitutional Affairs' website at:

   www.dca.gov.uk/judicial/appointments/jappinfr.htm

Chapter summary

The role of the judges

The judges play a central role under the British Constitution, providing a vital but sensitive control over the exercise of power by the state.

Judicial hierarchy

At the head of the judiciary is the President of the Courts of England and Wales. The most senior judges are the 12 Lords of Appeal in Ordinary. They currently sit in the House of Lords and the Privy Council. At the next level down, sitting in the Court of Appeal, are 37 judges known as Lord Justices of Appeal and Lady Justices of Appeal.

Appointing the judges

The way in which judges are appointed has been radically reformed by provisions in the Constitutional Reform Act 2005. The Act contains provisions for the establishment of a new Judicial Appointments Commission. It is hoped that the creation of this body will help to put an end to the breaches of the principle of the separation of powers and reinforce judicial independence. Depending on their rank, judges are appointed by the Queen on the advice of the Prime Minister or by the Lord Chancellor.

Training

Training is provided by the Judicial Studies Board.

Termination of appointment

There are five ways in which a judge may leave office:

- dismissal;
- discipline;
- resignation;
- retirement; or
- removal due to infirmity.

Independence of the judiciary

In our legal system, great importance is attached to the idea that judges should be independent and be seen to be independent. Section 3 of the Constitutional Reform Act 2005 states:

> 'The Lord Chancellor, other Ministers of the Crown and all with responsibility for matters relating to the judiciary or otherwise to the administration of justice must uphold the continued independence of the judiciary.'

There are real concerns that the independence of the judiciary is not sufficiently protected. The academic, Griffith, has accused judges of being biased towards the interests traditionally represented by the right wing of the political spectrum. The lawyer, Baroness Kennedy, has argued that the attitude of many judges to women is outdated and sometimes prejudiced. There is also concern that some judges are members of the Freemasons.

Criticisms of the judiciary

Judges are overwhelmingly white, male and middle- to upper-class, and frequently elderly, leading to accusations that they are unrepresentative of the society they serve. The appointments process has been criticised for being dominated by politicians, secretive and discriminatory. Judges receive very little training.

Question and answer guides

1. (a) Outline the theory of the separation of powers, illustrating your answer with examples.

Plan

- The theory was developed by Montesquieu in the eighteenth century.
- The three arms of the state are the legislature, the executive and the judiciary.
- Under the theory of the separation of powers, no single power should hold more than one form of power so that they can act as a check and balance on each other.
- Breach of the theory gives rise to the risk of an abuse of power.
- Examples of the theory being put into practice include: the protection of the independence of the judiciary; the judges respecting the intention of Parliament when interpreting statutes; and the supremacy of Parliament preventing the judges from questioning the legality of an Act of Parliament.
- Examples of each power controlling the other include the process of judicial review; the executive selecting the judiciary; the judiciary applying the golden rule of statutory interpretation when the literal rule would give an absurd result; the legislature controlling the conditions of employment of the judges and the legislative amending legislation where a minister has been found by the courts to have acted unlawfully.

Answer

The three arms of the state are the legislative, the executive and the judiciary. The legislative enacts and is represented by the Queen and Parliament. The executive consists of the government ministers and the civil service; and the judiciary is another name for the judges who settle disputes arising out of the application of the law in the courts. The eighteenth-century French philosopher, Montesquieu, developed the theory of the separation of powers. Under this theory, political liberty can be maintained only if the different agencies of the state are held in separate hands, so that each can keep a check on the other. If one arm could influence and control the other, there would be the risk of an abuse of power and ultimately of a dictatorship, as the government could influence or dictate judges' decisions and verdicts. The current crisis in Pakistan between the president and the lawyers can be viewed as an example of the tensions that can arise if the principle of the separation of powers is not respected.

This process of checks and balance seems to have operated successfully in the UK despite the historical role of the Lord Chancellor, who transcended each branch of power, but whose role has now been restricted to the executive and the legislative as he or she no longer acts as a judge. There are various ways in which the separation of powers is guaranteed under the English legal system. The judges benefit from independence, with that independence now being expressly provided for in the Constitutional Reform Act 2005. They have long enjoyed security of tenure, following the passing of the Act of Settlement in 1700, so that senior judges cannot be sacked by an executive which is unhappy with their decisions. Instead, a petition for the judges' removal has to be made to both Houses of Parliament in order for the Queen to remove them from their post. This has only happened once. Inferior court judges can be removed by the Lord Chancellor for inability or misbehaviour, which can include a drink-driving conviction.

Another example of the English legal system respecting the principle of the separation of powers in practice, is that the judges try to implement the intention of Parliament when they have to use the rules of statutory interpretation to give meaning to an Act. Since **Pepper** v **Hart** in 1993, the judges can use ministerial statements reported in *Hansard* to aid interpretation, but they have tended to prefer the literal approach as they are not then second-guessing Parliament's will. They always have the option of using the golden rule, which helps prevent an absurdity resulting from a strict, literal application of parliamentary law.

In addition, due to the principle of the supremacy of Parliament, the judges cannot question the legality of legislation. The unsuccessful challenge to the Hunting Act 2004 was based on the suggestion that the legislative process had not been correctly followed, so that the 2004 Act was not a genuine piece of parliamentary legislation.

As well as being able to see how each of the powers works separately and independently of the other, we can also see how each power provides a check and balance to the other, to avoid the abusive use of power. The judges are appointed by the executive, with an improved appointment process under the Judicial Appointments Commission, to try and make sure that the key criteria for appointment is merit. The appointment procedures are now more transparent and most appointments are made on the strength of a person's qualifications, work experience and performance at an assessment day. The legislative can change the law if the judges find that the executive has acted unlawfully. Finally, the judges can independently scrutinise the procedures of the executive through their judicial review function.

(b) Discuss the ways in which judges' independence is maintained.

(OCR Specimen Paper 2007, English Legal System Unit)

Plan

- The Constitutional Reform Act 2005, s. 3 states that government ministers must uphold the independence of the judiciary, and the Lord Chancellor and other ministers must not seek to influence a particular judicial decision through special access to the judiciary.

- Following the Act of Settlement 1700, senior judges can be dismissed only by the Queen following a petition of both Houses of Parliament.
- The Judicial Appointments Commission provides an appointment process based on merit.
- Judges can make decisions that are unpopular with politicians.
- They have high earnings to reduce the risk of being tempted by financial bribes.
- Judges must be seen to be impartial and a party can appeal against a case if the judge is found to have an interest in the outcome of the case. An example of this in practice is the case of **Re Pinochet** (1998) discussed at p. 259.
- Judges cannot be sued for what is said in court.
- Judges cannot stand for elections to become a member of Parliament and should avoid commenting in public on political issues.
- There is a convention that Law Lords only take part in House of Lords' debates on legislation which might subsequently be considered in court proceedings.
- Judges sometimes refuse to change the law where they feel there are public policy issues which it is up to Parliament to resolve.
- When interpreting statutes, the judges show respect for Parliament's intention.
- The future establishment of the Supreme Court should reinforce the independence of the judiciary from the legislative.

Group activity 1

The system for appointing judges has become more formalised and 'secret soundings' for judicial appointments are a thing of the past. Visit the website of the Judicial Appointments Commission:

www.judicialappointments.gov.uk

Which judicial appointments are they advertising at the moment? How will they select the successful candidate? Which (if any) job would you be interested in applying for and why?

Group activity 2

- Divide your friends (or class) into groups of two or three people.
- In your groups, visit the 'Learning Resources' pages of the website of the Judicial Communications Office – **www.judiciary.gov.uk/learning_resources** – and familiarise yourself with their contents.
- Note that the first of these pages contains the following statement: 'We are seeking your feedback to help us develop our Learning Resources pages. Please email us with any comments or suggestions.'
- In your groups, prepare a draft email to the JCO containing your comments and suggestions on the Learning Resources pages.
- Compare notes with the other groups and agree a final email for sending to the JCO.

Chapter 10
THE LEGAL PROFESSION

This chapter discusses:

- solicitors – their work, qualifications and training;
- possible educational reforms to help people from a wider range of social backgrounds to join the solicitor profession;
- the handling of complaints against solicitors;
- barristers – their work, qualifications and training;
- senior barristers, known as Queen's Counsel;
- the handling of complaints against barristers;
- the regulation of the profession;
- changes to the business structures in which the profession are organised;
- moves towards fusing the solicitor and barrister profession into a single profession.

Introduction

The British legal profession, unlike that of most other countries, includes two separate branches: barristers and solicitors (the term 'lawyer' is a general one which covers both branches). They each do the same type of work – advocacy, which means representing clients in court, and paperwork, including drafting legal documents and giving written advice – but the proportions differ, with barristers generally spending a higher proportion of their time in court.

In addition, some types of work have traditionally been available to only one branch (conveyancing to solicitors, and advocacy in the higher courts to barristers, for example), and barristers are not usually hired directly by clients. A client's first point of contact will usually be a solicitor, who then engages a barrister on their behalf if it proves necessary. As we shall see, however, these divisions are beginning to break down.

In the past, the two branches of the profession have been fairly free to arrange their own affairs, but over the last 15 years this situation has changed significantly, with the government increasingly passing legislation to control the professions.

As well as barristers and solicitors, an increasingly important profession is that of the legal executives.

Solicitors

There are around 98,000 solicitors in England and Wales. Their governing body is the Law Society. Until recently, the Law Society acted both as the representative of solicitors and as the solicitor's regulator. A government-commissioned report by Sir David Clementi (2004) (see p. 174 below) raised concerns that this dual function could cause a conflict of interests, with the Law Society putting the solicitor first, rather than the consumer, when making decisions regarding the regulation of the profession. In response to these concerns, in 2005 membership of the Law Society became voluntary and the Law Society decided to separate its representative function from its regulatory function. The profession is now regulated by the Law Society Regulation Board.

sourcebook p. 93 →

Work

For most solicitors, paperwork takes up much of their time. It includes conveyancing (when solicitors deal with the legal aspects of the buying and selling of houses and other property) and drawing up wills and contracts, as well as giving written and oral legal advice. Until 1985, solicitors were the only people allowed to do conveyancing work, but this is no longer the case – people from different occupations can qualify as licensed conveyancers, and the service is often offered by banks and building societies.

Solicitors have traditionally been able to do advocacy work in the magistrates' court and the county court, but not generally in the higher courts. This situation was changed by the Courts and Legal Services Act 1990 and the Access to Justice Act 1999. These Acts put in place the mechanics for equalising rights of audience between barristers and solicitors. Now all barristers and solicitors automatically

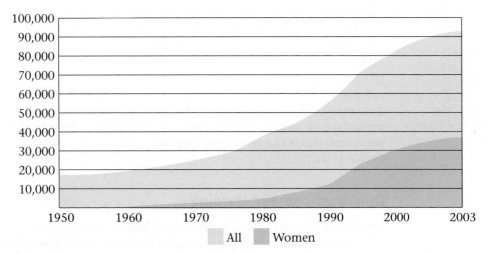

Figure 10.1 **Growth in the numbers of solicitors with practising certificates, 1950-2003**

Source: Law Society website. *Fact Sheet 2: Women in the profession* (www.lawsociety.org.uk). © The Law Society.

acquire full rights of audience, though they will be able to exercise these rights only on completion of the necessary training. There are currently 1,000 solicitor advocates. Many firms are sending their solicitors on courses, making advocacy training compulsory and designating individuals as in-house advocates. Thus, solicitors are increasingly doing the advocacy work themselves rather than sending it to a barrister. Where government funding has established fixed fees for work, solicitors are faced with a simple choice: keep the money or give it away. Even those solicitors who do not have full rights of audience can appear in the higher courts for a limited range of proceedings.

Traditionally, an individual solicitor did much less advocacy work than a barrister, but as more solicitors gain the necessary training, this is changing. In any case, solicitors as a group do more advocacy than barristers, simply because 98 per cent of criminal cases are tried in the magistrates' court, where the advocate is usually a solicitor.

> **✓ Know your terms 10.1**
>
> Define the following terms:
> 1 Law Society.
> 2 Conveyancing.
> 3 Rights of audience.
> 4 Solicitor advocate.

Solicitors can, and usually do, form partnerships, with other solicitors. Alternatively, since 2001, they can form a limited liability partnership (LLP). Under an ordinary partnership a solicitor can be personally liable (even after retirement) for a claim in negligence against the solicitor firm, even if he or she was not involved in the transaction giving rise to the claim. Under a limited liability partnership a partner's liability is limited to negligence for which he or she was personally responsible.

Solicitors work in ordinary offices, with, in general, the same support staff as any office-based business, and have offices all over England and Wales and in all towns. Practices range from huge London-based firms, dealing only with large corporations, to small partnerships or individual solicitors, dealing with the conveyancing, wills, divorces and minor crime of a country town. The top city law firms are known as the 'magic circle' and a Sweet & Maxwell survey found nearly a quarter of all law students wanted to join one when they qualified, though in practice a much smaller percentage will succeed in doing so. Most law firms are small, with 85 per cent of them having four or fewer partners, and nearly half having only one partner. Some solicitors work in law centres and other advice agencies, government departments, private industry and education rather than in private practice.

Figures published in the journal *Commercial Lawyer* in September 2000 show that an elite group of 100 City solicitors working in central London are earning more than £1 million per year. But this figure has to be seen in the context of a profession that has over 80,000 members. The average annual salary for a solicitor is £51,463.

Qualifications and training

Almost all solicitors have a university degree, though not necessarily in law. A number of universities introduced an admissions test in 2004, the National Admissions Test for Law, to help select students onto their popular law degrees. Students whose degree is not in law have to take a one-year conversion course leading to the Common Professional Examination (CPE).

The next step, for law graduates and those who have passed the CPE, is a one-year Legal Practice Course, designed to provide practical skills, including advocacy, as well as legal and procedural knowledge. The course costs between £5,000 and £9,000 and the vast majority of students are obliged to fund themselves or rely on loans.

After passing the Legal Practice exams, the prospective solicitor must find a place, usually in a solicitor firm, to serve a two-year apprenticeship under a training contract. There can be intense competition for these places, especially in times of economic difficulty, when firms are reluctant to invest in training. Trainee solicitors should receive a minimum salary of £15,332 outside London and £17,110 in London. In practice, the average salary for a trainee solicitor is £20,925. The work of a trainee solicitor can be very demanding, and a survey carried out for the Law Society found that a third work more than 50 hours a week.

It is possible to become a solicitor without a degree, by completing the one-year Solicitors First Examination Course, and the Legal Practice Course, and having a five-year training contract. Legal executives sometimes go on to qualify this way.

Solicitors are required to participate in continuing education throughout their careers. They have to undertake 16 hours of education a year, with the subjects covered depending on each individual's areas of interest or need.

Lord Woolf, an influential judge, has observed that the solicitor profession is becoming 'increasingly polarised', depending on the nature of the work carried out, with lawyers working in City firms earning significantly more than those in high street practices. Specialist LPC courses are now being offered for some City law firms. Lord Woolf has criticised this development, as he fears it could undermine the concept of a single solicitor profession with a single professional qualification.

Increasing diversity through educational reforms

The Solicitors Regulation Authority is considering introducing a radical reform to the way people qualify as solicitors. The Law Society has observed:

> 'The existing training pathway – a degree in law, one year on a Legal Practice Course and a two-year training contract – has worked well, and will continue to be the route to qualification for many. But it is a system that favours the young school leaver with a traditional academic education who is prepared to take on a five figure debt. It makes law a difficult career choice for the rest. That is discriminatory – and not good for the profession.'

sourcebook
p. 105 → In 2005 the Law Society published a consultation paper *Qualifying as a Solicitor: a framework for the future*. The consultation paper suggested that it should no longer be necessary for a future solicitor to complete a Legal Practice Course or, in fact, to have any academic legal qualifications (such as a law degree). Instead, candidates would simply need to demonstrate they had acquired the necessary skills and knowledge by passing assessments set by the Law Society.

These proposals were the subject of considerable criticism, in particular that, without the course structure for the Legal Practice Course, consistent standards would not be maintained. As a result, a further consultation paper was issued, *A new framework for work based learning* (2006). This paper recommended that the current academic and vocational training qualifications should essentially remain the same. Changes would be made, instead, to the work experience aspect of the qualification process. Currently, when a person completes the Legal Practice Course, they can only become fully qualified solicitors if they are able to find a training contract. Thousands of people each year fail to find such a position. The Solicitors Regulation Authority is considering establishing an alternative route to qualifying. Instead of having a training contract, individuals would be able to work in any legal environment and have that work supervised and accredited directly by the Authority. People taking this route could gain their work experience at any stage, including while they were actually studying on the Legal Practice Course. There would no longer be a requirement that the trainee solicitor gain their experience over two years; instead, the emphasis would be on the student demonstrating, through a portfolio of their work, that they had attained the relevant skills. In practice, this arrangement would allow paralegals to qualify as solicitors without having a training contract. Qualifying in this way is likely to take longer than the two-year training contract, and there is a risk that it might create a two-tier profession, with solicitors qualifying by the new route being viewed as inferior to those qualifying by the traditional route. This reform could help those people who pass their Legal Practice Course but are then unable to secure a training contract.

Changes would also be made to the training contract route to qualification, though it would still be necessary for these trainees to do the Legal Practice Course first. Law firms would have to apply to become accredited training organisations. The accredited firm would assess the work of trainee solicitors four times at regular six-monthly intervals.

The Solicitors Regulation Authority is proposing to carry out a small pilot scheme of its proposal in 2008 and review these proposals in 2010 in the light of the success (or otherwise) of the pilot. Sadly, the new proposals fail to tackle the problem of the cost of getting the academic and vocational qualifications, which will continue to act as a barrier to students from lower income families.

It is undoubtedly important that the legal profession should be a career option for all able students from a wide range of backgrounds, and that people should not be prevented from entering the profession because their family is not rich. But there are other ways that this can be achieved. The Charter 88 constitutional reform pressure group has argued that students should be funded throughout their legal training. The Law Society and the Bar Council have made representations to the Department of Education, pointing out that training for other professions such as medicine and teaching is paid or involves reduced fees. In her book, *Eve was Framed*, Helena Kennedy QC argues that selection for the Bar in particular has always been based too much on 'connections' and financial resources than on ability. She recommends public funding for legal education and that there should be incentives for barristers' chambers to take on less conventional candidates.

Michael Zander (1988) argued that both the academic and the vocational stages of training could be improved, with a consequent rise in professional standards. Law degrees should include at least preliminary training in areas such as drafting documents and developing interviewing skills. Both pupillage and training contracts can be 'infinitely variable' in quality, according to Zander, 'ranging from excellent to deplorable', depending on where they are undertaken. He suggested that a more integrated training was needed, like that undertaken by medical students, with better links between academic and vocational stages.

The former Advisory Committee on Legal Education and Conduct (ACLEC) examined the whole issue of legal training. Its 1996 report suggested that the two branches should no longer have completely separate training programmes at the post-graduate stage. Instead, after either a law degree or a degree in another subject plus the CPE, all students would take a Professional Legal Studies course, lasting around 18 weeks. Only then would they decide which branch of the profession to choose, going on to a Legal Practice Course (for solicitors) or Bar Vocational Course (for barristers), which would be only 15–18 weeks long. This, ACLEC suggested, would prevent the problem of students having to specialise too early. It also recommended that funding should be made available for the CPE course and the vocational stage of training.

Complaints

Complaints can be made to the Legal Complaints Service, to the Legal Services Ombudsman and/or by an action in negligence.

Legal Complaints Service

There have been on-going problems with the way complaints against solicitors are handled. The body responsible for dealing with these complaints has undergone numerous reforms and name changes over the years to deal with these problems. Until 1996, complaints about solicitors were handled by the Solicitors Complaints Bureau (SCB). The Bureau was widely criticised for delay and inefficiency, and a report by the National Consumer Council in 1994 suggested that its policy of attempting to conciliate the parties favoured solicitors over complainants, tending in many cases to impose a settlement or dismiss the complaint. The maximum compensation available to complainants was £1,000, and this was criticised as being too low. Another issue of concern was that the Solicitors Complaints Bureau was not sufficiently independent of the profession, as its powers were merely delegated to it by the Law Society.

Worried by these criticisms, the Law Society looked into the problems and in 1995 produced a report entitled *Supervision of Solicitors: the next decade*. The report found that the complaints process needed to be more efficient and customer-friendly, with a greater role for non-lawyers so that the process was independent of the profession. Its main recommendation was acted upon in 1996, when the Solicitors Complaints Bureau was replaced by the Office for the Supervision of Solicitors (OSS). This body was renamed the Consumer Complaints Service (CCS) in 2004.

However, the problems associated with the Solicitors Complaints Bureau remained. The complaints process has been repeatedly criticised by the Legal Services Ombudsman (discussed below). In his annual report for 2001/02, the Ombudsman stated he was dissatisfied with the handling of complaints in 32 per cent of the cases referred to him. The report concluded:

> '. . . it is apparent that sustained and continuing improvement in the Law Society's complaint-handling activities has not been achieved . . . Sometimes it seems that the OSS create problems for themselves and their customers by neglecting the very basics of complaint handling – like reading the information the complainant sends them.'

The CCS was criticised by the Consumers' Association magazine, *Which?*, for not being sufficiently independent of the profession: like the Solicitors Complaints Bureau, it was run by the Law Society, and its main decision-making committee was dominated by solicitors. The CCS's director also sat on the Law Society's management board. *Which?* suggested that complaints about solicitors should be handled by a completely independent organisation.

In 2007 the CCS was abolished and replaced by the Legal Complaints Service. This should provide an independent complaints handling service. It is also intended to be more efficient and consumer friendly. Unfortunately, spectators of this endlessly changing organisation may well be cynical as to whether this latest reform will succeed where its predecessors have failed. In 2007 the Solicitors Regulation Authority issued a new Code of Conduct for solicitors which states at rule 2.05 that a solicitor firm must have 'a written complaints procedure and that complaints are handled promptly, fairly and effectively in accordance with it'.

The problem of complaints handling was considered in Sir David Clementi's review of the legal professions in 2004. He recommended that an independent Office for Legal Complaints should be established which would handle all consumer complaints against any legal service provider (including solicitors and barristers). It would be supervised by a new Legal Services Board. The Legal Services Complaints Commissioner would be abolished. While the Law Society was happy with this proposal, the Bar Council is concerned that the new body may prove slower and more expensive than the existing arrangements. It commented:

> 'We have an extremely good record on complaints as confirmed by the Legal Services Ombudsman. We do not want the service provided to the public to be diminished by being sucked into a large bureaucratic Office for Legal complaints.'

The government has, however, accepted Sir David Clementi's recommendation, and provisions to establish this new body are contained in the Legal Services Act 2007. It has started to recruit people to work in the office for Legal Complaints, as the first step in the process of setting up the office itself.

Legal Services Ombudsman

The Office of the Legal Services Ombudsman was established in 1990. Its role is to oversee the handling of complaints by the professional regulatory bodies, and offers the final appeal regarding complaints against lawyers. Complainants who are dissatisfied with the way their grievances are handled by the CCS can ask the Legal Services Ombudsman to investigate. The number of cases being accepted for investigation by the Ombudsman is at an all-time high. In 2001/02 the Ombudsman received 1,677 new cases for investigation. If he or she is dissatisfied with the way the relevant professional body has handled the complaint, the Ombudsman can recommend that the relevant professional body reconsiders the complaint and/or order compensation to be paid.

In 1998 the performance of the Ombudsman's office itself came under scrutiny in a study commissioned by the Ombudsman, and the CCS might perhaps have been forgiven for indulging in a wry smile at the results. Although most members of the public seeking information and advice were happy with the service, and so were most lawyers who had professional contact with the Ombudsman's office, the majority of complainants who had their cases formally investigated were dissatisfied. They complained that they were not kept informed, that the processes of dealing with cases were complex and over-lengthy, and the role of the Ombudsman's service was unclear.

The Ombudsman promised that improvements would be made, and has since produced clearer information leaflets explaining the role of the service, and established new systems to keep complainants informed of the progress of their cases. However, she suggested part of the blame must lie with the professions themselves, in that lawyers' failure to resolve complaints more effectively in the first place naturally led to delay and dissatisfaction once complainants reached the Ombudsman's service.

Table 10.1 **Investigations where the Ombudsman found that complaint handling was satisfactory**

	Apr 2004 to Mar 2005	Apr 2003 to Mar 2004	Apr 2002 to Mar 2003	Apr 2001 to Mar 2002
Solicitors/Law Society	62.0%	53.3%	67.2%	57.9%
Barristers/GCB	78.7%	86.8%	88.4%	92.9%
Licensed conveyancers/CLC	33.3%	66.7%	61.5%	60.0%
All cases	63.8%	57.5%	69.2%	60.9%

Source: Annual Report of the Legal Services Ombudsman for England and Wales 2004/2005, p. 15.

A more recent report, commissioned by the Ombudsman in 2002, found that the Ombudsman was operating an efficient case load workflow system, consistent with best practice and appropriate for an organisation of its size and role.

Due to the government's dissatisfaction with the solicitors' complaints handling process, it has created a new Legal Services Complaints Commissioner (LSCC). The role of the LSCC is to oversee the operation of the Consumer Complaints Service, partly by setting its targets. He or she will have the power to impose large fines on the Law Society if these targets are not met. Ms Zahida Manzoor, the current Legal Services Ombudsman, has been formally appointed to hold this post as well. Her two roles, however, remain distinct: as Ombudsman she is concerned with individual complaints, as LSCC she supervises the complaints handling process as a whole.

Action for negligence

Solicitors can be sued for negligent work like most other professionals. Following the House of Lords' judgment in **Arthur J. S. Hall & Co** v **Simons** (2000), solicitors no longer enjoy any immunity from liability for work connected to the conduct of a case in court.

Quick quiz 10.2

1 How many solicitors are there?

2 Following the Access to Justice Act 1999, what rights of audience do solicitors have?

3 What percentage of criminal cases are heard in the magistrates' courts?

4 Which body currently has primary responsibility for considering complaints against solicitors?

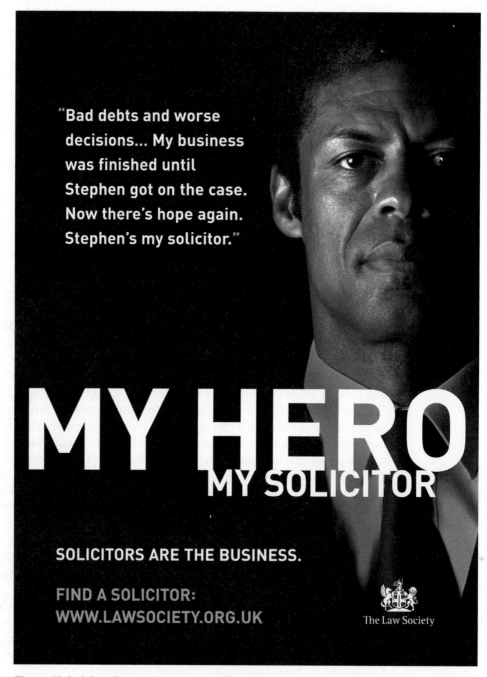

Figure 10.2 **Advertisement by the Law Society**

Source: By kind permission of The Law Society.

Barristers

There are around 14,000 barristers in independent practice, known collectively as the Bar. Their governing body is the Bar Council, which acts as a kind of trade union, safeguarding the interests of barristers. The Bar Council, like the Law Society, has tried to separate its representative functions from its regulatory functions, and has therefore established a Bar Standards Board responsible for regulating the Bar. The Board makes the rules and takes the decisions affecting entry to, training for, and practice at the Bar, including disciplinary issues.

Work

Advocacy is the main function of barristers, and much of their time will be spent in court or preparing for it. Until the changes made under the Courts and Legal Services Act in 1990, barristers were, with a few exceptions, the only people allowed to advocate in the superior courts – the House of Lords, the Court of Appeal, the High Court, the Crown Court and the Employment Appeal Tribunal. We have seen that this has now changed, and they are increasingly having to compete with solicitors for this work. Barristers also do some paperwork, drafting legal documents and giving written opinions on legal problems.

Barristers must be self-employed and, under Bar rules, cannot form partnerships, but they usually share offices, called chambers, with other barristers. All the barristers in a particular chambers share a clerk, who is a type of business manager, arranging meetings with the client and the solicitor and also negotiating the barristers' fees. Around 70 per cent of practising barristers are based in London chambers, though they may travel to courts in the provinces; the rest are based in the other big cities.

Not all qualified barristers work as advocates at the Bar. Like solicitors, some are employed by law centres and other advice agencies, government departments or private industry, and some teach. Some go into these jobs after practising at the Bar for a time, others never practise at the Bar.

Traditionally, a client could not approach a barrister directly, but had to see a solicitor first, who would then refer the case to a barrister. In 2004 the ban on direct access to barristers was abolished. Members of the public can now contact a barrister without using a solicitor as an intermediary. Barristers are today able to provide specialist advice, drafting and advocacy without a solicitor acting as a 'middleman', although the management of litigation will still generally be handled by solicitors. Direct access to the client is permitted where the barrister has been in practice for three years, and has undertaken a short course preparing them for this new mode of operation.

Barristers work under what is called the 'cab rank' rule. Technically, this means that if they are not already committed for the time in question, they must accept any case which falls within their claimed area of specialisation and for which a reasonable fee is offered. In practice, barristers' clerks, who take their bookings, may manipulate the rule to ensure that barristers are able to avoid cases they do not want to take. The cab rank rule does not apply where a barrister is approached directly by a potential client, rather than being referred to them by a solicitor. In these circumstances, barristers must follow a principle of non-discrimination, under which they must not refuse work because of the way it is funded or because the client is unpopular.

Qualifications and training

The starting point is normally an upper-second class degree. If this degree is not in law, applicants must do the one-year course leading to the Common Professional Examination (the same course taken by would-be solicitors with degrees in subjects other than law). Mature students may be accepted without a degree, but applications are subject to very stringent consideration, and this is not a likely route to the Bar.

All students then have to join one of the four Inns of Court: Inner Temple; Middle Temple; Gray's Inn; or Lincoln's Inn, all of which are in London. The Inns of Court first emerged in the thirteenth century and their role has evolved over time. Their main functions now cover the provision of professional accommodation for barristers' chambers and residential accommodation for judges, discipline, the provision of law libraries and the promotion of collegiate activities.

Students take the year-long Bar Vocational Course, which can now be taken at eight different institutions around the country. The course includes oral

Figure 10.3 One of the dining rooms of the Inns of Court
Source: Photograph by permission of the Masters of the Bench of The Honourable Society of Gray's Inn.

exercises, and tuition in interviewing skills and negotiating skills, and solicitors' training, more emphasis has been laid on these practical as recent years.

Around 1,600 people take the Bar Vocational Course each year, and each one has to pay approximately £7,000 for the course alone, and then find living expenses on top. Local authority grants are discretionary and only rarely available. Limited financial assistance is available from the Inns of Court.

Students have to dine at their Inn 12 times. This rather old-fashioned and much-criticised custom stems from the idea that students will benefit from the wisdom and experience of their elders if they sit among them at mealtimes. The dinners are now linked to seminars, lectures and training weekends, in order to provide genuine educational benefit.

After this, the applicant is called to the Bar, and must then find a place in a chambers to serve his or her pupillage. This is a one-year apprenticeship in which pupils assist a qualified barrister, who is known as their pupil master. Competition for pupillage places can be fierce, with only about 600 pupillage vacancies available each year. In the past funding for pupillage has been a problem. But pupils should now normally be paid a minimum of £10,000 a year. Pupils are required to take a further advocacy course before the end of pupillage, as part of the increased emphasis on practical skills.

Pupillage completed, the newly qualified barrister must find a permanent place in a chambers, known as a tenancy. This can be the most difficult part, and some are forced to 'squat' – remaining in their pupillage chambers for as long as they are allowed, without becoming a full member – until they find a permanent place. There are only around 300 tenancies available each year – one to every two pupils.

In 1993, the Royal Commission on Criminal Justice recommended that barristers should have to undertake further training during the course of their careers, after noting that both preparation of cases and advocacy were failing to reach acceptable standards. In response, the Bar Council introduced a continuing education programme. Barristers must now complete a minimum of 45 hours of continuing education in the prescribed subjects by the end of their first three years of practice. The Bar Council has also introduced an established practitioners programme under which all barristers who have been qualified for over three years must undertake each year a minimum of 12 hours' study.

Queen's Counsel

After ten years in practice, a barrister may apply to become a Queen's Counsel, or QC (sometimes called a silk, as they wear gowns made of silk). This usually means they will be offered higher-paid cases, and need do less preliminary paperwork. The average annual earnings of a QC are £270,000, with a small group earning over £1 million a year. Not all barristers attempt or manage to become QCs – those that do not are called juniors, even up to retirement age. Juniors may assist QCs in big cases, as well as working alone. Since 1995, solicitors can also be appointed as QCs, but there are currently only eight QCs who come from the solicitor profession.

Task 10.3

In July 2003 the government issued a Consultation Paper, *The Future of Queen's Counsel*. The Foreword to this Consultation Paper has been written by the former Minister for Constitutional Affairs, Lord Falconer. It states:

'There has long been a debate about the relevance and use of the rank of Queen's Counsel. The time has come to bring that debate to a head, and to reach conclusions, after full consultation on the way ahead. Over the last four centuries, the QC system has become a well-established part of our legal structure. But the legal system must meet the needs of the public. The system must be capable of identifying those with the skills and expertise to deal with any particular dispute. In particular, it should be able to recognise the wide variety of skills needed to provide the public with the legal service it needs. This paper therefore explores whether the current QC system is objectively in the public interest and whether it commands public confidence.'

Questions

The Consultation Paper asked for views from the public on a range of questions. Consider how you would respond to these questions asked by the government:

1 Do you consider that the rank of QC in its current form benefits the public? What are the reasons for your view?
2 Do you think that the current QC system should be abolished or changed? What are the reasons for your view?
3 If you consider that the QC rank should be abolished, do you consider that it should be replaced by another form of quality mark (whether it be granted by the state, the professions, an independent body or the Judicial Appointments Commission)?

Complaints

Until recently, barristers enjoyed an immunity from liability for negligent work in court. This immunity had been recognised by the courts in the case of **Rondel v Worsley** (1969). The main justification for the immunity was that clients would seek to use litigation against their barrister to indirectly reopen litigation that had already been lost. This immunity was dramatically abolished by the House of Lords in **Arthur J. S. Hall & Co v Simons** (2000). The House ruled that there was no longer any good reason to treat barristers any differently from other professionals, so that their negligence could give rise to liability in tort. Despite this judgment, in the most recent House of Lords' case on the point, **Moy v Pettman Smith** (2005), the House proceeded to treat a barrister more leniently than other professionals. A barrister had been sued for negligently failing to settle a case. The House concluded that she had not been negligent, and in reaching this conclusion it repeatedly referred to what could be expected from a barrister of her 'seniority and purported experience'. This is noticeably different from the way the work of other professionals has been judged in comparable situations. A doctor's work, for example, in a case of alleged negligence is usually judged by

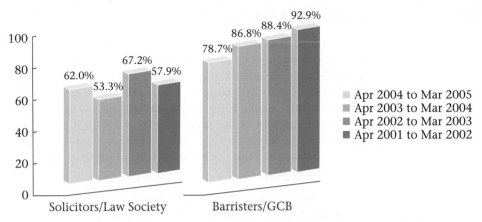

Figure 10.4 **Investigations where ombudsman complaint handling was satisfactory**
Source: *Annual Report of the Legal Services Ombudsman for England and Wales 2004/2005*, p. 56.

the standards of 'reasonably competent practitioners' and the courts ignore their level of seniority.

In the past the only avenue for complaints was the Bar Council but, if upheld, these complaints merely resulted in disciplinary action against the barrister, giving no redress to the client. In 1997 reforms were introduced. The complaints procedure is now overseen by a Complaints Commissioner. The Commissioner is not a lawyer and has complete independence from the Bar Council in the decisions that are made. If the Commissioner considers that the complaint may be justified, it will be referred to the Professional Conduct and Complaints Committee (PCC) for consideration. The PCC is a Committee of the Bar Council consisting of barristers and non-lawyers. If the PCC agrees that the complaint may be justified it sends the complaint to a disciplinary panel for a final decision on whether the complaint is justified.

> ✓ **Know your terms 10.4**
>
> Define the following terms:
> **1** Limited liability partnership.
> **2** Bar Council.
> **3** Pupillage.
> **4** Queen's Counsel.

If the complaint is successful, the barrister can be required to apologise, to repay fees or to pay compensation of up to £5,000 to a complainant where that complainant is the barrister's client. The barrister can be subjected to a fine or prevented from practising as a barrister either permanently or temporarily.

The Legal Services Ombudsman oversees the Bar's handling of complaints in the same way as with complaints about solicitors (see p. 165).

The future of the profession

A number of government reports have been published in recent years pushing for changes in the professions. In 2001 the Office of Fair Trading (OFT) issued a report entitled *Competition in the Professions* (2001). This looked primarily at the restrictive practices of barristers and solicitors. These professions were criticised for imposing unjustified restrictions on competition and urged to take prompt action to put an end to these practices.

Professor Zander (2001b) criticised the report, stating:

'What is deplorable about these developments is the simplistic belief that equating the work done by professional people to business will necessarily improve the position of the consumer, when the reality is that sometimes it may rather worsen it. Certainly one wants competition to ensure that professional fees are no higher than they need to be and that the professional rules did not unnecessarily inhibit efficiency. But what one looks for from the professional even more is standards, integrity and concern for the client of a higher order than that offered in the business world. To damage those even more important values in the name of value for the consumer in purely economic terms may be to throw out the baby with the bath water.'

The government accepted that the legal professions should be subject to competition law. It subsequently issued a consultation paper, *In the Public Interests?*, which questioned the competitiveness of legal services given primarily by solicitors working in solicitor firms.

The Bar Council has made some changes in the light of the OFT report, but has rejected many of its key recommendations. Direct access to the Bar has been increased. Employed barristers can now undertake litigation work for their employer. To exercise this right they will have to undertake 12 weeks' training with a practising litigator. The Office of Fair Trading considers this latter reform inadequate, and has confirmed it will continue to investigate the ban on independent barristers litigating without the intermediary of a solicitor. The stumbling block is over whether barristers should be allowed to handle clients' money – something the Bar Council is resolutely against.

In July 2003, the government established an independent review into the regulation of legal services. The review was chaired by Sir David Clementi and considered which regulatory framework 'would best promote competition, innovation and the public and consumer interest in an efficient, effective and independent legal sector'. Sir David published his final report in 2004, *Review of the regulatory framework for legal services in England and Wales*. The government subsequently published a White Paper in 2005 entitled *The Future of Legal Services – Putting Consumers First*, in which it accepted most of Clementi's recommendations. The Legal Services Act 2007 contains the key reforms, which will be considered in turn below.

sourcebook
p. 93 →

sourcebook
p. 103 →

Regulation of the legal professions

Sir David Clementi looked at how improvements in the provision of legal services could be made through changes to the regulation of the professions. At the moment, the professions regulate themselves through their professional bodies, the Law Society and the Bar Council. Clementi considered that the present regulatory arrangements did not prioritise the public's interest. He therefore considered whether the professions should be stripped of their right to regulate themselves and whether instead an independent regulator should be established. The professional bodies would have merely represented their professions and not regulated them. Clementi commented:

'Among the suggested advantages of this approach are the clear independence of the regulator, clarity of purposes for both regulator and representative bodies and consistency of rules and standards across the profession and services. An independent regulator would be well placed to make tough, fair enforcement decisions and to facilitate lay/consumer input into the decision making processes.

Disadvantages might include creating an overly bureaucratic and inefficient organisation, with consequent issues of costs and unwieldy procedure. A further argument is that it fails to recognise the significance of strong roots within the profession and their importance on the international stage. Divorcing the regulatory functions from the profession might lessen the feeling of responsibility professionals have for the high standard of their profession and their willingness to give time freely to support the system.'

Ultimately, Clementi concluded that an Independent Legal Services Board should be established, but this would just oversee the way the existing professional bodies regulated the professions. The Legals Services Board would have a duty to promote the public and consumer interests, and would be led by a part-time chair and a full-time chief executive, who would both be non-lawyers and the majority of the Board's members would be non-lawyers. All the members of the Board would be selected on merit by the relevant government minister. The professional bodies would be required to separate their regulatory and representative functions. They would still take care of the day-to-day regulation of the professions and disciplinary matters, though they could cease to be legally recognised if they failed to carry out their duties satisfactorily.

Sir David Clementi hopes that this reform would achieve consistency and transparency, while keeping costs down and leaving regulation close to those who provide the services. The proposal has been generally well received, though the Bar is unhappy that it is to lose the power to regulate itself. Front-line regulators, such as the Law Society and the Bar Council, are anxious that they should have primary responsibility for the day-to-day regulation of the professions, with the new Board taking only a light touch, supervisory approach to regulation (as recommended by Clementi), intervening merely when it is in the public interest. This light-touch approach would avoid costly duplication of effort, stifling innovation and burdening the front-line regulators. However, the Legal Services Act 2007 gives the Legal Services Board the power to set targets for front-line regulators and the power to remove a body's authorisation to regulate if the targets were not met. Front-line regulators have to apply to the Legal Services Board for permission to carry out regulatory functions, such as the regulation of alternative business structures.

The Law Society and Bar Council are also concerned that the Legal Services Board should be clearly independent of government politics, but the Act gives considerable power to the Minister of Justice, including making appointments to the Board. The Law Society has argued that members of the Legal Services Board should be appointed by an independent appointment panel. The Legal Aid Practitioners Group has commented that Clementi's proposals 'may give the government too much control over the lawyers whose challenges to them are essential in a free and democratic society'. For example, lawyers represent members of the public in criminal cases, when children are being taken into care and when local authorities seek to evict anti-social tenants.

With the passing of the Legal Services Act 2007, the Government has started the recruitment process for people to sit on the Legal Services Board, as the first stage in the process of setting up the Board itself.

Business structures

Currently, most legal services can be delivered to the public only by solicitors working in a law firm or by barristers in independent practice at the Bar. Sir David Clementi considered two new business structures through which legal services could be delivered to the public: legal disciplinary practices and multi-disciplinary partnerships. The government has decided to go one step further, with the introduction of 'alternative business structures' provided for in the Legal Services Act 2007. These provisions are likely to take effect in 2011.

Legal disciplinary practices

Legal disciplinary practices (LDPs) would consist of solicitors, barristers and legal executives being able to work together to provide legal services. Non-lawyers could be involved in the management and ownership of these practices. The OFT report, Sir David Clementi's report and the government's consultation document, *In the Public Interests?*, have all come out in favour of the creation of LDPs. At the moment, the regulations of the legal professions stop these being created, because they include rules that, for example, ban employed solicitors from giving advice directly to the public, and require that legal service providers to the public must be owned exclusively by lawyers.

If LDPs are introduced, solicitors could be employed by such organisations as supermarkets, banks, insurance firms and accountants to provide legal services directly to the public. Non-lawyers would simply need to pass a 'fit to own' test set by the Legal Services Board before they could invest in an LDP. Thus, to avoid a conflict of interest, a car insurance company would not be able to own a personal injury firm. The first people who are likely to become part of the management team of the new LDPs are people who are already senior employees in solicitor firms, such as finance directors, Human Resource managers and IT managers.

In support of this reform, Sir David Clementi has stated:

> *'The review favours a regulatory framework which permits a high degree of choice: choice both for the consumer, in where he goes for legal services, and for the lawyer, in the type of economic unit he works for.'*

The proposal has become known as the 'Tesco Law' because big organisations would be able to buy law firms. The government considers that bigger organisations might provide advice more efficiently. The Law Society sees the reform as an important means of attracting external investment into law firms and thereby facilitating business expansion.

However, the Bar Council is unhappy with this reform proposal. It has pointed out that outside commercial involvement does not always mean better and cheaper services. Large, wealthy companies would be allowed to employ a few solicitors and lots of paralegals (individuals with more limited legal qualifications) to offer these services. This could be primarily a telephone service, offered from a centralised location and focused on only the better paid work. Just as out of town supermarkets have forced the closure of local greengrocers and chemists, legal disciplinary practices could lead to the closure of many high street solicitor firms. The Lord Chancellor has admitted that the new proposed business structures could affect the future of small high street solicitor firms, but the government does not seem keen on small firms, pointing out in its 2005 White Paper that research by Paul Grout (2005) found that complaints about dishonest practice are disproportionately generated by smaller law firms.

The Bar Council has stated that the current ban on barristers forming partnerships actually promotes competition between the 10,000 barristers in private practice, and preserves their fundamental independence, which is at the core of the justice system. It is unhappy that non-lawyers could become owners and investors in legal practices. The Bar has argued that non-lawyers would not be bound by the ethical codes of standard that apply to legal professionals and that the independence of the legal practice would be put at risk. It considers that the current proposed safeguards would be inadequate to prevent improper interference by external investors with the delivery of legal services. The Bar Council would like to see corporate ownership restricted to a 25 per cent stake in a law firm.

Multi-disciplinary partnerships

Multi-disciplinary partnerships would bring together lawyers with other professionals, such as accountants, surveyors and estate agents. These organisations would be able to provide legal and non-legal services, so that they could be described as a 'one-stop shop', providing a range of services to their clients. Sir David Clementi has not recommended that these should be allowed. He was cautious about them and said the government should only consider introducing multi-disciplinary partnerships once some experience had been gained from the introduction of legal disciplinary practices. The Bar Council is opposed to the introduction of multi-disciplinary practices:

> 'The unravelling Enron case should remind us all of the strong public interest that resides in independent professions. Multi-disciplinary partnerships would be dominated by accountancy mega-firms, hungry for corporate consultancy work, and who would regard the independence of the Bar as a matter of secondary importance.'

Alternative business structures

The government's 2005 White Paper and Legal Services Act 2007 go much further than Sir David Clementi on this issue. The relevant provisions of the Act are likely to be brought into force in 2011 and will allow legal services to be provided to the public through a wide range of alternative business structures, which would include multi-disciplinary partnerships. The aim is to increase competition to the benefit of consumers and to increase investment in legal service providers, so that they can invest in such areas as the use of IT for the delivery of legal services and expand to provide a better quality of service to the consumer. The impact of these changes on business structures has been considered by research commissioned by the Department for Constitutional Affairs: James Dow and Carlos Lapuerta (2005) *The Benefits of Multiple Ownership Models in Law Services*. A central conclusion of this research was that external investment would lead to an increased use in IT for the delivery of legal services.

The Co-op, Halifax and the AA have publicly announced that, when the legislation has been brought into force, they intend to offer legal advice and assistance directly to the public. The Co-op plans to establish 'Co-operative Legal Services', offering a range of legal services, including conveyancing and will writing. It will be based in Bristol and employ approximately 150 people, including a team of 30 lawyers. It already offers a free legal services helpline to its customers, which has been praised by consumer groups but criticised by the Law Society for not offering face-to-face advice to its clients.

The Co-op's research into the legal market found that there was a general distrust of legal service providers. This is exacerbated by the media's portrayal of the legal system, but it also stems from clients' experiences. Unlike many other businesses, the solicitor profession has often not moved with the times to take into account the Internet and the mobile phone. The Co-op considers that it can succeed in this market because people like to deal with a business which they feel is a trusted brand, with which they have an existing relationship, and where they know what to expect. They want this combined with the professionalism, skill and gravitas of a properly qualified lawyer.

Halifax is proposing to launch 'Halifax Legal Solutions', which will provide a service whereby the public pay an annual membership fee of £89 for access to a 24-hour legal helpline. Additional services, such as conveyancing, will be available at fixed prices. Halifax has recognised that the banks and building societies, with their network of branded, highly visible shop fronts on every high street, have a huge advantage over local solicitors operating in isolation.

While the professions have been quick to attack the planned introduction of alternative business structures, it may be that the quality of their current services has made them vulnerable to this type of reform. Most people would be perfectly happy to go through life without ever having to instruct a solicitor. They only turn to a legal professional out of necessity and frequently at times of distress, for example, to get a divorce, or because they have been in an accident or have been arrested by the police. The Lord Chancellor's introduction to the White Paper, *The Future of Legal Services: Putting the Consumer First* (2005), observes:

> 'The professional competence of lawyers is not in doubt. The calibre of many of our legal professionals is among the best in the world. But despite this, too many consumers are finding that they are not receiving a good or a fair deal.'

In practice, much of the work in solicitor firms is already being done by paralegals rather than solicitors themselves. The personal contact between the solicitor and client has been reduced through the use of claims management companies, who refer cases to solicitors for a fee and the solicitor will have never met the client personally but merely receive a paper file on the case. Thus, solicitors themselves are not always providing a personal face-to-face service.

A parliamentary joint committee looked at the proposed introduction of alternative business structures contained in the Legal Services Bill when it was being passed through Parliament. It concluded that the government should take a more progressive approach to reform, allowing for the introduction first of partnerships between different types of lawyers (legal disciplinary partnerships) to see how they work in practice, before allowing for a wider range of owners and investors in legal practices. The committee was concerned that there was a risk of a conflict of interest between the different participants in alternative business structures and inappropriate pressure could be placed on lawyers within such structures to sell products, such as insurance policies, from other branches of the organisation. The evidence presented to the committee suggested that alternative business structures would not be allowed to practise in the US and some European countries.

Office for Legal Complaints

Sir David Clementi recommended that an Office for Legal Complaints should be created to hear complaints against all legal professions. This reform is discussed on p. 166.

Fusion of the professions

The divided legal profession dates from the nineteenth century, when the Bar agreed to give all conveyancing work and all direct access to clients to the solicitors, in return for sole rights of audience in the higher courts and the sole right to become senior judges for barristers. However, since the late 1960s, there have been a series of moves towards breaking down this division. Following the Access to Justice Act 1999, solicitors automatically have rights of audience, though they still have to undertake training in order to exercise these rights. It is likely that an increasing number of solicitors will undertake this training to become solicitor-advocates.

There has been much discussion over recent years as to whether the professions will eventually fuse. When the Courts and Legal Services Act 1990 was passed, it was thought that it might be the first step in government plans to fuse the two professions by legislation. Until 1985, the two branches had been largely left alone to divide work between themselves, and had made their own arrangements for this; the abolition of the solicitors' monopoly on conveyancing was the first major government interference in this situation, and the Courts and Legal Services Act was obviously a much bigger step towards regulation by government rather than the professions themselves. Even if the government did not force fusion, it has been suggested, it could happen anyway if large numbers of solicitors take up rights of audience.

Alternatively, it has been suggested that the Bar might survive, but in a much reduced form, and there is much debate about which areas would suffer most. Barristers generally fall into two groups: those who specialise in commercial fields, such as company law, tax and patents; and those who have what is called a common law practice, which means that they deal with a fairly wide range of common legal issues, such as crime, housing and family law. Some legal experts believed that commercial lawyers would be most likely to survive, since they have a specialist knowledge that solicitors cannot provide. However, for several years now, solicitors in city firms have been becoming more specialist themselves, and if able to combine specialist knowledge with rights of audience, they would clearly be a threat to the commercial Bar. In addition, such firms offer high incomes, without the insecurity of self-employment at the Bar, and therefore they are able to attract first-rate students who once would have automatically been attracted to the more prestigious Bar. As these entrants work their way up through law firms, the Bar's traditional claim to offer the best expertise in high-level legal analysis will be difficult to sustain.

Task 10.5

One day a week the quality papers have a section dedicated to looking at legal issues. *The Times* law section comes out every Tuesday. Job advertisements for work in the legal field are placed in this section. Select two job advertisements and consider:

■ Is the advertiser looking to recruit a barrister, solicitor or legal executive?
■ In what area of law would the person recruited work?
■ How much would they be paid?

Task 10.6

Professor Zander (2001) has criticised the report of the Office of Fair Trading on anti-competitive practices in the legal professions. He has written:

'What is deplorable about these developments is the simplistic belief that equating the work done by professional people to business will necessarily improve the position of the consumer, when the reality is that sometimes it may rather worsen it. Certainly one wants competition to ensure that professional fees are no higher than they need to be and that the professional rules do not unnecessarily inhibit efficiency. But what one looks for from the professions even more is standards, integrity and concern for the client of a higher order than that offered in the business world. To damage those even more important values in the name of value for the consumer in purely economic terms may be to throw out the baby with the bath water.'

Questions

1 In this context, who is the consumer?
2 What are the benefits identified of allowing competition among legal professionals?
3 What values does Zander argue need protecting by the legal professionals more than by the business world?
4 What is meant by the saying 'to throw out the baby with the bath water'?

Arguments for fusion of the professions

Expense

With the divided profession a client often has to pay both a solicitor and a barrister, sometimes a solicitor and two barristers, and as Michael Zander (1999) puts it: 'To have one taxi meter running is less expensive than to have two or three.' However, the Bar Council prepared a report entitled *The Economic Case for the Bar: A Comparison of the Costs of Barristers and Solicitors* (2000). This paper claimed that it was generally more economical to employ the services of a barrister, particularly a junior, for work within his or her area of expertise than to use a solicitor. In broad terms, it stated that the differences in charge-out rates make it from 25 per cent to 50 per cent cheaper to employ the services of a junior barrister than an assistant solicitor in London. A major factor is that barristers' overheads are approximately half those of solicitors. However, the paper is misleading, as without direct access to clients for barristers it is not an either/or situation. The reality is that a client does not pay for either a solicitor or a barrister, but if the client employs a barrister, the client must pay for both, along with the cost of the solicitor preparing the papers for the barrister.

Inefficiency

A two-tier system means work may be duplicated unnecessarily, and the solicitor prepares the case with little or no input from the barrister who will have to argue it in court. Barristers are often selected and instructed at the last moment: research by Bottoms and McLean in Sheffield revealed that in 96 per cent of cases where the plea was guilty, and 79 per cent where it was not guilty, clients saw their barrister for the first time on the morning of the trial. In this situation important points may be passed over or misunderstood.

Arguments against fusion

Independence

The Bar has traditionally argued that its cab-rank principle guarantees this, ensuring that no defendant, however heinous the charges against them, goes undefended; and that no individual should lack representation because of the wealth or power of the opponent. The fact that barristers operate independently, rather than in partnerships, also contributes. However, the Courts and Legal Services Act 1990 does provide for solicitors with advocacy certificates to operate on a cab-rank basis, which has somewhat weakened the Bar's argument. In addition, successful barristers do get round the cab-rank rule in practice.

Importance of good advocacy

Our adversarial system means that the presentation of oral evidence is important; judges have no investigative powers and must rely on the lawyers to present the case properly.

The 1979 Royal Commission suggested that fusion would lead to a fall in the quality of the advocacy, arguing that, although many solicitors were competent to advocate in the magistrates' and county courts, arguing before a jury required different skills and greater expertise, and if rights were extended it was unlikely that many solicitors would get sufficient practice to develop these.

Table 10.2 **Comparison of barristers and solicitors**

	Barrister	Solicitor
Number	14,000	98,000
Professional organisation	Bar Council	Law Society
Professional course	Bar Vocational Course (BVC)	Legal Practice Course (LPC)
Apprenticeship	Pupillage	Training contract

Reading on the web

Sir David Clementi's report, *Review of the Regulatory Framework for Legal Services in England and Wales*, is available at:

www.legal-services-review.org.uk

The consultation paper issued by the government in 2003 on the future of QCs is available on the former Department for Constitutional Affairs' website:

www.dca.gov.uk/consult/qcfuture/index.htm

The report of the Office of Fair Trading, *Competition in the Professions* (2001), is available on its website:

www.oft.gov.uk/shared_oft/reports/professional_bodies/oft328.pdf

The Bar Council's website can be found at:

www.barcouncil.org.uk/

The Law Society's website can be found at:

www.lawsociety.org.uk/home.law

The website of the Solicitors Regulation Authority is at:

www.sra.org.uk/about/strategy.page

Chapter summary

The two main professions in the legal field are:

- solicitors; and
- barristers.

Solicitors

- *Work*: traditionally solicitors focused primarily on paperwork but they are now doing more advocacy.
- *Qualifications and training*: usually a university degree, followed by a conversion course if this was not in law. They then take the one-year Legal Practice Course and a two-year training contract.

Increasing diversity through educational reforms

The Law Society is considering introducing a radical reform to the way people qualify as solicitors.

Barristers

- *Work*: traditionally advocacy, but they also do some paperwork.
- *Qualifications and training*: usually a university degree, followed by a conversion course if this is not in law. Then the one-year Bar Vocational Course and one-year pupillage.

The future of the profession

A number of government reports have been published in recent years pushing for changes in the professions. In July 2003, the government established an independent review into the regulation of legal services, chaired by Sir David Clementi. Following the enactment of the Legal Services Act 2007, a range of reforms is likely to be introduced in the near future with a view to modernising the professions.

Moves towards fusion?

Since the late 1960s, there has been a series of moves towards breaking down the division between barristers and solicitors.

Question and answer guides

1. Describe and explain the training and work of solicitors.

Plan

Training

- Academic stage – law degree (three years) or a non-law degree plus the CPE (one year).
- Vocational stage – Legal Practice Course (one year).
- Professional stage – training contract.
- Alternatively, non-graduates can take the ILEX route.
- Solicitors are not entered on the roll until they have completed their training contract.

Work

- Distinction between City law firms and high street law firms.
- General advice.
- Conveyancing.
- Drafting wills and probate.

- Family and domestic.
- Drafting contracts.
- Criminal.
- Commercial.
- Litigation.
- Advocacy in lower courts or in higher courts with appropriate qualification.

Answer

The 98,000 solicitors in England and Wales are the equivalent of the general practitioners of the medical profession, as they deal directly with members of the public and are usually the first point of call for people with a legal problem.

Solicitor training is divided into three stages. The vast majority of trainee solicitors are graduates who have either obtained a law degree over three years, or have taken another degree subject and then converted to law by completing the Common Professional Examination (CPE). The second stage of the qualification process is to undertake the Legal Practice Course (LPC), which is offered both at some universities and at some private colleges. This focuses on developing the student's practical legal skills, such as drafting, negotiation and advocacy. The majority of students have to fund themselves through this year, which is difficult without family support because the fees can be up to £10,000 a year, though generally the banks are happy to lend to students as they are expected to have a reliable career at the end of the qualification process. Finally, the students need to find a training contract with a solicitor firm. This is a two-year placement and a paid position. Competition is fierce for these training contracts, especially in the top London firms. The workload in these City firms is heavy, with trainees often working over 50 hours a week, but they are paid over £30,000 a year, which is more than the average trainee solicitor. Once their training contract is completed they are eligible to be entered onto the roll of solicitors, which is overseen by the Master of the Rolls. After qualifying, solicitors have to keep themselves up to date and develop their legal expertise by undertaking a certain number of hours of continuing professional development (CPD) in order to retain their status as practising solicitors.

Although the majority of solicitors are graduates, it is still possible to become a solicitor using the ILEX qualification route, after five years' work experience, the Solicitors First Examination course and the LPC.

The Law Society is currently reviewing the qualification and training process with a view to facilitating the qualification process for a more diverse range of people.

As regards the work of the solicitors, in practice the profession is divided between the minority who work in very large City law firms and the majority who work in smaller high street firms. The City law firms are primarily offering expensive, expert legal services to large international corporate and government clients. The high street law firms are primarily catering for the everyday legal problems of members of the public and smaller companies.

Many local solicitors work in a partnership in a law firm, though limited liability partnerships are becoming increasingly common as the lawyers try to limit their legal liability when things go wrong. Most solicitors work in high street offices and have clients who walk in off the street, as well as their regular clients who will have made appointments before their visit or who might well be dealt with by post.

Solicitors spend a lot of their time in their offices giving general advice and undertaking the legal paperwork on behalf of their clients for drafting wills and contracts and conveyancing (buying and selling houses). They assist clients on matters of family law and divorce. They prepare cases for litigation and increasingly carry out the advocacy in the courtroom, though they can choose to hand over this public speaking role to a barrister practising at the independent Bar. Historically, their courtroom appearances were limited to low level charges in the magistrates court, but since the 1990s solicitors who have had specialist advocacy training benefit from full rights of audience as solicitor advocates.

In criminal matters, the solicitor can attend police station interviews of arrested clients as well as representing them at court, particularly in the magistrates' court where solicitors undertake 98 per cent of the advocacy work.

Group activity 1

There is a lot of controversy over court dress for barristers and judges. It has been suggested that their garments are too formal and intimidating for other participants in the case and should be changed:

- What is the standard court dress for junior barristers, Queen's Counsel and for judges?
- Does a judge's dress alter according to their seniority?
- What do you think judges and barristers should wear in court?

Work in groups and allocate tasks to answer these questions. You could visit the following websites to help you research this subject:

lcjb.cjsonline.gov.uk/area21/library/Court_Dress.pdf
www.dca.gov.uk/consult/courtdress/annexd.htm
www.judiciary.gov.uk/about_judiciary/court_dress/examples/index.htm

Group activity 2

- Divide your friends (or class) into groups of two or three people.
- Each group should choose a firm of solicitors to research. If you do not already know of one, you can find lists in telephone directories or on the Internet (e.g. on the Law Society's website: **www.lawsociety.org.uk**).
- Using the Law Society's website, the firm's website, the firm's publicity material, media reports, etc., prepare a short profile of the firm, including information on its people, the type of work it does, and the number and location of its offices.
- Meet with the other groups to share and discuss profiles.

Chapter 11
MAGISTRATES

This chapter discusses:

- the existence of lay and professional magistrates;
- the selection and appointment of lay magistrates;
- their social background;
- the training provided;
- their role in criminal and civil cases;
- the work of justices' clerks and legal advisers;
- whether lay magistrates or professional judges should work in the magistrates' court.

Introduction

Lay magistrates have a long history in the English legal system, dating back to the Justices of the Peace Act 1361, which, probably in response to a crime wave, gave judicial powers to appointed lay people. Their main role then, as now, was dealing with criminals, but they also exercised certain administrative functions, and until the nineteenth century the business of local government was largely entrusted to them. A few of these administrative powers remain today.

There are over 28,000 lay magistrates (also called justices of the peace, or JPs), hearing over 1 million criminal cases a year – 95 per cent of all criminal trials, with the remaining being heard in the Crown Court. They are therefore often described as the backbone of the English criminal justice system. Lay magistrates do not receive a salary, but they receive travel, subsistence and financial loss allowances.

There are also 129 professional judges who sit in the magistrates' courts. These are now called 'district judges (magistrates' courts)' following a reform introduced by the Access to Justice Act 1999. They had previously been known as stipendiary magistrates. They receive a salary of over £90,000. Following the passing of the sourcebook p. 81 → Constitutional Reform Act 2005, the new Judicial Appointments Commission is involved in the appointment process of these professional judges. Applicants must have a relevant qualification and at least five years' post-qualification experience.

They act as sole judge in their particular court, mostly in the large cities, especially London. They are part of the professional judiciary, and most of the comments about magistrates in this chapter do not apply to them.

Selection and appointment

Lay magistrates are appointed by the Lord Chancellor in the name of the Crown, on the advice of Local Advisory Committees. For historical reasons, magistrates in Lancashire, Greater Manchester and Merseyside are appointed by the Chancellor of the Duchy of Lancaster in the name of the Crown. Candidates are interviewed by the committee, which then makes a recommendation to the minister, who usually follows the recommendation.

Members of the Local Advisory Committees are appointed by the Minister of Justice. Two-thirds of them are magistrates, and the minister is supposed to ensure that they have good local knowledge, and represent a balance of political opinion. Their identity was at one time kept secret, but names are now available to the public.

Candidates are usually put forward to the committee by local political parties, voluntary groups, trade unions and other organisations, though individuals may apply in person. The only qualifications laid down for appointment to the magistracy are that the applicants must be under 65 and live within 15 miles of the commission area in which they will work. These qualifications may be dispensed with if it is considered to be in the public interest to do so. In practice, they must also be able to devote an average of half a day a week to the task, for which usually only expenses and a small loss of earnings allowance are paid. Legal knowledge or experience is not required; nor is any level of academic qualification.

Certain people are excluded from appointment, including police officers, traffic wardens and members of the armed forces; anyone whose work is considered incompatible with the duties of a magistrate; anyone who owing to a disability could not carry out all the duties of a magistrate; people with certain criminal convictions; undischarged bankrupts; and those who have a close relative who is already a magistrate on the same Bench.

In 1998 the procedures for appointing lay magistrates were reviewed. The reforms aimed to make the appointment criteria open and clear. Thus, a job description for magistrates was introduced which declares that the six key qualities defining the personal suitability of candidates are: having good character, understanding and communication, social awareness, maturity and sound temperament, sound judgement and commitment and reliability. Positions are now advertised widely, including in publications such as *Inside Soaps*, to attract a wider range of people.

The new Judicial Appointments Commission established by the Constitutional Reform Act 2005 is not yet involved in the appointment of lay magistrates, but there are plans that at a future stage it will take over responsibility for their appointment. It is already responsible for the appointment of district judges (magistrates' court).

Quick quiz 11.1

1 Who appoints lay magistrates?

2 What is the role of the Local Advisory Committees?

3 What qualifications does a person need to become a magistrate?

4 In the future, which body will have responsibility for the appointment of lay magistrates?

Background

Class

The 1948 Report of the Royal Commission on Justices of the Peace showed that approximately three-quarters of all magistrates came from professional or middle-class occupations. Little seems to have changed since. Research carried out by Rod Morgan and Neil Russell (2000) found that more than two-thirds of lay magistrates were, or had been until retirement, employed in a professional or managerial position. Their social backgrounds were not representative of the community in which they served. For example, in a deprived metropolitan area, 79 per cent of the Bench members were professionals or managers compared with only 20 per cent in the local population.

 Know your terms 11.2

Define the following terms:

1 Stipendiary magistrate.
2 Justice of the Peace.
3 The Bench.
4 Royal Commission.

One of the reasons for this may be financial; while employers are required to give an employee who is appointed as a magistrate reasonable time off work, not all employers are able or willing to pay wages during the employee's absence. To meet this difficulty, lay magistrates receive a loss of earnings allowance, but this is not overly generous and will usually be less than the employee would have earned.

A further problem is that employees who take up the appointment against the wishes of their employer may find their promotion prospects jeopardised. This means that only those who are self-employed, or sufficiently far up the career ladder to have some power of their own, can serve as magistrates without risking damage to their own employment prospects. The outcome is that those outside the professional and managerial classes are proportionately under-represented on the Bench, which is still predominantly drawn from the more middle-class occupations. The maximum age for appointment has been raised to 65 in the hope that working-class people, who were prevented from serving during their working lives, will do so in retirement, though so far the change has had little impact.

In the past, the government sought to achieve a social balance on the Bench by taking into account a person's political affiliation when making appointments. This stemmed from the time when people tended to vote along class lines, with people from the working class voting predominantly for the Labour Party. Political opinion is no longer a reliable gauge of a person's social background and the government has therefore replaced the question about 'political associations' on the application form for magistrates. It has been replaced by a question about the applicant's employment. The Ministry of Justice believes that this will provide a better means of achieving a socially balanced Bench. The government has issued a White Paper, *Supporting Magistrates' Courts to Provide Justice*. This includes proposals to encourage the recruitment of more young magistrates to make them representative of the communities they serve. Legislation will be introduced to clarify the process of magistrates taking time off work to attend court, including a requirement for employers to explain a refusal to allow a person to take time off.

Age

There are few young magistrates – most are middle-aged or older. The average age of magistrates is 57, only 4 per cent are under the age of 40, and almost a third are in their 60s. The problems concerning employment are likely to have an effect on the age as well as the social class of magistrates; people at the beginning of their careers are most dependent on the goodwill of employers for promotion, and least likely to be able to take regular time off without damaging their career prospects. They are also more likely to be busy bringing up families.

While a certain maturity is obviously a necessity for magistrates, younger justices would bring some understanding of the lifestyles of a younger generation. The government is concerned that 11,000 magistrates are due to retire within the next ten years.

Table 11.1 **Ethnicity: lay magistrates and population generally**

	White	Black Caribbean, Black African, Black other	Indian, Pakistani, Bangladeshi, Chinese	Other	Not known	Total
Magistrates England and Wales						
Number	21,950	430	541	186	2,825	25,932
Percentage	85%	2%	2%	1%	11%	100%
General population for England and Wales (1991 census)	94%	2%	3%	1%	–	100%

The data excludes magistrates in the Duchy of Lancaster.

Source: R. Morgan and N. Russell (2000), *The Judiciary in the Magistrates' Courts*, Home Office RDS Occasional Paper No. 66.

Race

The government reported in 1987 that the proportion of black magistrates was only 2 per cent. The figures for 2003 show that lay magistrates increasingly reflect the ethnic diversity of contemporary Britain. Just over 6 per cent of magistrates come from ethnic minority communities, who make up 7.9 per cent of the

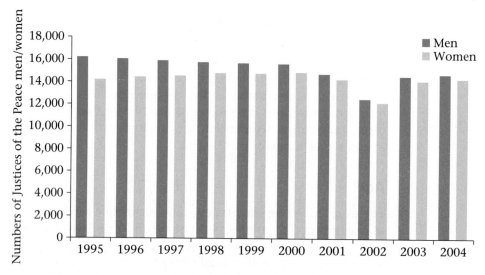

Figure 11.1 **Justices of the Peace, 1995-2004**[a]

[a] As at 1 January of each year. From 2000 onwards figures compiled on a financial year basis.

Source: K. Dibdin, A. Sealy and S. Aktar, *Judicial Statistics Annual Report 2004*, p. 128.

general population, but there is considerable variation locally and the fit between the local benches and the local communities they serve is, in several instances, very poor.

Sex

The sexes are fairly evenly balanced among lay magistrates, with 51 per cent men and 49 per cent women. However, district judges (magistrates' courts) are primarily male, with only 13 women holding this position.

Training

The Magistrates' Commission Committees are responsible for providing training under the supervision of the Judicial Studies Board. Magistrates are not expected to be experts on the law, and the aim of their training is mainly to familiarise them with court procedure, the techniques of chairing and the theory and practice of sentencing. They undergo a short induction course on appointment, and have to undergo basic continuous training comprising 12 hours every three years. Magistrates who sit in juvenile courts or on domestic court panels receive additional training. In order to chair a court hearing a magistrate must, since 1996, take a chairmanship course, the syllabus of which is set by the Judicial Studies Board. Since 1998 the training has included more 'hands on' practical experience, sessions in equality awareness and experienced magistrates act as monitors of more junior members of the Bench.

Role in criminal cases

Magistrates have three main functions in criminal cases:

- Hearing applications for bail.
- Trial: magistrates mainly try the least serious criminal cases (see p. 193). They are advised on matters of law by a justices' clerk, but they alone decide the facts, the law and the sentence.
- Appeals: in ordinary appeals from the magistrates' court to the Crown Court, magistrates sit with a judge. But, following a reform by the Access to Justice Act 1999, they no longer have this role in relation to appeals against sentence.

Magistrates also exercise some control over the investigation of crime, since they deal with applications for bail and requests by the police for arrest and search warrants.

Lay magistrates generally sit in groups of three. However, s. 49 of the Crime and Disorder Act 1998 provides that certain pre-trial judicial powers may be

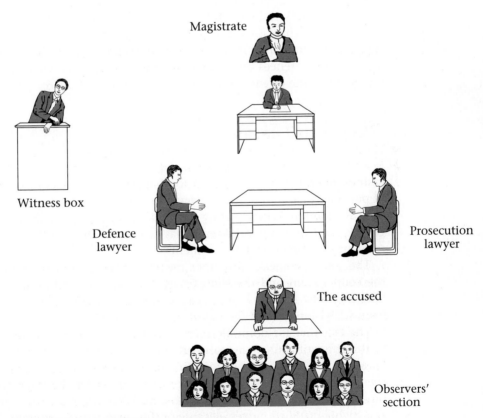

Magistrate

Witness box

Defence lawyer

Prosecution lawyer

The accused

Observers' section

Figure 11.2 Layout of a magistrates' court

Source: F. Mahar and M. J. Duffy, *AQA General Certificate of Education Law Teachers' Guide 2001/2.* © Fareen Mahar.

exercised by a single justice of the peace sitting alone. These include decisions to extend or vary the conditions of bail, to remit an offender to another court for sentence and to give directions as to the timetable for proceedings, the attendance of the parties, the service of documents and the manner in which evidence is to be given. These powers of single justices were tested in six pilot studies and, having proved to be successful, were applied nationally in November 1999.

The role of magistrates in the criminal justice system has been effectively increased in recent years. Some offences which were previously triable either way have been made summary only, notably in the Criminal Law Act 1977, where most motoring offences and criminal damage worth less than £2,000 were made summary only (since raised to £5,000 in the Criminal Justice and Public Order Act 1994). The government proposed at the time that thefts involving small amounts of money should also be made summary offences, but there was great opposition to the idea of removing the right to jury trial for offences which reflected on the accused's honesty. The proposal was dropped, but is still suggested from time to time.

The vast majority of new offences are summary only – there was controversy over the fact that the first offence created to deal with so-called 'joy-riding' was summary, given that the problem appeared to be a serious one, and critics assume that it was made a summary offence in the interests of keeping costs down. Since then, the more serious joy-riding offence, known as aggravated vehicle-taking, which occurs when joy-riding causes serious personal injury or death, has been reduced to a summary offence by the Criminal Justice and Public Order Act 1994. Other serious offences which are summary only include assaulting a police officer, and many of the offences under the Public Order Act 1986.

Role in civil cases

Magistrates' courts are responsible for granting licences to betting shops and casinos and hearing appeals from local authority decisions regarding the issuing of pub and restaurant licences. They also have jurisdiction over domestic matters such as adoption. When hearing such cases, they are known as family proceedings courts. The Child Support Agency has taken over most of their work in relation to fixing child maintenance payments.

The courts' domestic functions overlap considerably with the jurisdiction of the county court and the High Court, though some uniformity of approach is encouraged by the fact that appeals arising from these cases are all heard by the Family Division of the High Court.

The fact that for domestic matters different procedures and law are applied in the different courts, and cases are generally assigned to the magistrates' court because they fall within certain financial limits, has led to the criticism that there is a second class system of domestic courts for the poor, with the better off using the High Court and county courts where cases are heard by professional and highly qualified judges. Because of this, magistrates sitting in domestic cases must receive special training and the Bench must contain both male and female magistrates.

on the application form for magistrates. It has been replaced by a question about the applicant's employment. The Ministry of Justice believes that this will provide a better means of achieving a socially balanced Bench. The government has issued a White Paper, *Supporting Magistrates' Courts to Provide Justice*. This includes proposals to encourage the recruitment of more young magistrates to make them representative of the communities they serve. Legislation will be introduced to clarify the process of magistrates taking time off work to attend court, including a requirement for employers to explain a refusal to allow a person to take time off.

Age

There are few young magistrates – most are middle-aged or older. The average age of magistrates is 57, only 4 per cent are under the age of 40, and almost a third are in their 60s. The problems concerning employment are likely to have an effect on the age as well as the social class of magistrates; people at the beginning of their careers are most dependent on the goodwill of employers for promotion, and least likely to be able to take regular time off without damaging their career prospects. They are also more likely to be busy bringing up families.

While a certain maturity is obviously a necessity for magistrates, younger justices would bring some understanding of the lifestyles of a younger generation. The government is concerned that 11,000 magistrates are due to retire within the next ten years.

Table 11.1 **Ethnicity: lay magistrates and population generally**

	White	Black Caribbean, Black African, Black other	Indian, Pakistani, Bangladeshi, Chinese	Other	Not known	Total
Magistrates England and Wales						
Number	21,950	430	541	186	2,825	25,932
Percentage	85%	2%	2%	1%	11%	100%
General population for England and Wales (1991 census)	94%	2%	3%	1%	–	100%

The data excludes magistrates in the Duchy of Lancaster.

Source: R. Morgan and N. Russell (2000), *The Judiciary in the Magistrates' Courts*, Home Office RDS Occasional Paper No. 66.

Race

The government reported in 1987 that the proportion of black magistrates was only 2 per cent. The figures for 2003 show that lay magistrates increasingly reflect the ethnic diversity of contemporary Britain. Just over 6 per cent of magistrates come from ethnic minority communities, who make up 7.9 per cent of the

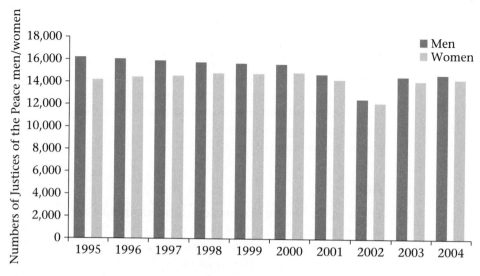

Figure 11.1 **Justices of the Peace, 1995–2004**[a]

[a] As at 1 January of each year. From 2000 onwards figures compiled on a financial year basis.

Source: K. Dibdin, A. Sealy and S. Aktar, *Judicial Statistics Annual Report 2004*, p. 128.

general population, but there is considerable variation locally and the fit between the local benches and the local communities they serve is, in several instances, very poor.

Sex

The sexes are fairly evenly balanced among lay magistrates, with 51 per cent men and 49 per cent women. However, district judges (magistrates' courts) are primarily male, with only 13 women holding this position.

Training

The Magistrates' Commission Committees are responsible for providing training under the supervision of the Judicial Studies Board. Magistrates are not expected to be experts on the law, and the aim of their training is mainly to familiarise them with court procedure, the techniques of chairing and the theory and practice of sentencing. They undergo a short induction course on appointment, and have to undergo basic continuous training comprising 12 hours every three years. Magistrates who sit in juvenile courts or on domestic court panels receive additional training. In order to chair a court hearing a magistrate must, since 1996, take a chairmanship course, the syllabus of which is set by the Judicial Studies Board. Since 1998 the training has included more 'hands on' practical experience, sessions in equality awareness and experienced magistrates act as monitors of more junior members of the Bench.

The government announced that it intended to put an end to the disparity in sentencing patterns in different areas, a situation which was described as 'postcode sentencing'. In order to do this, a Sentencing Guidelines Council has been established to ensure greater consistency in sentencing across England and Wales. This is not intended to be a threat to the independence of the magistracy who need to be able to take into account individual circumstances. But where circumstances are similar, the aim is to reduce the regional disparity in sentencing.

Inefficient

Most of the public sampled in the research by Rod Morgan and Neil Russell (2000) were largely unaware that there were two types of magistrate. When enlightened and questioned, a majority considered that magistrates' court work should be divided equally between the two types of magistrate or that the type of magistrate did not matter. However, professional court users have significantly greater levels of confidence in the district judges (magistrates' court). They regard these judges as quicker than lay justices, more efficient and consistent in their decision-making, better able to control unruly defendants and better at questioning CPS and defence lawyers appropriately. In practice, straightforward guilty pleas to minor matters are normally dealt with by panels of lay magistrates, whereas serious contested matters are increasingly dealt with by a single, professional judge who decides questions of both guilt and sentence. Morgan and Russell question whether the work should be distributed in the opposite way.

Bias towards the police

Police officers are frequent witnesses, and become well known to members of the Bench, and it is alleged that this results in an almost automatic tendency to believe police evidence. One magistrate was incautious enough to admit this: in **R v Bingham J J, ex parte Jowitt** (1974), a speeding case where the only evidence was that of the motorist and a police constable, the chairman of the Bench said: 'Quite the most unpleasant cases that we have to decide are those where the evidence is a direct conflict between a police officer and a member of the public. My principle in such cases has always been to believe the evidence of the police officer, and therefore we find the case proved.' The conviction was quashed on appeal because of this remark.

Magistrates were particularly criticised in this respect during the 1984 miners' strike, for imposing wide bail conditions which prevented attendance on picket lines, and dispensing what appeared to be conveyor-belt justice.

Background

Despite the recommendations of two Royal Commissions (1910 and 1948) and the *Review of the Criminal Courts* (2001) that magistrates should come from varied social backgrounds, magistrates still appear to be predominantly middle-class and middle-aged, with a strong Conservative bias.

The selection process has been blamed for the general narrowness of magistrates' backgrounds: Elizabeth Burney's 1979 study into selection methods concluded that the process was almost entirely dominated by existing magistrates who, over and over again, simply appointed people with similar backgrounds to their own.

Table 11.2 **The cost of appearing before lay and professional magistrates (per appearance)**

	Lay magistrates £	Professional magistrates £
Direct costs (salary, expenses, training)	3.59	20.96
Indirect costs (premises, administration staff, etc.)	48.51	40.82
Direct and indirect costs	52.10	61.78

Source: R. Morgan and N. Russell (2000), *The Judiciary in the Magistrates' Courts*, Home Office RDS Occasional Paper No. 66.

Lay involvement

Lay magistrates are an ancient and important tradition of voluntary public service. They can also be seen as an example of participatory democracy. Lay involvement in judicial decision-making ensures that the courts are aware of community concerns. However, given the restricted social background of magistrates, and their alleged bias towards the police, the true value of this may be doubtful. Magistrates do not have the option, as juries do, of delivering a verdict according to their conscience.

Weight of numbers

The simple fact that magistrates must usually sit in threes may make a balanced view more likely.

Local knowledge

Magistrates must live within a reasonable distance of the court in which they sit, and therefore may have a more informed picture of local life than professional judges.

Criticism of lay magistrates

Inconsistent

There is considerable inconsistency in the decision-making of different Benches. This is noticeable in the differences in awards of state funding and the types of sentences ordered. To achieve the fundamental goal of a fair trial similar crimes committed in similar circumstances by offenders with similar backgrounds should receive a similar punishment. But in Teeside, 20 per cent of convicted burglars are sentenced to immediate custody, compared to 41 per cent in Birmingham.

In 1985, the Home Office noted in *Managing Criminal Justice* (edited by David Moxon) that, though Benches tried to ensure their own decisions were consistent, they did not strive to achieve consistency with other Benches. The researchers Flood-Page and Mackie found in 1998 that district judges (magistrates' courts) sentenced a higher proportion of offenders to custody than lay magistrates after allowing for other factors. There are also marked variations in the granting of bail applications: in 1985, magistrates' courts in Hampshire granted 89 per cent of bail applications, while in Dorset only 63 per cent were allowed.

Lay magistrates versus professional judges

In recent years there has been some discussion as to whether lay magistrates should be replaced by professional judges. There have been suspicions that this may be on the government's political agenda. These suspicions have been fuelled by the increasing role of justices' clerks and the commission of research in the field by Rod Morgan and Neil Russell. Their report, *The Judiciary in the Magistrates' Courts* (2000), has provided some useful up-to-date information to support the debate on the future role of lay magistrates in the criminal justice system. That research concluded:

> *'At no stage during the study was it suggested that . . . the magistrates' courts do not work well or fail to command general confidence. It is our view, therefore, that eliminating or greatly diminishing the role of lay magistrates would not be widely understood or supported.'*

Advantages of lay magistrates

Cost

It has traditionally been assumed that, because lay magistrates are unpaid volunteers, they are necessarily cheaper than their professional colleagues. However, it is not clear that this is the case. The research by Rod Morgan and Neil Russell (2000) found that a simple analysis of the direct costs for the Magistrates' Courts Service of using the two types of magistrates shows that lay magistrates are extraordinarily cheap compared to professional judges. The direct average cost of a lay justice is £495 per annum, that of a district judge £90,000. However, lay magistrates incur more indirect costs than professional judges. They are much slower than professional judges in hearing cases – one professional judge handles as much work as 30 lay magistrates. Lay magistrates therefore make greater proportionate use of the court buildings. They need the support of legally qualified legal advisers. Administrative support is required for their recruitment, training and rota arrangements. When all the overheads are brought into the equation, the cost per appearance for lay and professional magistrates becomes £52.10 and £61.78 respectively. These figures have to be seen in the context that professional judges are currently more likely to send someone to prison which is more expensive than the alternative sentences frequently imposed by lay magistrates. They are almost twice as likely to remand defendants in custody and they are also twice as likely to sentence defendants to immediate custody, a finding that may be partly attributable to their hearing the most serious cases.

Switching to Crown Court trials would be extremely expensive. The Home Office Research and Planning Unit has estimated that the average cost of a contested trial in the Crown Court is around £13,500, with guilty pleas costing about £2,500. By contrast, the costs of trial by lay magistrates are £1,500 and £500 respectively. This is partly a reflection of the more serious nature of cases tried in the Crown Court, but clearly Crown Court trials are a great deal more expensive overall.

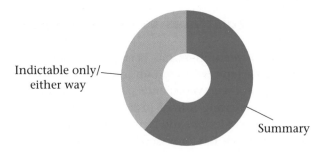

Figure 11.3 **Magistrates' courts: types of cases**
Source: 'Crown Prosecution Service Annual Report 2005-06 p. 36, Chart 2.

The justices' clerk and legal advisers

The primary function of the justices' clerk and legal adviser is to advise the lay magistrates on law and procedure. They are not supposed to take any part in the actual decision of the Bench; legal and procedural advice should be given in open court, and the justices' clerk and legal adviser should not accompany the magistrates if they retire to consider their decision.

Task 11.3

Visit a magistrates' court. You can find the address of a local magistrates' court by looking in a telephone directory. Write up a report of your visit by answering the following questions:

About the court
1 What was the name and address of the court?
2 What was the court building like? Was it old or modern? Was it clean and in good decorative order? Were the waiting areas comfortable? Was there access to refreshments? Was it easy to find your way around the building, with rooms clearly signposted and labelled?
3 Did you find the court staff helpful? Were there any explanatory leaflets available?

About the proceedings
Take one of the cases that you watched and answer the following questions:

1 Were the proceedings heard by lay magistrates or a professional judge? Were they male or female and what was their approximate age? What did they wear? Were they polite to the parties?
2 Was the case a civil or criminal matter?
3 Were the parties represented by a lawyer?
4 What was the case about?
5 Did any witnesses give evidence?
6 If you heard the whole case, what was its outcome?
7 Did you think that the court came to the right decision?

The effect of their narrow background on the quality and fairness of magistrates' decisions is unclear. A survey of 160 magistrates by Bond and Lemon (1979) found no real evidence of significant differences in approach between those of different classes, but they did conclude that political affiliation had a noticeable effect on magistrates' attitudes to sentencing, with Conservatives tending to take a harder line. The research did not reveal whether these differences actually influenced the way magistrates carried out their duties in practice, but there is obviously a risk that they would do so.

In 1997, there was a slight controversy when, on winning the General Election, the Labour Lord Chancellor called for more Labour-voting candidates to be recommended for appointment as magistrates by Advisory Committees. His reasoning was that the political make-up of the magistrates needed to reflect that of the general population, which had shifted towards Labour. The Labour government has now reversed its position, having concluded that it is no longer necessary to seek a political balance among magistrates because people no longer vote along class lines.

Some feel that the background of the Bench is not a particular problem: in *The Machinery of Justice in England* (1989), Jackson points out that: 'Benches do tend to be largely middle to upper class, but that is a characteristic of those set in authority over us, whether in the town hall, Whitehall, hospitals and all manner of institutions.'

However, a predominantly old and middle-class Bench is unrepresentative of the general public and may weaken confidence in its decisions, on the part of society in general as well as the defendants before them. Jackson's argument that those 'set in authority over us' always tend to be middle to upper class is not a justification for doing nothing.

Quick quiz 11.4

1 Describe the three main functions of the magistrates in criminal matters.

2 How many lay magistrates normally sit to hear a case?

3 What is the role of the justices' clerk?

4 In what way has the magistrates' decision-making been found to be inconsistent?

Reading on the web

The research of Rod Morgan and Neil Russell, *The Judiciary in the Magistrates' Courts* (2000), is available on the Home Office website in the section dedicated to the Research Development and Statistics Directorate:

www.homeoffice.gov.uk/rds/pdfs/occ-judiciary.pdf

The website of the Magistrates' Association, which represents the interests of magistrates, is available at:

www.magistrates-association.org.uk

General information about magistrates is available on the former Department for Constitutional Affairs' website:

www.dca.gov.uk/magistrates.htm

The report, *Delivering simple, speedy, summary justice - an evaluation of the magistrates' courts tests*, is available at:

www.dca.gov.uk/publications/reports_reviews/mag_courts_evaluation.pdf

Chapter summary

Introduction

There are over 28,000 lay magistrates and 129 professional judges who sit in the magistrates' courts.

Selection and appointment

Lay magistrates are appointed by the Lord Chancellor in the name of the Crown, on the advice of Local Advisory Committees.

Background

More than two-thirds of lay magistrates are employed in a professional or managerial position, or were until they retired. Almost a third of magistrates are in their sixties. Lay magistrates do, however, increasingly reflect the ethnic diversity of contemporary Britain.

Training

The Magistrates' Commission Committees are responsible for providing training under the supervision of the Judicial Studies Board.

Role in civil and criminal cases

Magistrates are primarily concerned with criminal matters but they exercise a limited jurisdiction over some civil matters.

The justices' clerk and legal adviser

The primary function of the justices' clerk and legal adviser is to advise the lay magistrates on law and procedure. They are not supposed to take any part in the actual decision of the Bench.

Lay magistrates versus professional judges

In recent years there has been some discussion as to whether lay magistrates should be replaced by professional judges.

Question and answer guides

1. Explain the role of magistrates in both civil and criminal cases.

Plan

- There are both lay magistrates and professional magistrates – known as district judges (magistrates' court).
- Primarily concerned with criminal cases.
- Decide bail.
- Conduct plea before venue, mode of trial hearings and transfer for trial hearings.
- For summary trials they decide the verdict where the defendant pleads not guilty.
- Following conviction in the magistrates' court, they either sentence offenders or send them to the Crown Court to be sentenced when they think their sentencing powers are inadequate.
- Issue warrants for arrest and/or the search of premises.
- Approve extensions to the detention period of people being questioned at a police station.
- Sit in youth courts where they have undertaken the additional training required.
- Magistrates have a more limited role in civil cases.
- They deal with some family proceedings.
- They issue licences for casinos and appeals against licencing decisions for pubs, clubs and restaurants.
- Proceedings are brought before them for unpaid council tax and TV licence fees.

Answer

The magistrates' court has a very wide jurisdiction, covering both criminal and civil proceedings, and magistrates can be either three local people or a professional district judge sitting alone. Lay magistrates have a long history in the English courts and their function was formally codified by statute in the fourteenth century. They are entrusted with the job of regulating many aspects of social life, ranging from keeping the peace (hence the other term for magistrates – Justice of the Peace) to dealing with those accused of breaking the criminal law. They are an invaluable part of the criminal justice system and deal with 95 per cent of criminal cases going to court. They provide a relatively cheap system of justice because lay magistrates are unpaid.

There are three broad types of criminal cases heard by magistrates: those that start and finish in the magistrates' court, those that begin there but are sent to the Crown Court for trial or sentence, and those involving young offenders. The magistrates also have an important role to play in authorising pre-trial actions related to the criminal process, such as arrest, continued detention, and the search and seizure of property.

The Youth court deals with cases where the accused is between the ages of 10 and 18. The lay magistrates sitting in the youth court are selected from a trained panel and must include magistrates from both sexes. They sit *in camera*, which means that members of the general public are not allowed in the courtroom.

Criminal cases take up the bulk of the magistrates' workload. Before a trial, they can grant or refuse bail and they can issue a summons for a person to attend court. Where a person fails to attend court – breaching their bail or failing to respond to a summons – they can issue a warrant for their arrest, which the police are then expected to act upon. As part of a police investigation, they can issue a warrant for a person's arrest, for the search of premises and the seizure of property. In practice, today the police are more likely to rely on their power to arrest without a warrant during an investigation, rather than go to the magistrates to seek a warrant. If the police wish to detain a person for questioning beyond 36 hours, they must get an extension order from the magistrates' court authorising this. Reasons for continued detention must be given.

All summary offences are tried in the magistrates' court along with those either way offences where both the defendant and the magistrates agree to the case being heard in the magistrates' court. At these trials the magistrates decide what the true facts are in the case, they have a legal adviser in court who can advise them on the law, but they reach their own verdict. If the defendant is convicted the magistrates will usually sentence the offender themselves, but they have the option of sending the offender to the Crown Court if they consider that their sentencing powers are inadequate to reflect the gravity of the case.

As Justices of the Peace, magistrates have an ancient power to keep public order, and to this end they can impose orders on individuals to keep the peace (known as a bind over). This can be imposed regardless of whether a person is convicted of any crime.

As regards their civil jurisdiction, magistrates can hear some family cases, though the magistrates need to have undertaken extra training to handle these sensitive cases and they sit *in camera*. They used to issue licences for the sale of alcohol but these licences are now granted by local authorities with the magistrates only hearing appeals from these initial decisions. They continue to grant licences for casinos and betting shops. Proceedings can be brought before the magistrates' court for unpaid council tax and where a person has failed to pay their TV licence fee.

The Auld review of criminal justice suggested that improvements could be made by making the magistrates benches more accurately reflect their local communities rather than the stereotypical JP, who is white, middle-class and close to retirement.

Group activity 1

Have a look at the following website providing information about being a lay magistrate:

www.dca.gov.uk/magistrates/index.htm

- Would you be interested in becoming a magistrate, now or in the future? If in the future, at what stage in the future?
- If you decided that you would like to become a magistrate, what would you need to do to make this idea a reality?

- What qualifications would you need?
- Once you had been selected to become a magistrate, what training would you be offered?
- If you were working, could you insist that your employer gave you time off so that you could sit as a magistrate?

Group activity 2

- Divide your friends (or class) into groups of two or three people.
- Each group should visit 'The Magistrates' Blog', also known as 'The Law West of Ealing Broadway', at **http://tlwoeb.blogspot.com**. This blog describes itself as 'Musings and Snippets from an English Magistrate'.
- Dip into the blog (do not attempt to read it all!) and make notes summarising the things that the author appears to like/dislike most about his/her work as a magistrate.
- Compare your notes with the other groups to see if you have missed anything.
- If you know any magistrates, ask them what they like/dislike most about their work and see how they compare with the blogger.
- **Warning**: When reading this blog, bear in mind that it is anonymous and therefore we do not know whether the author is indeed a magistrate.

Visit **www.mylawchamber.co.uk/elliottocr** to access questions, quizzes and activities to test yourself on this chapter.

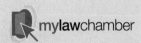

This chapter discusses:

- the role of the jury in civil and criminal cases;
- how the jury works in secret and reaches its verdict;
- the jury selection process;
- the advantages and disadvantages of jury service;
- some possible ways that the jury system could be reformed;
- alternatives to using a jury.

Introduction

The jury system was imported to Britain after the Norman Conquest. Today the jury is considered a fundamental part of the English legal system though, as we shall see, only a minority of cases are tried by a jury. The main Act that now governs jury trial is the Juries Act 1974.

Today, the jury has attained symbolic importance, so that Lord Devlin wrote in 1956: 'Trial by jury is more than an instrument of justice and more than one wheel of the constitution; it is the lamp that shows that freedom lives.' This statement led to a classic rebuttal by the academic Penny Darbyshire (1991), who wrote an article entitled 'The Lamp that shows that Freedom Lives – Is it worth the Candle?'. She argued in that article that juries are not random, not representative, but anti-democratic, irrational and haphazard legislators, whose erratic and secret decisions run counter to the rule of law.

At the trial the jurors have to weigh up the evidence and decide what are the true facts of the case – in other words, what actually happened. The judge directs them as to what is the relevant law, and the jury then have to apply the law to the facts that they have found and thereby reach a verdict. If it is a criminal case and the jury have given a verdict of guilty, the judge will then decide on the appropriate sentence. In civil cases the jury decide on how much money should be awarded in damages.

In reaching their decision, the jury are only entitled to consider evidence that arose in court, they cannot consider in the jury room evidence that has not been introduced in court. This issue arose in **R** *v* **Marshall and Crump** (2007). Two defendants had been convicted of offences including robbery and manslaughter. After their conviction, material printed off the Internet, was found in the jury room. The defendants appealed on the basis that their convictions were unsafe as they had not had any opportunity to discuss this material in open court. While it was accepted that, in principle, a jury should not consider material that had not been considered in court, on the facts of the case the evidence had been printed off legitimate websites to which the public had general access and concerned only issues as to sentencing. Therefore, on the facts of the particular case, the convictions were found to have been safe.

The role of the jury in criminal cases

Although juries are symbolically important in the criminal justice system, they actually operate only in a minority of cases and their role is constantly being reduced to save money. Criminal offences are classified into three groups: summary only offences, which are tried in the magistrates' courts; indictable offences, which are tried in the Crown Court; and either way offences, which, as the name suggests, may be tried in either the magistrates' courts or the Crown Court. The majority of criminal offences are summary only, and because these are, in general, the least serious offences, they are also the ones most commonly committed (most road traffic offences, for example, are summary only). As a result, 95 per cent of criminal cases are heard in the magistrates' courts, where juries have no role (this proportion also includes cases involving either way offences where the defendant chooses to be tried by magistrates). Juries only decide cases heard in the Crown Court. Even among the 5 per cent of cases heard there, in a high proportion of these the defendant will plead guilty, which means there is no need for a jury and, on top of that, there are cases where the judge directs the jury that the law demands that they acquit the defendant, so that the jury effectively makes no decision here either. The result is that juries actually decide only around 1 per cent of criminal cases.

On the other hand, it is important to realise that even this 1 per cent amounts to 30,000 trials, and that these are usually the most serious ones to come before the courts – though here too the picture can be misleading, since some serious offences, such as assaulting a police officer or drink-driving, are dealt with only by magistrates, while even the most trivial theft can be tried in the Crown Court if the defendant wishes.

Despite its historical role in the English legal system, and the almost sacred place it occupies in the public imagination, the jury has come under increasing attack in recent years. Successive governments have attempted to reduce the use of juries in criminal cases in order to save money. The Criminal Law Act 1977 removed the right to jury trial in a significant number of offences, by making most driving offences and relatively minor criminal damage cases summary only. Since 1977, more and more offences have been removed from the realm of jury trial by being made summary only. The sentencing powers of magistrates have been increased by the Criminal Justice Act 2003. Prior to that Act, magistrates could only sentence a person to six months' imprisonment for a single offence.

Following the passing of the 2003 Act, magistrates can sentence offenders to up to 12 months' imprisonment for a single offence, and this could be increased further to 18 months by delegated legislation. The government hopes that, by increasing the magistrates' sentencing powers, more cases will be tried in the magistrates' court rather than being referred up to the Crown Court to be tried by an expensive jury. The Criminal Justice Act 2003 also allows trial by judge alone in the Crown Court in two situations:

sourcebook
p. 136

- where a serious risk of jury tampering exists (s. 44); or
- where the case involves complex or lengthy financial and commercial arrangements (s. 43).

In this second scenario, trial by judge alone would be possible where the trial would be so burdensome upon a jury that it is necessary in the interests of justice for the case to be heard without a jury. Alternatively, it would be possible where the trial would be likely to place an excessive burden on the life of a typical juror. While s. 44 has been brought into force, the government agreed with the opposition not to implement s. 43 while alternative proposals for specialist juries and judges sitting in panels were investigated. The relevant legislative provisions can be brought into force only by a parliamentary order approving its implementation, which will require debates and a vote in both Houses of Parliament. This process was initiated at the end of 2005, but following strong opposition the provision was not brought into force. Instead, in 2006 the government introduced a single issue Bill, the Fraud (Trials without Jury) Bill, aimed solely at abolishing the jury in a limited range of serious and complex fraud trials. This Bill did not complete its progress through Parliament before Parliament closed for the summer of 2007. It may be that the Government will not try to push through this piece of regislation as no mention was made of it in the Queen's SPeech when Parliament re-opened in November 2007 and it has not been reintroduced to Parliament.

The role of the jury in civil cases

In the past, most civil cases were tried by juries, but trial by jury in the civil system is now almost obsolete. The erosion of the use of juries in civil cases was very gradual and appears to have started in the middle of the nineteenth century, when judges were given the right, in certain situations, to refuse to let a case be heard before a jury and insist that it be heard in front of a sole judge instead. Now less than 1 per cent of civil cases are tried by a jury. Today, the Supreme Court Act 1981 gives a qualified right to jury trial of civil cases in four types of case:

- libel and slander;
- malicious prosecution;
- false imprisonment; and
- fraud.

In these cases jury trial is to be granted, unless the court is of the opinion that the trial requires any prolonged examination of documents or accounts, or any scientific or local investigation which cannot conveniently be made with a jury. This right is exercised most frequently in defamation actions, although its use may be

Figure 12.1 **The Old Bailey, the Central Criminal Court in London**
Source: © EMPICS.

more limited now that the Defamation Act 1996 has introduced a new summary procedure for claims of less than £10,000, which can be heard by a judge alone.

In all other cases, the right to jury trial is at the discretion of the court. In **Ward v James** (1966) the Court of Appeal stated that, in personal injury cases (which constitute the majority of civil actions), trial should be by judge alone unless there were special considerations. In **Singh v London Underground** (1990) an application for trial by jury of a personal injury claim arising from the King's Cross underground fire of November 1987 was refused on the ground that a case involving such wide issues and technical topics was unsuitable for a jury.

There has been criticism of the distinction drawn between the four types of case which carry a qualified right to trial by jury and other civil cases. The Faulks Committee on Defamation (1975) rejected arguments for the complete abolition of juries in defamation cases, but recommended that in such cases the court should have the same discretion to order jury trial as it does in other civil cases, and that the function of the jury should be limited to deciding issues of liability, leaving the assessment of damages to the judge.

The secrecy of the jury

Once they retire to consider their verdict, jurors are not allowed to communicate with anyone other than the judge and an assigned court official, until after the verdict is delivered. Afterwards they are forbidden by s. 8 of the Contempt of Court Act 1981 from revealing anything that was said or done during their deliberations. Breach of this section amounts to a criminal offence.

The arguments in favour of secrecy have been stated by McHugh J as:

- it ensures freedom of discussion in the jury room;
- it protects jurors from outside influences, and from harassment;
- if the public knew how juries reached a verdict, they might respect the decision less;
- without secrecy, citizens would be reluctant to serve as jurors;
- it ensures the finality of the verdict;
- it enables jurors to bring in unpopular verdicts;
- it prevents unreliable disclosures by jurors and misunderstanding of verdicts.

The arguments against secrecy and in favour of disclosure are that this reform would:

- make juries more accountable;
- make it easier to enquire into the reliability of convictions and rectify injustices;
- show where reform is required;
- educate the public;
- ensure each juror's freedom of expression.

The verdict

Ideally, juries should produce a unanimous verdict, but in 1967 majority verdicts were introduced of ten to two (or nine to one if the jury has been reduced during the trial). This is now provided for in the Juries Act 1974. When the jury withdraws to consider its verdict, it must be told by the judge to reach a unanimous verdict. If, however, the jury has failed to reach a unanimous verdict after what the judge considers a reasonable period of deliberation, given the complexity of the case (not less than two hours), the judge can direct that it may reach a majority verdict. The foreman of the jury must state in open court the numbers of the jurors agreeing and disagreeing with the verdict.

Qualification for jury service

Before 1972, only those who owned a home which was over a prescribed rateable value were eligible for jury service. The Morris Committee in 1965 estimated that 78 per cent of the names on the electoral register did not qualify for jury service under this criteria, and 95 per cent of women were ineligible. This was either because they lived in rented accommodation or because they were the wife or other relative of the person in whose name the property was held. The Committee recommended that the right to do jury service should correspond with the right to vote. This reform was introduced in 1972, but nevertheless there continued to be a problem that, in practice, juries were not truly representative of the society which they served. While it was understandable that some people with criminal convictions were disqualified from jury service, a wide range of other people were either excluded or excused from jury service.

The basis of the use of juries in serious criminal cases is that the 12 people are randomly selected, and should therefore comprise a representative sample of the population as a whole. This ideal came closer with the abolition of the property qualification and with the use of computers for the random selection process. Despite this, research carried out for the Home Office (*Jury Excusal and Deferral* (2000)) found that each year only two-thirds of the people summoned for jury service made themselves available to do it. About 15 per cent of summoned jurors failed to attend court on the day or had their summonses returned as 'undelivered'. Because enforcement has been poor, it became widely known that a jury summons could be ignored with impunity.

sourcebook
p. 130 →

In his *Review of the Criminal Courts* (2001), Sir Robin Auld argued that the many exclusions and excusals from jury service deprived juries of the experience and skills of a wide range of professional and successful people. Their absence created the impression that jury service was only for those not important or clever enough to get out of it. He was keen to make juries more representative of the general population. He wanted jury service to become a compulsory public duty for all, to stop middle-class professionals opting out. He proposed that everyone should be eligible for jury service, save for the mentally ill.

The government accepted these recommendations. The Criminal Justice Act 2003, s. 321 and Sch. 33 amended the Juries Act 1974. This Act now provides that potential jury members must be:

- aged 18 to 70;
- on the electoral register;
- resident in the UK, Channel Islands or Isle of Man for at least five years since the age of 13;
- not a mentally disordered person; and
- not disqualified from jury service.

Most of the grounds for ineligibility and excusal have been removed. Only military personnel can be excused from jury service and only the mentally ill are ineligible for jury service. The rules disqualifying people with certain criminal convictions from jury service remain. As a result, in future juries should become much more representative of society. Following these reforms, increasing participation in the jury system, an appeal was brought before the Court of Appeal (**R v Abdroikov** (2005)), arguing that a trial was unfair where a police officer or employee of the Crown Prosecution Service acted as jurors. This appeal was rejected, as the court stated that such individuals were required to behave in the same way as any other randomly selected juror.

Sir Robin Auld also recommended that potential jurors should no longer only be selected from the electoral register. Many people are not registered to vote in elections, even though they are entitled to do so. To reach as many people as possible he therefore proposed that a range of publicly maintained lists and directories should be used. The government has not adopted this recommendation.

Quick quiz 12.1

1 Does the jury decide the sentence of an offender?

2 What age group can sit on a jury?

3 Can a police officer sit as a juror?

4 Do the jury have to reach a unanimous verdict in order to convict a defendant?

Summoning the jury

Every year almost half a million people are summoned to do jury service. In 2001 a Central Juror Summoning Bureau was established to administer the juror-summoning process for the whole of the country. Computers are used to produce a random list of potential jurors from the electoral register. Summons are sent out (with a form to return confirming that the person does not fall into any of the disqualified or ineligible groups), and from the resulting list the jury panel is produced. This is made public for both sides in forthcoming cases to inspect, though only names and addresses are shown. It is at this stage that jury vetting may take place (see below). Jurors also receive a set of notes which explain a little of the procedure of the jury service and the functions of the juror.

Jury service is compulsory and failure to attend on the specified date, or unfitness for service through drink or drugs, is contempt of court and can result in a fine.

The jury for a particular case is chosen by random ballot in open court – the clerk has each panel member's name on a card, the cards are shuffled and the first 12 names called out. Unless there are any challenges (see p. 000), these 12 people will be sworn in. In a criminal case there are usually 12 jurors and there must never be fewer than nine. In civil cases in the county court there are eight jurors.

Jury vetting

Jury vetting consists of checking that potential jurors do not hold 'extremist' views which some feel would make them unsuitable for hearing a case. It is done by checking police, Special Branch and security service records.

Attorney-General's guidelines exist stating when jurors should be vetted. These state that vetting might be necessary in certain special cases, such as terrorism. Authorisation is required by the Attorney-General, who will be acting on the advice of the Director of Public Prosecutions. Checking whether a person has a criminal record is permissible in a much wider range of cases without special permission.

Vetting for any purpose remains controversial. Supporters claim that it can promote impartiality by excluding those whose views might bias the other members of the jury, and make them put pressure on others, as well as protecting national security and preventing disqualified persons from serving. Opponents say it infringes the individual's right to privacy, and gives the prosecution an unfair advantage, since it is too expensive for most defendants to undertake, and they do not have access to the same sources of information as the prosecution.

Challenges

As members of the jury panel are called, and before they are sworn in, they may be challenged in one of two ways:

1 **Challenge for cause.** Either side may challenge for cause, on the grounds of privilege of peerage, disqualification, ineligibility or assumed bias. Jurors cannot be questioned before being challenged to ascertain whether there are grounds

for a challenge. A successful challenge for cause is therefore only likely to succeed if the juror is personally known, or if jury vetting has been undertaken. If a challenge for cause is made, it is tried by the trial judge.

2 **Stand by.** Only the prosecution may ask jurors to stand by for the Crown. Although there are specified grounds for this, in practice no reason need be given, and this is generally how the information supplied by jury vetting is used.

This limited process of challenging the jury should be contrasted with the system in the US, where it can take days to empanel a jury, particularly where the case has received a lot of pre-trial media coverage. Potential jury members can be asked a wide range of questions about their attitudes to the issues raised by a case, and a great deal of money may be spent employing special consultants who claim to be able to judge which way people are likely to vote, based on their age, sex, politics, religion and other personal information.

In a high-profile case, **R v Andrews** (1999), the defence wanted to use the American approach to establish whether members of the jury panel were likely to be biased against the defendant. She was accused of murdering her boyfriend, and the case had received an enormous amount of publicity, since Ms Andrews had initially told police that her boyfriend was killed by an unknown assailant in a 'road rage' incident, sparking off a media hunt for the killer. Her lawyers wanted to issue questionnaires to the jury panel to check whether any of them showed a prejudice against her. The trial judge refused the request and when Ms Andrews was convicted, she appealed, arguing that the failure to allow questioning of the jury meant her conviction was unsafe. The argument was rejected by the Court of Appeal, which stated that questioning of the jury panel, whether orally or by written questionnaire, should be avoided in all but the most exceptional cases, such as where potential jurors might have a direct or indirect connection to the facts of the trial (for example, if they were related to someone involved in the trial, or had lost money as a result of the defendant's actions).

Figure 12.2 Tracie Andrews, the defendant in **R v Andrews** (1998), arrives at the High Court in London to find out if her Court of Appeal bid for freedom has succeeded, after being jailed for life for murdering her fiancé, Lee Harvey, who she had claimed was killed by a mystery motorist in a road rage attack

Source: © EMPICS.

Advantages of the jury system

Public participation

Juries allow the ordinary citizen to take part in the administration of justice, so that verdicts are seen to be those of society rather than of the judicial system, and satisfy the constitutional tradition of judgment by one's peers. Lord Denning described jury service as giving 'ordinary folk their finest lesson in citizenship'.

The Home Office has carried out research into the experience of being a juror: Matthews, Hancock and Briggs, *Jurors' Perceptions, Understanding, Confidence and Satisfaction in the Jury System: a study in six courts* (2004). The research questioned 361 jurors about their jury service. More than half (55 per cent) said they would be happy to do it again, 19 per cent said they would not mind doing jury service again, but 25 per cent said they would never want to be a juror again. About two-thirds felt that their experience had boosted their opinion of the jury system and they were impressed by the professionalism and helpfulness of the court staff and the performance of the judge. A minority were unhappy with the delays in the system, the trivial nature of some cases and the standard of facilities. Thirty-six per cent of jurors felt intimidated or very uncomfortable in the courtroom, primarily because they were worried about meeting defendants or their family members coming out of court or in the street.

When questioned by Professor Lloyd-Bostock about their experience, the jurors in the collapsed Jubilee line case were found to be enthusiastic about their role, committed to it, and furious when the trial was aborted. They were a remarkably cooperative and mutually supportive group. Two compared being on the jury with being on *Big Brother*. However, as the trial progressed, the jurors felt increasingly like 'jury fodder', on tap but not informed. They would be telephoned at short notice and told not to turn up for several days but no explanation would be given. Even more frustrating was when they turned up for jury service and then, after a lengthy delay, sent home again. The main difficulties suffered by the jurors were in relation to their employment. All seven jurors who were employed said their employers were very unhappy about the long trial. Most felt that the court should have more responsibility for communicating directly with their employers rather than placing the onus on the jurors. Uncooperative employers could cause problems over claims for allowances. One juror had been made redundant, one was in an employment dispute, one had missed a definite and much-desired promotion and was required to undertake extensive retraining, and one had been signed off by his doctor as suffering from stress as a result of his work situation. Most of the jurors had suffered financially as a result of the trial. One suggestion is that a juror liaison person could be appointed for long jury trials whose remit is to look after jurors' needs and alleviate the burden of jury service as much as possible.

Certainty

The jury adds certainty to the law, since it gives a general verdict which cannot give rise to misinterpretation. In a criminal case the jury simply states that the accused is guilty or not guilty, and gives no reasons. Consequently, the decision is not open to dispute.

Ability to judge according to conscience

A major milestone in the history of the jury was in **Bushell's Case** (1670). Before this, judges would try to bully juries into convicting the defendant, particularly where the crime had political overtones, but in **Bushell's Case** it was established that the jury's members were the sole judges of fact, with the right to give a verdict according to their conscience, and could not be penalised for taking a view of the facts opposed to that of the judge. The importance of this power now is that juries may acquit a defendant, even when the law demands a guilty verdict.

Because juries have the ultimate right to find defendants innocent or guilty, they have been seen as a vital protection against oppressive or politically motivated prosecutions, and as a kind of safety valve for those cases where the law demands a guilty verdict, but genuine justice does not. For example, in the early nineteenth century, all felonies (a classification of crimes used at the time, marking out those considered most serious) were in theory punishable by death. Theft of goods or money above the value of a shilling was a felony, but juries were frequently reluctant to allow the death penalty to be imposed in what seemed to them trivial cases, so they would often find that the defendant was guilty, but the property stolen was worth less than a shilling.

There are several well-known recent cases of juries using their right to find according to their consciences, often concerning issues of political and moral controversy, such as **R v Kronlid** (1996). The defendants were three women who broke into a British Aerospace factory and caused damage costing over £1.5 million to a Hawk fighter plane. The women admitted doing this – they had left a video explaining their actions in the plane's cockpit – but claimed that they had a defence under s. 3 of the Criminal Law Act 1967, which provides that it is lawful to commit a crime in order to prevent another (usually more serious) crime being committed, and that this may involve using 'such force as is reasonable in all the circumstances'.

The defendants pointed out that the plane was part of a consignment due to be sold to the government of Indonesia, which was involved in oppressive measures against the population of East Timor, a region forcibly annexed by Indonesia in 1975. They further explained that Amnesty International had estimated that the Indonesians had killed at least a third of the population of East Timor, and that the jet was likely to be used in a genocidal attack against the survivors. Genocide is a crime and therefore, they argued, their criminal damage was done in order to prevent a crime. However, the prosecution gave evidence that the Indonesian government had given assurances that the planes would not be used against the East Timorese, and the British government had accepted this and granted an export licence. Acquitting the women was therefore a criticism of the British government's position on the issue, as well as the actions of the Indonesian government, and in the face of the clear evidence that they had caused the damage, they were widely expected to be convicted. The jury found them all not guilty.

Other cases have involved what were seen to be oppressive prosecutions in cases involving the government, such as **R v Ponting** (1985), where the defendant, a civil servant, was prosecuted for breaking the Official Secrets Act after passing confidential information to a journalist – even though doing so exposed a matter of public interest, namely the fact that the then government had lied to Parliament. Ponting was acquitted.

Quick quiz 12.2

1 Give three arguments in favour of the secrecy of the jury and three arguments against.

2 What is the minimum number of jurors who must vote in favour of a conviction or an acquittal in order to reach a verdict?

3 Can juries carry out independent research into a case?

4 Give an example of a case where the jurors may have decided a case according to their conscience rather than the law.

Task 12.3

The Judicial Studies Board has issued a specimen direction which judges can give to a jury to explain their different roles during a jury trial. This specimen direction is as follows:

'Our functions in this trial have been and remain quite different. Throughout this trial the law has been my area of responsibility, and I must now give you directions as to the law which applies in this case. When I do so, you must accept those directions and follow them.

I must also remind you of the prominent features of the evidence. However, it has always been your responsibility to judge the evidence and decide all the relevant facts of this case, and when you come to consider your verdict you, and you alone, must do that.

You do not have to decide every point which has been raised; only such matters as will enable you to say whether the charge laid against the defendant has been proved. You will do that by having regard to the whole of the evidence and forming your own judgement about the witnesses, and which evidence is reliable and which is not.

The facts of this case are your responsibility. You will wish to take account of the arguments in the speeches you have heard, but you are not bound to accept them. Equally, if in the course of my review of the evidence, I appear to express any views concerning the facts, or emphasise a particular aspect of the evidence, do not adopt those views unless you agree with them; and if I do not mention something which you think is important, you should have regard to it, and give it such weight as you think fit. When it comes to the facts of this case, it is your judgement alone that counts.'

Questions

1 Does the jury have to follow the judge's directions on the law?
2 Does the jury have to follow the judge's view of the facts?

Criticisms of the jury system

Lack of competence

Lord Denning argued, in *What Next in the Law?* (1982), that the selection of jurors is too wide, resulting in jurors that are not competent to perform their task. Praising the 'Golden Age' of jury service when only 'responsible heads of household from a select band of the middle classes' were eligible to serve, he claimed that the 1972 changes have led to jurors being summoned who are not sufficiently intelligent or educated to perform their task properly. In one unfortunate case, a jury hearing a murder trial had apparently set up an ouija board in an attempt to make contact with the spirit of the deceased: **R v Young** (1995). Denning suggested that jurors should be selected in much the same way as magistrates are, with interviews and references required. This throws up several obvious problems: a more complicated selection process would be more time-consuming and costly; finding sufficient people willing to take part might prove difficult; and a jury that is intelligent and educated can still be biased, and may be more likely to be so if drawn from a narrow social group.

Particular concern has been expressed about the average jury's understanding of complex fraud cases. The Roskill Committee concluded that trial by random jury was not a satisfactory way of achieving justice in such cases, with many jurors 'out of their depth'. However, the Roskill Committee was unable to find accurate evidence of a higher proportion of acquittals in complex fraud cases than in any other kind – many of their conclusions were based on research by Baldwin and McConville (1979), yet none of the questionable acquittals reported there was in a complex fraud case.

The academic, Terry Honess (2003), conducted an extended simulation study of jurors' comprehension of some of the evidence in the Maxwell fraud trial. He estimated that four out of five of the participants could be regarded as competent to serve on a major fraud trial, and concluded that abolition of the jury system for complex fraud trials was not justified on the grounds of 'cognitive unfitness'.

Following the collapse of the trial of six men prosecuted for alleged fraud in the awarding of contracts for the construction of the extension to the Jubilee underground line, **R v Rayment and others** (2005), the jurors were questioned about their experience of the trial as part of a government review of the case. This review found that 'when the case collapsed this jury, taken as a group, had a good understanding of the case, the issues and the evidence so far, as presented to them'. The jurors said they had no problem with technical language or documents. They displayed quite impressive familiarity with the charges, issues and evidence, and were able to engage in detailed discussion of the prosecution case nearly a year after it had closed. The chief difficulty expressed by the jurors was not in finding evidence too technical or complex, but in finding the pace of the trial extremely slow and parts of the defence evidence tedious. It is questionable whether the trial needed to be unmanageably long. In the preface to his report on the case, Stephen Wooler (2006) describes it as 'probably one of the best examples' of cases 'which are neither sufficiently complex to be beyond the comprehension of juries, nor necessarily lengthy'. Discussion was evidently facilitated by the provision of a jury deliberating room for much of the trial, where the jury went whilst at court but not in court. The jurors said they found discussion much more difficult, if not impossible, when they did not have use of this room. The jurors were not allowed to take their notes from the courtroom and several said it would have been helpful to do so. The academic, Professor Findlay, has noted that juror comprehension and memory for complex evidence can be assisted through, for example, the use of visual aids. Discussion amongst jurors, taking notes and asking questions can enhance juror comprehension (Horowitz (2001)). Professor Lloyd-Bostock has concluded:

> '. . . where the jury is concerned, the "problem" with the Jubilee Line case was not the jury's ability to cope, but the unnecessarily excessive length of the case with its consequences for the jurors' lives, together with some aspects of their treatment at court . . . Taken in context, the jurors' perspective on the ill-fated Jubilee Line trial does not indicate that the solution is to abandon jury trial for such cases. Rather, it confirms that jury trial is valued, and that improvements through trial preparation, and trial and jury management, should be fully explored before the jury itself is threatened.'

The 'perverse verdicts' problem

It is a matter of fact that juries acquit proportionately more defendants than magistrates do. Research from the Home Office Planning Unit suggests that an acquittal is approximately twice as likely in a jury trial. Many critics of the jury system argue that this is a major failing on the part of juries, arising either from their inability to perform their role properly, as discussed above, or from their sympathy with defendants, or both.

This is a difficult area to research, as the Contempt of Court Act 1981 prohibits asking jurors about the basis on which they reached their decision. What research there is generally involves comparing actual jury decisions with those reached by legal professionals, or by shadow juries, who sit in on the case and reach their own decision just as the official jurors are asked to do.

A piece of research commissioned by the Roskill Committee on fraud trials concluded that jurors who found difficulty in comprehending the complex issues involved in fraud prosecution were more likely to acquit. They suggested that the jurors characterised their own confusions as a form of 'reasonable doubt' leading them to a decision to acquit.

A study by McCabe and Purves, *The Jury at Work* (1972), looked at 173 acquittals, and concluded that 15 (9 per cent) defied the evidence, the rest being attributable to weakness of the prosecution case or failure of their witnesses, or the credibility of the accused's explanation. McCabe and Purves viewed the proportion of apparently perverse verdicts as quite small and, from their observations of shadow juries, concluded that jurors did work methodically and rationally through the evidence, and tried to put aside their own prejudices.

However, Baldwin and McConville's 1979 study (*Jury Trials*) examined 500 cases, both convictions and acquittals, and found that up to 25 per cent of acquittals were questionable (as well as 5 per cent of convictions), and concluded that, given the serious nature of the cases concerned, this was a problem. They describe trial by jury as 'an arbitrary and unpredictable business'.

Zander (1988) points out that the high rate of acquittals must be seen in the light of the high number of guilty pleas in the Crown Court. It must also be noted that many acquittals are directed or ordered by the judge: according to evidence from the Lord Chancellor's Department to the Runciman Commission, in 1990–1, 40 per cent of all acquittals were ordered by the judge because the prosecution offered no evidence at the start of the trial. A further 16 per cent of the acquittals were directed by the judge after the prosecution had made its case as there was insufficient evidence to leave to the jury. Thus the jury was only responsible for 41 per cent of the acquittals, which was merely 7 per cent of all cases in the Crown Court. Bearing in mind the pressures on defendants to plead guilty, it is not surprising that those who resist tend to be those with the strongest cases – and, of course, the standard of proof required is very high. Nor is it beyond the bounds of possibility that part of the difference in conviction rates between magistrates and juries is due to magistrates convicting the innocent rather than juries acquitting the guilty.

In a high-profile case the Court of Appeal overturned a jury decision in civil proceedings on the basis that the jury decision had been perverse. In **Grobbelaar v News Group Newspapers Ltd** (2001) a jury had awarded the professional goal-keeper, Bruce Grobbelaar, £85,000 on the basis that he had been defamed in *The Sun* newspaper. *The Sun* had published a story claiming that Grobbelaar had received cash to fix football matches. It had obtained secretly taped videos of Grobbelaar, in which he apparently admitted receiving money in the past to lose matches, and appeared to accept cash following a proposal to fix matches in the future. A criminal prosecution of Grobbelaar had failed and he sued in the civil courts for defamation. Grobbelaar accepted that he had made the confessions and accepted cash, but claimed that he had done so as a trick in order to bring the other person to justice. The jury accepted his claim and awarded damages. *The Sun's* appeal was allowed on the basis that the jury's decision had been perverse. The Court of Appeal found Grobbelaar's story 'incredible'. The House of Lords allowed a further appeal. It considered it wrong to overturn the jury's verdict as perverse, as the verdict could have been given an alternative explanation.

Bias

Jurors may be biased for or against certain groups – for example, they may favour attractive members of the opposite sex, or be prejudiced against the police.

Bias appears to be a particular problem in libel cases, where juries prejudiced against newspapers award huge damages, apparently using them punitively rather than as compensation for the victim. Examples include the £500,000 awarded to Jeffrey Archer in 1987, and the £300,000 to Koo Stark a year later, as well as **Sutcliffe v Pressdram Ltd** (1991), in which *Private Eye* was ordered to pay £600,000 to the wife of the Yorkshire Ripper. In the latter case, Lord Donaldson described the award as irrational, and suggested that judges should give more guidance on the amounts to be awarded – not by referring to previous cases or specific amounts, but by asking juries to think about the real value of money (such as what income the capital would produce, or what could be bought with it). The Courts and Legal Services Act 1990 now allows the Court of Appeal to reduce damages considered excessive.

For a discussion of cases concerned with potentially racist jurors, see p. 221.

Representation of ethnic minorities

Black defendants have no right to have black people sitting on the jury. In **R v Bansal** (1985) the case involved an Anti-National Front demonstration and the trial judge ordered that the jury should be drawn from an area with a large Asian population. However, this approach was rejected as wrong in **R v Ford** (1989). The Court of Appeal held that race could not be taken into account when selecting jurors, and that a judge could not discharge jurors in order to achieve a racially representative jury.

Manipulation by defendants

The government's consultation paper, *Determining Mode of Trial in Either Way Cases* (1998), suggests that manipulation of the right to jury trial by defendants is a major problem. It claims that many guilty defendants choose jury trial in a bid to make use of the delay such a choice provides. The report puts forward three reasons why guilty defendants want to do this. First, delay may put pressure on the Crown Prosecution Service to reduce the charge in exchange for the defendant pleading guilty and so speed up the process. Secondly, it may make it more likely that prosecution witnesses will fail to attend the eventual trial, or at least weaken their recollections if they do attend, so making an acquittal more likely. Thirdly, if a defendant is being held on remand, he or she is kept at a local prison, and allowed additional visits and other privileges not given to convicted prisoners. Time spent on remand is deducted from any eventual prison sentence, so for a defendant on remand who calculates that he or she is likely to be found guilty and sentenced to imprisonment, putting off the trial for as long as possible will maximise the amount of the sentence that can be spent under the more favourable conditions. Such manipulation is obviously undesirable from the point of view of justice, and it also wastes a great deal of time and money, since many defendants who manipulate the system in this way end up pleading guilty at the last minute (resulting in what is known as a 'cracked trial'), so that the time and money spent preparing the prosecution's case is wasted; in most cases, state funding will also have been spent on the defence case.

However, those who support jury trials argue that this is a declining problem. In 1987, defendants choosing jury trial accounted for 53 per cent of either-way cases sent to the Crown Court, but by 1997, the proportion had fallen to 28 per cent.

Jury nobbling

This problem led to the suspension of jury trials for terrorist offences in Northern Ireland, and has caused problems in some English trials. In 1982 several Old Bailey trials had to be stopped because of attempted 'nobbling', one after seven months, and the problem became so serious that juries had to sit out of sight of the public gallery, brown paper was stuck over the windows in court doors, and jurors were warned to avoid local pubs and cafés and eat only in their own canteen. In 1984, jurors in the Brinks-Mat trial had to have police protection to and from the court, and their telephone calls intercepted.

A new criminal offence was created under the Criminal Justice and Public Order Act 1994 to try to give additional protection to the jury. This provides under s. 51 that it is an offence to intimidate or threaten to harm, either physically or financially, certain people involved in a trial including jurors.

A more radical reform was introduced in the Criminal Procedure and Investigations Act 1996. Section 54 of the Act provides that where a person has been acquitted of an offence and someone is subsequently convicted of interfering with or intimidating jurors or witnesses in the case, then the High Court can quash the acquittal and the person can be retried. This is a wholly exceptional development in the law since traditionally acquittals were considered final, and subsequent retrial a breach of fundamental human rights. Following the Criminal Justice Act 2003, where there is a real risk of jury nobbling a case can be heard by a single judge.

Absence of reasons

When judges sit alone their judgment consists of a detailed and explicit finding of fact. When there is a jury it returns an unexplained verdict which simply finds in favour of one party or another. The former is more easily reviewed by appellate courts because the findings and the inferences of the trial judge can be examined. But when the appellate court is faced with a jury's verdict, it must support that verdict if there is any reasonable view of the evidence which leads to it.

Article 6 of the European Convention on Human Rights requires courts to give reasons for their judgments. In his review of the criminal courts, Sir Robin Auld considered this matter in relation to the unreasoned jury verdict. However, he concluded that the European Court of Human Rights would take into account the way the British jury trial works as a whole and not find a violation of Art. 6.

Problems with compulsory jury service

Jury service is often unpopular but a refusal to act as a juror amounts to a contempt of court. Resentful jurors might make unsatisfactory decisions: in particular, jurors keen to get away as soon as possible are likely simply to go along with what the majority say, whether they agree or not.

Excessive damages

In the past, juries in civil cases have awarded very high damages. The Court of Appeal now has the power either to order a new trial on the ground that damages awarded by a jury are excessive or, without the agreement of the parties, to substitute for the sum awarded by the jury such sum as appears to the court to be proper.

Cost and time

A Crown Court trial currently costs the taxpayer around £7,400 per day, as opposed to £1,000 per day for trial by magistrates. The jury process is time-consuming for all involved, with juries spending much of their time waiting around to be summoned into court.

Distress to jury members

Juries trying cases involving serious crimes of violence, particularly rape, murder or child abuse, may have to listen to deeply distressing evidence, and in some cases to inspect graphic photographs of injuries. One juror in a particularly gruesome murder case told a newspaper how he felt on hearing a tape of the last words of the victim as, fatally injured, she struggled to make herself understood on the phone to the emergency services:

> *'It was your worst nightmare. I've watched American police programmes where you have a murder every 15 seconds, pools of blood, chalk lines where the bodies were . . . that's nothing compared to the sound of this tape. You cannot believe the shock that runs through you, the fear when you know this is what happened.'* (The Sunday Times, *13 April 1997*)

At the end of the case, most members of the jury were in tears, and after delivering their verdict, it was over an hour before they could compose themselves sufficiently to leave the jury room. The problem is made worse by the fact that jurors are told not to discuss the case with anyone else.

The potential for distress to jurors was recognised in the recent trials of Rosemary West and the killers of James Bulger, where the jurors were offered counselling afterwards, and since these cases the Ministry of Justice has provided that court-appointed welfare officers should be made available. However, these are provided only in cases judges deem to be exceptional, and only if jurors request their help.

Quick quiz 12.4

1 On what basis did the Court of Appeal allow the appeal of *The Sun* newspaper in the case of **Grobbelaar v News Group Newspapers Ltd** (2001)?

2 Does the failure of the jury to give reasons violate the right to a fair trial contained in Art. 6 of the European Convention on Human Rights?

3 Which is cheaper, a Crown Court trial or a trial in a magistrates' court?

4 Do black defendants have a right to at least one black juror sitting on the jury to hear their case?

Reform of the jury

A wide range of reform proposals have been put forward for the reform of the jury system.

Serious fraud trials

The government would like to remove jury trials from most serious fraud cases (see p. 204), a reform that has been heavily criticised. There has been an on-going debate as to whether juries are suitable for such cases. Public attention was drawn to this issue by the collapse of the trial of six men accused of fraud relating to the awarding of contracts for the construction of the Jubilee Line extension on the London Underground system (**R** v **Rayment** (2005)). The trial lasted two years – the longest ever jury trial – before it collapsed, having cost the taxpayer £60 million. It had suffered from a range of delays due to illness, scheduled holidays and paternity leave among the jury and lawyers, since it began in February 2000. Legal arguments also involved substantial periods where the jury was not required to hear evidence. In the last seven months before the case was dropped, the jury heard evidence on only 13 days of the 140 available. The prosecution eventually dropped the case after deciding there had been so many interruptions that a fair trial had become impossible.

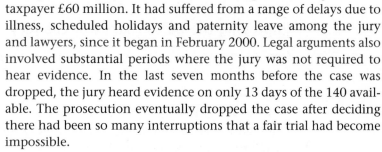

Know your terms 12.5

Define the following terms:

1 Jury vetting.
2 Stand by.
3 Summary offence.
4 Jury nobbling.

sourcebook
p. 127 →

To try to prevent such a waste of time and money occurring again, the Lord Chief Justice issued a protocol requiring judges to exercise strong case management over cases likely to last more than eight weeks, including strict deadlines. The aim is to reduce the length of such trials to a maximum of three months. Trials would only be allowed to go on longer than six months in 'exceptional circumstances'. In addition, since April 2005 large criminal cases are monitored by a case management panel chaired by the Director of Public Prosecutions.

But the government decided not to wait to see whether this new Protocol led to shorter fraud trials with juries sitting, and instead decided to remove juries from such cases by trying to push it through Parliament the Fraud (Trials Without Jury) Bill. However, it faced strong opposition and the Bill has not been enacted.

The use of a single judge has the advantages of making trials quicker, reducing the likelihood of 'perverse' verdicts, and defeating the problem of jury nobbling (in Northern Ireland single judges have long been used in some cases because of the problem of jury nobbling). However, the benefits of public participation in the legal system would be lost, and all the problems associated with judicial bias and the restricted social background of judges (described in Chapter 10) would be let loose on cases which involve vital questions for both the individuals concerned and society as a whole. The Bar Council believes that juries should be retained in all cases where the defendant faces serious loss of liberty or reputation. It considers that fraud cases can appear complex, but if they are properly managed, juries are capable of deciding the case, which usually comes down to determining whether the defendant has been dishonest.

Using a bench of perhaps three or five judges would give a little more protection against individual bias, but would still not give the benefit of community participation that the jury offers (and would also require massive investment to train the increased number of judges that would be required).

Task 12.6

If you were charged with committing a fraud, what type of trial would you prefer?

- Would you prefer your case to be heard in a magistrates' court or a Crown Court?
- Would you want your case to be heard by a professional judge, by a jury or by a combination of lay people sitting with a judge and jointly deciding your guilt?

Why would you prefer this type of trial?

Improving the performance of the jury

Sir Robin Auld has made a range of specific recommendations to improve the performance of the jury.

Help the jury to work effectively

The Auld Review recommended that, in order to assist a jury in their work, the prosecution and defence advocates should prepare a written summary of the case and the issues that needed to be decided. This 'case and issues' summary would be agreed by the judge and distributed to the jurors at the start of the trial.

The judge would sum up the case at the end of the trial by forming questions which needed to be considered by the jurors. Juries would reach verdicts by answering these questions during their deliberations. Where the judge thought it appropriate he or she would be able to require the jury publicly to answer each of the questions and to declare a verdict in accordance with those answers. Sir Robin Auld argues that this would strengthen the jury as a tribunal of fact, provide a reasoned basis for jury verdicts and reduce the risk of perverse verdicts. While there can only be benefits from presenting the case more clearly to the jury, the use of questions which the jury may be forced to answer publicly seems to be an unnecessary restriction on the jurors' freedom to reach a decision in accordance with their conscience as well as in accordance with the law.

Professor Zander (2001) has criticised these recommendations. He argues persuasively that Sir Robin Auld demonstrates:

> 'an authoritarian attitude that disregards history and reveals a grievously misjudged sense of the proper balance of the criminal justice system. For centuries the role of the jury has included the power to stand between the citizen and unjust law . . . [G]etting it right does not necessarily mean giving the verdict a judge would have given. . . . To want to inquire whether they reached their decision in the "right" way, is foolish because it ignores the nature of the institution.'

Prevent perverse verdicts

The Auld Review was concerned by the risk of juries reaching perverse verdicts. Rather than seeing these as a potential safeguard of civil liberties, the review seems to consider these as an insult to the law. It has therefore recommended that legislation should declare that juries have no right to acquit defendants in defiance of the law or in disregard of the evidence. The prosecution would be given a right to appeal against what it considered to be a perverse acquittal by a jury.

Sir Robin Auld recommended that, where appropriate, the trial judge and the Court of Appeal should be allowed to investigate any alleged impropriety or failure in the way the jury reached its verdict, even where this is supposed to have happened during the traditionally secret deliberations of the jury. Such an investigation might look at accusations that some jurors ignored or slept through the deliberation or that the jury reached its verdict because of an irrational prejudice or whim, deliberately ignoring the evidence.

These recommendations show insufficient respect for the jurors and have been rejected by the government.

Reserve jurors

One recommendation of the *Review of the Criminal Courts* (2001) was that, where appropriate, for long cases judges should be able to swear in extra jurors. These reserve jurors would be able to replace jurors who are unable to continue to hear a case because, for example, of illness.

Black jurors

It has been argued by the Commission for Racial Equality that consideration needs to be given to the racial balance in particular cases. They suggest that where a case has a racial dimension and the defendant reasonably believes that he or she cannot receive a fair trial from an all-white jury, then the judge should have the power to order that three of the jurors come from the same ethnic minority as the defendant or the victim. Both the Runciman Commission (1993) and Sir Robin Auld's *Review of the Criminal Courts* (2001) have given their endorsement to this proposal but it has never been implemented.

The Society of Black Lawyers had, in addition, submitted to the Runciman Commission that there should always be a right to a multiracial trial and that certain cases with a black defendant should be tried by courts in areas with high black populations, and panels of black jurors who would be available at short notice should be set up. These proposals have not been implemented either.

The problems caused by lack of racial representation on juries can be seen in the high-profile Rodney King case in Los Angeles, where a policeman was found not guilty of assaulting a black motorist despite a videotape of the incident showing brutal conduct. The case was tried in an area with a very high white population, while the incident itself had occurred in an area with a high black population. However, the decision in **R** v **Ford** (1989), that there is no principle that a jury should be racially balanced, still holds.

Alternatives to juries

It can be argued that, since juries decide only 1 per cent of criminal cases, the system really no longer needs them at all and they should be abolished. The pros and cons of this argument naturally depend on what would be put in their place.

The government's 1998 consultation paper on the criminal justice system considered four possible options for serious fraud trials:

- abolishing the use of juries in fraud trials completely and replacing them with a specially trained single judge and two lay people with expertise in commercial affairs;
- replacing juries with a specially trained single judge or panel of judges, possibly with access to advisers on commercial matters;
- retaining jury trial but restricting the jury's role to deciding questions of dishonesty, with the judge deciding other matters; or
- replacing the traditional, randomly selected jury with a special jury, selected on the basis of qualifications or tests, or drawn from those who can demonstrate specialist knowledge of business and finance.

Reading on the web

The *Report on Interviews with Jurors in the Jubilee Line Case* (2006) by Professor Sally Lloyd-Bostock is available on the website of Her Majesty's Crown Prosecution Service Inspectorate at:

www.hmcpsi.gov.uk/reports/JLJury_IntsRep.pdf

The *Review of the Investigation and Criminal Proceedings Relating to the Jubilee Line Case* (2006) by Stephen Wooler is available on the website of Her Majesty's Crown Prosecution Service Inspectorate at:

www.hmcpsi.gov.uk/reports/JubileeLineReponly.pdf

The consultation document, *Jury Research and Impropriety* (2005), considering when the law should allow the secrecy of jury deliberations to be broken, can be found on the former Department for Constitutional Affairs' website at:

www.dca.gov.uk/consult/juryresearch/_cp0405.pdf

Leaflets on jury service are published on the Court Service website at:

www.hmcourts_service.gov.uk/

Chapter summary

The role of the jury

Juries decide only about 1 per cent of criminal cases and a very small number of civil cases.

The secrecy of the jury

Once they retire to consider their verdict, jurors are not allowed to communicate with anyone other than the judge and an assigned court official, until after the verdict is delivered.

The verdict

Ideally, juries should produce a unanimous verdict, but in 1967 majority verdicts were introduced of ten to two (or nine to one if the jury has been reduced during the trial).

Qualifications for jury service

Potential jury members must be:

- aged 18 to 70;
- on the electoral register; and
- resident in the UK, Channel Islands or Isle of Man for at least five years since the age of 13.

Jury vetting

Jury vetting consists of checking that the potential juror does not hold 'extremist' views which some feel would make them unsuitable for hearing a case. It is done by checking police, Special Branch and security service records.

Advantages of the jury system

Juries allow ordinary citizens to participate in the administration of justice and decide cases according to their conscience.

Disadvantages of the jury system

In practice, juries are not representative of the general population. Some of their judgments are perverse; they can be biased and susceptible to manipulation.

Reform of the jury

Proposals have been put forward for restricting the role of juries or abolishing juries altogether. Significant reform proposals were drawn up by Sir Robin Auld but many of these have been rejected by the government. Parliament considered the Fraud (Trials Without Jury) Bill but this Bill to abolish the use of juries in many fraud trials, has not been passed.

Question and answer guides

1. (a) Explain the role of juries in both criminal cases and civil cases.

Plan

Criminal cases

- Juries hear criminal trials in the Crown Court of indictable offences and some either-way offences where the defendant pleads not guilty.

- They consider the evidence presented at court.
- The judge directs the jury on the law.
- The jury reach a verdict as to the defendant's guilt or innocence.
- The verdict is usually reached unanimously, though a majority verdict is possible.
- The judge can direct the jury to find the defendant not guilty where there is insufficient evidence for a reasonable jury to reach a guilty verdict.
- Only the judge decides the sentence.
- The jury need no legal qualifications as they are intended to represent the public.

Civil cases

- Today, juries play only a very limited role in the civil courts.
- Occasionally, they sit in the High Court and exceptionally the county court.
- A claimant has a right to a jury trial in cases of defamation, false imprisonment, malicious prosecution and civil fraud, although judges can refuse a jury trial if they consider it unsuitable and a claimant can expressly ask for a trial by judge rather than by jury.
- In civil cases the jury decide both the defendant's liability and the amount of damages to be awarded.

Answer

A jury holds an important symbolic role in the English legal system, as they represent justice being handed down by one's peers. The jury system dates back to the days of the Norman Conquest and was described by Lord Devlin as 'the lamp that shows that freedom lives'. In practice, the role of the jury today is very limited, particularly with regard to civil matters. It is governed by the Juries Act 1974.

Looking first at the jury role in criminal cases, they only sit in the Crown Court where they hear indictable offences and offences triable either way if either the defendant or the magistrate have elected a Crown Court trial. They are not required to do anything if the defendant pleads guilty. As only 5 per cent of all criminal cases are heard in the Crown Court, with the rest being heard in the magistrates' court, this means statistically juries are hearing only a small fraction of criminal cases. These are, however, the most important cases, including all murders, rapes and serious terrorist charges.

The jury consists of 12 independent people with no previous knowledge of the case or the parties. They are chosen at random from the electoral register and must therefore be entitled to vote. Anyone aged between 18 and 70 can be called and most of the past disqualifications and exemptions were removed by the Criminal Justice Act 2003. It is now possible for a Crown Court trial to have two judges in the courtroom – one managing the case and the other sitting as a citizen on a jury.

The jury decides the case on the basis of evidence presented before them in court. They have to decide whether the defendant is guilty or not guilty beyond reasonable doubt based on the facts given in the evidence. Juries can consider only the evidence presented and there have been some disturbing cases including one in which a jury was found to have used a ouija board to help decide a verdict (**R v Young**). If the judge decides that there is insufficient evidence in law upon which to reach a verdict, he or she can instruct the jury to formally find the defendant not guilty.

The judge directs the jury as to the relevant law for the case and sums up the case once all the evidence has been heard. The jury's verdict does not have to be explained to the court and their deliberations are in secret. In 80 per cent of cases a verdict is unanimous, although if after a few hours of deliberations there is no prospect of a unanimous verdict, judges can instruct that they are prepared to accept a majority verdict where at least 10 of the standard 12 jurors agree. If jurors are unable to reach even a majority verdict then they must be discharged and a new trial can be ordered with a different jury. If a defendant is convicted, the judge alone decides the sentence.

As regards the role of the jury in civil cases, claimants have a qualified right to a civil jury in High Court cases involving libel, false imprisonment, malicious prosecution or fraud. In other civil cases the appointment of a jury is at the discretion of the judge, who will take into account the sums involved in the case. Juries should not generally be used in personal injury claims unless there are special considerations that could justify the presence of a jury. Juries can also be used in coroners' courts to determine the cause of death at an inquest. A jury in a coroner's court will have between 7 and 11 jurors. A jury is currently hearing the inquest into the death of Princess Diana.

(b) Discuss the arguments for abolishing juries.

(OCR Specimen Paper 2007, English Legal System Unit)

Plan

Note that this question asked you only to discuss the arguments *in favour* of the abolition of the jury, arguments against its abolition were therefore not relevant and should not be mentioned.

- Some cases are too complex and time-consuming for juries, particularly serious fraud.
- You could discuss the collapsed Jubilee Line trial and the waste of taxpayers' money.
- Jurors are not required to have legal qualifications, or in fact any qualifications at all.
- Historically, they were clearly important, but today they are only used in a small minority of cases.
- They are expensive compared to, for example, magistrates.
- Sir Robin Auld found that many middle-class people were effectively opting out of jury service, but the government has subsequently tried to tighten up participation, otherwise the concept of judgment by one's peers is undermined.
- Participation on a jury can be distressing, owing to the nature of the case and also cause financial difficulties and family problems for the jury members.
- The size of the jury may be too big for an effective discussion.
- Sir Robin Auld was unhappy with 'perverse' verdicts which did not match the law.

- Risk of the jury's prejudices influencing their verdicts leading to a miscarriage of justice.
- It is difficult to bring an effective appeal against a jury verdict because they do not give reasons for their decision.

Group activity 1

Imagine you receive a letter in the post one morning informing you that you have been summoned to act as a juror.

- What should you do next?
- Why were you selected?
- When you are sitting in the jury box, how many other people will be sitting next to you?
- How long will you be required to sit as a juror?
- What happens if you have already booked a holiday which clashes with your jury service?

The government website on the criminal justice system will provide you with some useful information to help you think about the answers to these questions:

www.cjsonline.gov.uk/juror/

Group activity 2

- With your friends (or class), prepare a brief but balanced summary of the arguments for and against the use of juries in the English criminal justice system. The summary should be written in a style that can be understood by someone who knows nothing about the law.
- Divide your friends (or class) into groups of two or three people.
- Each group should invite six people of at least 18 years of age, having no knowledge of law, to read the summary and then answer the following questions. Try to get your interviewees to give reasoned answers, rather than just 'Yes' or 'No'.
  - Q1: Do you think that the use of juries in the English criminal justice system is a good thing?
  - Q2: Do you think that there should be any changes made to the use of juries in the English criminal justice system?
  - Q3: Would you be happy to serve on a jury if asked to do so?
  - Q4: Have you ever served on a jury before and, if so, what did you think of the experience?
- With your friends (or class), prepare a table summarising all the answers obtained by all the groups.
- Does this summary cause you to reconsider your own views on the jury system?

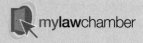

Visit **www.mylawchamber.co.uk/elliottocr** to access questions, quizzes and activities to test yourself on this chapter.

mylawchamber

Chapter 13
PAYING FOR LEGAL SERVICES

This chapter discusses:

- private funding of legal services;
- the Community Legal Service providing state funding for civil cases;
- the Criminal Defence Service providing state funding for criminal cases;
- the Public Defender Service;
- conditional fee agreements as an alternative method of funding legal proceedings;
- alternative sources of legal advice;
- criticisms and reform of the current funding arrangements.

Introduction

When people have a legal problem or requirement then they may decide to see a lawyer. They may be able to pay for that lawyer out of their own savings or because they have insurance which covers their legal expenses in the case. If they are paying from their private funds then they will be able to choose the lawyer that they can afford and that they consider will be best able to do the job for them. For example, they might want a lawyer to do the conveyancing work on the sale of a house and a neighbour might recommend a good lawyer to them. But lawyers can be expensive and sometimes the state is prepared to foot the bill rather than expecting private individuals to pay because it is important that everyone should be able to enforce their legal rights.

Unfortunately, cost is not the only thing which stops many ordinary people from using the legal system. Other issues, such as awareness of legal rights, the elitist image of the legal profession and even its geographical situation, all contribute to the problem which legal writers call 'unmet legal need' – where people have a legal problem, but fail to see a lawyer to resolve that problem.

State-funded legal services

The system of state-funded legal help in this country goes back over half a century. After the Second World War, the Labour government introduced a range of measures designed to address the huge inequalities between rich and poor. These included the National Health Service, the beginnings of today's social security system and, in 1949, the first state-funded legal aid scheme. The legal aid scheme was designed to allow poorer people access to legal advice and representation in court: this would be provided by solicitors in private practice, but the state, rather than the client, would pay all or part of the fees. By the 1980s, the system had developed into six different schemes, covering most kinds of legal case, and administered by the Legal Aid Board. But the growing cost of these schemes was causing concern. In the 1990s the Conservative government sought to keep the escalating costs down by reducing financial eligibility for the schemes, which in turn led to criticisms that they were also reducing access to justice. As a result of all this, the Labour government passed the Access to Justice Act 1999, which made major changes to the system.

With the passing of this legislation the government hoped to improve the quality and accessibility of the legal services on offer, while keeping a tighter control on their budget. On 1 April 2000 the Legal Aid Board was replaced by the Legal Services Commission. It currently has a budget of approximately £2 billion a year – effectively each taxpayer is contributing £100 annually to legal aid work. The Commission is an executive non-departmental public body reporting to the Minister of Justice. The minister provides guidance to the Commission on his priorities but is not allowed to give guidance about the handling of any individual case.

The schemes

The Legal Services Commission administers two schemes: the Community Legal Service, which is concerned with civil matters, and the Criminal Defence Service, which is concerned with criminal matters. These two schemes will be considered in turn.

The Community Legal Service

Funding

Before 1999, legal aid in civil cases was available on a demand-led basis (meaning that all cases which met the merits and means tests would be funded). There is now a Community Legal Service Fund, containing a fixed amount of money, set each year as part of the normal round of government spending plans.

The detailed way in which the fund is to be spent is decided by a Funding Code, drawn up by the Legal Services Commission and approved by the Lord Chancellor, which sets out the criteria and procedures to be used when deciding

*Community
Legal Service*

Figure 13.1
**The logo of
the Community
Legal Service**
Source: Legal
Services
Commission.

whether a particular case should be funded. The Commission has a duty to obtain the best value for money, which the explanatory notes to the Access to Justice Act 1999 define as taking into account 'a combination of price and quality'. In other words, the Commission is not obliged to choose the cheapest possible service, but it is not obliged to choose the best quality one either; it has to find the best balance between the two.

Levels of funded legal services

Only solicitors or advice agencies holding a contract with the Legal Services Commission are able to provide advice or representation directly funded by the Commission. For specialist areas of law, such as family law, immigration, mental health and clinical negligence, only specialist firms are funded to do the work. The merits test for civil legal aid has been replaced by the new Funding Code discussed above. This code lays down the rules as to which cases should receive funding. Direct funding is provided for different categories of legal service, as follows:

Legal Help

Legal Help provides initial advice and assistance with any legal problem. A means test is applied. This level of service covers work previously carried out under the 'green form' scheme.

Legal Representation

Funding is available for a person to be represented in court proceedings. Both a means and a merits test are applied. This scheme replaces civil legal aid.

Help at Court

Help at Court allows somebody (a solicitor or adviser) to speak on another's behalf at certain court hearings, without formally acting for them in the whole proceedings. A means test is applied.

Approved Family Help

Approved Family Help provides help in relation to a family dispute, including assistance in resolving that dispute through negotiation or otherwise. This overlaps with the services covered by Legal Help, but also includes issuing proceedings and representation where necessary to obtain disclosure of information from another party, or to obtain a consent order where the parties have reached an agreement.

Family Mediation

This level of service covers mediation for a family dispute, including finding out whether mediation appears suitable or not.

Coverage

Certain types of case have been removed from the state-funded system altogether. These are:

- Personal injury cases (with the exception of clinical negligence cases). Instead, these are funded by conditional fee agreements, which are discussed later in this chapter.
- Cases of defamation and malicious falsehood. Legal aid was never available for defamation. When the legal aid system was first established in 1949, defamation was excluded because the Attorney-General of the day was concerned that it would produce frivolous and unnecessary claims. While he accepted that the reputation of a poor person is just as deserving of legal protection as that of a wealthy person, he was worried that the legal aid scheme would be seriously overloaded if every slander uttered across the back garden wall could be pursued at the expense of the state. In some cases, behaviour which would normally be classed as defamation could be categorised as the related tort of malicious falsehood, for which legal aid was available. Now, neither is eligible for state funding. Under the Access to Justice Act 1999, legal aid can exceptionally be made available for such cases, but this has only happened once. Proceedings for defamation and malicious falsehood can, instead, be brought under a conditional fee agreement, discussed at p. 242.
- Disputes arising in the course of a business. Business traders can insure against the cost of having to bring or defend a legal action, and the government believes that taxpayers should not be required to meet the legal costs of those who fail to do so.
- Matters concerning the law relating to companies, partnerships, trusts (trusts are a way of holding property, and as such, tend mainly to affect wealthier people), or boundary disputes (for example, disputes between neighbours as to where each party's garden begins and ends).

The government considers that none of these types of case is sufficiently important to justify public funding. Approximately 80,000 people are injured each year at work, on the road or during a leisure activity. It has been estimated that personal injury cases accounted for around 60 per cent of cases previously funded by legal aid. However, the Access to Justice Act 1999 provides that a government minister can direct the Commission to provide services for excluded categories in exceptional circumstances.

Eligibility

Both a merits test and a means test are applied to determine whether funding for civil legal services will be awarded. A single means test applies. State funding is not available if a person earns more than £2,288 per month and if a person has £8,000 in savings.

The merits test is set out in the Funding Code and reflects the fact that certain cases should be given a higher priority for funding than others. For example, the chances of success might be relevant in many types of case, but would not be in cases about whether a child should be taken into local authority care.

Suppliers

In the past, a person who wanted help with a problem covered by legal aid could go to any lawyer and, provided the client met the relevant means and merits tests, that lawyer would be paid by the government for the help given in that particular case. This situation was beginning to change even before the 1999 Act was passed. Now only solicitors and advice agencies holding contracts with the Legal Services Commission are able to get state funding. Once they hold a contract, they are paid by the hour for their work.

The 1999 Act also gives the Commission power to make grants to service providers, such as advice centres, and to employ staff directly to deliver legal services to the public. This latter point means that the Commission could, if it wished, create a system of lawyers employed by the state to provide legal help to the public, though there appear to be no plans to do so with regard to civil cases at the moment.

Community Legal Advice

In 2004, Community Legal Advice was established. This is a national telephone and website service providing free legal advice on civil law matters. Members of the public can telephone the helpline on 0845 345 4345 for advice on such matters as housing, social security benefits and debt. Alternatively, they can visit the website at **www.clsdirect.org.uk**. This website is visited over 50,000 times each month. Community Legal Advice is intended to provide an alternative to face-to-face advice, which will be particularly attractive to those with mobility problems, caring responsibilities or accommodation in a remote area. In addition, some people may feel more comfortable talking about their problems with the relative anonymity of a telephone line, rather than in a face-to-face meeting.

Quick quiz 13.1

1 When was the Community Legal Service established?

2 What is the name of the body that administers the Community Legal Service?

3 What is the Funding code?

4 What are the five different categories of legal service that get direct funding as part of the Community Legal Service?

The Criminal Defence Service

In April 2001 a Criminal Defence Service was introduced, replacing the old system of criminal legal aid. This Criminal Defence Service is administered by the Legal Services Commission.

Funding

Unlike legal aid in civil cases, state-funded criminal defence work is still given on a demand-led basis; there is no set budget and all cases which fit the merits criteria and the means test are funded.

Levels of funded legal services

As part of this service, the Commission directly funds the provision of criminal legal services, employs public defenders and pays for duty solicitor schemes. Thus, under the Criminal Defence Service, legal services are provided by both lawyers in private practice and employed lawyers. The government believes that a mixed system of public and private lawyers will provide the best value for money for the taxpayer. The salaried service is intended to provide a benchmark to assess whether prices charged by private practice lawyers are reasonable, as well as filling in gaps in the system.

Direct funding

Only solicitor firms having a contract with the Legal Services Commission are able to offer state-funded criminal defence work. Unlike the contracts for civil matters, the contracts for criminal defence matters do not limit the number of cases that can be taken on, nor the total value of the payments that may be made. Contracted solicitors will be paid for all work actually undertaken in accordance with the contract. Solicitors with a contract should be able to provide the full range of criminal defence services, from the time of arrest until the end of the case (unlike under the previous system, where defendants could receive assistance relating to the same alleged offence under several different schemes, each resulting in a separate payment for the lawyers involved). In certain cases – such as serious fraud trials – there are panels of firms or individual lawyers who specialise in the relevant type of case, and defendants will be required to choose from that panel. State funding can support three types of service.

Advice and assistance. Funding is available for the provision of advice and assistance from a solicitor, including giving general advice, writing letters, negotiating, getting a barrister's opinion and preparing a written case. A means test is applied, but people who are eligible do not have to make any contribution to the legal costs. It does not cover representation in court.

When a person is questioned by the police, he or she has a right to free legal advice from a contracted solicitor and no means test is applied.

Advocacy assistance. Advocacy assistance covers the costs of a solicitor preparing a client's case and initial representation in certain proceedings in both the magistrates' court and the Crown Court and in certain other circumstances. There is no means test but there is a merits test.

Representation. When a person has been charged with a criminal offence, representation covers the cost of a solicitor to prepare the person's defence and to represent him/her in court. It may also be available for a bail application. It will sometimes pay for a barrister, particularly for the Crown Court and for the cost of an appeal.

Decisions to grant representation in individual cases are made by the magistrates' courts. Representation will be granted when it is in the 'interests of justice'. The court may decide that it is in the interests of justice to grant representation where, for example, the case is so serious that, on conviction, a person is likely to be sent to prison or to lose their job, where there are substantial questions of law to be argued, or where the defendant is unable to follow the proceedings and explain their case because they do not speak English well enough or are suffering from a psychiatric illness.

Means test

Before the Access to Justice Act 1999, criminal legal aid was means tested. The means test was criticised because most defendants were too poor to pay for their defence lawyers – only 1 per cent of applicants were refused criminal legal aid. As a result, the cost of administering the means test was more than the sum that was collected by defendants and the process also caused delays in the criminal system. The 1999 Act therefore abolished the means test for criminal cases. Instead, for cases heard in the Crown Court, orders could be issued at the end of a trial to recover the defence costs against wealthy people who have been convicted of an offence. Abolition of the means test led to concern in the media that some wealthy defendants were receiving legal aid when they could have comfortably afforded to pay themselves. Following such criticisms, the Criminal Defence Service Act 2006 has reintroduced a means test for criminal cases (apart from the first hearing, to avoid court delays). There remains a risk that these reforms will cause delays in the criminal system, both because evidence of means will need to be obtained and because the number of unrepresented defendants is likely to increase. The Criminal Justice and Immigration Bill contains some provisions to try and improve how means testing works in practice.

Public defender service

 Know your terms 13.2

Define the following terms:

1 Approved Family Help.
2 Means test.
3 Criminal Defence Service.
4 Public defender.

Since May 2001, the Legal Services Commission directly employs a number of criminal defence lawyers, known as public defenders. The public defenders can provide the same services as lawyers in private practice and have to compete for work.

There was strong opposition to the introduction of public defenders. The explanatory notes to the Access to Justice Act state that the idea is to provide flexibility, so that employed lawyers could be used if, for example, there is a shortage of suitable private lawyers in remoter areas. The notes point out that using salaried lawyers will also give the Commission better information about the real costs of providing the services. Public defenders will provide an element of competition with solicitors in private practice. They are required to follow a code of conduct guaranteeing certain standards of professional behaviour, including duties to avoid discrimination, to protect the interests of those whom they are defending, to avoid conflicts of interest and to maintain confidentiality.

The government had planned eventually to set up a national network of public defender offices. People suspected of crime would then have had a choice only between these public defenders and lawyers who had a contract with the Legal Services Commission, though within that limited range it was intended that there would be some choice in all but the most exceptional circumstances. However, following research carried out by Lee Bridges and others, entitled

Evaluation of the Public Defender Service in England and Wales (2007), the government concluded that four of the public defender offices were not delivering value for money and decided to close these down. It noted that all of the offices that were earmarked to be closed operated in areas with alternative criminal defence services, which was probably why they did not capture enough work to be cost effective. There are therefore four offices remaining and no plans at the moment to expand the scheme.

Duty solicitor schemes

Duty solicitors are available at police stations and magistrates' courts and offer free legal advice.

Criminal Defence Service Direct

A telephone service, known as Criminal Defence Service Direct (CDSD), was established in 2005 to provide telephone advice primarily to people detained by police for non-imprisonable offences who do not request to see their own lawyer. In addition, three pilot schemes have been established where telephone advice can be provided to any individual detained in a police station who is charged with a summary or either-way offence. For minor offences on the pilot scheme, the suspect will not be entitled to see their own solicitor, but will be obliged to use the telephone service. If these pilot schemes are successful, the role of the CDSD will be expanded nationally. The Legal Services Commission considers that telephone advice is a modern and appropriate way to assist people detained at police stations who are accused of less serious offences. It is also much cheaper than face-to-face advice. CDSD attempts to contact the client within 15 minutes of being informed of the case. In over half of cases the police fail to pick up the telephone, which causes delay.

Advice agencies

There are a number of non-profit-making agencies which give legal advice and sometimes representation, and initiatives by the legal profession and other commercial organisations also address the issue of access to justice.

Law centres

Law centres offer a free, non-means-tested service to people who live or work in their area. They aim to be accessible to anyone who needs legal help, and in order to achieve this usually operate from ground floor, high street premises, stay open beyond office hours, employ a high proportion of lay people as well as lawyers and generally encourage a more relaxed atmosphere than that found in most private solicitors' offices. Most law centres are run by a management committee drawn from the local area, so that they have direct links with the community.

The first law centres were established in 1969; today there are around 50 of them. The Law Society allowed them to advertise (before the restriction on advertising was lifted for solicitors in general) in exchange for the centres not undertaking certain areas of work which were the mainstay of the average high street solicitor – small personal injury cases, wills and conveyancing. Their main areas of work are housing, welfare, immigration and employment.

Law centres are largely funded by grants from central and local government, though a few have also managed to secure some financial support from large local private firms. This method of funding means that they do not have to work on a case-by-case basis but can allocate funding according to community priorities.

Because they do not depend on case-by-case funding, law centres have developed innovative ways of solving legal problems. As well as dealing with individual cases, they run campaigns designed to make local people aware of their legal rights, act as a pressure group on local issues such as bad housing, and take action where appropriate on behalf of groups as well as individuals. The reasoning behind this approach is that resources and time are better used tackling problems as a whole, rather than aspects of those problems as they appear case by case. For example, if a council has failed to replace lead piping or asbestos in its council houses, it would seem more efficient to approach the council about all the properties rather than take out individual cases for each tenant as they become aware that they have a problem.

Law centres also provide valuable services in areas not covered by the statutory schemes, such as inquests, and several have set up duty solicitor schemes to deal with housing cases in the county court and help prevent evictions. They may offer a 24-hour general emergency service.

Most law centres face long-term problems with funding; several have closed, and others go through periodic struggles for survival. It is hoped that the Access to Justice Act, with its emphasis on making the most of voluntary advice services, will mean better funding in future. The danger is that local authorities will withdraw funding as funding becomes available from the Legal Services Commission.

Community Legal Advice Centres

In 2006 the Legal Service Commission established two pilot Community Legal Advice Centres (CLACs); it aims to establish a total of 75 in the future. The result would be a national network of legal aid suppliers working like the National Health Service. The idea is to tackle the full range of social welfare problems (such as debt, housing and employment) in a 'one-stop shop' for clients. CLACs will be situated in deprived areas. The director of the Law Centres Federation has observed that CLACs look remarkably like Law Centres and suggests that the government would be better off building on the strengths of the law centre 'brand' and funding more law centres, rather than creating competitors under a new brand.

Citizens' Advice Bureaux

There are around 700 Citizens' Advice Bureaux (CAB) across the country, offering free advice and help with a whole range of problems, though the most common areas at the moment are social security and debt. They are largely staffed by trained volunteers, who can become expert in the areas they most frequently deal with. Where professional legal help is required, some bureaux employ solicitors, some have regular help from solicitor volunteers and others refer individuals to local solicitors who undertake state-funded work. The bureaux are overseen by the National Association of Citizens' Advice Bureaux and must conform to its standards and codes of practice.

Task 13.3

Imagine that you are homeless with two children. You want to find out whether you have any rights to accommodation. Go to the Legal Services Commission website at **www.clsdirect.org.uk** and see whether you can find any useful information.

The Citizens' Advice Bureau provides advice online at **www.adviceguide.org.uk.** Compare the information that is available on this website.

One of the major advantages of CABs is a very high level of public awareness – because they are frequently mentioned in the press and have easily recognisable high street offices, most people know where they are and what they do.

Like law centres, they have come under considerable financial pressure in recent years, with the result that many can only open for a very limited number of hours a week. The Access to Justice Act may mean better funding in future.

Alternative sources of legal advice

Some local authorities run money, welfare, consumer and housing advice centres to provide both advice and a mechanism for dealing with complaints, while charities such as Shelter, the Child Poverty Action Group and MIND often offer legal help in their specialist areas. Other organisations, such as trade unions, motoring organisations, such as the AA and RAC, and the Consumers' Association give free or inexpensive legal help to their members. Some university law faculties run 'law clinics', where students, supervised by their tutors, give free help and advice to members of the public.

There are a number of internet sites giving basic legal advice for free, and some magazines publish legal advice lines, which charge a premium rate for readers to phone and get one-to-one legal advice from qualified solicitors. It is also possible to insure against legal expenses, either as a stand-alone policy or, more usually, as part of household, credit card or motor insurance.

As we saw earlier, cost is not the only cause of unmet legal need; a reluctance among many ordinary people to bring problems to lawyers is also recognised. In recent years, the profession has taken steps to address the issue, including the use of advertising and public relations campaigns. Many high street firms now advertise their services locally, while some of the firms currently involved in suing cigarette manufacturers for illnesses caused by smoking attracted potential clients by advertising specifically for people with smoking-related diseases.

Task 13.4

In 2003 the government issued a consultation paper, *Delivering Value for Money in the Criminal Defence Service*. The government wished to consult the public on proposed changes to the Criminal Defence Service. The end of the document contained a list of questions on which it wished to know the public's views before proceeding to introduce any reforms. These questions included the following:

1 Do you consider that access to free police station advice should be reduced? Would this adversely affect the rights of clients?
2 What types of police station advice should still be funded?
3 What impact would restricting the court duty solicitor scheme have upon the rights of the defendants?
4 What impact do you consider restricting the court duty solicitor scheme would have on the administration of the magistrates' courts?
5 What impact do you consider restricting the court duty solicitor scheme would have upon the number of defendants appearing without representation?

If you were preparing a response to the government, how would you answer these questions?

The Access to Justice Act: an assessment

The Access to Justice Act 1999 was the subject of much opposition during the legislative process, and though some of the criticisms were addressed during the passing of the Act, some of this opposition remains. Below we detail the main criticisms, but first we look at some of the advantages claimed for the reformed system.

Advantages of the Access to Justice Act reforms

Control of costs

Before 1999 the cost of the legal aid system was considered a major problem. The government claims that the issuing of contracts, the fixed budget for state funding in civil cases and the fact that the Funding Code sets out clear criteria which reflect agreed priorities, will help keep costs under control.

A report from the National Audit Office (2003) has identified significant improvements that have taken place in the administration of state funding of legal services, with the creation of the Community Legal Service. The new funding arrangements have led to greater control and targeting of resources and better scrutiny of suppliers.

Better allocation of resources

The Funding Code for civil matters is designed to reflect agreed priorities, so money can be channelled into those areas which the government considers best reflect the needs of society.

Higher standards of work

By limiting state funding to contracted lawyers and firms who have passed quality control standards, the government claims that standards of work should be consistently high. The quality assurance mark will be used to spread high standards beyond law firms, to any organisation which might offer legal advice to the public. In addition, the Lord Chancellor suggested (*The Times*, 7 September 1999) that the creation of defence lawyers employed by the Commission would create a 'healthy rivalry' with private criminal lawyers and so stimulate them to give a better service.

Disadvantages of the reforms

Access to justice

The reforms were intended to improve access to justice, but they seem to have achieved the opposite. Because many state-funded legal services can only be obtained from lawyers who have a contract with the Legal Services Commission, members of the public are finding it increasingly difficult to find a state-funded lawyer with the relevant expertise close to their home.

Part of the problem is that many law firms have in the past done a small amount of legal aid work alongside their privately funded work. Such firms have not wanted to bid for block contracts because they have not wanted to increase the amount of comparatively poorly paid state-funded work they take on. There are now only 5,000 solicitor firms offering state-funded legal services, compared with 11,000 under the old legal aid system. Between January 2000 and June 2003 the number of civil contracts offered for housing law fell by a third from 743 to 489. In the same period, contracts for debt law fell by more than half, from 462 to 206. One result, many fear, will be the creation of a two-tier legal profession, with one set of firms doing poorly paid state-funded work and another doing exclusively private work.

The National Audit Office (2003) has identified a problem of lawyers opting out of contracting in family work. It also points to a need for more lawyers to undertake work in community care, housing and mental health. A study undertaken by the Citizens' Advice Bureaux (2004) has reinforced this picture of growing gaps in the supply of state-funded legal services, what it calls 'advice deserts'. Their survey found that people were often having to travel up to 50 miles to find a lawyer. Over two-thirds of Citizens' Advice Bureaux said they had difficulty finding a legal aid immigration lawyer for clients, and 60 per cent reported problems finding solicitors to deal with housing and family law problems. The Legal Services Commission has, however, rejected the suggestion that there are legal aid 'advice deserts'. It has pointed out that almost 95 per cent of the population lives within five miles of a civil legal aid provider. It has also stated that the number of people who received civil legal help in 2005/06 was at a six-year high.

State funding is not available for legal representation at most tribunals.

Problems with conditional fee agreements

The Access to Justice Act 1999 removed personal injury cases from the state funding system, so that these can only be funded privately or by a conditional fee agreement. Much of the criticism of the current funding arrangements is concerned with the use of these conditional fee agreements, which are discussed at pp. 242–248.

Cost-cutting

Critics, including the legal professions and some MPs, have accused the government of putting cost-cutting before access to justice. The chairperson of the Legal Aid Practitioners Group, Richard Miller, told *The Lawyer* newspaper in December 1998 that he believed the fixed budget for civil matters was designed to make it easy for the government to cut the amount spent in later years: 'The Legal Services Commission will simply be able to say, this is the budget and if there are any more cases, tough luck.'

Public defenders

The legal profession has fiercely opposed the idea of the Commission employing its own lawyers to do criminal defence work. Both the Bar Council and the Criminal Law Solicitors Association have expressed concern that lawyers who are wholly dependent on the state for their income cannot be sufficiently independent to defend properly people suspected of crime – people who, by definition, are on the opposite side to the state.

The experience of foreign jurisdictions such as the US and Canada shows that any system of public defenders must be properly funded and staffed if it is to retain the confidence of providers, users and the courts. Unfortunately, they are frequently under-funded in practice, relying as a result on inexperienced lawyers with excessive case loads and who are not respected by their clients, opponents or the court.

sourcebook
p. 192 → Research carried out by Cyrus Tata and others (2004) has evaluated the success of the Public Defence Solicitors Office in Scotland in its first three years. The research compared the performance of the public defenders with that of solicitors in private practice receiving state funding. The conclusions of this research were mixed. It found that public defender clients pleaded guilty earlier than clients of solicitors in private practice. But it found no evidence to suggest that public defenders put explicit pressure on clients to plead guilty. Instead, the clients criticised the public defenders for being too neutral and too willing to go along with whatever the client decided. The change in economic incentives involved in receiving a salary rather than a legal aid payment appeared to produce a change in behaviour, because solicitors in private practice earn very little if a client immediately pleads guilty, so ending the case, compared to where there is a late guilty plea. Public defender clients were more likely to be convicted. Representation by a public defender increased the chances of a client being convicted from around 83 per cent to 88 per cent. This was primarily because clients of private solicitors were more likely to plead late, allowing for a greater chance in the meantime for the case against them to be dropped by the prosecution, for example because a witness fails to attend the trial. There was no difference between the sentences handed down.

The levels of trust and satisfaction expressed by public defender clients who had not volunteered to use the service, but been obliged to do so, was consistently lower than those expressed by clients using private practitioners. They were less likely to say that their solicitor had done 'a very good job' in listening to what they had to say; telling them what was happening; being there when they wanted them; or having enough time for them. They were also less likely to agree strongly that the solicitor had told the court their side of the story or treated them as though they mattered. Part of the problem appears to have been that clients resented not being able to choose their solicitor and this choice has now been reinstated. Those who had chosen to use the public defender service were more positive about the service. However, they were still significantly less likely than private clients to agree strongly that their lawyer had told the court their side of the story or had treated them as if they mattered, rather than as 'a job to be done'. Public defenders tended to be seen as more 'business-like' and less personally committed than private solicitors. Public defender clients were less likely to say that they would use the service again compared to clients of private solicitors.

The research concluded:

> 'From a managerial perspective, the fact that public defenders resolved cases at an earlier stage has advantages. It has the potential to save legal aid costs and also reduce court and prosecution costs, inconveniencing fewer witnesses. Clients were spared the wait and worry of repeated court [hearings] and were less likely to be held in detention pending the resolution of their case.'

At the moment, surprisingly, the public defender service is proving more expensive than private solicitors. The average cost of a case handled by the public defender service is over £800, compared to £506 for private practice. The Legal Aid Practitioners Group has suggested that this is because the taxpayer has to pay the salary of public defenders even if they have failed to attract clients, while private solicitors are only paid for the work they do.

Poorer standards of work

A survey carried out in 1999 for the Legal Aid Practitioners Group found that 84 per cent of legal aid firms believed the Act's reliance on exclusive contracts would reduce the quality of legal services.

The Consumers' Association undertook research in 2001 into the experiences of people seeking help from the Community Legal Service. The research consisted of in-depth interviews of people who had sought help from the service, particularly those from vulnerable groups in society. It found that community centres and law centres provided the best help and advice, but many people felt that the legal system gave them a second-rate service. The research criticised the apparent lack of commitment and poor communication of some solicitors. There were still not enough solicitors and advisers specialising in areas like social security, housing, disability discrimination, employment and immigration law. People with disabilities complained of poor physical access to buildings.

The Legal Services Commission has paid for some research into the impact of different funding arrangements on the quality of the provision of legal services (Moorhead (2001) *Quality and Cost: Final Report on the Contracting of Civil, Non-family Advice and Assistance Pilot*). A study was undertaken over two years of

80,000 cases handled by 43 not-for-profit agencies and 100 solicitor firms. The solicitor firms were randomly allocated to one of three payment groups: those who continued to be paid as under the old green form system; those paid a fixed sum and left to determine how many cases it was reasonable for them to do for the money; and those paid a fixed sum and given a specific number of cases which had to be undertaken. The research concluded that where the payment system gave firms an incentive to do work cheaply, the quality of work suffered. Thus, firms in the third group performed worst on most indicators, with 20 per cent of the contracted advisers doing poor quality work. Group 2, in general, performed better than Group 1.

In his *Review of the Criminal Courts* (2001), Sir Robin Auld has recommended that changes should be made to the arrangements for the payment of defence lawyers so that they are rewarded for carrying out adequate case preparation.

Quick quiz 13.5

1 Give three advantages of the Access to Justice Act 1999 reforms.

2 Give three disadvantages of the Access to Justice Act 1999 reforms.

3 Research carried out by the Consumers' Association raised concerns about the standards of work carried out by the Community Legal Service. What were these concerns?

4 What does the Citizens Advice Bureau mean by an 'advice desert'.

Over-billing

Lawyers may be charging the government too much for their work. Audits conducted by the Legal Services Commission of case files kept by suppliers suggest that 35 per cent of suppliers were claiming 20 per cent more than they should have been, although some suppliers have complained about the basis of some of these decisions.

The cost of criminal cases

It seems that currently 1 per cent of criminal cases consume 49 per cent of the budget for the Criminal Defence Service. Following the publication of a consultation paper, *Delivering Value for Money in the Criminal Defence Service* (Lord Chancellor's Department, 2003), the government has tried to reduce the cost of these cases. Lawyers working on cases lasting more than five weeks, or costing more than £150,000 have to negotiate contracts for payment at each stage of the case.

The government paper, *A Fairer Deal for Legal Aid* (2005), gives details of plans to reduce the length of high cost criminal cases, by for example, removing juries from serious fraud cases and improving case management by judges. Lawyers will not be paid for time spent when a trial overruns.

Criminal barristers consider that they are underpaid for their work and in 2005 they effectively took strike action (they could not officially strike because they were self-employed and not members of a trade union). Fixed fees for Crown Court trials lasting up to ten days were introduced in 1997. The remuneration for these cases has been frozen since it came into force and this represents a 22.5 per cent pay cut in real terms. It has been estimated that junior criminal barristers relying on legal aid work, with up to five years' experience, are earning only between £15,000 and £30,000 a year. They are paid just £46.50 to attend a Crown Court hearing which is not a trial, even though this can take up a whole day due to court delays.

At the moment, the government allocates a single budget to both civil and criminal state funding of legal services. Within this budget criminal defence work takes priority. So while the cost of criminal legal aid is expanding, this leaves less and less for civil legal aid. In 2004 the national legal aid budget was £2 billion, and 60 per cent of this was spent on criminal legal aid. Spending on civil legal aid fell by 22 per cent between 1997 and 2006.

Conditional fee agreements

In the US, a great many cases brought by ordinary individuals are funded by what are called contingency fees, or 'no win, no fee' agreements. Lawyers can agree with clients that no fee will be charged if they lose the case, but if they win, the fee will be an agreed percentage of the damages won. This obviously gives the lawyer a direct personal interest in the level of damages, and there have been suggestions that this is partly responsible for the soaring levels of damages seen in the US courts.

In the English legal system, contingency fees are banned, but in 1990 the Courts and Legal Services Act (CLSA) made provision for the introduction of conditional fee agreements. Under a conditional fee agreement, solicitors can agree to take no fee or a reduced fee if they lose, and raise their fee by an agreed percentage if they win, up to a maximum of double the usual fee. The solicitor calculates the extra fee (usually called the 'uplift' or 'success fee') on the basis of the size of the risk involved – if the client seems very likely to win, the uplift will generally be lower than in a case where the outcome is more difficult to predict. The rule that the losing party must pay the winner's costs remains, so a party using a conditional fee agreement will usually take out insurance to cover this if he or she should lose.

 Know your terms 13.6

Define the following terms:

1 Duty solicitor.
2 Pilot scheme.
3 Law centre.
4 Conditional fee agreement.

The Access to Justice Act 1999 makes some changes to the arrangements for conditional fee agreements in order to promote their use. Where a person who has made a conditional fee agreement wins his or her case, it will be possible for the court to order the losing party to pay the success fee, as well as the normal legal costs. Thus, the success fee is now only ever payable by the losing party, which is a complete reversal of the previous situation. This provision is designed to meet the criticism that damages are calculated to compensate the litigant for the damage done to him or her, so if the 'uplift' has to come out of the client's damages, the amount left will be less than the court calculated as necessary for the purpose of full compensation.

Similarly, where a winning litigant has taken out insurance to provide for payment of the other side's costs if he or she loses, the court can order that the other side also pays the cost of the insurance premium. As a result, people who are bringing actions for remedies other than the payment of money can use a conditional fee arrangement. These changes have caused problems in practice. The cost of after-the-event insurance has increased considerably, and some clients are finding it difficult to obtain such insurance. There has been a lot of litigation over paying these extra costs by the losing party. To try to reduce this problem, new rules of court have been written, which fix the success fee for particular types of litigation, such as road traffic accidents, depending on the circumstances of the case. For example, where litigation involves an accident at work and the employee brings a claim on the basis of a conditional fee agreement; if that action is successful, the employer's insurer will pay the employee's solicitor their normal costs, plus a success fee of 25 per cent of these costs if the case settled before trial, and a 100 per cent success fee for a riskier case that went to trial. It might be better if the sums were simply covered by judges increasing the award of damages to take into account these extra expenses.

There is no means test to determine whether a person is entitled to bring litigation on the basis of a conditional fee agreement. Naomi Campbell had brought legal proceedings against the publishers of the *Daily Mirror*. The case claimed that the newspaper had breached her right to privacy because it had published pictures of her leaving a support group for recovering drug users. Her claim was rejected by the Court of Appeal and she proceeded to appeal to the House of Lords. To pay for this appeal she reached a conditional fee agreement with her solicitors and her barrister. Her appeal to the House of Lords was successful and the publishing company was ordered to pay her £3,500 in damages and her costs. Her costs were £1,086,295.47 in total. The size of the bill for the appeal to the House of Lords was particularly high because the conditional fee agreement allowed for a success fee of 95 per cent for her solicitor and 100 per cent for her barrister. The publishers contested these costs, arguing that the success fee was so disproportionate that it infringed their rights to free speech under Art. 10 of the European Convention on Human Rights. They argued that, as Naomi Campbell was a rich celebrity, she could have afforded to fund her litigation without a conditional fee agreement, while the conditional fee agreement scheme was intended to help people who could not otherwise afford to sue. The House of Lords rejected this argument – conditional fee agreements were not means tested, and the publishers had to pay all the costs.

The Access to Justice Act 1999 made conditional fee agreements available for all cases apart from medical negligence. The government is now considering stopping state funding for medical negligence actions, so that these too would fall within the remit of conditional fee agreements. The consultation paper, *A New Focus for Civil Legal Aid: encouraging early resolution; discouraging unnecessary litigation* (2005), suggests that medical negligence cases could be transferred to the conditional fee agreement system after research into the possible impact of this change has been completed. It is questionable whether conditional fees are appropriate for such cases. They are generally very difficult for claimants to win – the success rate is around 17 per cent, compared with 85 per cent for other personal injury claims (often caused by road accidents). While the outcome of litigation arising from a road accident is often reasonably easy to predict, medical negligence cases require detailed reports before anyone can hazard a guess about whether any party is to blame. The evidence is that solicitors will only take on a case under a conditional fee agreement if they estimate there is at least a 70 per cent chance of being successful. It can cost between £2,000 and £5,000 simply to do the initial investigations necessary to assess accurately whether the case is worth pursuing. As a result, solicitors would be very unlikely to want to take on such cases on a conditional fee basis and, even if they did, the uncertainty of outcome means that insurance against losing would be extremely expensive, possibly amounting to thousands of pounds. On the other hand, removing state funding could be an effective way of reducing the National Health Service's legal costs. In 2003 the NHS was facing a record £4.4 billion bill in outstanding negligence claims.

The government is currently considering introducing collective conditional fee agreements. These are designed for bulk users of legal services such as trade unions and insurers.

Advantages of conditional fee agreements

Cost to the state

Conditional fee agreements cost the state nothing – the costs are entirely borne by the solicitor or the losing party, depending on the outcome. By removing the huge number of personal injury cases from state funding and promoting conditional fee agreements for them instead, the government claims it can devote more resources to those cases which still need state funding, such as tenants' claims against landlords, and direct more money towards suppliers of free legal advice, such as Citizens' Advice Bureaux.

Wider access to justice

The government believes that conditional fee agreements will allow many people to bring or defend cases, who would not have been eligible for state funding and who could not previously have afforded to bring cases at their own expense. As long as they can afford to insure against losing, and can persuade a solicitor that the case is worth the risk, anyone will be able to bring or defend a case for damages. Critics point out that there are a number of problems with this argument (see below).

Performance incentives

Supporters claim conditional fees encourage solicitors to perform better, since they have a financial interest in winning cases funded this way.

Wider coverage

Conditional fee agreements are allowed for defamation actions, and cases brought before tribunals: two major gaps in the provision of state funding.

Public acceptance

The Law Society suggests that clients have readily accepted conditional fee agreements in those areas where they have been permitted in the past. Within two years of the agreements being introduced, almost 30,000 conditional fee agreements had been signed, and by 1999 around 25,000 were in operation.

Fairness to opponents

There are restrictions on the costs state-funded clients can be made to pay to the other side, which can give them an unfair advantage, particularly in cases where both sides are ordinary individuals but only one has qualified for state funding. The requirement for insurance in conditional fee cases solves this problem.

Disadvantages of conditional fee agreements

Uncertain cases

Most of those who have criticised the legislation on conditional fee agreements accept that they are a good addition to the state-funded system, but are concerned that they may not be adequate as a substitute. In particular, critics – including the Bar, the Law Society, the Legal Action Group, and the Vice-Chancellor of the Supreme Court, Sir Richard Scott – have expressed strong concerns that certain types of case will lose out under the new rules. They suggest that solicitors will only want to take on cases under conditional fee agreements where there is a very high chance of winning. It was for this reason that medical negligence cases have been kept within the state-funded system.

Unfair trials

sourcebook
p. 187 → Where legal aid is refused, a subsequent trial may prove to be unfair if one party is unrepresented by a lawyer as a result, and the other party benefited from legal representation. This can amount to a breach of Art. 6 of the European Convention, which guarantees the right to a fair trial. The problem was highlighted by the case which has come to be known as the McLibel Two (**Steel *v* United Kingdom** (2005)). The defendants were two environmental campaigners who had distributed leaflets outside McDonalds' restaurants. These leaflets criticised the nutritional content of the food sold in the restaurants. McDonald's sued the two defendants for defamation. The defendants were refused legal aid because it is not generally available for defamation cases (see p. 230). They therefore represented themselves throughout the proceedings, with only limited help from some sympathetic lawyers who provided a small amount of assistance for free. McDonald's were represented by a team of specialist lawyers. The libel trial lasted for 313 days and was the longest civil action in English legal history. The defendants lost the case and were ordered to pay £60,000 in damages (later reduced to £40,000 on appeal). They challenged the fairness of the UK proceedings in the European Court of Human Rights. That challenge was successful. The European Court held that the McLibel Two had not had a fair trial in breach of Art. 6 of the European Convention on Human Rights and there had been a breach of their right to freedom of expression under Art. 10 of the Convention.

Claimants misled

The Citizens Advice Bureau has issued a report entitled *No Win, No Fee, No Chance* (2005). This expresses concern that consumers are being misled by the term 'no win, no fee'. Often consumers find that the system costs them more than they gain. Consumers are subjected to aggressive and high-pressured sales tactics from unqualified employees of claims management companies. These companies receive a fee from solicitors for passing them a case. Consumers can be subjected to inappropriate marketing tactics, for example, accident victims have been approached in hospital. Consumers are not informed clearly of the financial risks that the legal proceedings will involve, and are misled into believing that the system will genuinely be 'no win, no fee'. In fact, consumers may need to take out an insurance policy to offset any legal expenses incurred if they lose the case and are required to pay the other side's costs. If the claim is, for example, against the council for failure to repair a council flat, a building surveyor may need to be paid as well as the lawyers. These legal expenses can be artificially inflated by unscrupulous claims management companies. The consumer can be encouraged to take out a loan to pay the monthly instalments of the insurance policy. The consumer frequently discovers that these expenses have wiped out any compensation they win. The injured person does not as a result benefit from the compensation they are entitled to. In some cases, the consumer even ends up owing money. In one case handled by the Citizens Advice Bureau a woman was left with just £15 from a £2,150 compensation payout, and in another case a man received compensation of £1,250 for an accident at work, but owed nearly £2,400 for insurance relating to the litigation.

In **Bowen and ten others** *v* **Bridgend County Borough Council** (2004) the litigation had arisen when employees of a claims management company had knocked on council tenants' doors suggesting that claims could be made. An action was brought against the council for failing to carry out housing repairs. The claimants had taken out loans to pay for insurance policies to cover any legal expenses they incurred. The average compensation paid to claimants was £1,631, but the claimants' solicitors sought an average of £8,000 in costs against the local authority. In fact, the court only ordered £250 to be paid, holding that many of the legal fees were unjustified and not payable.

The government has issued a consultation paper, *Making Simple CFAs a Reality* (2004). This is looking at how conditional fee agreements can be improved. It is also intending to improve the regulation of claims management companies through

provisions contained in the Compensation Act 2006.

Insurance costs

There are concerns that insurance against losing can be expensive. In the area of personal injury, the Law Society provides an affordable insurance scheme, but in other areas the only suppliers are private insurance companies, which charge according to risk, so that clients with cases where the outcome is uncertain may be faced with very high premiums.

Both the Law Society and the Bar have suggested that a better idea would be the establishment of a self-financing contingency fund, which would pay for cases on the understanding that successful litigants would pay a proportion of their damages back to the fund. As mentioned above, this is allowed by the Act, but the government has said it has no plans to use the power at the moment.

Insurance pressures

There may also be pressure to settle from insurance companies, some of which have been known to threaten to withdraw their cover if a client refuses to accept an offer of settlement that the insurance company considers reasonable. Clearly, the insurance company's primary interest will be to avoid having to pay out, so it is not difficult to see that their idea of a reasonable settlement might be very different from the client's – or from what the client could expect to get if the case continued.

Financial involvement of lawyers

The Bar has criticised the idea of allowing lawyers a financial interest in the outcome of a case. In a letter to the Lord Chancellor, the Chair of the Bar Council argued that, since clients generally lack the knowledge to assess their chances of winning their case, lawyers will be able to charge whatever they think they can get away with (within the set limits). This seems a rather strange argument for a representative of the legal profession to put forward, and critics have widely suggested that the real reason behind this and the other criticisms made by the legal profession is that lawyers were reluctant to lose the no-risk income that state-funded legal aid allowed them.

The evidence on solicitors' approach to the uplift on fees is currently rather inconclusive. A 1997 report by Yarrow for the Policy Studies Institute on the effects of the changes made under the Courts and Legal Services Act 1990 found that the average uplift was 43 per cent, less than half the 100 per cent maximum allowed – but within that average, one in ten solicitors was charging between 90 per cent and 100 per cent. The author of the study, Stella Yarrow, commented that the number of cases assessed as having a low chance of success was surprisingly large, suggesting that solicitors might be underestimating the chances of winning in order to increase the uplift.

In 1999, the Forum of Insurance Lawyers (FOIL) suggested that the chance to make extra money was encouraging solicitors to push clients into conditional fee agreements, even where the clients did not need such an agreement. Around 17 million people in Britain have some form of legal expenses insurance attached to their home, car or credit card insurance, and in many cases this will pay their legal costs for them. However, FOIL points out, many people have this insurance without realising it, and it claims that instead of suggesting that clients check whether they have it, solicitors are persuading them into unnecessary conditional fee agreements.

Abuse in defamation proceedings

There is concern that conditional fee agreements are being used inappropriately in defamation proceedings, and thereby threatening the right to freedom of expression. Following a critical newspaper article, it is easy for a person to bring proceedings for defamation at no expense to themselves, but the newspaper is forced to incur considerable expense to defend such a claim. While it may be clear that a newspaper article damages the reputation of the claimant, the burden of proof will pass to the defendant to show, for example, that the article was true or fair comment. As a result, there needs to be strong case management by judges in defamation cases and the capping of costs where appropriate.

Lord Carter's reforms

In 2005, the Lord Chancellor asked Lord Carter to carry out a review of the legal aid system. Major reforms to the system have now been recommended by Lord Carter in his report, *Legal aid: a market-based approach to reform* (2006). Immediately after the publication of this report, the government issued a consultation paper, *Legal Aid: a sustainable future* (2006). This latter paper considers many of Lord Carter's recommendations.

Lord Carter has recommended that a new procurement regime should be introduced in 2009. To prepare for this procurement process a national system of peer review should be undertaken from 2007. Peer review means that law firms are assessed for the quality of their service by their peers, in other words other experienced and independent solicitors. This process of assessment would become the responsibility of the Law Society. The peer review system would identify firms who had attained the requisite quality thresholds, known as preferred suppliers, and they would be invited to apply for a contract with the Legal Services Commission. The tendering competition would be decided according to which firm bid to do the most work for the lowest price. A pilot scheme of a preferred supplier system, involving 25 firms throughout 2004–5, was shown to reduce bureaucracy and raise standards of service, as well as improve the relationship between the Legal Services Commission and legal aid firms. Legal aid lawyers have been strongly opposed to the introduction of competitive tendering and have pointed to hospital cleaning, school dinners and prison transport as examples of why tendering should not be used as a procurement mechanism.

Lord Carter criticised the current criminal legal aid system for spending money on 'unproductive time and anomalies in the system'. Payment is calculated on the basis of the number of hours spent on a case, and does not therefore reward efficiency. He recommends that criminal legal aid lawyers should no longer be paid by the hour, but by the case. Fixed fees will be introduced across the board for criminal cases, calculated according to the type of case. Fees will be front-loaded to encourage early preparation and discourage trials. It is argued that a fixed fee regime allows efficient firms to be more profitable since they expend less input to produce the same quality service and get the same fee as a less efficient firm.

'Fixed pricing rewards efficiency and suppliers who can deliver increased volumes of work. However, pricing should be graduated for more complex work so that cases genuinely requiring more expertise and effort are priced fairly.'

Also, under the new proposals, efficient firms would be able to win new contracts in the best value tendering process.

Lord Carter is also of the view that large law firms are more efficient than small ones. He predicts that his recommendations for procurement contracts, combined with the implementation of Sir David Clementi's recommendations (see p. 174) will lead to 'an increase in the average size of firms through growth and mergers, rationalization and harmonization of the way separate services are delivered'. To encourage this move towards larger law firms, the Legal Services Commission is proposing to grant legal aid contracts which are worth at least £25,000. Contracts could be awarded to either individual firms or a collection of firms formed to deliver the benefits of scale. Thus, there will be a move towards granting fewer and larger contracts. The number of people involved might not change dramatically but they would work for fewer employers.

Lord Carter considers that it is uneconomic for both the Legal Services Commission and solicitors to deliver small amounts of legal aid work. Grants should be made available to support this transition, including money for investment in computer technology and modernisation. The government's consultation paper suggests that it would be prepared to provide some practical support to law firms during this period of transition but not financial grants. Lord Carter argues that this reorganisation will be in the interests of legal aid lawyers, saying that sole practitioners (lawyers working in an office on their own) are likely to earn between £36,000 and £55,000, while equity partners in a legal aid firm with 40 fee earners could expect to earn between £120,000 and £150,000.

The aim of these reforms is to control the cost and quality of legal aid and to promote efficiency of service in the public interest. Lord Carter predicts that implementation of his proposals could lead to a saving of £100 million a year, with criminal legal aid costing 20 per cent less than in 2005. He suggests that, without these new procurement reforms, the same sort of price inflation as seen in the past decade would more than likely be repeated in the future.

The reform proposals have been the subject of considerable criticism from legal aid lawyers. Respondents to a consultation paper on price-competitive tendering issued by the Legal Services Commission in 2005, found that 85 per cent of respondents were opposed to this system. Sixty per cent said the proposals would have a negative effect on the quality of legal advice. Lord Carter's strategy has been dismissed by critics as 'pile them high, sell them cheap'. Black and minority ethnic solicitors frequently work as sole practitioners or in small legal aid firms, and this has led to concern that such firms may suffer if these reforms are introduced. The reforms are likely to lead to a legal aid client having a narrower choice of lawyer. The contracts will only last for one or two years. Initially, there will be intense competition to obtain one of these contracts. Once the contracts have been allocated, a monopoly will have been created in each geographical area for the contract period – economically, an extremely unhealthy market structure and quite the opposite of the 'diverse and competitive market' intended. A criminal law firm which fails to get a contract, is unlikely to survive six months and it will be difficult for any new solicitor to enter the market given the emphasis on larger firms being preferred suppliers.

Reading on the web

The report of the Constitutional Affairs Committee criticising the government's plans to implement Lord Carter's legal aid reforms, *Implementation of the Carter Review of Legal Aid* (2007), is available on Parliament's website at:

www.publications.parliament.uk/pa/cm200607/cmselect/cmconst/223/223i.pdf

The report by Lee Bridges and others, *Evaluation of the Public Defender Service in England and Wales* (2007), is available on the website of the Legal Services Commission at:

www.legalservices.gov.uk/docs/pds/Public_Defenders_Report_PDFVersion6.pdf

Lord Carter's report, *Legal aid: a market-based approach to reform* (2006), is available at:

www.legalaidprocurementreview.gov.uk/publications.htm

The consultation paper, *Legal Aid: a sustainable future* (2006), is available at:

www.dca.gov.uk/consult/legal-aidsf/sustainable-future.htm

The website of Community Legal Advice is:

www.communitylegaladvice.org.uk

The judgment of the European Court of Human Rights in the McLibel Two case, was application number 6841/01 and can be found on the court's website at:

www.echr.coe.int/echr

The website of the Legal Services Commission is:

www.legalservices.gov.uk/

The website of the Community Legal Service is:

www.legalservices.gov.uk/civil.asp

Chapter summary

State funding of legal services

With the passing of the Access to Justice Act 1999, the Labour government introduced some major reforms to the provision of state-funded legal services. On 1 April 2000, the Legal Aid Board was replaced by the Legal Services Commission.

The Legal Services Commission administers two schemes: the Community Legal Service which is concerned with civil matters and the Criminal Defence Service which is concerned with criminal matters.

The Community Legal Service

Direct funding is provided for different categories of legal service as follows:

- Legal Help;
- Legal Representation;
- Help at Court;
- Approved Family Help; and
- Family Mediation.

The Criminal Defence Service

State funding can provide direct funding for three types of service in the criminal field:

- Advice and assistance;
- Advocacy assistance; and
- Representation.

In addition, the Legal Services Commission employs public defenders and pays for duty solicitor schemes.

Conditional fee agreements

In 1990 the Courts and Legal Services Act made provision for the introduction of conditional fee agreements. The scope for their use was increased by the Access to Justice Act 1999.

Reform

In his report, *Legal aid: a market-based approach to reform* (2006), Lord Carter has recommended the introduction of some important, money-saving reforms to the system of state-funded legal services.

Question and answer guides

Jane is a bank clerk and has been arrested on suspicion of stealing £10,000 from her employer.

(a) Describe the types of public funding available for advice and representation in a criminal case.

Plan

Demonstrate good knowledge of the Criminal Defence Service:

- The Legal Services Commission was established under the Access to Justice Act 1999 to provide state-funded legal services.
- The Criminal Defence Service administers state-funded legal services.
- State-funded legal help for criminal cases is provided by contracted solicitors or salaried public defenders.
- Under the duty solicitor scheme at the police station, suspects receive free legal advice and no means or merits test is applied.
- Under the duty solicitor scheme at the magistrates' court, defendants receive state-funded legal advice, which will, for example, assist them with a bail application.
- State-funded legal representation for criminal court hearings. A merits test is applied based on the interests of justice. A means test is applied looking at the defendant's disposable income and capital. Depending on their financial circumstances, a defendant can be required to contribute to their legal expenses.
- Lord Carter's reform proposals.

Answer

The Legal Services Commission was established under the Access to Justice 1999, replacing the old Legal Aid Board. The Commission established the Criminal Defence Service to administer state funding for legal services in criminal matters. The purpose of the Criminal Defence Service is to ensure that people suspected or accused of a crime have access to advice, assistance and representation, as the interests of justice require. Approximately three-quarters of a million people receive legal funding from this body every year. Private practice solicitors are only able to carry out criminal defence work funded by the Commission if they have a General Criminal Contract. Firms are audited to ensure they continue to meet quality assurance standards.

A contracted solicitor is able to provide three levels of service: Advice and Assistance, Advocacy Assistance, and Representation. Looking first at Advice and Assistance, this covers the cost of a solicitor giving general advice, writing letters, negotiating, getting a barrister's opinion and preparing a written case. It enables people of restricted means to get help from a solicitor. It is not available during criminal court proceedings, after charge or summons. It does not cover representation in court. The Advice and Assistance scheme covers £500-worth of work by a solicitor.

Advocacy Assistance covers some advice and some representation at court. It covers the cost of a solicitor preparing a case and initial representation in certain proceedings in both the magistrates' court and the Crown Court.

Representation covers the preparation of a criminal case and representation in court. This is subject to a means and merits test. The merits test looks at whether it would be in the interests of justice to award state funding, whether the individual would be likely to lose their liberty or livelihood; whether the case involves a substantial question of law; whether the proceedings may involve the tracing, interviewing or expert cross-examination of witnesses; and whether it is in the interests of another person that the individual be represented. The means test looks at the income and capital of the defendants and, depending on their financial situation, they can be required to make a contribution to their legal expenses.

Public defender pilot schemes with salaried lawyers have been running in several areas in England and Wales since 2001. Public defenders provide exactly the same service as a defendant would receive from lawyers in private practice. Solicitors in private practice were unhappy with this development, fearing that public defenders would constitute unfair competition and pull their earnings down. In fact, the government itself has concluded that some of the public defender offices were too expensive and not providing value for money. Four have been closed down and there are currently no plans to expand the existing schemes.

The first contact that a suspect is likely to have with the state-funded criminal legal aid system is at the time of their arrest and detention in the police station. Under the duty solicitor scheme, any individual arrested and held in custody, or attending a police station 'voluntarily' while suspected of a criminal offence, is eligible to ask for advice and assistance from the duty solicitor. The duty solicitor can advise clients as to their rights, ensure fair treatment, and assist them in applying for bail and/or full legal aid – though increasingly this advice is only provided over the telephone. There is also usually a duty solicitor available in the magistrates' courts to provide state-funded legal services where defendants risk losing their liberty or their employment.

Under the relatively new scheme called Criminal Defence Service Direct, a person detained for a non-imprisonable offence, who has not requested a lawyer, can use a telephone helpline for advice. This helpline is often staffed by retired police officers who have a legal advice qualification.

The state-funding arrangements for criminal legal proceedings are currently being reformed following an important report by Lord Carter, *Legal aid: a market-based approach to reform* (2006). This is likely to restrict the availability of state-funded criminal legal services to a smaller number of larger law firms in order to save money.

(b) Explain to Jane what problems she might encounter with the public funding of her defence.

(OCR Specimen Paper 2007, English Legal System Unit)

Plan

- In practice, the police subtly discourage suspects in the police station from seeking assistance from a duty solicitor and often this advice is now given over the

253

phone. Historically, there had been concerns about the quality of the advice given, but training for this role has since been improved.

- Duty solicitors in the magistrates' court are not consistently available, though they could be useful for Jane's application for bail.
- Where applicable, the means test thresholds are low so that Jane, as a bank clerk, is likely to have to contribute to the cost of her legal expenses.
- Where the merits test applies, Jane has no automatic right to state funding, her entitlement depends on how the merits test is applied to her case. On the facts one would expect her to satisfy this test because, if convicted, she is likely to lose her job and could face a prison sentence. If state funding was refused, she could appeal.
- Jane's choice of lawyer is restricted to those who have a contract with the Legal Services Commission.
- Public defenders are available in a few areas and there has been controversy over their impartiality and quality of service. Research by Cyrus Tata and others has not found any significant problems in this respect, though generally defendants felt they received a more personal and supportive service from solicitors in private practice.

Group activity 1

- Divide your friends (or class) into groups of two or three people.
- Each group should choose a Law Centre in England & Wales from the list on the website of The Law Centres Federation – **www.lawcentres.org.uk**. It should prepare a profile of its chosen Law Centre, focusing on the types of legal problems with which it can help, the range of legal services that it offers, and the extent to which its services are funded by the state.
- The groups should then meet to compare profiles, looking for any common themes.

Visit **www.mylawchamber.co.uk/elliottocr** to access questions, quizzes and activities to test yourself on this chapter.

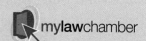

Unit 2

SOURCES OF LAW

English law stems from four main sources, though these vary a great deal in importance. The basis of our law today is case law, a mass of judge-made decisions which
lay down rules to be followed in future court cases. For many centuries it was the main
form of law and it is still very important today. However, the most important source
of law, in the sense that it prevails over most of the others, are Acts of Parliament.
Delegated legislation is made by the administration rather than the legislature, and
tends to lay down detailed rules to implement the broader provisions of Acts of
Parliament.

An increasingly important source of law is the legislation of the European Union,
which is the only type of law that can take precedence over Acts of Parliament in
the UK.

This Unit concludes with a discussion of the process of law reform, whereby these
sources of law can be changed to reflect the changes taking place in society.

Chapter 14
JUDICIAL PRECEDENT

This chapter contains:

- an introduction to judicial precedent;
- an explanation of case names and law reporting;
- a description of the hierarchy of the courts and judicial precedent;
- an analysis of how judicial precedent works in practice;
- a discussion of whether the judges actually make the law, rather than simply declaring the law;
- an overview of the advantages and disadvantages of binding precedent.

Introduction

Judicial precedent, often known as case law, comes from the decisions made by judges in the cases before them. In deciding a case, there are two basic tasks; first, establishing what the facts are, meaning what actually happened; and, secondly, how the law applies to those facts. It is the second task that can make case law. Once a decision has been made on how the law applies to a particular set of facts, similar facts in later cases should be treated in the same way. This is the principle of *stare decisis*, which is a Latin term meaning 'let the decision stand'. This is obviously fairer than allowing each judge to interpret the law differently, and also provides predictability, which makes it easier for people to live within the law. In developing case law, the judges follow the decisions that preceded them and set precedents for the future, hence the name judicial precedent.

English judgments are frequently quite long, containing quite a lot of comment which is not strictly relevant to the case, as well as an explanation of the legal principles on which the judge has made a decision. The explanation of the legal principles on which the decision is made is called the *ratio decidendi* – Latin for the 'reason for deciding'. It is this part of the judgment, known as binding precedent, which forms case law.

All the parts of the judgment which do not form part of the *ratio decidendi* of the case are called *obiter dicta* – which is Latin for 'things said by the way'. These are often discussions of hypothetical situations: for example, the judge might say: 'Jones did this, but if she had done that, my decision would have been . . .' None of the *obiter dicta* forms part of the judicial precedent, though judges in later cases may be influenced by it, and it is said to be a persuasive precedent.

In deciding a case, a judge must follow any decision that has been made by a higher court in a case with similar facts. The rules concerning which courts are bound by which are known as the rules of judicial precedent, or *stare decisis*. As well as being bound by the decisions of courts above them, some courts must also follow their own previous decisions; they are said to be bound by themselves.

> ✓ **Know your terms 14.1**
>
> Define these Latin terms:
> 1 *Stare decisis.*
> 2 *Ratio decidendi.*
> 3 *Obiter dicta.*

Case names

Each legal case that is taken to court is given a name. The name of the case is usually based on the family name of the parties involved. In essays, the name of the case should normally be put into italics or underlined, though in this book we have chosen to put them in bold.

If Ms Smith steals Mr Brown's car, then a criminal action is likely to be brought by the state against her. The written name of the case would then be **R** *v* **Smith**. The letter 'R' stands for the Latin *Rex* (King) or *Regina* (Queen), depending on whether there was a king or queen in office at the time of the decision. Sometimes the full Latin terms are used rather than the simple abbreviation R, so that the case **R** *v* **Smith**, if brought now while Queen Elizabeth is in office, could also be called **Regina** *v* **Smith**.

The 'v' separating the two parties' names is short for 'versus' (against), in the same way as one might write Manchester United *v* Arsenal Football Club when the two teams are going to play a match against each other. When speaking, instead of saying 'R versus Smith', one should really say 'The Crown against Smith'.

In civil law, if Mr Brown is in a neighbour dispute with Ms Smith and decides to bring an action against Ms Smith, the name of the case will be **Brown** *v* **Smith**.

The law reports

Because some cases lay down important legal principles, over 2,000 each year are published in law reports. Some of these law reports date back over 700 years. Perhaps the most respected series of law reports are those called *The Law Reports*, because before publication the report of each case included in them is checked for accuracy by the judge who tried it. It is this series that should be cited before a court in preference to any other.

The hierarchy of the courts

The European Court of Justice

Decisions of the European Court of Justice (ECJ) are binding on all English courts. It appears not to be bound by its own decisions.

The House of Lords

Apart from cases concerning European law, this is the highest appeal court on civil and criminal matters, and all other English courts are bound by it. It was traditionally bound by its own decisions but, in 1966, the Lord Chancellor issued a **Practice Statement** saying that the House of Lords was no longer bound by its previous decisions. In practice, the House of Lords only rarely overrules one of its earlier decisions. This reluctance to do so is illustrated by the case of **R v Kansal (No. 2)** (2001). In that case the House of Lords held that it had probably got the law wrong in its earlier decision of **R v Lambert** (2001). The latter case had ruled that the **Human Rights Act 1998** would not have retrospective effect in relation to appeals heard by the House of Lords after the Act came into force, but which had been decided by the lower courts before the Act came into force. Despite the fact that the majority thought the earlier judgment of **Lambert** was wrong, the House decided in **Kansal** to follow it. This was because **Lambert** was a recent decision, it represented a possible interpretation of the statute which was not unworkable and it only concerned a temporary transitional period.

There are, however, a range of cases where the House of Lords has been prepared to apply the 1966 Practice Statement. For example, in **R v R** (1991), it held that rape within marriage is a crime, overturning a legal principle that had stood for centuries.

In **Arthur JS Hall & Co v Simons** (2000), the House of Lords refused to follow the earlier case of **Rondel v Worsley** (1969), which had given barristers immunity against claims for negligence in their presentation of cases.

In **R v G and another** (2003), the House of Lords overruled an established criminal case of **R v Caldwell** (1981). Under **R v Caldwell**, the House had been prepared to convict people for criminal offences where the prosecution had not proved that the defendant personally had intended or seen the risk of causing the relevant harm, but had simply shown that a reasonable person would have had this state of mind on the facts. This was particularly harsh where the actual defendant was incapable of seeing the risk of harm, because, for example, they were very young or of low intelligence. **Caldwell** had been heavily criticised by academics over the years, but when the House of Lords originally reconsidered the matter in 1992 in **R v Reid**, it confirmed its original decision. However, when the matter again came to the House of Lords in 2003 in **R v G**, the House dramatically admitted that it had got the law wrong. It stated:

> *'The surest test of a new legal rule is not whether it satisfies a team of logicians but how it performs in the real world. With the benefit of hindsight the verdict must be that the rule laid down by the majority in* **Caldwell** *failed this test. It was severely criticised by academic lawyers of distinction. It did not command respect among practitioners and judges. Jurors found it difficult to understand; it also sometimes offended their sense of justice. Experience suggests that in* **Caldwell** *the law took a wrong turn.'*

An important case is **Re Pinochet** (1998), where the House of Lords stated that it had the power to reopen an appeal where one of the parties has been subjected to an unfair procedure. The case was part of the litigation concerning General Augusto Pinochet, the former Chilean president. The Lords reopened the appeal because one of the Law Lords who heard the original appeal, Lord Hoffmann, was connected with the human rights organisation, Amnesty International, which had been a party to the appeal. This meant that there was a possibility of bias and so the proceedings could be viewed as unfair. The Lords stressed, however, that there was no question of them being able to reopen an appeal because the decision made originally was thought to be wrong; the Pinochet appeal was reopened because it could be said that there had not been a fair hearing, and not because the decision reached was wrong (although at the second hearing of the appeal, the Lords did in fact come to a slightly different decision).

The government intends to abolish the House of Lords and replace it with a Supreme Court. This reform is contained in the Constitutional Reform Act 2005 and is discussed at p. 32.

sourcebook p. 326 →

Task 14.2

Visit the House of Lords' judicial business website at:

www.publications.parliament.uk/pa/ld/ldjudgmt.htm

Find the judgment **Re Pinochet** (1998). Who were the judges in that case?

Figure 14.1 **Demonstrators in favour of the deportation of the former Chilean President Augusto Pinochet**

Source: © EMPICS.

Privy Council

The Privy Council was established by the Judicial Committee Act 1833. It is the final appeal court for many Commonwealth countries. The Privy Council currently has jurisdiction to hear devolution cases relating to the powers of the devolved legislative and executive authorities in Scotland, Northern Ireland and Wales. Once the Supreme Court has been established, this domestic jurisdiction will be transferred to the new court.

Under the traditional rules of precedent, the decisions of the Privy Council do not bind English courts, but have strong persuasive authority because of the seniority of the judges who sit in the Privy Council (**de Lasala** *v* **de Lasala** (1980)). This well-established rule of precedent has been thrown into doubt by the recent Court of Appeal judgment of **R** *v* **James and Karimi** (2006). The Court of Appeal held that in exceptional circumstances a Privy Council judgment can bind the English Courts and effectively overrule an earlier House of Lords' judgment. This conflicts with the traditional approach to such judgments, confirmed by the House of Lords in **Miliangos** *v* **George Frank (Textiles) Ltd** (1976) that 'the only judicial means by which decisions of this House can be reviewed is by this House itself'.

The Court of Appeal case of **James and Karimi** was concerned with provocation, which can be a partial defence to murder. The defence is laid down in s. 3 of the Homicide Act 1957. This section has been interpreted as laying down a two-part test. The first part of the test requires the defendant to have suffered from a sudden and temporary loss of self-control when he or she killed the victim. The second part of the test provides that the defence will be available only if a reasonable person would have reacted as the defendant did. This is described as an objective test, because it is judging the defendant's conduct according to objective standards, rather than their own standards. However, in practice, reasonable people almost never kill, so if this second requirement was interpreted strictly the defence would rarely succeed. As a result, in **R** *v* **Smith (Morgan)** (2001) the House of Lords held that, in determining whether a reasonable person would have reacted in this way, a court could take into account the actual characteristics of the defendant. So if the defendant had been depressed and was of low intelligence, then the test would become whether a reasonable person suffering from depression and of low intelligence would have reacted by killing the victim.

sourcebook p. 9
In an appeal from Jersey on the defence of provocation, **Attorney-General for Jersey** *v* **Holley** (2005), the Privy Council had refused to follow the case of **Smith (Morgan)**, stating that the case misinterpreted Parliament's intention when it passed the Homicide Act 1957. It considered that the only characteristics that should be taken into account when considering whether the defendant had reacted reasonably, were characteristics that were directly relevant to the provocation itself, but not general characteristics which simply affected a person's ability to control him or herself.

The Court of Appeal in **James and Karimi** (2006) has now decided to apply the Privy Council's judgment in **Holley** rather than the House of Lords' judgment in **Smith (Morgan)**. The Court of Appeal acknowledged that this went against the established rules of judicial precedent. It gives various justifications for treating this as an exceptional case, in which those established rules should not apply. It pointed out that the Privy Council had realised the importance of its judgment and had chosen to have an enlarged sitting of nine judges, all drawn from the House of Lords:

> *'The procedure adopted and the comments of members of the Board in **Holley** suggest that a decision must have been taken by those responsible for the constitution of the Board in **Holley** . . . to use the appeal as a vehicle for reconsidering the decision of the House of Lords in **Morgan Smith**, not just as representing the law of Jersey but as representing the law of England. A decision was taken that the Board hearing the appeal to the Privy Council should consist of nine of the twelve Lords of Appeal in Ordinary.'*

The emphasis on the enlarged formation of the Privy Council potentially leaves the status of its decisions dependent upon an administrative decision as to how many judges should sit, a decision which has never been the subject of any legal controls.

The judges in **Holley** were divided in their verdict six to three. The start of the first judgment of the majority stated:

> *'This appeal, being heard by an enlarged board of nine members, is concerned to resolve this conflict [between the House of Lords and the Privy Council] and clarify definitively the present state of English law, and hence Jersey law, on this important subject.'*

The dissenting judges stated: 'We must however accept that the effect of the majority decision is as stated in paragraph 1 of the majority judgment.' Thus, even the dissenting judges appear to accept that the majority decision lays down the law in England.

The Court of Appeal also considered that if an appeal was taken to the House of Lords, the outcome was 'a foregone conclusion' and the House would take the same approach as **Holley**:

> *'Half of the Law Lords were party to the majority decision in **Holley**. Three more in that case accepted that the majority decision represented a definitive statement of English law on the issue in question. The choice of those to sit on the appeal might raise some nice questions, but we cannot conceive that, whatever the precise composition of the Committee, it would do other than rule that the majority decision in **Holley** represented the law of England. In effect, in the long term at least, **Holley** has overruled **Morgan Smith**.'*

This argument would be more convincing if the **Holley** case had been decided by a unanimous verdict. In fact, there are still potentially six House of Lords judges who could prefer the **Smith (Morgan)** approach: the three dissenting judges and the three House of Lords' judges who did not hear the **Holley** case.

Lord Woolf recognised in **R v Simpson** (2003) that the rules of judicial precedent must provide certainty but at the same time they themselves must be able to evolve in order to do justice:

> *'The rules as to precedent reflect the practice of the courts and have to be applied bearing in mind that their objective is to assist in the administration of justice. They are of considerable importance because of their role in achieving the appropriate degree of certainty as to the law. This is an important requirement of any system of justice. The principles should not, however, be regarded as so rigid that they cannot develop in order to meet contemporary needs.'*

The Court of Appeal presumably concluded in **James and Karimi** that this was a situation where justice could only be achieved by shifting the established rules of judicial precedent. The actual outcome of the case makes it more difficult for a partial defence to murder, reducing liability to manslaughter, to succeed. This may be considered to achieve justice for victims' families, but it may be an injustice to the mentally ill defendant.

The Court of Appeal

This is split into Civil and Criminal Divisions; they do not bind each other. Both divisions are bound by the House of Lords.

The Civil Division is usually bound by its own previous decisions, but there are four exceptions to this where:

1 the previous decision was made in ignorance of a relevant law (it is said to have been made *per incuriam*);
2 there are two previous conflicting decisions;
3 there is a later, conflicting House of Lords decision;
4 a proposition of law was assumed to exist by an earlier court and was not subject to argument or consideration by that court.

The first three of these exceptions were laid down in **Young** *v* **Bristol Aeroplane Co. Ltd** (1944). The fourth was added by **R** *v* **Brent London Borough Housing Benefit Review Board, ex parte Khadim** (2001).

In the Criminal Division, the results of cases heard may decide whether or not an individual goes to prison, so the Criminal Division takes a more flexible approach to its previous decisions and does not follow them where doing so could cause injustice.

Lord Denning would have liked the Court of Appeal to have had the power to overrule its own previous decisions wherever it felt it had got the law wrong, in the same way as the House of Lords has this power following the Practice Statement of 1966. He put forward this view in **Davis** *v* **Johnson** (1979). The Court of Appeal has not been prepared to take this stance, and Lord Simon was of the view that any such change to the rules of precedent concerning the Court of Appeal would require an Act of Parliament (**Miliangos** *v* **George Frank (Textiles) Ltd** (1976)).

The High Court

This court is divided between the Divisional Courts and the ordinary High Court. All are bound by the Court of Appeal and the House of Lords.

The Divisional Courts are the Queen's Bench Division, which deals with criminal appeals and judicial review, the Chancery Division and the Family Division, which both deal with civil appeals. The two civil Divisional Courts are bound by their previous decisions, but the Divisional Court of the Queen's Bench is more flexible about this, for the same reason as the Criminal Division of the Court of Appeal. The Divisional Courts bind the ordinary High Court.

The ordinary High Court is not bound by its own previous decisions. It can produce precedents for courts below it, but these are of a lower status than those produced by the Court of Appeal or the House of Lords.

The Crown Court

The Crown Court is bound by all the courts above it. Its decisions do not form binding precedents, though when High Court judges sit in the Crown Court, their judgments form persuasive precedents, which must be given serious consideration in subsequent cases, though it is not obligatory to follow them. Since the Crown Court cannot form binding precedents, it is obviously not bound by its own decisions.

Magistrates' and county courts

These are called the inferior courts. They are bound by the High Court, Court of Appeal and House of Lords. Their own decisions are not reported, and cannot produce binding precedents, or even persuasive ones; like the Crown Court, they are therefore not bound by their own decisions.

European Court of Human Rights

The European Court of Human Rights (ECtHR) is an international court based in Strasbourg. It hears cases alleging that there has been a breach of the European Convention on Human Rights. This court does not fit neatly within the hierarchy of the courts. Under s. 2 of the Human Rights Act 1998 an English court is required to 'take account of' the cases decided by the ECtHR, though its decisions

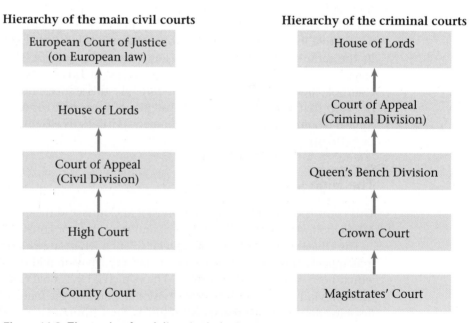

Hierarchy of the main civil courts

European Court of Justice
(on European law)

↑

House of Lords

↑

Court of Appeal
(Civil Division)

↑

High Court

↑

County Court

Hierarchy of the criminal courts

House of Lords

↑

Court of Appeal
(Criminal Division)

↑

Queen's Bench Division

↑

Crown Court

↑

Magistrates' Court

Figure 14.2 **The routes for civil and criminal cases**

do not bind the English courts. In practice, when considering a Convention right, the domestic courts try to follow the same interpretation as that given by the ECtHR. In **R (Alconbury)** *v* **Secretary of State for the Environment, Transport and the Regions** (2001) the House of Lords said:

> *'In the absence of some special circumstances it seems to me the court should follow any clear and constant jurisprudence of the European Court of Human Rights. If it does not do so there is at least a possibility the case will go to that court which is likely in the ordinary case to follow its own constant jurisprudence.'*

Despite this, the House of Lords has refused to follow an earlier decision of the ECtHR. In **Morris** *v* **United Kingdom** (2002) the ECtHR ruled that the courts martial system (which is the courts system used by the army) breached the European Convention on Human Rights, as it did not guarantee a fair trial within the meaning of Art. 6 of the European Convention. Subsequently, in **Boyd** *v* **Army Prosecuting Authority** (2002), three soldiers who had been convicted of assault by a court martial argued before the House of Lords that the court martial had violated their right to a fair trial under the Convention. Surprisingly, the argument was rejected and the House of Lords refused to follow the earlier decision of the ECtHR. It stated:

> *'While the decision in **Morris** is not binding on the House, it is of course a matter which the House must take into account (s. 2(1)(a) of the Human Rights Act 1998) and which demands careful attention, not least because it is a recent expression of the European Court's view on these matters.'*

The House considered that the ECtHR was given 'rather less information than the House' about the courts martial system, and in the light of this additional information it concluded that there had been no violation of the European Convention.

Where there is a conflict between a decision of the ECtHR and a national court which binds a lower court, then the lower court should usually follow the decision of the binding higher national court, but give permission to appeal. Thus, in **Kay** *v* **London Borough of Lambeth** (2006) the Court of Appeal had been faced with a binding precedent of the House of Lords which conflicted with a decision of the ECtHR. The Court of Appeal had applied the House of Lords' decision but given permission to appeal. In the subsequent appeal the House had agreed that this was the appropriate course of action.

How judicial precedent works

When faced with a case on which there appears to be a relevant earlier decision the judges can do any of the following:

- **Follow.** If the facts are sufficiently similar, the precedent set by the earlier case is followed, and the law applied in the same way to produce a decision.
- **Distinguish.** Where the facts of the case before the judge are significantly different from those of the earlier one, then the judge distinguishes the two cases and need not follow the earlier one.
- **Overrule.** Where the earlier decision was made in a lower court, the judges can overrule that earlier decision if they disagree with the lower court's statement

sourcebook
p. 31

of the law. The outcome of the earlier decision remains the same, but will not be followed. We have seen at p. 259 that the House of Lords has the power to overrule its own previous decisions and the case of **Pepper *v* Hart** (1993), discussed on p. 314, is an example of this.

■ **Reverse.** If the decision of a lower court is appealed to a higher one, the higher court may change it if they feel the lower court has wrongly interpreted the law. Clearly, when a decision is reversed, the higher court is usually also overruling the lower court's statement of the law.

In practice, the process is rather more complicated than this, since decisions are not always made on the basis of only one previous case; there are usually several different cases offered in support of each side's view of the question.

How do judges really decide cases?

The independence of the judiciary was ensured by the Act of Settlement 1700, which transferred the power to sack judges from the Crown to Parliament. Consequently, judges should theoretically make their decisions based purely on the logical deductions of precedent, uninfluenced by political or career considerations.

The eighteenth-century legal commentator, William Blackstone, introduced the declaratory theory of law, stating that judges do not make law, but merely, by the rules of precedent, discover and declare the law that has always been. He thought there was always one right answer to a legal question, to be deduced from an objective study of precedent.

Today, however, this position is considered somewhat unrealistic. If the operation of precedent is the precise science Blackstone suggests, a large majority of cases in the higher courts would never come to court at all. The lawyers concerned could simply look up the relevant case law and predict what the decision would be, then advise whichever of the clients would be bound to lose not to bother bringing or fighting the case. In civil litigation no good lawyer would advise a client to bring or defend a case that they had no chance of winning. Evidence that more than one solution is possible is provided by reading a judgment of the Court of Appeal, argued as though it were the only possible decision in the light of the cases that had gone before, and then discover that this apparently inevitable decision has promptly been reversed by the House of Lords.

In practice, then, judges' decisions may not be as neutral as Blackstone's declaratory theory suggests: they have to make choices which are by no means spelt out by precedents. Yet, rather than openly stating that they are choosing between two or more equally relevant precedents, the courts find ways to avoid awkward ones, which give the impression that the precedents they do choose to follow are the only ones that could possibly apply. In theory, only the House of Lords, which can overrule its own decisions as well as those of other courts, can depart from precedent: all the other courts must follow the precedent that applies in a particular case, however much they dislike it. In fact, there are a number of ways in which judges may avoid awkward precedents that at first sight might appear binding.

- By distinguishing the awkward precedent on its facts – arguing that the facts of the case under consideration are different in some important way from those of the previous case, and therefore the rule laid down does not apply to them. Since the facts are unlikely to be identical, this is the simplest way to avoid an awkward precedent, and the courts have made some extremely narrow distinctions in this way.

- By distinguishing the point of law – arguing that the legal question answered by the precedent is not the same as that asked in the present case.

- By stating that the precedent has been superseded by more recent decisions, and is therefore outdated.

- By giving the precedent a very narrow *ratio decidendi*. The only part of a decision that forms binding precedent is the *ratio*, the legal principle on which the decision is based. Since judges never state 'this is the *ratio decidendi*', it is possible to argue at some length about which bits of the judgment actually form the *ratio* and therefore bind courts in later cases. Judges wishing to avoid an awkward precedent may reason that those parts of the judgment which seem to apply to their case are not part of the *ratio*, and are only *obiter dicta*, which they are not obliged to follow.

- By arguing that the precedent has no clear *ratio decidendi*. There are usually three judges sitting in Court of Appeal cases, and five in the House of Lords. Where each judge in the former case has given a different reason for coming to the same decision, or where, for example, two judges of the House of Lords take one view, two more another, and the fifth agrees with none of them, it can be argued that there is no one clear *ratio decidendi* for the decision.

- By claiming that the precedent is inconsistent with a later decision of a higher court, and has been overruled by implication.

- By stating that the previous decision was made *per incuriam*, meaning that the court failed to consider some relevant statute or precedent. This method is used only rarely, since it clearly undermines the status of the court below.

- By arguing that the precedent is outdated, and no longer in step with modern thinking. The best-known example of this approach (which is not frequently used) is the case of **R** *v* **R** (1991), when the House of Lords overturned a centuries-old common law rule that rape within marriage was not a crime (see p. 259).

We can see that there is considerable room for manoeuvre within the doctrine of precedent, which has led to the suggestion that the judges are actually able to make the law rather than simply declaring it.

Do judges make law?

Although judges have traditionally seen themselves as declaring or finding rather than creating law, and frequently state that making law is the prerogative of Parliament, there are several areas in which they clearly do make law.

In the first place, historically, a great deal of our law is and always has been case law, made by judicial decisions. Contract and tort law are still largely judge-made, and many of the most important developments – for example, the development of negligence as a tort – have had profound effects. Even though statutes have later been passed on these subjects, and occasionally Parliament has attempted to embody whole areas of common law in statutory form, these still embody the original principles created by the judges.

Secondly, the application of law, whether case law or statute, to a particular case is not usually an automatic matter. Terminology may be vague or ambiguous, new developments in social life have to be accommodated, and the procedure requires interpretation as well as application. As we have suggested, judicial precedent does not always make a particular decision obvious and obligatory – there may be conflicting precedents, their implications may be unclear, and there are ways of getting round a precedent that would otherwise produce an undesirable decision. If it is accepted that Blackstone's declaratory theory does not apply in practice, then clearly the judges do make law, rather than explaining the law that is already there.

Where precedents do not spell out what should be done in a case before them, judges nevertheless have to make a decision. They cannot simply say that the law is not clear and refer it back to Parliament, even though in some cases they point out that the decision before them would be more appropriately decided by those who have been elected to make decisions on changes in the law. This was the case in **Airedale NHS Trust** *v* **Bland** (1993), where the House of Lords considered the fate of Tony Bland, the football supporter left in a coma after the Hillsborough stadium disaster. The court had to decide whether it was lawful to stop supplying the drugs and artificial feeding that were keeping Mr Bland alive, even though it was known that doing so would mean his death soon afterwards. Several Law Lords made it plain that they felt that cases raising 'wholly new moral and social issues' should be decided by Parliament, the judges' role being to 'apply the principles which society, through the democratic process, adopts, not to impose their standards on society'. Nevertheless, the courts had no option but to make a decision one way or the other, and they decided that the action was lawful in the circumstances, because it was in the patient's best interests.

Thirdly, our judges have been left to define their own role, and the role of the courts generally in the political system, more or less as they please. They have, for example, given themselves the power to review decisions of any public body, even when Parliament has said those decisions are not to be reviewed. Also, despite their frequent pronouncements that it is not for them to interfere in Parliament's law-making role, the judges have made it plain that they will not, unless forced by very explicit wording, interpret statutes as encroaching on common law rights or judge-made law (see p. 312). They also control the operation of case law without reference to Parliament: an obvious example is that the 1966 Practice Direction announcing that the House of Lords would no longer be bound by its own decisions, which made case law more flexible and thereby gave the judges more power, was made on the court's own authority, without needing permission from Parliament.

The House of Lords has explained its approach to judicial law-making in the case of **C (A Minor)** *v* **DPP** (1995), which raised the issue of children's liability for crime. The common law defence of *doli incapax* provided that a defendant aged between 10 and 14 could be liable for a crime only if the prosecution could prove that the child knew that what he or she did was seriously wrong. On appeal from the magistrates' court, the Divisional Court held that the defence was outdated and should no longer exist in law. An appeal was brought before the House of Lords, arguing that the Divisional Court was bound by precedent and not able to change the law in this way. The House of Lords agreed, and went on to consider whether it should change the law itself (as the 1966 Practice Statement clearly allowed it to do), but decided that this was not an appropriate case for judicial law-making. Explaining this decision, Lord Lowry suggested five factors were important:

■ where the solution to a dilemma was doubtful, judges should be wary of imposing their own answer;
■ judges should be cautious about addressing areas where Parliament had rejected opportunities of clearing up a known difficulty, or had passed legislation without doing so;
■ areas of social policy over which there was dispute were least likely to be suitable for judicial law-making;
■ fundamental legal doctrines should not be lightly set aside;
■ judges should not change the law unless they can be sure that doing so is likely to achieve finality and certainty on the issue.

This guidance suggests that the judges should take quite a cautious approach to changing the law. In practice, however, the judges do not always seem to be following these guidelines. For example, in an important criminal case of **R v Dica** (2004), the Court of Appeal overruled an earlier case of **R v Clarence** (1888) and held that criminal liability could be imposed on a defendant for recklessly infecting another person with AIDS. This change in the law was made despite the fact that the Home Office had earlier decided that legislation should not be introduced which would have imposed liability in this situation (*Violence: Reforming the Offences Against the Person Act 1861* (1998)). The Home Office had observed that 'this issue had ramifications going beyond the criminal law into wider considerations of social and public health policy'.

Some commentators feel that the judiciary's current approach is tending to go too far, and straying outside its constitutional place. Writing in the *New Law Journal* in 1999, Francis Bennion, a former parliamentary counsel, criticised what he called the 'growing appetite of some judges for changing the law themselves, rather than waiting for Parliament to do it'. Bennion cites two cases as examples of this. The first, **Kleinwort Benson Ltd v Lincoln City Council** (1998), concerns contract law, and in particular, a long-standing rule, originating from case law, that where someone made a payment as a result of a mistake about the law, they did not have the right to get the money back. The rule had existed for nearly two centuries, and been much criticised in recent years – so much so that a previous Lord Chancellor had asked the Law Commission to consider whether it should be amended by legislation, and they had concluded that it should. This would normally be taken by the courts as a signal that they should leave the issue alone and wait for Parliament to act, but in this case the Lords decided to change the rule. In doing so, Lord Keith expressed the view that 'a robust view of judicial development of the law' was desirable. Bennion argues that, in making this decision, the Lords were usurping the authority which constitutionally belongs to Parliament. He also points out that judicial, rather than parliamentary, change of the law in this kind of area causes practical difficulties, because it has retrospective effect; a large number of transactions which were thought to be settled under the previous rule can now be reopened. This would not usually be the case if Parliament changed the law.

The second case Bennion criticises is **DPP** *v* **Jones** (1999), which concerned a demonstration on the road near Stonehenge. In that case the Lords looked at another long-held rule, that the public have a right to use the highway for 'passing and repassing' (in other words, walking along the road), and for uses which are related to that, but that there is no right to use the highway in other ways, such as demonstrating or picketing. In **Jones**, the House of Lords stated that this rule placed unrealistic and unwarranted restrictions on everyday activities, and that the highway is a public place that the public has a right to enjoy for any reasonable purpose. This decision clearly has major implications for the powers of the police to break up demonstrations and pickets.

Bennion argues that, in making decisions like these, the judiciary are taking powers to which they are not constitutionally entitled, and that they should not extend their law-making role into such controversial areas.

Quick quiz 14.3

1 What are the four main sources of English law?

2 In what year did the House of Lords declare that it was no longer bound by its previous decisions?

3 What are the four situations where the Court of Appeal Civil Division is not bound by its own decisions?

4 Which of the following courts can create a binding precedent: the High Court, Crown Court, magistrates' court and county court?

5 What is the difference between a court overruling a previous decision and a court reversing a previous decision?

6 Which legal writer is traditionally associated with the declaratory theory of law?

Task 14.4

Read the Practice Statement that was issued by the House of Lords in 1966, stating that it was no longer bound by its previous decisions, and then answer the questions below.

'Their Lordships regard the use of precedent as an indispensable foundation upon which to decide what is the law and its application to individual cases. It provides at least some degree of certainty upon which individuals can rely in the conduct of their affairs, as well as a basis for orderly development of legal rules.

Their Lordships nevertheless recognise that the rigid adherence to precedent may lead to injustice in a particular case and also unduly restrict the proper development of the law. They propose, therefore, to modify their present practice and while treating former decisions of this House as normally binding, to depart from a previous decision when it appears right to do so.

In this connection they will bear in mind the danger of disturbing retrospectively the basis on which contracts, settlement of property and fiscal arrangements have been entered into and also the especial need for certainty as to the criminal law.

This announcement is not intended to affect the use of precedent elsewhere than in the House.'

Questions

1 Define the term 'retrospectively'.
2 What did the House of Lords consider to be the advantages of the doctrine of judicial precedent?
3 What disadvantages did they recognise exist in the strict application of the rules of judicial precedent?
4 In which areas of law did their Lordships state that they would be less willing to change their previous decisions?

Advantages of binding precedent

Certainty

Judicial precedent means litigants can assume that like cases will be treated alike, rather than judges making their own random decisions, which nobody could predict. This helps people plan their affairs.

Detailed practical rules

Case law is a response to real situations, as opposed to statutes, which may be more heavily based on theory and logic. Case law shows the detailed application of the law to various circumstances, and thus gives more information than statute.

Just and impartial rules

If the judges are accepted as independent and follow the rules of judicial precedent then if we accept Blackstone's declaratory theory, their decisions should be just and impartial.

Free market in legal ideas

The right-wing philosopher Hayek (1982) has argued that there should be as little legislation as possible, with case law becoming the main source of law. He sees case law as developing in line with market forces; if the *ratio* of a case is seen not to work, it will be abandoned, if it works, it will be followed. In this way the law can develop in response to demand. Hayek sees statute law as imposed by social planners, forcing their views on society whether they like it or not, and threatening the liberty of the individual.

Flexibility

Law needs to be flexible to meet the needs of a changing society, and case law can make changes far more quickly than Parliament. The most obvious signs of this are the radical changes the House of Lords has made in the field of criminal law, since announcing in 1966 that it would no longer be bound by its own decisions.

Disadvantages of binding precedent

Complexity and volume

There are hundreds of thousands of decided cases, comprising several thousand volumes of law reports, and more are added all the time. Judgments themselves are long, with many judges making no attempt at readability, and the *ratio decidendi* of a case may be buried in a sea of irrelevant material. This can make it very difficult to pinpoint appropriate principles.

Rigid

The rules of judicial precedent mean that judges should follow a binding precedent even where they think it is bad law, or inappropriate. This can mean that bad judicial decisions are perpetuated for a long time before they come before a court high enough to have the power to overrule them.

Illogical distinctions

The fact that binding precedents must be followed unless the facts of the case are significantly different can lead to judges making minute distinctions between the facts of a previous case and the case before them, so that they can distinguish a precedent which they consider inappropriate. This in turn leads to a mass of cases all establishing different precedents in very similar circumstances, and further complicates the law.

Unpredictable

The advantages of certainty can be lost if too many of the kind of illogical distinctions referred to above are made, and it may be impossible to work out which precedents will be applied to a new case.

Dependence on chance

Case law changes only in response to those cases brought before it, so important changes may not be made unless someone has the money and determination to push a case far enough through the appeal system to allow a new precedent to be created.

Unsystematic progression

Case law develops according to the facts of each case and so does not provide a comprehensive code. A whole series of rules can be built on one case, and if this is overruled the whole structure can collapse.

Lack of research

When making case law the judges are presented only with the facts of the case and the legal arguments, and their task is to decide on the outcome of that particular dispute. Technically, they are not concerned with the social and economic implications of their decisions, and so they cannot commission research or consult experts as to these implications, as Parliament can when changing the law. In the US, litigants are allowed to present written arguments containing socio-economic material.

Retrospective effect

Changes made by case law apply to events which happened before the case came to court, unlike legislation, which usually only applies to events after it comes into force. This may be considered unfair, since if a case changes the law, the parties concerned in that case could not have known what the law was before they acted. US courts sometimes get round the problems by deciding the case before them according to the old law, while declaring that in future the new law will prevail: or they may determine with what degree of retroactivity a new rule is to be enforced.

In **SW *v* United Kingdom** (1996), two men, who had been convicted of the rape and attempted rape of their wives, brought a case before the European Court of Human Rights, alleging that their convictions violated Art. 7 of the European Convention on Human Rights, which provides that criminal laws should not have retrospective effect. The men argued that, when the incidents which gave rise to their convictions happened, it was not a crime for a man to force his wife to have sex; it only became a crime after the decision in **R *v* R** (1991) (see p. 267). The court dismissed the men's argument: Art. 7 did not prevent the courts from clarifying the principles of criminal liability, provided the developments could be clearly foreseen. In this case, there had been mounting criticism of the previous law, and a series of cases which had chipped away at the marital rape exemption, before the **R *v* R** decision.

The same issue came before the courts again in **R *v* C** (2004). In that case the defendant was convicted in 2002 of raping his wife in 1970. On appeal, he argued that this conviction breached Art. 7 of the European Convention and tried to distinguish the earlier case of **SW *v* United Kingdom** (1996). He said that, while in **SW *v* United Kingdom** the defendant could have foreseen in 1989 when he committed his offence that his conduct would be regarded as criminal, this was not the case in 1970. This argument was rejected by the Court of Appeal. It claimed, rather unconvincingly, that a husband in 1970 could have anticipated this development in the law. In fact, the leading textbooks at the time clearly stated that husbands were not liable for raping their wives.

Recent criminal cases have shown that the retrospective effect of case law can also work to the benefit of the defendant. In **R v Powell and English** (1998) the House of Lords clarified the law that should determine the criminal liability of accomplices. An earlier controversial case that had involved the criminal liability of an accomplice was that of **R v Craig and Bentley** (1952), whose story was made into the Hollywood film *Let Him Have It*. Bentley was caught and arrested after being chased across rooftops by police. Craig had a gun, and Bentley is alleged to have said to Craig, 'Let him have it'. Craig then shot and killed a policeman. Craig was charged with murdering a police officer (at that time a hanging offence) and Bentley was charged as his accomplice. In court Bentley argued that when he shouted 'Let him have it', he was telling Craig to hand over his gun, rather than, as the prosecution claimed, encouraging him to shoot the police officer. Nevertheless, both were convicted. Craig was under the minimum age for the death sentence, and was given life imprisonment. Bentley, who was older, was hanged. The conviction was subsequently overturned by the Court of Appeal in July 1998, following a long campaign by his family. In considering the trial judge's summing up to the jury, the Court of Appeal said that criminal liability 'must be determined according to the common law as now understood'. The common law that applied in 1998 to accomplice liability was more favourable than the common law that applied in 1952. The danger in practice is that every time the common law shifts to be more favourable to defendants the floodgates are potentially open for defendants to appeal against their earlier convictions.

Undemocratic

Lord Scarman pointed out in **Stock v Frank Jones (Tipton Ltd)** (1978) that a judge cannot match the experience and vision of the legislator; and that unlike the legislator a judge is not answerable to the people. Theories, like Griffith's (1997), which suggest that precedent can actually give judges a good deal of discretion, and allow them to decide cases on grounds of political and social policy, raise the question of whether judges, who are unelected, should have such freedom.

Reading on the web

The House of Lords' recent judgments are available on the House of Lords' judicial business website at:

www.publications.parliament.uk/pa/ld/ldjudgmt.htm

Some important judgments are published on the Court Service website at:

www.hmcourts-service.gov.uk/cms/

Chapter summary

Introduction

In deciding a case, a judge must follow any decision that has been made by a higher court in a case with similar facts. Judges are bound only by the part of the judgment forming the legal principle that was the basis of the earlier decision, known as the *ratio decidendi*. The rest of the judgment is known as *obiter dicta* and is not binding.

The hierarchy of the courts

The European Court of Justice is the highest authority on European law, in other matters the House of Lords is the highest court in the UK. Following the 1966 Practice Statement, the House of Lords is not bound by its previous decisions.

How do judges really decide cases?

According to the traditional declaratory theory laid down by William Blackstone, judges do not make law but merely discover and declare the law that has always been, but this is open to debate.

Do judges make the law?

While judges have traditionally seem themselves as declaring or finding the law, in practice on occasion they clearly make the law.

Advantages of binding precedent

The doctrine of judicial precedent provides:

■ certainty;
■ detailed practical rules;
■ just and impartial rules;
■ a free market in legal ideas; and
■ flexibility.

Disadvantages of binding precedent

Case law has been criticised because of its:

■ complexity and volume;
■ rigidity;
■ illogical distinctions;
■ unpredictability;
■ dependence on chance;
■ retrospective effect; and
■ undemocratic character.

Question and answer guides

Read the source material below and answer parts (a) to (c) which follow.

Exercise on Judicial Precedent

SOURCE A

At first sight, it may seem that the doctrine of precedent means that the common law will almost never alter. But it would be an oversimplification to see the common law as a process of mechanically applying and restating rules of law that have already been created in the past. From time to time, cases arise that are so unusual that there is little or nothing in the way of case law to apply. In addition, judges find ways to   5
avoid applying an existing precedent. No two cases have identical facts. Judges generally have to choose which of a number of precedents to apply to the current case. Earlier cases that are similar, but are in some crucial respect different, need to be *distinguished* from valid precedents. Some courts may *overrule* the decisions of other courts (or themselves) and some courts may *reverse* the decision of lower courts.   10

SOURCE B

There are two factors to bear in mind when trying to establish the *ratio* of any particular case. Taken together, these factors indicate why there may be scope for debate as to what the *ratio* is and, often, why there is no simple black and white answer to the question. First, written judgments do not have headings. There is never a clear heading, the '*ratio decidendi*'. The judgments in appeal cases can often run to   5
a dozen or more pages. As a result, it is not always clear what is *ratio* and what are *obiter dicta*. Second, there is always more than one judge in the appeal courts. In the House of Lords there may be up to seven. Each judge is likely to give a separate judgment containing a different set of reasons for deciding the case and a different view of the law. Which judgment provides the *ratio*?

Adapted from: 'Law in Focus', Simon Jackson, Causeway Press, 2003

(OCR Specimen Paper 2007, Sources of Law Unit)

(a) Source B refers to the terms *ratio decidendi* and *obiter dicta*.

Describe and illustrate what is meant by *both* of these terms.

Plan

Ratio decidendi:

- The *ratio decidendi* is the reason for a decision.
- It is the most important part of a judgment.
- It binds future cases with similar facts in lower courts.
- Almost any case law could be used to illustrate the concept, for example if you have studied contract law you could consider the case of **Carlill *v* Carbolic Smoke Ball Co. Ltd** (1892). The *ratio* of that case was that a unilateral offer to contract can be accepted by performing the conduct stipulated in the offer. Another illustration could be **Donoghue *v* Stevenson** (1932) in tort law.

Obiter dicta:

- *Obiter dicta* means things said by the way.
- Any observations on the law that do not fall within the *ratio decidendi* of the case can be described as falling within the *obiter dicta*.
- These statements are not binding on future cases, but may be treated as of interest and may influence future developments in the law.
- *Obiter dicta* often consists of speculation by a judge of what the decision would have been had the facts been different or how the law could be improved. Interesting *obiter dicta* can be found in the contract case of **Central London Property Trust Ltd *v* High Trees House Ltd** (1947).

Answer

The doctrine of judicial precedent is known in Latin as *stare decisis,* meaning 'let the previous decision stand'. Under this doctrine, the lower courts have to follow the legal principles decided in earlier cases by higher courts.

The legal statements in a court judgment can be divided into its *ratio decidendi* (the reason for the decision) and its *obiter dicta* (things said by the way). Sometimes it is not easy to identify what the *ratio decidendi* of a case is, especially where a number of judges have handed down judgments in an appellate court giving different reasons for the decision of the court.

The *ratio decidendi* of a case is the binding part of the decision, binding future decisions of the lower courts. When judges deliver their judgment in a case they tend to outline their findings of fact and then apply the law to these facts which is the reason for their final decision: the *ratio*. Although the judges do give reasons for their decision, often their judgments are quite lengthy and it can be difficult to identify precisely what the *ratio decidendi* is for the case. It will be the task for the future judges to elicit the *ratio* from the judgment. There may be disagreement over what the *ratio* is, there may be more than one *ratio*, and it will be up to the lawyers to persuade the judge to interpret the case in a way that is favourable to their client. The resulting discretion enjoyed by the judges provides an element of flexibility in the system of judicial precedent which can help judges achieve justice on the facts of a particular case before them.

Two cases will be considered to illustrate the concept of a *ratio decidendi*. In contract law, a leading case is **Carlill *v* Carbolic Smoke Ball Co Ltd** (1892). The *ratio* of that case was that a unilateral offer to contract can be accepted by performing the conduct stipulated in the offer. In tort law, a leading case is **Donoghue *v* Stevenson** (1932). The *ratio* of that case was that manufacturers owe a duty of care to the end user of their goods.

Judges may speculate about what their decision might have been if the facts of the case or the law had been different. These observations fall within the *obiter dicta* of the case, as they are 'things said by the way'. Obiter is persuasive precedent which can always be helpful to a creative judge needing some flexibility and looking to distinguish or otherwise avoid a binding precedent. It is arguable that the neighbour principle contained in **Donoghue *v* Stevenson** actually forms part of the *obiter* of that case.

The *obiter dictum* is not binding on later cases because it was not strictly relevant to the matter in issue in the original case. However, an *obiter dictum* may be of interest and influence future developments in the law.

(b) Source A identifies various methods by which judges avoid having to apply past precedents.

Explain which method of avoidance is most suited to each of the scenarios below. Illustrate your answer where appropriate:

(i)　The House of Lords wish to depart from a past decision of their own;

Plan

Following the House of Lords' Practice Statement of 1966, the House can overrule its own previous decisions. **R v R** (1991) criminalising marital rape, and **Pepper v Hart** (1993) allowing the courts to refer to *Hansard* when interpreting a statute, are examples of where the House of Lords overruled its earlier decisions.

The House of Lords is reluctant to overrule its own previous decisions – this reluctance is illustrated by the case of **R v Kansal (No. 2)** (2001) discussed on p. 259. It might therefore seek instead to distinguish its earlier decision on the facts of the case.

(ii)　on appeal, the Court of Appeal disagrees with a ruling of the High Court and wishes to replace it with a different decision;

Plan

The Court of Appeal could reverse the decision of a lower court on appeal in the same case and the High Court is lower in the hierarchy of the courts than the Court of Appeal. It could then replace the earlier decision with its own decision where it comes to a different view of the law.

(iii)　a judge in the Crown Court does not wish to follow a past precedent of a higher court as she feels that the facts are slightly different.

Plan

Judges in all courts are entitled to distinguish the facts of a case from an earlier case and are not then required to follow it under the rules of judicial precedent. Examples of this happening could be provided, for example, from contract law and the cases of **Balfour v Balfour** (1919) and **Merritt v Merritt** (1971). These cases considered whether the parties to a domestic agreement had an intention to make a legally binding contract.

(c) **With reference to Sources A and B:**

(i)   describe the justifications for judges following binding precedents.

Plan

Justifications for following binding precedents include:

- **Certainty**: litigants know that the judges will follow earlier reported decisions. The outcome of the case may be predictable, which will help the parties decide whether to settle out of court. This provides an excellent environment in which companies can do business. The reluctance of the House of Lords to overrule its own previous decisions reflects the emphasis given to the value of certainty.
- **Consistency**: like cases should be treated alike. This is fair and encourages respect in the law.
- **Flexibility**: within the rules of binding precedent, judges still retain a level of discretion which allows the law to change to reflect changes in society. This flexibility was reinforced by the House of Lords' Practice Statement of 1966.
- **Efficiency**: once a legal principle has been established this can be followed, rather than trying to recreate the law with each new decision. With a system of binding precedent an appeal is less likely, because the parties can predict the probability of an appeal being successful.
- **Detailed practical rules**: the law has developed from real life cases.
- **Free market in legal ideas**: Hayek (1982) has argued that case law develops in line with market forces.

(ii)   discuss the disadvantages of the doctrine of precedent.

Plan

- **Complexity**: there is a huge amount of reported cases and within each case it can be difficult to determine the *ratio decidendi*, particularly where more than one judge heard the case in an appellate court.
- **Rigidity**: because lower courts are bound by the higher courts and the House of Lords is still reluctant to overturn its own previous decisions despite the Practice Statement of 1966.
- **Illogical distinctions**: the courts can resort to drawing minute distinctions in an effort to avoid an earlier authority.
- **Slow and unpredictable**: change depends on the random chance of a case reaching an appellate court.
- **Lack of research**: while legislation can be based on careful research on the law in practice, the judges do not have such resources to rely on when developing the law.
- **Retrospective effect**: changes in case law affect conduct committed prior to the date of the case, which can create particular complications in the context of the criminal law.
- **Undemocratic**: judges are not elected.

Group activity 1

Look at Lord Bingham's judgment in the House of Lords' case **R (Countryside Alliance and others)** *v* **Attorney General** (2007). Which strategies does he use to avoid following these cases:

- **Pretty** *v* **United Kingdom** (2002);
- **Buckley** *v* **United Kingdom** (1996); and
- **Chapman** *v* **United Kingdom** (2001)?

Group activity 2

- With your friends (or class), prepare a chart depicting the English civil court hierarchy in as simple a form as possible. It should make clear that all civil cases are tried in either the High Court or a county court, and that appeals go to the Court of Appeal and then to the House of Lords.
- Divide your friends (or class) into groups of two or three people.
- Each group should invite six people, having no knowledge of law, to study the chart and then answer the following questions. Try to get your interviewees to give reasoned answers, rather than just 'Yes' or 'No'.

  Q1(a): Do you think that a court on the chart should be bound by the earlier decisions of a court that is higher than it? (You will need to explain what 'bound' means!)

  Q1(b): Do you think that there should be any situations in which a court on the chart should be able to overrule an earlier decision of a court that is higher than it?

  Q2(a): Do you think that a court on the chart should be bound by its own previous decisions?

  Q2(b): Do you think that there should be any situations in which a court on the chart should be able to overrule one of its own previous decisions?

- With your friends (or class), prepare a table summarising all the answers obtained by all the groups.
- To what extent do these answers accurately reflect the legal position and what conclusions can you draw from this as to the current rules of judicial precedent?

Visit **www.mylawchamber.co.uk/elliottocr** to access questions, quizzes and activities to test yourself on this chapter.

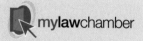

Chapter 15
ACTS OF PARLIAMENT

This chapter discusses:

- how an Act of Parliament is made;
- the supremacy of Parliament;
- the advantages and disadvantages of Parliamentary law-making.

Introduction

The most important laws in the UK are made by Parliament. These laws are known as Acts of Parliament or statutes. Parliament is the democratically elected governing body for the nation. It consists of the House of Commons, the House of Lords and the monarch (currently Queen Elizabeth). A lengthy process of informal and formal debate needs to be carried out before an Act of Parliament becomes law. The informal process starts outside Parliament, when different organisations and people try to influence the government to decide what new laws are needed in the country to tackle a particular problem. For example, a newspaper might publish headlines suggesting that new offences should be created to tackle the problem of drug abuse. The government might accept this and commence a formal legislative process through Parliament to pass an Act of Parliament creating new drug offences.

Making an Act of Parliament

When a government has identified a policy objective, which may have been drawn to its attention in one of the ways described above, then it may choose to include this in an official consultation document, known as a Green Paper. This document puts forward tentative proposals for reform, often through the use of parliamentary legislation, which interested parties may consider and give their views on. The Green Paper will be followed by a White Paper, which contains the specific reform plans.

Bills

All statutes begin as a Bill, which is a proposal for a piece of legislation. There are three types of Bill:

1 **Public Bills.** These are presented to Parliament by government ministers and change the general law of the whole country. They are written by lawyers known as parliamentary counsel, who specialise in drafting legislation.
2 **Private members' Bills.** These are prepared by an individual backbench MP (someone who is not a member of the Cabinet). MPs wanting to put forward a Bill have to enter a ballot to win the right to do so, and then persuade the government to allow enough parliamentary time for the Bill to go through. Consequently, very few such Bills become Acts, and they tend to function more as a way of drawing attention to particular issues. Some, however, have made important contributions to legislation, an example being the Abortion Act 1967, which stemmed from a private member's Bill put forward by David Steel.
3 **Private Bills.** These are usually proposed by a local authority, public corporation or large public company, and normally affect only that sponsor. An example might be a local authority seeking the right to build a bridge or road.

The actual preparation of Bills is done by expert draftsmen known as Parliamentary Counsel.

Task 15.1

Public Bills that are currently being considered by Parliament are available at:

www.parliament.the-stationery-office.co.uk/pa/pabills.htm

Visit this website and find a public Bill that is before Parliament.

First reading

The title of the prepared Bill is read to the House of Commons. This is called the first reading, and acts as a notification of the proposed measure.

Second reading

At the second reading, the proposals are debated fully, and may be amended, and members vote on whether the legislation should proceed. In practice, the whip system (party officials whose job is to make sure MPs vote with their party) means that a government with a reasonable majority can almost always get its legislation through at this and subsequent stages.

Committee stage

The Bill is then referred to a committee of the House of Commons for detailed examination, bearing in mind the points made during the debate. At this point, further amendments to the Bill may be made.

ELIZABETH II

c. **4**

Criminal Defence Service (Advice and Assistance) Act 2001

2001 CHAPTER 4

An Act to clarify the extent of the duty of the Legal Services Commission under section 13(1) of the Access to Justice Act 1999.　　　　[10th April 2001]

B E IT ENACTED by the Queen's most Excellent Majesty, by and with the advice and consent of the Lords Spiritual and Temporal, and Commons, in this present Parliament assembled, and by the authority of the same, as follows:—

1 **Extent of duty to fund advice and assistance**

(1) Subsection (1) of section 13 of the Access to Justice Act 1999 (c. 22) (duty of Legal Services Commission to fund advice and assistance as part of Criminal Defence Service) shall be treated as having been enacted with the substitution of the following for paragraph (b) and the words after it—

"(b) in prescribed circumstances, for individuals who—

(i) are not within paragraph (a) but are involved in investigations which may lead to criminal proceedings,

(ii) are before a court or other body in such proceedings, or

(iii) have been the subject of such proceedings;

and the assistance which the Commission may consider appropriate includes assistance in the form of advocacy."

(2) Regulations under subsection (1) of section 13 (as amended above) may include provision treating them as having come into force at the same time as that subsection.

2 **Short title**

This Act may be cited as the Criminal Defence Service (Advice and Assistance) Act 2001.

Figure 15.1 **Criminal Defence Service (Advice and Assistance) Act 2001**

Source: © Crown Copyright 2001.

Report stage

The committee then reports back to the House, and any proposed amendments are debated and voted upon.

Third reading

The Bill is re-presented to the House. There may be a short debate, and a vote on whether to accept or reject the legislation as it stands.

House of Lords

The Bill then goes to the House of Lords, where it goes through a similar process of three readings. If the House of Lords alters anything, the Bill returns to the Commons for further consideration. The Commons then responds with agreement, reasons for disagreement, or proposals for alternative changes.

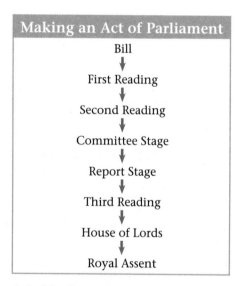

Figure 15.2 **Making an Act of Parliament**

At one time, legislation could not be passed without the agreement of both Houses, which meant that the unelected House of Lords could block legislation put forward by the elected House of Commons. The Parliament Acts of 1911 and 1949 lay down special procedures by which proposed legislation can go for Royal Assent without the approval of the House of Lords after specified periods of time. These procedures are only rarely used, because the House of Lords usually drops objections that are resisted by the Commons, though their use has increased in recent years. Only four Acts of Parliament have been passed to date relying on the Parliament Act 1949. It is of particular note that the procedures were used to pass the controversial Hunting Act 2004. This Act bans hunting wild animals with dogs and a form of hunting known as hare coursing. It was passed despite the House of Lords' opposition, by using the Parliament Act 1949.

Task 15.2

Recent legislation is published on The Stationery Office website. Visit this site at:

www.opsi.gov.uk/acts.htm

Find s. 46 of the Criminal Justice and Court Services Act 2000. What is the definition of an exclusion order?

Explanatory notes provide guidance as to the implications of new legislation. These are available at:

www.opsi.gov.uk/legislation/uk-expa.htm

Find the explanatory notes that accompany the Criminal Justice and Court Services Act 2000. What guidance is given in relation to s. 46?

Royal Assent

In the vast majority of cases, agreement between the Lords and Commons is reached, and the Bill is then presented for Royal Assent. Technically, the Queen must give her consent to all legislation before it can become law, but in practice that consent is never refused.

The Bill is then an Act of Parliament, and becomes law, though most do not take effect from the moment the Queen gives her consent, but on a specified date in the near future or when a commencement order has been issued by a government minister. Acts of Parliament are referred to by their short title and the year in which they were passed, for example, the Police and Criminal Evidence Act 1984.

Quick quiz 15.3

Put the following events into chronological order for the ordinary process of passing a public Bill:

- Second reading in the House of Commons.
- Royal Assent.
- House of Lords considers the Public Bill.
- Public Bill drafted.
- First reading in the House of Commons.
- Report stage.
- Green Paper.
- Committee stage in the House of Commons.
- Third reading.

 Know your terms 15.4

Define the following terms:

1 Hereditary peer.
2 Royal Assent.
3 Public Bill.

The supremacy of Parliament

The supremacy of Parliament (also known as the 'sovereignty of Parliament') is a fundamental principle of our constitution. This means that Parliament is the highest source of English law; so long as a law has been passed according to the

Figure 15.3 **Houses of Parliament**
Source: © Copyright 2002 Parliamentary Education Unit (House of Commons).

rules of parliamentary procedure, it must be applied by the courts. So if, for example, Parliament had passed a law stating that all newborn boys had to be killed, or that all dog owners had to keep a cat as well, there might well be an enormous public outcry, but the laws would still be valid and the courts would, in theory at least, be obliged to uphold them. The reasoning behind this approach is that Parliament, unlike the judiciary, is democratically elected, and therefore ought to have the upper hand when making the laws that every citizen has to live by.

This approach is unusual in democratic countries. Most comparable nations have what is known as a Bill of Rights. This is a statement of the basic rights which citizens can expect to have protected from state interference and takes precedence over other laws. The courts are able to refuse to apply legislation which infringes any of the rights protected by it.

Britain does not have a Bill of Rights but, under the Human Rights Act 1998, the European Convention on Human Rights has been incorporated into domestic law. The Act does not give the Convention superiority over English law, however. It requires that, wherever possible, legislation should be interpreted in line with the principles of the Convention, but it does not allow the courts to override statutes that are incompatible with it, nor does it prevent Parliament from making laws that are in conflict with it.

Section 19 of the Act requires that when new legislation is made, a government minister must make a statement before the second reading of the Bill in either House of Parliament, saying either that in their view the provisions of the Bill are compatible with the Convention, or that even if they are not, the government wishes to proceed with the Bill anyway. Although the implication is obviously that, in most cases, ministers will be able to say that a Bill conforms with the Convention, the Act's provision for the alternative statement confirms that parliamentary supremacy is not intended to be overridden. The Act does make one impact on parliamentary supremacy, though a small one: s. 10 allows a minister of the Crown to amend by order any Act which has been found by the courts to be incompatible with the Convention, whereas normally an Act of Parliament could only be changed by another Act. However, there is no obligation to do this and a piece of legislation which has been found to be incompatible with the Convention would remain valid if the government chose not to amend it.

By contrast, a definite erosion of parliamentary supremacy has been brought about by Britain's membership of the European Union. The EU can only make laws concerning particular subject areas, but in those areas, its law must take precedence over laws made by Parliament, and in this respect Parliament is no longer strictly speaking the supreme source of law in the UK. In areas of law not covered by the EU, however, Parliament remains supreme.

In 1998 some important constitutional changes were made, which passed some of the powers of the Westminster Parliament to new bodies in Scotland and Northern Ireland. The new Scottish Parliament, created by the Scotland Act 1998, can make laws affecting Scotland only, in many important areas, including health, education, local government, criminal justice, food standards and agriculture, though legislation on foreign affairs, defence, national security, trade and industry and a number of other areas will still be made for the whole of the UK by the Westminster Parliament. The Northern Ireland Act 1998 similarly gives the Northern Ireland Assembly power to make legislation for Northern Ireland in some areas, though again, foreign policy, defence and certain other areas are still to be covered by Westminster.

In the same year, the Government of Wales Act established a new body for Wales, the Welsh Assembly, but unlike the other two bodies, the Welsh Assembly does not have the power to make primary legislation; legislation made in Westminster will continue to cover Wales. However, the Welsh Assembly is able to make what is called delegated legislation (discussed in Chapter 16).

Advantages of parliamentary law-making

Democratic process

A key advantage of the parliamentary process is that the House of Commons has been democratically elected and therefore the legislation that it issues should reflect the will of the majority of the general public.

Open debate

The legislative process takes place in public and there is an opportunity through the consultative processes for the public to directly influence the content of the legislation.

Disadvantages of parliamentary law-making

The House of Lords

Membership of the House of Lords is currently in transition. Historically, this body has not been elected and therefore has not been democratic. The Labour government has reduced the role of people who sat in the House of Lords simply because of who their parents were (known as hereditary peers) and in the future the intention is that at least some of its members will be elected.

Limited time

The parliamentary process is relatively slow and sometimes people would accept that law reform is necessary but no time is available for Parliament to pass the legislation. This has been particularly frustrating for the Law Commission, which has produced lengthy and well-argued documents arguing for a specific law reform and while the government accepts that such a reform is necessary, no parliamentary time is made available to push through this reform.

Task 15.5

Read the following article and then answer the questions that follow:

Many of the measures announced by Tony Blair to tackle terrorism in the wake of the London suicide bombings could and should have been taken long ago. Announcing plans for new legislation and more extensive use of existing powers to deport those who advocate terrorism, the Prime Minister twice said 'the rules of the game' are changing. By this, he seemed to mean the 'rules' within international human rights law and the Human Rights Act needed changing. That impression was strengthened when the Lord Chancellor, Lord Falconer, warned that British judges might have to be instructed by Act of Parliament on how to interpret and apply Article 3 of the European Convention on Human Rights (prohibiting torture) more restrictively than the European Court of Human Rights.

  Our courts need no instruction from government or parliament about how to interpret and apply the Human Rights Act. Contrary to the intemperate and ignorant attacks on the judiciary by Michael Howard, they have not been guilty of 'aggressive judicial activism', 'thwarting the will of parliament'. Our courts are in a weaker position than those of the rest of Europe and the common-law world. In deference to parliamentary sovereignty, they cannot strike down Acts of Parliament, but can only give declarations of incompatibility, leaving it to ministers and parliament to decide what to do. British courts have interpreted and applied the Human Rights Act wisely, without encroaching on the executive and legislative branches of government.

Source: Adapted from an article by Anthony Lester in *The Observer*, 14 August 2005.

1 Why is Art. 3 of the European Convention important?
2 Who is Michael Howard?
3 Why are our judges in a weaker position than their European counterparts?
4 Who do you think should have the most power, the judges or Parliament?

Reading on the web

Copies of Public Bills currently being considered by Parliament can be found at:

www.parliament.uk/business/bills_and_legislation.cfm

Copies of recent legislation can be found at:

www.opsi.gov.uk/acts.htm

Useful explanatory notes prepared by the government to explain the implications of recent legislation can be found at:

www.opsi.gov.uk/legislation/uk-expa.htm

John Halliday has produced a report on the work of the Law Commission which has been published on the internet at:

www.dca.gov.uk/majrep/lawcom/halliday.htm

The Law Commission's website is:

www.lawcom.gov.uk/

Chapter summary

Introduction

The most important laws in the UK are made by Parliament.

Making an Act of Parliament

All statutes begin as a Bill. There are three types of Bill:

- Public Bills.
- Private members' Bills.
- Private Bills.

The legislative process usually starts in the House of Commons and proceeds as follows:

- First reading.
- Second reading.
- Committee stage.
- Report stage.
- Third reading.
- House of Lords.
- Royal Assent.

Role of the House of Lords

The Parliament Acts of 1911 and 1949 lay down special procedures by which proposed legislation can go for Royal Assent without the approval of the House of Lords after specified periods of time. These procedures are only rarely used, because the House of Lords usually drops objections that are resisted by the Commons, though their use has increased in recent years.

The supremacy of Parliament

This means that Parliament is the highest source of English law, and statutes must be applied by the courts. Britain does not have a Bill of Rights which could restrict Parliament's powers to make laws. The Human Rights Act 1998 incorporated the European Convention on Human Rights but this does not give the Convention superiority over English law. Statutes which breach the Convention must still be applied by the courts.

One limit on parliamentary supremacy is now European law. As part of a process of devolution, Parliament has chosen to give legislative powers to the Scottish Parliament and the Northern Ireland Assembly. In theory, Parliament could take back these legislative powers and therefore remains supreme.

Advantages of parliamentary law-making

- A democratic process.
- An opportunity for open debate.

Disadvantages of parliamentary law-making

- Problems with the House of Lords.
- Parliament only has limited time.

Question and answer guides

1 (a) Describe how Acts of Parliament are made by the House of Commons, the House of Lords and the Crown.

Answer

Before Parliament becomes directly involved in the legislative process, there is frequently a preliminary preparatory stage when the idea for a new piece of legislation is generated. This idea might seek to deal with an issue of social concern or reflect new developments in society. A change in the law can be promoted by a pressure group, such as the Campaign for Nuclear Disarmament and Liberty, or might come from a branch of the civil service. Legislation might have been promised by a political party in their election manifesto. Once it has been decided that legislation is desirable then a Bill can be prepared. Three types of Bill can be presented to Parliament: a public Bill, which is presented by a government minister, a private member's Bill, which is presented by a Member of Parliament selected by an annual lottery to introduce a Bill of their personal choice; and a private Bill.

A Bill is generally introduced for its first reading to the House of Commons by its promoter who reads out the title to the House. The Bill is also subjected to a second reading which traditionally must be at least two clear weeks later to allow MPs time to read the published Bill. A full debate takes place at the second reading and this is possibly the most important stage of the legislative process. A vote will be called, which is sometimes shown on television when the Speaker calls 'clear the lobbies'. There is usually a whipped vote in the Commons, which means that the MPs are pressurised to vote according to their party's instructions. Sometimes a Bill is not considered to be a party political issue, in which case the MP is allowed to vote according to their personal morals, for example, in relation to legislation on abortion.

The Bill then passes to a House of Commons Committee, the composition of which usually reflects party numbers in the House of Commons, to scrutinise the Bill in minute detail. The Committee makes amendments, putting forward additions or deletions to clarify or improve the Bill. It then reports back to the Commons with its suggestions and the amendments can be debated and voted by MPs. This report stage is then followed by the third reading, where the Bill is re-read to MPs and any final changes voted on. The House of Commons then hands the Bill over to the House of Lords.

The House of Lords has changed in formation recently. It used to include a large number of unelected peers, but the Labour government brought in the House of Lords Act 1999 and all but 92 unelected peers remain, the rest are appointed life peers, bishops and Law Lords. Their role is to act as a check and balance on the work of government but with many life peers being put forward by politicians, there is a possibility of the Lords reflecting party affiliations. The stages the Bill passes through in the Lords are almost identical to those in the Commons: first reading, second reading, committee stage (though the committee is actually the whole House) and final reading. The Lords can reject a bill or delay it and if the government does not want to push through the legislation in the face of the House of Lords' opposition, it will be shelved. If, however, the government wants the Bill on the statute books (as with the Hunting Act 2004), it can push the Bill through Parliament by invoking the Parliament Acts 1911 and 1949, despite opposition from the House of Lords.

A Bill can be started in the House of Lords instead of the House of Commons but the procedures followed are exactly the same.

The Bill then goes to the Crown for Royal Assent. Traditionally, the Queen signs every Bill presented to her, so the Royal Assent has become a mere formality. Once Royal Assent has been given, the Act becomes law and will come into force immediately unless the Act provides that it is to come into force at a later date.

(b) Consider the advantages and disadvantages of the parliamentary legislative process.

Plan

Advantages:

- A democratic process.
- Transparent and open to the public.
- Consultation with the public.
- Careful debate inside Parliament.
- Sufficient time to consider the impact of the proposed legislation.
- Full media coverage.
- Respected tradition.

Disadvantages:

- Principles of democracy undermined by composition of the House of Lords.
- Slow.
- Insufficient time for all important legislation, so reforms proposed by, for example, the Law Commission are frequently not presented to Parliament.
- Too much delegated legislation because of shortage of parliamentary time, which is not subject to such tight controls.
- Politicians controlled by their party whips, rather than entering into a genuine debate.
- Acts are poorly drafted, with complex language which the public (and lawyers) find difficult to understand.
- Limited post-legislative scrutiny.

Group activity 1

Working in groups, look at the website of the Office of Public Sector Information to investigate the passage of the Hunting Act 2004 through Parliament:

www.opsi.gov.uk/acts/acts2004/20040037.htm

- Was the Hunting Bill preceded by a formal consultation process?
- What type of Bill was it?
- What problems did the Bill encounter on its way through Parliament?
- What does the Act state its purpose to be?

Group activity 2

Consider the following statement: 'This country has no need for the House of Lords as a legislative chamber and it should be abolished.'

Divide your friends (or class) into two groups. Choose one person to be the judge. One group must argue in favour of the House of Lords being retained as a legislative chamber and the other group must argue in favour of it being abolished. The judge will act as a referee, choosing who can speak and deciding at the end which group put forward the strongest arguments.

Chapter 16
DELEGATED LEGISLATION

This chapter discusses:

- the three forms of delegated legislation;
- the reasons for delegating legislative powers;
- how delegated legislation is controlled;
- the criticism made of delegated legislation.

Introduction

In many cases, the statutes passed by Parliament lay down a basic framework of the law, with creation of the detailed rules delegated to government departments, local authorities, or public or nationalised bodies. There are three main forms of delegated legislation:

Statutory instruments

These are made by government departments.

Bye-laws

These are made by local authorities, public and nationalised bodies. Bye-laws have to be approved by central government.

Orders in Council

These are made by government in times of emergency. They are drafted by the relevant government department, approved by the Privy Council and signed by the Queen. Under the Civil Contingency Act 2004 (replacing the Emergency Powers Act 1920), Orders in Council can be issued at times of emergency. This has tended to happen in the past when there have been major strikes, so that soldiers can provide services during the strike action.

On an everyday basis, delegated legislation is an extremely important source of law. The output of delegated legislation far exceeds that of Acts of Parliament, and its provisions include rules that can substantially affect the day-to-day lives of huge numbers of people – safety laws for industry, road traffic regulations, and rules relating to state education, for example.

The power to make delegated legislation

Ordinary members of the public cannot decide on a whim to make delegated legislation. Instead, usually an Act of Parliament is required, known as an enabling Act, which gives this power to a branch of the state. The Act can be quite specific giving a limited power to make legislation on a very narrow issue, or it can be quite general and allow for a wide range of delegated legislation to be made. An example

sourcebook p. 35 → of such a general provision is the European Communities Act 1972, s. 2, which allows the executive to make delegated legislation to bring into force in the UK relevant European legislation.

Parliament has recently passed an Act which gives the executive very wide powers to make delegated legislation, the Legislative and Regulatory Reform Act 2006. This Act was introduced following a report of the Better Regulation Taskforce, *Regulation – Less is More* (2005). The official aim of the Act is to make it simpler and faster to amend existing legislation. It will allow ministers to issue statutory instruments to amend existing legislation or implement recommendations of the Law Commission (with the possibility of some changes being added by the government). No vote in Parliament would be required, though the statutory instrument could be blocked by a new parliamentary committee. The first draft of the Bill was severely criticised by a panel of MPs for giving excessive powers to make delegated legislation which were disproportionate to the Bill's stated aims. In the light of these criticisms, some amendments were made, but concerns remain that this is an unnecessary shift of power from a democratically elected Parliament, to the executive. The director of the pressure group, Justice, has commented:

> *'In its original form, the Bill went well beyond what the government says it wanted and was one of the most appallingly drafted Bills I've ever seen. It was just amazingly wide. Either that was the government's intention, in which case they really were trying to accumulate a major increase in power, or it wasn't, in which case it's pretty incompetent.'*

Task 16.1

Statutory instruments are published on the office for Public Sector Information website at:

www.opsi.gov.uk/stat.htm

Go to this website and find the Data Protection Act 1998 (Commencement) Order 2000 (SI 2000/183). This statutory instrument brought the main provisions of the Data Protection Act 1998 into force.

1 Under which legislative provisions was this piece of delegated legislation made?
2 On what date did these provisions come into force?

The reasons for delegating legislative powers

Delegated legislation is necessary for a number of reasons.

Insufficient parliamentary time

Parliament does not have the time to debate every detailed rule necessary for efficient government.

Speed

It allows rules to be made more quickly than they could by Parliament. Parliament does not sit all the time, and its procedure is slow and cumbersome. Delegated legislation often has to be made in response to emergencies and urgent problems.

Technicality of the subject matter

Modern legislation often needs to include detailed, technical provisions – those in building regulations or safety at work rules, for example. MPs do not usually have the technical knowledge required, whereas delegated legislation can use experts who are familiar with the relevant areas.

Need for local knowledge

Local bye-laws, in particular, can only be made effectively with awareness of the locality. Recognition of the importance of local knowledge can be found with the new devolved assemblies for Scotland, Wales and Northern Ireland. These new democratic bodies have important powers to make delegated legislation.

Flexibility

Statutes require cumbersome procedures for enactment, and can only be revoked or amended by another statute. Delegated legislation, however, can be put into action quickly, and be easily revoked if it proves problematic.

Future needs

Parliament cannot hope to foresee every problem that might arise as a result of a statute, especially concerning areas such as health provision or welfare benefits. Delegated legislation can be put in place as and when such problems arise.

Control of delegated legislation

Because it is not directly made by elected representatives, delegated legislation is subject to the following range of controls, designed to ensure that the power delegated is not abused.

Consultation

Those who make delegated legislation often consult experts within the relevant field, and those bodies who are likely to be affected by it. In the case of road traffic regulations, for example, ministers are likely to seek the advice of police, motoring organisations, vehicle manufacturers and local authorities before making the rules. Often, the relevant statute makes such consultation obligatory and names the bodies who should be consulted. Under the National Insurance Act 1946, for example, draft regulations must be submitted to the National Insurance Advisory Committee, and any minister proposing to make rules of procedure for a tribunal within a department is required by the Tribunals and Inquiries Act 1971 to consult the Council on Tribunals. In other cases there may be a general statutory requirement for 'such consultation as the minister thinks appropriate with such organisations as appear to him to represent the interest concerned'.

Publication

All delegated legislation is published, and therefore available for public scrutiny. Alongside the statutory instrument, the government now publishes an explanatory memorandum detailing the statutory instrument's policy objective and legislative context.

Supervision by Parliament

There are a number of ways in which Parliament can oversee delegated legislation.

Revocation

Parliamentary sovereignty means that Parliament can at any time revoke a piece of delegated legislation itself, or pass legislation on the same subject as the delegated legislation.

The affirmative resolution procedure

Enabling Acts dealing with subjects of special, often constitutional, importance may require Parliament to vote its approval of the delegated legislation. This is called the affirmative resolution procedure, whereby delegated legislation is laid before one or both Houses (sometimes in draft), and becomes law only if a motion approving it is passed within a specified time (usually 28 or 40 days). Since a vote has to be taken, the procedure means that the government must find parliamentary time for debate, and opposition parties have an opportunity to raise any objections. In practice, though, it is very rare for the government not to achieve a majority when such votes are taken.

The negative resolution procedure

Much delegated legislation is put before Parliament for MPs under the negative resolution procedure. Within a specified time (usually 40 days), any member may put down a motion to annul it. An annulment motion put down by a back-bencher is not guaranteed to be dealt with, but one put down by the Official

Opposition (the party with the second largest number of MPs) usually will be. If, after debate, either House passes an annulment motion, the delegated legislation is cancelled.

Parliamentary Scrutiny Committees

Several parliamentary committees monitor new delegated legislation. The Joint Committee on Statutory Instruments watches over the making of delegated legislation and reports to each House on any delegated legislation which requires special consideration, including any regulations made under an Act that prohibit challenge by the courts, or which seem to make unusual or unexpected use of the powers granted by the enabling Act. However, the committee may not consider the merits of any piece of delegated legislation. This is the responsibility of the House of Lords' Merits of Statutory Instruments Committee. In addition, the House of Lords' Select Committee on Delegated Powers and Deregulation looks at the extent of legislative powers proposed to be delegated by Parliament to government ministers. It is required to report on whether the provision of any Bill inappropriately delegates legislative power, or subjects the exercise of legislative power to an inappropriate level of parliamentary scrutiny.

Questions from MPs

MPs can ask ministers questions about delegated legislation at a ministerial question time, or raise them in debates.

The House of Lords

Although the House of Lords cannot veto proposed Acts, the same does not apply to delegated legislation. In 1968 the House of Lords rejected an order imposing sanctions against the Rhodesian government made under the Southern Rhodesia Act 1965.

Control by the courts: judicial review

While the validity of a statute can never be challenged by the courts because of parliamentary sovereignty, delegated legislation can. In a judicial review hearing the courts undertake a review of the process that has been followed in making a decision and can make sure that the public authority had the power to make this decision. Delegated legislation may be challenged on any of the following grounds under the procedure for judicial review.

Procedural *ultra vires*

The term *ultra vires* is Latin and can be translated as 'beyond the powers'. It refers to the situation where a public authority has overstepped its powers. Procedural *ultra vires* occurs where the procedures laid down in the enabling Act for producing delegated legislation have not been followed. In **Agricultural, Horticultural and Forestry Training Board** *v* **Aylesbury Mushrooms Ltd** (1972), an order was declared invalid because the requirement to consult with interested parties before making it had not been properly complied with.

Substantive *ultra vires*

This is usually based on a claim that the measure under review goes beyond the powers Parliament granted under the enabling Act. In **Customs and Excise Commissioners** *v* **Cure & Deeley Ltd** (1962), the powers of the Commissioners to make delegated legislation under the Finance (No. 2) Act 1940 were challenged. The Act empowered them to produce regulations 'for any matter for which provision appears to them necessary for the purpose of giving effect to the Act'. The Commissioners held that this included allowing them to make a regulation giving them the power to determine the amount of tax due where a tax return was submitted late. The High Court invalidated the regulation on the grounds that the Commissioners had given themselves powers far beyond what Parliament had intended; they were empowered only to collect such tax as was due by law, not to decide what amount they thought fit.

R *v* **Secretary of State for Social Security, ex parte Joint Council for the Welfare of Immigrants** (1996) concerned the Asylum and Immigration Appeals Act 1993, which provided a framework for determining applications for asylum, and for appeals after unsuccessful applications. It allowed asylum seekers to apply for social security benefits while they were waiting for their applications or appeals to be decided, at a cost of over £200 million per year to British taxpayers. This led to concern from some quarters that the provisions might attract those who were simply seeking a better lifestyle than that available in their own countries (often called economic migrants), as opposed to those fleeing persecution, whom the provisions were actually designed to help.

In order to discourage economic migrants, the then Secretary of State for Social Security exercised his powers to make delegated legislation under the Social Security (Contributions and Benefits) Act 1992, and produced regulations which stated that social security benefits would no longer be available to those who sought asylum after they had entered the UK, rather than immediately on entry, or those who had been refused leave to stay here and were awaiting the outcome of appeals against the decision.

The Joint Council for the Welfare of Immigrants challenged the regulations, claiming that they fell outside the powers granted by the 1992 Act. The Court of Appeal upheld the claim, stating that the 1993 Act was clearly intended to give asylum seekers rights which they did not have previously. The effect of the regulations was effectively to take those rights away again, since without access to social security benefits, most asylum seekers would have either to return to the countries from which they had fled, or to live on nothing while their claims were processed. The court ruled that Parliament could not have intended to give the Secretary of State powers to take away the rights it had given in the 1993 Act: this could only be done by a new statute, and therefore the regulations were *ultra vires*.

The decision was a controversial one, because the regulations had themselves been approved by Parliament, and overturning them could be seen as a challenge to the power of the legislature, despite the decision being explained by the court as upholding that power.

Unreasonableness

If rules are manifestly unjust, have been made in bad faith (for example, by some-one with a financial interest in their operation) or are otherwise so perverse that no reasonable official could have made them, the courts can declare them invalid.

Quick quiz 16.3

1 Name the three main forms of delegated legislation.

2 Give three reasons why delegated legislation is necessary.

3 Explain what is meant by the affirmative resolution procedure.

4 Name the three grounds on which delegated legislation can be challenged before the courts.

Criticism of delegated legislation

Lack of democratic involvement

This argument is put forward because delegated legislation is usually made by civil servants, rather than elected politicians. This is not seen as a particular problem where the delegated legislation takes the form of detailed administrative rules, since these would clearly take up impossible amounts of parliamentary time otherwise. However, in the last years of the last Conservative government there was increasing concern that delegated legislation was being used to implement important policies.

Overuse

Critics argue that there is too much delegated legislation; this is linked to the point above, as there would be little problem with increasing amounts of delegated legislation if its purpose was merely to flesh out technical detail.

Sub-delegation

Delegated legislation is sometimes made by people other than those who were given the original power to do so.

Lack of control

Despite the above list of controls over delegated legislation, the reality is that effective supervision is difficult. First, publication has only limited benefits, given that the general public are frequently unaware of the existence of delegated legisla-tion, let alone on what grounds it can be challenged and how to go about doing so. This in turn has an effect on the ability of the courts to control delegated legisla-tion, since judicial review relies on individual challenges being brought before the courts. This may not happen until years after a provision is enacted, when it finally affects someone who is prepared and able to challenge it. The obvious result is that legislation which largely affects a class of individuals who are not given to questioning official rules, are unaware of their rights, or who lack the financial resources to go to court, will rarely be challenged.

A further problem is that some enabling Acts confer extremely wide discretionary powers on ministers; a phrase such as 'the minister may make such regulations as he sees fit for the purpose of bringing the Act into operation' would not be unusual. This means that there is very little room for anything to be considered *ultra vires*, so judicial review is effectively frustrated. Even where judicial review is available, this is frequently a slow and expensive process.

The main method of control over delegated legislation is therefore parliamentary, but this too has its drawbacks. Although the affirmative resolution procedure usually ensures that parliamentary attention is drawn to important delegated legislation, it is rarely possible to prevent such legislation being passed. The Select Committee on the Scrutiny of Delegated Powers makes an important contribution, and has been able to secure changes to a number of important pieces of legislation. However, it too lacks real power, as it is unable to consider the merits of delegated legislation (as opposed to whether the delegated powers have been correctly used) and its reports have no binding effect.

Reading on the web

Statutory instruments are published on the Office for Public Sector Information website at:

www.opsi.gov.uk/stat.htm

Chapter summary

There are three main forms of delegated legislation:

- statutory instruments;
- bye-laws; and
- Orders in Council.

The reasons for delegating legislative powers

Delegated legislation is necessary because it saves parliamentary time, constitutes a quick form of legislation, and is suited to technical subject areas or where local knowledge is needed.

Control of delegated legislation

Delegated legislation is controlled through:

- the consultation of experts;
- publication of the legislation;
- supervision by Parliament; and
- the courts with the judicial review procedure.

Criticism of delegated legislation

Delegated legislation has been criticised due to:

- lack of democratic involvement;
- overuse;
- sub-delegation; and
- lack of controls.

Question and answer guides

Read the source material below and answer parts (a) to (c) which follow.

Exercise on Delegated Legislation

SOURCE A

Delegated legislation consists of laws created under the authority of Parliament but not actually created by Parliament. There are three types: Statutory Instruments, Bye-laws and Orders in Council.

***Kruse v Johnson* (1898)**

Kent County Council made a bye-law, under the Local Government Act 1888, provid-   5
ing that 'No person shall sound or play upon any musical or noisy instrument or sing in any public place or highway within fifty yards of any dwelling-house after being required by any constable or by an inmate of such house personally or by his or her servant to stop doing so'.

SOURCE B

Delegated legislation is necessary for a number of reasons. Local bye-laws can only be made effectively with awareness of the locality. The new assemblies for Scotland, Wales and Northern Ireland have important powers to make delegated legislation. Also, modern legislation often needs to include detailed technical provisions and MPs do not usually have the technical skill required. Delegated legislation can be made by   5
experts who are familiar with the relevant areas.

However, the main criticism of delegated legislation is that there is a lack of demo-cratic involvement due to the fact that most delegated legislation is made by civil servants rather than elected politicians.

Adapted from: 'English Legal System', Catherine Elliott and Frances Quinn, Longman

(OCR Specimen Paper 2007, Sources of Law Unit)

(a) Source A refers to a bye-law.

Describe and illustrate bye-laws and two other types of delegated legislation.

Plan

Bye-laws

■ Made by local authorities to cover local matters such as residents car parking and cycling in a local park.
■ Occasionally made by public corporations and certain companies for matters within their remit that affect the public using their services, for example, banning people from dropping litter on railway lines.
■ The case of **Kruse** v **Johnson** (1898) concerned a bye-law made by Kent County Council restricting the playing of music in the street near residential housing.

Statutory instruments

■ Made by government departments with the authority of an enabling Act.
■ Over 3,000 passed every year.
■ Either the affirmative or the negative procedure followed (discussed on p. 296).
■ Acts of Parliament often brought into force by a statutory instrument.
■ Much of the detailed provision regarding the state funding of legal services is introduced by statutory instrument.
■ The case of **Customs and Excise Commissioners** v **Cure & Deeley Ltd** (1962) and **R** v **Secretary of State for Social Security, ex parte Joint Council for the Welfare of Immigrants** (1996), which are discussed on p. 298, were both concerned with the legality of statutory instruments made by a government minister under the apparent authority of an enabling Act.

Orders in Council

■ Usually drafted by a government department, approved by the Privy Council and signed by the Queen.
■ Made at times of emergency. During a fuel crisis in September 2000, Parliament put the Privy Council on alert in case emergency legislation was necessary.
■ The use of Orders in Council has been extended recently – as from 2007, legislation put before the Welsh Assembly will be enacted through Orders in Council after following the affirmative resolution procedure.
■ Orders in Council were controversially used in 2004 to attempt to legalise the removal of the residents of the Chagossian island, which forms part of the British Indian Ocean Territory. However, the Court of Appeal held that this use of the Order in Council was unlawful.

Answer

This essay will consider three forms of delegated legislation: bye-laws, statutory instruments and Orders in Council. Looking first at bye-laws, these can be made by local authorities to cover matters of local concern, for example, controlling resident car parking permits and the use of bicycles in local parks. Bye-laws are made under the authority of an enabling Act and an important enabling Act for local authorities is the Local Government Act 1972.

Bye-laws are sometimes made by public corporations (such as Transport for London) and certain companies for matters within their remit. For example, Parliament has passed enabling legislation allowing the Gas Regulatory Board to make bye-laws fixing minimum standards for gas installations.

The case of **Kruse** *v* **Johnson** (1898) concerned a bye-law made by Kent County Council restricting the playing of music in the street near residential housing. The bye-law was found by the court to be unlawful because it was unreasonable.

Statutory instruments are generally introduced by ministers of government departments under powers given in an enabling Act. This is a major method of law-making – some 3,000 are brought into force each year and with that volume the media and ordinary citizens have a very hard job to try to keep track of them. A minister can read reports from technical experts in his or her department's field and can create secondary legislation more competently than if Parliament tried to undertake this role. Some EU Directives are brought into force through the use of statutory instruments, which can lead to some controversial issues being brought into force without a full debate in this country. The introduction of horse passports was an example of this. The EU issued a Directive that all animals in the human food chain needed to be individually identifiable with a list of drugs administered. The UK does not have horses in the human food chain and live export is banned, but horse owners had to acquire passports for all horses at their own cost.

Statutory instruments can be introduced by either an affirmative resolution procedure (which requires parliamentary debate) or a negative resolution procedure (under which the statutory instrument becomes law in the absence of any objections being submitted within 40 days of it being laid before Parliament). The Hunting Act, for example, provides that secondary legislation issued under its authority needs to go through an affirmative resolution procedure.

Orders in Council are usually drafted by a government department, approved by the Privy Council and signed by the Queen. They can refer to constitutional matters such as the Orders in Council authorising the transfer of some powers from Westminster to the Scottish Parliament and Welsh Assembly following devolution. The use of Orders in Council has recently been extended; as from 2007, legislation put before the Welsh Assembly will be enacted through Orders in Council after following the affirmative resolution procedure. Orders in Council are particularly important at times of emergency and when Parliament is not sitting. For example, during the fuel crisis of September 2000, Parliament put the Privy Council on alert in case emergency legislation was required. Orders in Council were also issued to authorise the deployment of the military in the UK to assist with the logistics and labour needed during the foot and mouth crisis. Orders in Council were controversially used in 2004, to attempt to legalise the removal of the residents of the Chagossian island which forms part of the British Indian Ocean Territory. However, the Court of Appeal held that this use of the Order in Council was unlawful.

(b) Identify and explain which type of delegated legislation would be most appropriate to introduce a law relating to each of the following:

(i)   parking restrictions in a district or town;
(ii) the implementation of regulations outlined in an enabling Act relating to the use of mobile phones in cars;
(iii) powers needed to deal with an emergency situation.

Plan

(i)   A bye-law would be the most suitable as local authorities can make these to cover local matters.
(ii) A statutory instrument made by a government minister would be the most suitable because delegated legislation laying down rules for the whole country is required.
(iii) An Order in Council is generally used for emergency situations and these can be made quickly, even when Parliament is not sitting.

(c) With reference to Source B and your knowledge of delegated legislation:

(i)   state the reasons why delegated legislation is needed;
(ii) discuss the disadvantages of delegated legislation.

Plan

(i)

- Insufficient parliamentary time.
- Speed.
- Technicality of the subject matter, such as health and safety. Source B mentions that delegated legislation can be made by 'experts who are familiar with the relevant areas'.
- Need for local knowledge – Source B refers to an 'awareness of the locality'.
- Flexibility to amend or revoke.
- Orders in Council can respond quickly to emergency situations.
- Respond to future needs which Parliament cannot predict when passing the primary legislation.
- The use of delegated legislation as part of the devolution process for Scotland and Wales is mentioned by Source B.

(ii)

- 'Lack of democratic involvement' is main criticism made in Source B.
- Inadequate debate and publicity.
- Overuse.
- Sub-delegation to unelected civil servants – passing reference made to this in Source B.
- Lack of control.

- Limitations of judicial review.
- Large amount that is inaccessible and badly drafted.

Group activity 1

You will often find new bye-laws listed in the classified section of the local news-papers. Take a look at your local newspaper and see if you can find a bye-law mentioned that has been passed recently. Alternatively, you could look at your local council website and look up bye-laws on the site index and select a recent bye-law from the website.

- What was the name of the bye-law?
- What was its purpose?
- Which enabling Act empowered the local authority to pass the bye-law?

Split up into small groups and report back your findings.

Group activity 2

- Divide your friends (or class) into groups of two or three people.
- Each group should visit the web page of the Joint Committee on Statutory Instruments: **www.parliament.uk/parliamentary_committees/joint_committee_ on_statutory_instruments.cfm**
- Read one of the Committee's recent reports, with each group choosing a different report.
- Make notes summarising your chosen report's contents.
- Compare your notes with those of the other groups.
- In the light of this comparison, how useful do you think the Committee is in controlling delegated legislation?

Visit **www.mylawchamber.co.uk/elliottocr** to access questions, quizzes and activities to test yourself on this chapter.

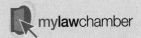

Chapter 17
STATUTORY INTERPRETATION

When judges are faced with a new piece of legislation, its meaning is not always clear and they have to interpret it. Often, when interpreting the Act, the judges say that they are looking for Parliament's intention. In this chapter we will consider:

- the meaning of parliamentary intention;
- the rules of statutory interpretation;
- internal aids to statutory interpretation;
- external aids to statutory interpretation.

Introduction

Although Parliament makes legislation, it is left to the courts to apply it. The general public imagines that this is simply a case of looking up the relevant law and ruling accordingly, but the reality is not so simple. Despite the fact that Acts of Parliament are carefully written by expert draftsmen, there are many occasions on which the courts find that the implications of a statute for the case before them are not at all clear.

Where the meaning of a statute is uncertain, the job of the courts – in theory at least – is to discover how Parliament intended the law to apply and put that into practice. This is because, in our constitution, Parliament is the supreme source of law (excluding European law, which will be discussed later), and therefore the judiciary's constitutional role is to put into practice what it thinks Parliament actually intended when Parliament made a particular law, rather than simply what the judges themselves might think is the best interpretation in the case before them. However, as we shall see, the practice is not always as straightforward as the constitutional theory suggests.

What is parliamentary intention?

While the judges often say, when interpreting a piece of legislation, that they are looking for the intention of Parliament, it is not really clear what is meant by this. The idea of parliamentary intention is a very slippery concept in practice. Is it the intention of every individual member of Parliament at the time the law was passed? Obviously not, since not every MP will have voted for the legislation or even necessarily been present when it was passed. The intention of all those who did support a particular piece of legislation is no easier to assess; it is not feasible to conduct a questionnaire every time a legislative provision is found to be unclear. When judges say they are looking for the intention of Parliament, often what they really mean is that they are looking for the meaning of the words that Parliament used. They are seeking not what Parliament meant, but the true meaning of the words they used.

Statutory interpretation and case law

Once the courts have interpreted a statute, or a section of one, that interpretation becomes part of case law in just the same way as any other judicial decision, and subject to the same rules of precedent. A higher court may decide that the interpretation is wrong, and reverse the decision if it is appealed, or overrule it in a later case, but unless and until this happens, lower courts must interpret the statute in the same way.

Rules of interpretation

Parliament has given the courts some sources of guidance on statutory interpretation. The Interpretation Act 1978 provides certain standard definitions of common provisions, such as the rule that the singular includes the plural and 'he' includes 'she', while interpretation sections at the end of most modern Acts define some of the words used within them – the Police and Criminal Evidence Act 1984 contains such a section. A further source of help has been provided since the beginning of 1999: all Bills passed since that date are the subject of special explanatory notes, which are made public. These detail the background to the legislation and explain the effects particular provisions are intended to have.

Apart from this assistance, it has been left to the courts to decide what method to use to interpret statutes, and three basic approaches have developed, in conjunction with certain aids to interpretation.

The literal rule

This rule gives all the words in a statute their ordinary and natural meaning, on the principle that the best way to interpret the will of Parliament is to follow the literal meaning of the words it has used. Under this rule, the literal meaning must be followed, even if the result is absurd.

Advantages of the literal rule

The literal rule respects parliamentary sovereignty, giving the courts a restricted role and leaving law-making to those elected for the job.

Disadvantages of the literal rule

Where use of the literal rule does lead to an absurd or obviously unjust conclusion, it can hardly be said to be enacting the will of Parliament, since Parliament is unlikely to have intended absurdity and injustice.

Examples of the literal rule

Whiteley *v* **Chapell** (1868). A statute aimed at preventing electoral malpractice made it an offence to impersonate 'any person entitled to vote' at an election. The accused was acquitted because he impersonated a dead person and a dead person was clearly not entitled to vote!

sourcebook
p. 26 →

    Fisher *v* **Bell** (1961). After several violent incidents in which the weapon used was a flick-knife, Parliament decided that these knives should be banned. The Restriction of Offensive Weapons Act 1959 consequently made it an offence to 'sell or offer for sale' any flick-knife. The defendant had flick-knives in his shop window and was charged with offering these for sale. The court held that 'offers for sale' must be given its ordinary meaning in law, and that in contract law this was not an offer for sale but only an invitation to people to make an offer to buy. The defendant was therefore not guilty of a crime under the Act, despite the fact that this was obviously just the sort of behaviour the Act was set up to prevent.

In addition, the literal rule is useless where the answer to a problem simply cannot be found in the words of the statute.

The Law Commission in 1969 pointed out that interpretation based only on literal meanings 'assumes unattainable perfection in draftsmanship'; even the most talented and experienced draftsmen cannot predict every situation to which legislation may have to be applied. The same word may mean different things to different people, and words also shift their meanings over time.

In the case of **R (Haw)** *v* **Secretary of State for the Home Department** (2006), the Court of Appeal refused to apply a literal interpretation to a new piece of legislation, as it considered that this would not reflect the intention of Parliament. The case was concerned with Brian Haw, who had been holding a protest in Parliament Square, opposite Parliament, against the war in Iraq since June 2001. He lived on the pavement and displayed a large number of placards protesting about government policy in Iraq. The demonstration had earlier been held to be lawful since it neither caused an obstruction nor gave rise to any fear that a breach of the peace might arise. The Serious Organized Crime and Police Act 2005 was subsequently passed, s. 133(1) of which required any person who intended to organise a demonstration in the vicinity of Parliament to apply to the police for authorisation to do so. Section 132(1) provided that a person who carried on a demonstration in the designated area was guilty of an offence if, when the demonstration started, appropriate authorisation had not been given:

'Any person who –
(a) organises a demonstration in a public place in the designated area; or
(b) takes part in a demonstration in a public place in the designated area; or

*(c) carries on a demonstration by himself in a public place in the designated area is guilty of an offence if, when the demonstration **starts**; authorisation for the demonstration has not been given under section 134(2).'*

Haw argued that the Act did not apply to his demonstration because it had started before the Act came into force. The Court of Appeal held that the Act did in fact apply to Haw's demonstration: 'Any other conclusion would be wholly irrational and could fairly be described as manifestly absurd.' Construing the statutory language in context, Parliament's intention was clearly to regulate all demonstrations in the designated area, whenever they began. Thus, rather than following a literal interpretation of the legislation, the courts looked at its context to determine the intention of Parliament. The court gave particular weight to the fact that the 2005 Act repealed a provision in the Public Order Act 1986. That provision had provided for controls to be placed on public demonstrations and would have applied to demonstrations which had been started since 1986. The Court of Appeal thought it was inconceivable that Parliament would have intended to repeal that power to control demonstrations started before 2006 and replace it with legislation which could only control demonstrations started after 2006, as this would leave a significant gap in the power of the state to control demonstrations. Conditions have now been imposed on Haw's demonstration in accordance with the provisions of the 2005 Act, aimed primarily at restricting the size of the demonstration. It is accepted that Haw's demonstration in itself does not pose a security risk, but if a large number of people joined his demonstration, this could be an opportunity for terrorists to join in and conceal an explosive device.

The golden rule

This provides that if the literal rule gives an absurd result, which Parliament could not have intended, then (and only then) the judge can substitute a reasonable meaning in the light of the statute as a whole.

Advantages of the golden rule

The golden rule can prevent the absurdity and injustice caused by the literal rule, and help the courts put into practice what Parliament really means.

Disadvantages of the golden rule

The Law Commission noted in 1969 that the 'rule' provided no clear meaning of an 'absurd result'. As in practice that was judged by reference to whether a particular interpretation was irreconcilable with the general policy of the legislature, the golden rule turns out to be a less explicit form of the mischief rule (discussed below).

Examples of the golden rule

R *v* **Allen** (1872). Section 57 of the Offences Against the Person Act 1861 stated that: 'Whosoever being married shall marry any other person during the life of the former husband or wife . . . shall be guilty of bigamy.' It was pointed out that it was impossible for a person already married to 'marry' someone else – he or she might go through a marriage ceremony, but would not actually be married; using the literal rule would make the statute useless. The court therefore held that 'shall marry' should be interpreted to mean 'shall go through a marriage ceremony'.

sourcebook p. 28 → **Adler** v **George** (1964). The defendant was charged under s. 3 of the Official Secrets Act 1920, with obstructing a member of the armed forces 'in the vicinity of any prohibited place'. He argued that the natural meaning of 'in the vicinity of' meant near to, whereas the obstruction had actually occurred in the prohibited place itself, an air force station. The court held that, while in many circumstances 'in the vicinity' could indeed only be interpreted as meaning near to, in this context it was reasonable to construe it as including being within the prohibited place.

Inco Europe Ltd v **First Choice Distribution** (2000). The House of Lords stated that words could be added to a statute by the judge to give effect to Parliament's intention where an obvious error had been made in drafting a statute.

The mischief rule

This rule was laid down in **Heydon's Case** in the sixteenth century, and provides that judges should consider three factors:

- what the law was before the statute was passed;
- what problem, or 'mischief', the statute was trying to remedy;
- what remedy Parliament was trying to provide.

Examples of the mischief rule

sourcebook p. 29 → **Smith** v **Hughes** (1960). The Street Offences Act 1958 made it a criminal offence for a prostitute to solicit potential customers in a street or public place. In this case, the prostitute was not actually in the street, but was sitting in a house, on the first floor, and tapping on the window to attract the attention of the men walking by. The judge decided that the aim of the Act was to enable people to walk along the street without being solicited, and since the soliciting in question was aimed at people in the street, even though the prostitute was not in the street herself, the Act should be interpreted to include this activity.

Elliott v **Grey** (1960). The Road Traffic Act 1930 provided that it was an offence for an uninsured car to be 'used on the road'. The car in this case was not being used on the road, but jacked up, with its battery removed, but the court held that as it was nevertheless a hazard of the type which the statute was designed to prevent, it was covered by the phrase 'used on the road'.

The judge should then interpret the statute in such a way as to put a stop to the problem that Parliament was addressing.

Advantages of the mischief rule

The mischief rule helps avoid absurdity and injustice, and promotes flexibility. It was described by the Law Commission in 1969 as a 'rather more satisfactory approach' than the other two established rules.

Disadvantages of the mischief rule

Heydon's Case (1584) was the product of a time when statutes were a minor source of law, compared to the common law. Drafting was by no means as exact a process as it is today, and the supremacy of Parliament was not really established. At that time, too, statutes tended to include a lengthy preamble, which more or less spelt out the 'mischief' with which the Act was intended to deal. Judges of the time were very well qualified to decide what the previous law was and what problems a statute was intended to remedy, since they had usually drafted statutes on behalf of the king, and Parliament only rubber-stamped them. Such a rule may be less appropriate now that the legislative situation is so different.

Quick quiz 17.1

Complete the following table by giving one case to illustrate each of the rules of interpretation.

Literal rule	
Golden rule	
Mischief rule	

Table 17.1 **The three rules of statutory interpretation**

Literal rule	The words are given their ordinary and natural meaning.
Golden rule	If the literal rule gives an absurd result that Parliament cannot have intended, then the judge can substitute a reasonable meaning in the light of the statute as a whole.
Mischief rule	This rule was laid down in **Heydon's Case.** Judges should consider three factors: ■ what the problem was before the statute was passed; ■ what problem, or 'mischief', the statute was trying to remedy; ■ what remedy Parliament was trying to provide. The judge should then interpret the statute in such a way as to put a stop to the problem that Parliament was addressing.

Aids to interpretation

Whichever approach the judges take to statutory interpretation, they have at their disposal a range of material to help. Some of these aids may be found within the piece of legislation itself, or in certain rules of language commonly applied in statutory texts – these are called internal aids. Others, outside the piece of legislation, are called external aids.

Internal aids

The literary rule and the golden rule both direct the judge to internal aids, though they are taken into account whatever the approach applied.

The statute itself

To decide what a provision of the Act means, the judge may draw a comparison with provisions elsewhere in the statute. Clues may also be provided by the long title of the Act or the subheadings within it.

Rules of language

Developed by lawyers over time, these rules are really little more than common sense, despite their intimidating names. As with the rules of interpretation, they are not always precisely applied. Some examples are given below.

Ejusdem generis

General words which follow specific ones are taken to include only things of the same kind. For example, if an Act used the phrase 'dogs, cats and other animals', the phrase 'and other animals' would probably include other domestic animals, but not wild ones.

Expressio unius est exclusio alterius

Express mention of one thing implies the exclusion of another. If an Act specifically mentioned 'Persian cats', the term would not include other breeds of cat.

Noscitur a sociis

A word draws meaning from the other words around it. If a statute mentioned 'cats, kittens and food', it would be reasonable to assume that 'food' meant cat food, and dog food was not covered by the relevant provision.

Presumptions

The courts assume that certain points are implied in all legislation. These presumptions include the following:

- statutes do not change the common law;
- the legislature does not intend to remove any matters from the jurisdiction of the courts;
- existing rights are not to be interfered with;
- laws which create crimes should be interpreted in favour of the citizen where there is ambiguity;
- legislation does not operate retrospectively: its provisions operate from the day it comes into force, and are not backdated.

 It is always open to Parliament to go against these presumptions if it sees fit – for example, the European Communities Act 1972 makes it clear that some of its provisions are to be applied retrospectively. But unless the wording of a statute makes it absolutely clear that Parliament has chosen to go against one or more of the presumptions, the courts can assume that the presumptions apply.

External aids

The mischief rule directs the judge to external aids, including the following:

Historical setting

A judge may consider the historical setting of the provision that is being interpreted, as well as other statutes dealing with the same subjects.

Dictionaries and textbooks

These may be consulted to find the meaning of a word, or to gather information about the views of legal academics on a point of law.

Explanatory notes

Acts passed since the beginning of 1999 are provided with explanatory notes, published at the same time as the Act.

Reports

Legislation may be preceded by a report of a Law Commission or a public inquiry. The House of Lords stated in **Black Clawson International Ltd** (1975) that official reports may be considered as evidence of the pre-existing state of the law and the mischief that the legislation was intended to deal with.

 The Human Rights Act 1998

This Act incorporates into UK law the European Convention on Human Rights, which is an international treaty signed by most democratic countries, and designed to protect basic human rights. In many countries, the Convention has been incorporated into national law as a Bill of Rights, which means that the courts can overrule domestic legislation which is in conflict with it. This is not the case in the UK. Instead, s. 3(1) of the Human Rights Act requires that: 'So far as it is possible to do so, primary and subordinate legislation must be read and given effect in a way which is compatible with the Convention rights.' This means essentially that where a statutory provision can be interpreted in more than one way, the interpretation which is compatible with the European Convention should be the one chosen. Section 2 further requires that in deciding any question which arises in connection with a right protected by the Convention, the courts should take into account any relevant judgments made by the European Court of Human Rights. If it is impossible to find an interpretation which is compatible with the Convention, the court concerned can make a declaration of incompatibility. This does not affect the validity of the statute in question, but it is designed to draw attention to the conflict so that the government can change the law to bring it in line with the Convention (although the Act does not oblige the government to do this). There is a special 'fast track' procedure by which a minister can make the necessary changes.

To clarify interpretation, when new legislation is made, the relevant Bill must carry a statement from the relevant minister, saying either that its provisions are compatible with the Convention, or that even if they are not, the government wishes to go ahead with the legislation anyway. In the latter case, the government would be specifically saying that the legislation must override Convention rights if there is a clash, but clearly any government intent on passing such legislation would be likely to face considerable opposition and so would have to have a very good reason, in the eyes of the public, for doing so.

Hansard

This is the official daily report of parliamentary debates, and therefore a record of what was said during the introduction of legislation. For over 100 years, the judiciary held that such documents could not be consulted for the purpose of statutory interpretation. During his career, Lord Denning made strenuous efforts to do away with this rule, and in **Davis** *v* **Johnson** (1979) justified his interpretation of a piece of legislation by reference to the parliamentary debates during its introduction. The House of Lords, however, rebuked him for doing so, and maintained that the rule should stand.

sourcebook p. 30 →
In 1993, the case of **Pepper** *v* **Hart** overturned the rule against consulting *Hansard*, and such consultation is clearly now allowed. The case was between teachers at a fee-paying school (Malvern College) and the Inland Revenue, and concerned the tax which employees should have to pay on perks (benefits related to their job). Malvern College allowed its teachers to send their sons there for one-fifth of the usual fee, if places were available. Tax law requires employees to pay tax on perks, and the amount of tax is based on the cost to the employer of providing the benefit, which is usually taken to mean any extra cost that the employer would not otherwise incur. The amount paid by Malvern teachers for their sons' places covered the extra cost to the school of having the child there (in books, food, etc.), but did not cover the school's fixed costs, for paying teachers, maintaining buildings and so on, which would have been the same whether the teachers' children were there or not. Therefore the perk cost the school little or nothing, and so the teachers maintained that they should not have to pay tax on it. The Inland Revenue disagreed, arguing that the perk should be taxed on the basis of the amount it saved the teachers on the real cost of sending their children to the school.

The reason why the issue of consulting parliamentary debates arose was that during the passing of the Finance Act 1976, which laid down the tax rules in question, the then Secretary to the Treasury, Robert Sheldon, had specifically mentioned the kind of situation that arose in **Pepper** *v* **Hart**. He had stated that where the cost to an employer of a perk was minimal, employees should not have to pay tax on the full cost of it. The question was, could the judges take into account what the minister had said? The House of Lords convened a special court of seven judges, which decided that they could look at *Hansard* to see what the minister had said, and that his remarks could be used to decide what Parliament had intended.

The decision in **Pepper** *v* **Hart** was confirmed in **Three Rivers District Council** *v* **Bank of England (No. 2)** (1996), which concerned the correct interpretation of legislation passed in order to fulfil obligations arising from an EC Directive. Although the legislation was not itself ambiguous, the claimants stated that, if interpreted in the light of the information contained in *Hansard*, the legislation imposed certain duties on the defendants, which were not obvious from the legislation itself. The defendants argued that *Hansard* could only be consulted where legislation contained ambiguity, but the court disagreed, stating that where legislation was passed in order to give effect to international obligations, it was important to make sure that it did so, and consulting legislative materials was one way of helping to ensure this. The result would appear to be that *Hansard* can be consulted not just to explain ambiguous phrases, but to throw light on the general purpose of legislation.

In **R v Secretary of State for the Environment, Transport and the Regions, ex parte Spath Holme Ltd** (2001) the House of Lords gave a restrictive interpretation of the application of **Pepper v Hart**. The applicant was a company that was the landlord of certain properties. It sought judicial review of the Rent Acts (Maximum Fair Rent) Order 1999, made by the Secretary of State under s. 31 of the Landlord and Tenant Act 1985. The applicant company contended that the 1999 Order was unlawful as the Secretary of State had made it to alleviate the impact of rent increases on certain categories of tenants, when a reading of *Hansard* showed that Parliament's intention was that such orders would only be made to reduce the impact of inflation. On the use of *Hansard* to interpret the intention of Parliament, the House of Lords pointed out that the case of **Pepper v Hart** was concerned with the meaning of an expression used in a statute ('the cost of a benefit'). The minister had given a statement on the meaning of that expression. By contrast, the present case was concerned with a matter of policy, and in particular the meaning of a statutory power rather than a statutory expression. Only if a minister were, improbably, to give a categorical assurance to Parliament that a power would not be used in a given situation would a parliamentary statement on the scope of a power be admissible.

sourcebook
p. 32 → In **Wilson v Secretary of State for Trade and Industry** (2003) the House of Lords again gave a restrictive interpretation to **Pepper v Hart**. It held that only statements in *Hansard* made by a minister or other promoter of legislation could be looked at by the court, other statements recorded in *Hansard* had to be ignored.

Under the British constitution, Parliament and the courts have separate roles. Parliament enacts legislation, the courts interpret and apply it. Owing to the principle of the separation of powers (see p. 148), neither institution should stray into the other's domain. Thus, Art. 9 of the Bill of Rights 1689 provides that 'the freedom of speech and debates or proceedings in Parliament ought not to be impeached or questioned in any court or place out of Parliament'. In **Wilson v Secretary of State for Trade and Industry** (2003) the House of Lords emphasised the importance of the courts not straying into Parliament's constitutional role. It concluded from this that *Hansard* could be used only to interpret the meaning of words in legislation; it could not be used to discover the reasons for the legislation. The Court of Appeal in **Wilson** had used *Hansard* to look at the parliamentary debates concerning a particular Act. It was not trying to discover the meaning of words, as their meaning was not in doubt, but to discover the reason which led Parliament to think that it was necessary to pass the Act. The House of Lords held that the Court of Appeal had been wrong to do this. Referring to *Hansard* simply to check the meaning of enacted words supported the principle of parliamentary sovereignty (see p. 285). Referring to *Hansard* to discover the reasoning of Parliament, where there was no ambiguity as to the meaning of the words, would go against the sovereignty of Parliament.

The Human Rights Act 1998 requires the courts to exercise a new role in respect of Acts of Parliament. This new role is fundamentally different from interpreting and applying legislation. The courts are now required to determine whether the legislation violates a right laid down in the European Convention on Human

Rights. If the Act does violate the Convention, the courts have to issue a declaration of incompatibility. In order to determine this question, the House of Lords stated in **Wilson** that the courts can only refer to *Hansard* for background information, such as the social policy aim of the Act. Poor reasoning in the course of parliamentary debate was not a matter which could count against the legislation when determining the question of compatibility.

Although it is now clear that *Hansard* can be referred to in order to find evidence of parliamentary intention, there is still much debate as to how useful it is, and whether it can provide good evidence of what Parliament intended.

Arguments for the use of Hansard

■ **Usefulness**

Lord Denning argued in **Davis v Johnson** (1979) that to ignore the parliamentary debates would be to 'grope in the dark for the meaning of an Act without switching on the light'. When such an obvious source of enlightenment was available, it was ridiculous to ignore it.

■ **Media reports**

Parliamentary proceedings are reported in newspapers and on radio and television. Since judges are as exposed to these as anyone else, it seems ridiculous to blinker themselves in court, or to pretend that they are blinkered.

Arguments against the use of Hansard

■ **Lack of clarity**

The House of Lords, admonishing Lord Denning for his behaviour in **Davis v Johnson**, and directing that parliamentary debates were not to be consulted, stated that the evidence provided by the parliamentary debates might not be reliable; what was said in the cut and thrust of public debate was not 'conducive to a clear and unbiased explanation of the meaning of statutory language'.

■ **Time and expense**

Their Lordships also suggested that if debates were to be used, there was a danger that the lawyers arguing a case would devote too much time and attention to ministerial statements and so on, at the expense of considering the language used in the Act itself.

> 'It would add greatly to the time and expense involved in preparing cases involving the construction of a statute if counsel were expected to read all the debates in Hansard, and it would often be impracticable for counsel to get access to at least the older reports of debates in select committees in the House of Commons; moreover, in a very large proportion of cases such a search, even if practicable, would throw no light on the question before the court . . .'

■ **Parliamentary intention**

The nature of parliamentary intention is difficult, if not impossible, to pin down. Parliamentary debates usually reveal the views of only a few members, and even then, those words may need interpretation too.

Lord Steyn, a judge in the House of Lords, has written an article entitled '*Pepper v Hart: A Re-examination*' (2001). In that article he criticises the way the use of *Hansard* in **Pepper** *v* **Hart** gives pre-eminence to the government minister's interpretation of the statute and ignores any dissenting voices by opposition MPs. The minister only spoke in the House of Commons and the detail of what he said was unlikely to have been known by the House of Lords. He therefore queries how the minister's statement can be said to reflect the intention of Parliament, which is made up of both Houses. He points to the nature of the parliamentary process:

> *'The relevant exchanges sometimes take place late at night in nearly empty chambers. Sometimes it is a party political debate with whips on. The questions are often difficult but politician warfare sometimes leaves little time for reflection. These are not ideal conditions for the making of authoritative statements about the meaning of a clause in a Bill. In truth a Minister speaks for the government and not for Parliament. The statements of a Minister are no more than indications of what the Government would like the law to be. In any event, it is not discoverable from the printed record whether individual members of the legislature, let alone a plurality in each chamber, understood and accepted a ministerial explanation of the suggested meaning of the words.'*

This criticism has been partly tackled by the House of Lords in **Wilson** *v* **Secretary of State for Trade and Industry** (2003). The House stated that the courts must be careful not to treat the ministerial statement as indicative of the intention of Parliament.

> *'Nor should the courts give a ministerial statement, whether made inside or outside Parliament, determinative weight. It should not be supposed that members necessarily agreed with the Minister's reasoning or his conclusions.'*

The House emphasised that the will of Parliament is expressed in the language used in its enactments.

 Quick quiz 17.2

1 Name the three main rules of statutory interpretation.

2 Give three examples of internal aids to statutory interpretation.

3 Give three examples of external aids to statutory interpretation.

4 What is the legal significance of the House of Lords' decision in **Pepper** *v* **Hart**?

How do judges really interpret statutes?

The so-called 'rules of interpretation' are not rules at all, but different approaches. Judges do not methodically apply these rules to every case, and the fact that the rules can conflict with each other and produce different results necessarily implies some choice as to which is used. The idea that statutory interpretation is an almost scientific process that can be used to produce a single right answer is simply nonsense. There is room for more than one interpretation (otherwise the question would never reach the courts) and judges must choose between them. For clear evidence of this, there is no better example than the recent litigation concerning Augusto Pinochet, the former President of Chile. He had long been accused of crimes against humanity, including torture and murder and conspiracy to torture and to murder. When he made a visit to the UK, the Spanish government requested his extradition to Spain so that it could put him on trial. This led to a protracted sequence of litigation concerning whether it was legal for Britain to extradite him to Spain, and eventually the question came before the House of Lords. Pinochet's defence argued on the basis of the State Immunity Act 1978, which gives other states with immunity from prosecution in English courts; the Act provides that 'states' includes heads of state. The Lords were therefore asked to decide whether this immunity extended to Pinochet's involvement in the acts he was accused of and, by a majority of three to two, they decided that it did not. Yet when the appeal was reopened (because one of the judges, Lord Hoffmann, was found to have links with Amnesty International, which was a party to the case), this time with seven Law Lords sitting, a different decision was reached. Although the Lords still stated that the General did not have complete immunity, by a majority of six to one, they restricted his liability to those acts which were committed after 1978, when torture committed outside the UK became a crime in the UK. This gave General Pinochet immunity for the vast majority of the torture allegations, and complete immunity for the allegations of murder and conspiracy to murder.

The reasoning behind both the decisions is complex and does not really need to concern us here; the important point to note is that in both hearings, the Lords were interpreting the same statutory provisions, yet they came up with significantly different verdicts. Because of the way it was reopened, the case gives us a rare insight into just how imprecise and unpredictable statutory interpretation can be, and it is hard to resist the implication that if you put any other case involving statutory interpretation before two separate panels of judges, they might well come up with different judgments too. Given then that judges do have some freedom over questions of statutory interpretation, what influences the decisions they make? The academic Griffith (1997) claims that where there is ambiguity, the judges choose the interpretation that best suits their view of policy and are therefore making a political decision.

The purposive approach

Over the past three decades, the judiciary has come to acknowledge that it does have some degree of discretion in interpreting statutes, but there is still considerable debate as to how far it can, and should, take this.

Lord Denning was in the forefront of moves to establish a more purposive approach, aiming to produce decisions that put into practice the spirit of the law, even if that meant paying less than usual regard to the letter of the law, the actual words of the statute. He felt that the mischief rule could be interpreted broadly, so that it would not just allow the court to look at the history of the case, but would also allow the court to carry out the intention of Parliament, however imperfectly this might have been expressed in the words used.

Denning stated his view in **Magor and St Mellons *v* Newport Corporation** (1952):

'We do not sit here to pull the language of Parliament to pieces and make nonsense of it ... we sit here to find out the intention of Parliament and carry it out, and we do this better by filling in the gaps and making sense of the enactment than by opening it up to destructive analysis.'

This approach was roundly criticised by the House of Lords, with Lord Simonds describing 'filling in the gaps' as 'a naked usurpation of the judicial function, under the guise of interpretation ... If a gap is disclosed, the remedy lies in an amending Act'.

Denning's views nevertheless contributed to the growth of a more purposive approach which has gained ground in the last 20 years, with courts seeking to interpret statutes in ways which will promote the general purpose of the legislation. However, the courts still maintain that this cannot be taken too far.

The introduction of the Human Rights Act 1998 is likely to prompt a shift to a purposive interpretation of legislation, as the courts weigh up important issues concerning the rights of the individual against the state, and take into account the judgments of the European Court of Human Rights, which itself takes a purposive approach to interpretation. Some experts have predicted that the House of Lords' role will become increasingly like that of the American Supreme Court, dealing with vital questions for society and the individual, rather than the detailed and technical commercial and taxation matters which form the bulk of its current work.

Interpretation of European legislation

Under Art. 234 of the Treaty of Rome, the European Court is the supreme tribunal for the interpretation of European Union law. Section 3(1) of the European Communities Act 1972 states that questions as to the validity, meaning or effect of European legislation are to be decided in accordance with the principles laid down by the European Court.

In the light of these provisions, Lord Denning stated that, when interpreting European law, English courts should take the same approach as the European Court would:

*'No longer must they examine the words in meticulous detail. No longer must they argue about the precise grammatical sense. They must look to the purpose or intent. To quote the words of the European Court in the **Da Costa** case they must deduce from the wording and the spirit of the Treaty the meaning of the Community rules ... They must divine the spirit of the Treaty and gain inspiration from it. If they find a gap, they must fill it as best they can. They must do what the framers of the instrument would have done if they had thought about it. So we must do the same.' (**Bulmer** v **Bollinger** (1974))*

In other words, he was saying that, rather than using the literal rule, the courts should apply a broadly interpreted mischief rule – which was, of course, the same approach that he felt should be applied to domestic legislation.

If the English courts are uncertain as to how a piece of European legislation should be interpreted they can, and sometimes must, refer it to the European Court of Justice for interpretation. In such circumstances the case is adjourned, until the European Court directs the English one on how to interpret the European legislation. The English court then reopens the case in England and applies this interpretation.

Effect of EU membership on the interpretation of UK law

Section 2(4) of the European Communities Act 1972 provides that all parliamentary legislation (whether passed before or after the European Communities Act) must be construed and applied in accordance with Union law. The case of **R v Secretary of State for Transport, ex parte Factortame** (1990) makes it clear that the English courts must apply European law which is directly effective even if it conflicts with English law, including statute law (these issues are discussed more fully in Chapter 18).

Reading on the web

Hansard is available at:

    www.publications.parliament.uk/pa/pahansard.htm

Chapter summary

Parliamentary intention

When interpreting statutes the courts are looking for the intention of Parliament, but this intention is frequently difficult to find.

Rules of statutory interpretation

There are three rules of statutory interpretation:

- the literal rule;
- the golden rule; and
- the mischief rule.

Internal aids to statutory interpretation

Internal aids consist of the statute itself and rules of language.

External aids

These include:

- dictionaries and textbooks;
- the explanatory notes;
- reports that preceded the legislation;
- treaties; and
- *Hansard*, following the decision of **Pepper v Hart**.

How do judges really interpret statutes?

The idea that statutory interpretation is an almost scientific process that can be used to produce a single right answer is simply nonsense. There is room for more than one interpretation (otherwise the question would never reach the courts) and judges must choose between them. The academic Griffith (1997) claims that where there is ambiguity, the judges choose the interpretation that best suits their view of policy and are therefore making a political decision.

The purposive approach

During his judicial career, Lord Denning was in the forefront of moves to establish a more purposive approach to statutory interpretation, aiming to produce decisions that put into practice the spirit of the law, even if that meant paying less than usual regard to the letter of the law, the actual words of the statute.

Interpretation of European legislation

Under Art. 234 of the Treaty of Rome, European legislation can be referred to the European Court of Justice for interpretation.

Question and answer guides

Read the source material below and answer parts (a) to (c) which follow:

SOURCE A
A knife was displayed in a shop window with a price ticket attached to it. The shop-keeper was charged with offering for sale a flick knife contrary to s. 1(1) of the Restriction of Offensive Weapons Act 1959, which provides:

'Any person who manufactures, sells or hires or offers for sale or hire, or lends to any other person – 5
(a) any knife which has a blade which opens automatically by hand pressure applied to a button, spring or other device in or attached to the handle of the knife, sometimes known as a "flick knife"... shall be guilty of an offence.'

The court had to decide whether the shopkeeper was guilty of 'offering the knife for sale' (he had not actually sold any). Applying the literal rule to the facts of the case, the 10
court held that the display of the knife in the shop window was not 'offering for sale' – merely an invitation to treat. Hence the shopkeeper was not guilty of the offence.
   Fisher v Bell [1961] 1 QB 394

SOURCE B
'Some may say ... that judges should not pay attention to what is said in Parliament. They should grope around in the dark for the meaning of an Act without switching on the light. I do not agree with this view.'

Adapted from the judgment of Lord Denning in Davis v Johnson [1979] AC 264

(OCR Specimen Paper 2007, Sources of Law Unit)

(a) Source B refers to Lord Denning's dissatisfaction with the ban on the use of the external aid Hansard prior to 1993. Explain what Hansard is and the circumstances in which courts may make a reference to it.

Plan

- *Hansard* is the official report of what is said in Parliament.
- It is available online as well as in printed volumes.
- Historically, the courts were not allowed to refer to *Hansard*.
- Following **Pepper v Hart** in 1993 the courts are allowed to refer to *Hansard* in limited circumstances.
- *Hansard* cannot be referred to where the words of the legislation are ambiguous, obscure or lead to absurdity.
- Only clear statements made by the minister or other promoter of the Bill can be considered.
- The statements to be relied upon are clear.
- Cases on the subject include **R v Secretary of State for the Environment, Transport and the Regions, ex parte Spath Holme Ltd, Wilson v Secretary of State for Trade and Industry** and **Davis v Johnson**.

Answer

Hansard is the official daily record of parliamentary debates and provides a verbatim record of what was said during the passage of all legislation through Parliament. It has existed since the early nineteenth century, but is now available online as well as in printed volumes. It provides an accurate record of ministers' speeches when a new Bill is introduced to Parliament or during parliamentary debates. It had been the case that a judge faced with a statute to interpret was limited to using the standard rules of interpretation and a limited range of aids to interpretation. They could not use *Hansard* to learn what the minister had explained was the purpose of the Bill when it was being considered by Parliament.

Some judges, like Lord Denning, were striving for ways to interpret Acts according to parliamentary intention and considered that not using *Hansard* was like 'groping around in the dark without turning on the lights'. Others, such as Lord Simonds in **Magor and St Mellons v Newport Corporation** (1952), considered such an approach would be 'a naked usurpation of the legislative function under the thin disguise of interpretation'.

Lord Denning and other progressive Court of Appeal judges continued their quest, but their view that it was valid to consult *Hansard* as an aid to interpretation was rejected by five Law Lords in **Davis v Johnson**. Eventually, in the case of **Pepper v Hart** in 1993 the House of Lords, made up of seven judges because of the importance of the case, decided that it was acceptable for a judge to consult *Hansard* where the legislation was ambiguous, obscure, or could lead to absurdity and there were statements in Parliament which would clarify the meaning for the court. The House of Lords in that case was concerned with the interpretation of the Finance Act 1976 with regard to the taxation of discounted perks for employees.

Any issue of judges interpreting statute law has always been handled cautiously by the courts, as there should be safeguards to maintain the separation of powers, so that the judiciary do not indirectly become the legislator through their role of interpreting the statute.

This acceptance of using *Hansard* as another extrinsic aid to interpretation was confirmed in **Three Rivers DC v Bank of England (No. 2)**, which concerned the correct interpretation of legislation used to bring in an EU Directive. Since then, the approach in **Pepper v Hart** has been tightened. In **Wilson v Secretary of State for Trade and Industry** it was held that only statements of the minister or the MP promoting the Bill should be looked at when they are making statements providing background information as to the social aims of the legislation.

(b) Read Source A lines 4–9. Using your knowledge of statutory interpretation, consider whether any of the following 'sells or hires or offers for sale or hire or gives to any other person – any knife which has a blade which opens automatically by hand pressure applied to a button, spring or other device in or attached to the handle of the knife' and therefore commits an offence under s. 1(1) of the Restriction of Offensive Weapons Act 1959:

(i)   **Jane, a youth worker, confiscates a flick knife from a member of her youth club and gives it to her supervisor.**

(ii) **Tony, an antique dealer, displays an old military knife with a spring opening device in his shop window with a price ticket attached to it.**

(iii) **Fola buys a 'job lot' box of kitchen utensils from a car boot sale. Without examining the contents closely she donates the box to a charity shop. The box is found to contain a flick knife.**

Plan

(i)   Applying a literal interpretation, Jane could be guilty of an offence. If the legislation is interpreted applying the mischief rule or the purposive approach, then she could avoid liability, as it was not the intention of Parliament to punish those who were trying to prevent the use of these weapons.

(ii) This situation is factually very similar to **Fisher v Bell**. Applying s. 1(1), Tony is not guilty of an offence under the literal rule. If the mischief rule is applied and, given the greater willingness of Parliament to look at *Hansard* and the purpose of the legislation, then a different outcome to such a case is likely today. Following the decision of **Fisher v Bell**, the problem was resolved with the passing of the Restriction of Offensive Weapons Act 1961, criminalising the display of such goods in a shop window.

(iii) A strict application of the literal rule to s. 1(1) would result in Fola being convicted as she 'gives' the flick knife to the charity shop. The charity shop would not yet be guilty of an offence, as it has not yet offered it for sale. However, Fola is unaware of the presence of the weapon and the courts might conclude that the literal rule has created an absurd result and move on to the golden rule, under which they could decide that Parliament intended a requirement of intention to be implied for the offence to be committed.

(c) With reference to Source A and other cases consider the problems that can be created by using the literal rule of interpretation and any advantages to be gained by using the modern purposive approach.

Plan

Problems with the literal rule
- The literal rule gives words their literal meaning.
- While the literal rule respects the principle of the separation of powers, it does not always respect the intention of Parliament, as can be seen in the case of **Fisher v Bell**.
- Examples of the literal rule being applied in practice include **Whiteley v Chappell**.

Advantages of the purposive approach
- The purposive approach looks behind the words of the statute to find the purpose for which the Act was passed. This is the normal approach to statutory interpretation for European law.
- It respects the intention of Parliament, which is the democratically elected law maker.
- In **Royal College of Nursing v DHSS**, the purposive interpretation allowed the courts to take into account social and technological developments since the relevant Act was passed.

Group activity 1

Look at the bye-law on the website below restricting multiple dog walking:

www.wandsworth.gov.uk/Home/EnvironmentandTransport/Dogs/dogwalking.htm

Split up into three groups. One group should apply a literal interpretation to the bye-law, one should apply the golden rule and one should apply the mischief rule. Compare how each group interpreted the bye-law. Did you come to different conclusions as to its meaning depending on which approach was used?

Group activity 2

In **Royal College of Nursing v DHSS** (1980) the House of Lords had to interpret s. 1 of the Abortion Act 1967.

- Divide your friends (or class) into five groups.
- Each group should read one of the five Law Lords' judgments in the case. (You will find all the judgments at **www.bailii.org/uk/cases/UKHL/1980/10.html**, but each group should only read one!)
- Each group should prepare notes stating what interpretation 'its' Law Lord put on s. 1 and summarising the reasons they gave for choosing that interpretation.
- The groups should then meet to compare notes.
- What conclusions can you draw from this comparison about the process of statutory interpretation?

Chapter 18
EUROPEAN LAW

This chapter discusses:

- the four key institutions of the European Union: the Council, the Commission, the European Parliament and the European Court of Justice;
- how European law is made;
- the four main sources of European law: treaties, regulations, directives and decisions;
- the impact of European Union law on the UK.

Introduction

The European Union currently comprises 27 western European countries. The original six member countries got together in 1951 to try to create political unity within Europe and prevent another world war. Today, the European Union also aims to weld Europe into a single prosperous area by abolishing all restrictions affecting the movement of people, of goods and money between Member States, producing a single market of over 370 million people, available to all producers in the Member States. This, it is hoped, will help Europe to compete economically with Japan, China and the US, the Member States being stronger as a block than they could possibly be on their own. Along with these closer economic ties, it is intended that there should be increasing political unity, though there is some disagreement – particularly, though not exclusively, in Britain – as to how far this should go.

Task 18.1

Find a newspaper article about the European Union in a quality newspaper that was published this week. Write a summary of the article.

The institutions of the European Union

There are four key European institutions: the Commission, the Council, the European Parliament and the European Court of Justice. Each of these institutions will be considered in turn, and then we look briefly at the efforts to reform the institutions so that they can work effectively with the enlarged membership of the EU.

The Commission

The Commission is composed of 27 members, called Commissioners, who are each appointed by the Member States, subject to approval by the European Parliament, for five years. They must be nationals of a Member State, and in practice there tend to be two each from the largest states – France, Germany, Italy, Spain and the UK – and one each from the rest. However, the Commissioners do not represent their own countries: they are independent, and their role is to represent the interests of the EU overall. The idea is that the Commission's commitment to furthering EU interests balances the role of the Council, whose members represent national interests.

In addition to its part in making EU legislation (see p. 330), the Commission is responsible for ensuring that Member States uphold European law, and has powers to investigate breaches by Member States and, where necessary, bring them before the Court of Justice. It also plays an important role in the relationship of the EU with the rest of the world, negotiating trade agreements and the accession of new members, and draws up the annual draft budget for the EU. It is assisted in all these functions by an administrative staff, which has a similar role to that of the civil service in the UK.

The Council

The Council represents the interests of individual Member States. It is the most powerful body in Europe and plays an important role in the passing of legislation. It does not have a permanent membership – in each meeting, the members, one from each country, are chosen according to the subject under discussion (so, for example, a discussion of matters relating to farming would usually be attended by the Minister of Agriculture of each country). Presidency of the Council rotates among the Member States every six months.

The Council may be questioned by the European Parliament, but the chief control is exercised by national governments controlling their ministers who attend the Council.

The European Parliament

The Parliament is composed of 785 members (MEPs), who are directly elected in their own countries. Elections are held every five years.

As well as taking part in the legislative process (discussed below), the Parliament has a variety of roles to play in connection with the other institutions. It

Figure 18.1 The European Parliament building, Strasbourg
Source: © EMPICS.

exercises a supervisory power over the Commission. It has a right of veto over the appointment of the Commission as a whole, and can also dismiss the whole Commission by a vote of censure.

The Council is not accountable to Parliament in the same way, and Parliament has only very limited controls over its activities.

The Parliament appoints an Ombudsman, who investigates complaints of mal-administration by EU institutions from individuals and MEPs.

The European Court of Justice (ECJ)

The ECJ has the task of supervising the uniform application of European law throughout the Member States, and in so doing it can create case law. It is important not to confuse it with the European Court of Human Rights, which deals with alleged breaches of human rights by countries who are signatories to the European Convention on Human Rights. That court is completely separate, and not an institution of the European Union.

The ECJ, which sits in Luxembourg, has 27 judges, appointed by agreement among Member States for a period of six years (which may be renewed). The judges are assisted by eight Advocates General, who produce opinions on the cases assigned to them, indicating the issues raised and suggesting conclusions. These are not binding, but are nevertheless usually followed by the court. Both judges and Advocates General are chosen from those who are eligible for the highest judicial posts in their own countries.

Most cases are heard in plenary session, that is with all the judges sitting together. Only one judgment will be delivered, giving no indication of the extent of agreement between the judges, and these often consist of fairly brief propositions, from which it can be difficult to discern any *ratio decidendi*. Consequently, lawyers seeking precedents often turn to the opinions written by the Advocates General.

The majority of cases heard by the ECJ are brought by Member States and institutions of the Community, or are referred to it by national courts. It has only limited power to deal with cases brought by individual citizens, and such cases are rarely heard.

The ECJ has two separate functions: a judicial role, deciding cases of dispute; and a supervisory role.

The judicial role of the ECJ

The ECJ hears cases of dispute between parties, which fall into two categories: proceedings against Member States, and proceedings against European institutions.

Proceedings against Member States may be brought by the Commission, or by other Member States, and involve alleged breaches of European law by the country in question. For example, in **Re Tachographs: EC Commission** *v* **UK** (1979), the ECJ upheld a complaint against the UK for failing to implement a European regulation making it compulsory for lorries used to carry dangerous goods to be fitted with tachographs (devices used to record the speed and distance travelled, with the aim of preventing lorry drivers from speeding, or for driving for longer than the permitted number of hours). The Commission usually gives the Member State the opportunity to put things right before bringing the case to the ECJ.

Proceedings against European institutions may be brought by Member States, other European institutions and, in limited circumstances, by individual citizens or organisations. The procedure can be used to review the legality of regulations, directives or decisions, on the grounds that proper procedures have not been followed, the provisions infringe a treaty or any rule relating to its application, or powers have been misused. In **United Kingdom** *v* **Council of the European Union** (1996) the UK sought to have the directive on the 48-hour working week annulled on the basis that it had been unlawfully adopted by the Council. The application was unsuccessful.

Decisions made in these kinds of cases cannot be questioned in UK courts. Member States can be fined for failure to implement a judgment of the European Court.

The supervisory role of the ECJ

Under Art. 234 of the Treaty of Rome any court or tribunal in a Member State may refer a question on European law to the ECJ if it considers that 'a decision on that question is necessary to enable it to give judgment'. The object of this referral system is to make sure that the law is interpreted in the same way throughout Europe.

A reference must be made if the national court is one from which there is no further appeal – so, in Britain, the House of Lords must refer such questions, while the lower courts usually have some discretion about whether or not to do so.

Attempts have been made to set down guidelines by which a court can determine when a reference is necessary. In **Bulmer v Bollinger** (1974), Lord Denning set down guidelines on the points which should be taken into account in considering whether a reference was necessary. He emphasised the cost and delay that a reference could cause, and stated that no reference should be made:

- where it would not be conclusive of the case, and other matters would remain to be decided;
- where there had been a previous ruling on the same point;
- where the court considers that point to be reasonably clear and free from doubt;
- where the facts of the case had not yet been decided.

Unless the point to be decided could be considered 'really difficult and important', said Lord Denning, the court should save the expense and delay of a reference and decide the issue itself.

Denning's view has since been criticised by academics, who point out that it can be cheaper and quicker to refer a point at an early stage, than to drag the case up through the English courts first. In addition, the clear and consistent interpretation of European law can come to depend on whether individual litigants have the resources to take their cases all the way up to the House of Lords.

Although the judiciary still uses Denning's **Bulmer** guidelines, there now appears to be a greater willingness to refer cases to the ECJ. In **R v International Stock Exchange, ex parte Else** (1993) Lord Justice Bingham said that if, once the facts have been found, it is clear that an issue of European law is vital to a court's final decision, that court should normally make a reference to the ECJ. English courts should only decide such issues without referral if they have real confidence that they can do so correctly, without the help of the ECJ.

Where a case is submitted, proceedings will be suspended in the national court until the ECJ has given its verdict. This verdict does not tell the national court how to decide the case, but simply explains what European law on the matter is. The national court then has the duty of making its decision in the light of this.

Regardless of which national court submitted the point for consideration, a ruling from the ECJ should be followed by all other courts in the EU.

The court's decisions can be changed only by its own subsequent decision or by an amendment of the Treaty. Decisions of the European Court cannot be questioned in English courts.

An illustration of the use of Art. 234 is the case of **Marshall v Southampton and South West Hampshire Area Health Authority** (1986). Miss Marshall, a dietitian, was compulsorily retired by the Authority from her job when she was 62, although she wished to continue to 65. It was the Authority's policy that the normal retiring age for its employees was the age at which state retirement pensions became payable: for women this was 60, though the Authority had waived the rule for two years in Miss Marshall's case. She claimed that the Authority was discriminating against women by adopting a policy that employees should retire at state pension age, hence requiring women to retire before men. This policy appeared to be legal under the relevant English legislation but was argued to be contrary to a Council directive providing for equal treatment of men and women. The national court made a reference to the ECJ, asking for directions on the meaning of the directive. The ECJ found that there was a conflict with UK law, and the UK later changed its legislation to conform.

Sources of European law

The Council, the Commission and the European Parliament all play a role in making European legislation. A complicated range of different procedures has been developed to make these laws. All legislation starts with a proposal from the Commission and the Council enjoys the most power in the legislative process.

Parliament's legislative role was historically purely advisory, with the Commission and the Council having a much more powerful role in the legislative process. This led to concern over the lack of democracy within Europe, for while the Parliament is directly elected by the citizens of Europe, the Commission and Council members are not.

Table 18.1 Membership of the European institutions

Commission	27 Commissioners.
Council	It does not have a permanent membership. For each meeting one minister is chosen from each country according to the subject of the meeting.
European Parliament	785 members of the European Parliament (MEPs).
European Court of Justice	27 judges.

The role of the European Parliament in the passing of European legislation has gradually been increased over the years, but problems still remain. There are still areas of law on which Parliament does not even have the right to be consulted. Where Parliament is consulted by the Council, it normally has no power to block the legislation, but can merely delay it.

The Council plays an important role in the passing of European legislation. There are three systems of voting in the Council:

- Unanimity, where proposals are only passed if all members vote for them.
- Simple majority, where proposals only require more votes for than against.
- Qualified majority, which allows each country a specified number of votes (the larger the country, the more votes it has), and provides that a proposal can only be agreed if there are a specified number of votes in its favour. The number is calculated to ensure that larger states cannot force decisions on the smaller ones.

These voting procedures have been controversial, because where unanimity is not required a Member State can be forced to abide by legislation for which it has not voted, and which it believes is against its interests. This is seen as compromising national sovereignty. However, requiring unanimity makes it difficult to get things done quickly (or sometimes at all). Increasingly, only a qualified majority is required.

There is a range of different forms of European legislation: treaties, regulations, directives and decisions. In considering the impact of this legislation on UK law, a distinction has to be drawn between *direct applicability* and *direct effect*. Direct applicability refers to the fact that treaty articles, regulations and some decisions immediately become part of the law of each Member State. Directives are not directly applicable.

Where European legislation has direct effect, it creates individual rights which national courts must protect without any need for implementing legislation in that Member State. In the UK the national courts were given this power under s. 2(1) of the European Communities Act 1972.

sourcebook
p. 35 →

There are two types of direct effect: *vertical direct effect* gives individuals rights against governments; and *horizontal direct effect* gives rights against other people and organisations.

Provisions of treaties, regulations and directives only have direct effect if they are clear and unconditional and their implementation requires no further legislation in Member States. These conditions were first laid down in the context of treaties in **Van Gend en Loos *v* Nederlandse Tariefcommissie** (1963).

The ability of individuals to rely on European law before their national courts greatly enhances its effectiveness. National courts can quickly apply directly effective legislation and can draw on a wide range of remedies. Where legislation does not have direct effect, the only method of enforcement available in the past was an action brought by the Commission or a Member State against a Member State before the European Court of Justice. This process can be slow and provides no direct remedy for the individual.

However, in the 1990s the European Court of Justice recognised the right of individuals to be awarded damages by their national courts for breach of European legislation by a Member State, even where the legislation did not have direct effect. Originally, in **Francovich *v* Italy** (1991), this right was applied where directives had not been implemented, but it has been developed to extend to any violation of European law.

??? Quick quiz 18.2

1 How many countries are members of the European Union?

2 Name the four key institutions of the European Union.

3 Explain the supervisory role of the European Court of Justice.

4 What are the three systems of voting in the Council?

Treaties

These are the highest source of European law and, as well as laying down the general aims of the European Union, they themselves create some rights and obligations. The existing treaties are the three treaties of Rome that established the framework for Europe (the European Coal and Steel Community Treaty, the Euratom Treaty and the European Community Treaty), the Single European Act, the Treaty on European Union (known as the Maastricht Treaty because it was signed in Maastricht), and the Treaty of Amsterdam. The article numbers of the European

Community Treaty were changed by the Treaty of Amsterdam, as old articles had been repealed and new articles added since it had been originally drafted.

The case of **Van Gend en Loos** (1963) decided that a treaty provision has direct effect if it is unconditional, clear and precise as to the rights or obligations it creates, and leaves Member States no discretion on implementing it. Treaty provisions which are unconditional, clear and precise, and allow no discretion on implementation have both horizontal and vertical direct effect. An example of a directly effective treaty provision is Art. 139 of the EC Treaty. This provides that 'men and women shall receive equal pay for equal work'. In **Macarthys** *v* **Smith** (1979), Art. 139 was held to give a woman in the UK the right to claim the same wages as were paid to the male predecessor in her job, even though she had no such right under the UK equal pay legislation passed in 1970, before the UK joined Europe.

Treaty provisions which are merely statements of intent or policy, rather than establishing clear rights or duties, require detailed legislation to be made before they can be enforced in the Member States.

Regulations

A regulation is the nearest that European law comes to an English Act of Parliament. Regulations apply throughout the EU, usually to people in general, and they become part of the law of each member nation as soon as they come into force, without the need for each country to make its own legislation. Regulations must be applied even if the Member State has already passed legislation which conflicts with them.

Directives

Directives are less precisely worded than regulations, because they aim to set out broad objectives, leaving the Member States to create their own detailed legislation in order to put those objectives into practice (within specified time limits). As a result, it was originally assumed by most Member States that directives could not have direct effect, and would not create individual rights until they had been translated into domestic legislation. However, the European Court of Justice has consistently refused to accept this view, arguing that direct effect is an essential weapon if the EU is to ensure that Member States implement directives.

> ✔ **Know your terms 18.3**
>
> Define the following terms:
> 1 Advocate General.
> 2 Veto.
> 3 European Commission.
> 4 Directive.

sourcebook p. 38 → The case which initially established direct effect for directives was **Van Duyn** *v* **Home Office** (1974). The Home Office had refused Van Duyn permission to enter the UK, because she was a member of a religious group, the Scientologists, which the government wanted to exclude from the country at the time. Van Duyn argued that her exclusion was contrary to provisions in the Treaty of Rome on freedom of movement. The government responded by pointing out that the treaty allowed exceptions on public policy grounds, but Van Duyn then relied on a later directive which said that public policy could only be invoked on the basis of personal conduct, and Van Duyn herself had done nothing to justify exclusion. The case was referred to the ECJ, which found that the obligation conferred on the government was clear and unconditional, and so created enforceable rights.

Directives have vertical direct effect but not horizontal direct effect. This means that they impose obligations on the state and not individuals. A directive with direct effect can be utilised by an individual against the state when the state has failed to implement the directive properly or on time.

The issue of direct effect was important in the high-profile case of **R (Westminster City Council) *v* Mayor of London** (2002). Westminster Council had applied for judicial review of the decision to introduce a congestion charge to enter central London. The decision had been taken by the Mayor of London, Ken Livingstone. The High Court rejected the application. Westminster Council had sought to rely on a provision of a directive. The High Court stated that the Council could not do this, as when directives had direct effect they only gave rights to individuals and not to government institutions.

The ECJ has found a number of ways to widen access where the principle of vertical direct effect applies. First, it has defined 'the state' very broadly to include all public bodies, including local authorities and nationalised industries. This meant, for example, that in **Marshall *v* Southampton and Southwest Hampshire Area Health Authority** (1986), discussed on p. 332, Miss Marshall was able to take advantage of the relevant directive even though she was not suing the government itself, because her employer was a health authority and therefore considered a public body.

Secondly, in **Von Colson *v* Land Nordrhein-Westfalen** (1984), the court introduced the principle of indirect effect, stating that national courts should interpret national law in accordance with relevant directives, whether the national law was designed to implement a directive or not. The principle was confirmed in **Marleasing SA *v* La Comercial Internacional de Alimentacion SA** (1990).

Thirdly, some recent cases have allowed an unimplemented directive to act as a shield though not as a sword to the benefit of private individuals. In other words, the directive could be relied upon to provide a defence but not to provide a right of action. For example, **CIA Security International SA *v* Signalson** (1996) concerned the failure by the Belgian government to notify the Commission of its law on security systems in accordance with a European directive on the subject (Notification Directive 98/34). Litigation arose between two private companies, CIA Security and Signalson. Signalson tried to prevent CIA from marketing an alarm system which had not been approved under Belgian law. CIA successfully argued that the Belgian law did not apply because the Commission had not been notified about it in accordance with the European directive. Thus, CIA were able to rely on the directive to provide a defence in the litigation between two private individuals. On the surface it looked as if the directive was being given horizontal direct effect in breach of established principles of European law, but in fact the case has been interpreted as merely allowing a directive to give private individuals a defence. Another interpretation of the case was that Signalson was effectively acting as an agent of the state, bringing proceedings for the withdrawal of a product which potentially did not conform with Belgian law.

In **R (Wells) *v* Secretary of State for Transport, Local Government and the Regions** (2005), there was a plan by a private company to reopen a quarry in an environmentally sensitive area. No environmental impact assessment had been carried out by the state in accordance with the Environmental Impact Assessment

Directive (Directive 85/337). A local resident asked the Secretary of State to remove or modify the planning permission pending the carrying out of the assessment, but he refused. In the subsequent litigation, the court had to consider whether the local resident could rely on the directive. It acknowledged that a directive cannot be used as a sword to impose obligations on a private individual. But a directive could be used as a shield, even if in doing so there would be a negative impact on a private individual; in this case the quarry owners would have to stop work on the quarry until the completion of the environmental impact assessment. As the quarry owners were not required to carry out an obligation, this did not amount to the imposition of direct horizontal effect.

Table 18.2 **Impact of European legislation**

Impact	Meaning of term
Direct applicability	Legislative provisions immediately become part of the law of each Member State.
Direct effect	Legislation creates individual rights which national courts must protect without any need for implementing legislation in the Member State.
Horizontal direct effect	Legislation gives rights against governments, individuals and private organisations.
Vertical direct effect	Legislation gives rights against governments.
Indirect effect	National courts should interpret national law in accordance with relevant European legislation.

Decisions

A decision may be addressed to a state, a person or a company and is binding only on the recipient. Examples include granting, or refusing, export licences to companies from outside the European Union.

The impact of EU law on the UK

One view of the influence of UK membership of Europe on our national law was given by Lord Denning, in poetic mood, in **Bulmer v Bollinger** (1974): 'The Treaty is like an incoming tide. It flows into the estuaries and up the rivers. It cannot be held back.' Lord Scarman, obviously in an equally lyrical frame of mind, commented:

'For the moment, to adopt Lord Denning's imagery, the incoming tide has not yet mingled with the home waters of the common law: but it is inconceivable that, like the Rhone and the Arve where those two streams meet at Geneva, they should move on, side by side, one grey with the melted snows and ice of the distant mountains of our legal history, the other clear blue and clean, reflecting modern opinion. If we stay in the Common Market, I would expect to see its principles of legislation and statutory interpretation, and its conception of an activist court whose role is to strengthen and fulfil the purpose of statute law, replace the traditional attitudes of English judges and lawyers to statute law and the current complex style of statutory drafting.'

What Lord Scarman was referring to was the difference in approach between the English legal system and those in mainland Europe. When drafting statutes, for example, English law has tended towards tightly written, very precise rules, whereas the continental style is looser, setting out broad principles to be followed. As a result, the continental style of statutory interpretation takes a very purposive approach, paying most attention to putting into practice the spirit of the legislation, and filling in any gaps in the wording if necessary, as opposed to the more literal style traditionally associated with English judges. The ECJ tends to take the continental approach, and it has been suggested that, as time goes on, this will influence our own judges more and more, leading to more creative judicial decision-making, with corresponding changes in the drafting of statutes.

Following the **Factortame** litigation, there was concern that Europe was threatening the sovereignty of the UK Parliament, as the ECJ ruling had caused an Act of Parliament to be set aside. Lord Denning revised his description of European law as like an 'incoming tide' and stated:

> *'No longer is European law an incoming tide flowing up the estuaries of England. It is now like a tidal wave bringing down our sea walls and flowing inland over our fields and houses – to the dismay of all.'* (The Independent, *16 July 1996*)

In **R *v* Secretary of State for Foreign and Commonwealth Affairs, ex parte Rees-Mogg** (1994) an unsuccessful attempt was made to demonstrate that the UK could not legally ratify the Maastricht Treaty. In rejecting this claim, the court pointed out that the treaty did not involve the abandoning or transferring of powers, so that a government could choose later to denounce the treaty, or fail to honour its obligations under it.

sourcebook
p. 42 →

Institutional Reform

The European institutions were expected to be modernised to cope with the European Union's expanded membership through the passing of a new European Constitution. However, referendums in the Netherlands and France rejected the Constitution so it is uncertain which reforms will be introduced and when.

The Constitution contained a wide range of provisions. It would have explicitly stated for the first time that European law had primacy over national law. EU legal instruments would have been re-classified, to establish a clear hierarchy and to distinguish between legislative and administrative acts. Constitutional law would be the highest source of law, amendable only under treaty amendment procedures. European laws and framework laws would be binding legislative acts (similar to the current regulations and directives), regulations and decisions would be binding administrative acts; and recommendations and opinions would not be binding.

The European Union would have had a stronger political profile through the creation of two new posts: a Commission President and a Minister for Foreign Affairs. The Commission President would have been elected by the European Parliament. The Minister for Foreign Affairs would have been elected by the European Council. The President of the Council of Ministers would no longer have been held for six months, instead a team presidency would have been established consisting of three individuals appointed for 18 months. The number of Commissioners would have been reduced to two-thirds of the number of Member States. Membership of the European Parliament would have been restricted to 750. The European Parliament's legislative role would have been strengthened to make the legislative process more democratic. The rotating six-monthly presidency of the European Council would have been abolished and replaced by a person appointed for a renewable period of two and a half years.

Within the European Council the emphasis would have been on qualified majority voting, with a view to reducing the current number of national vetoes. The existing system of weighted votes for calculating a qualified majority would have been replaced by a 'double majority' system. This would have required the support of 55 per cent of Member States which also represented at least 65 per cent of the EU population. To prevent two or three large countries blocking a vote, a blocking minority would require at least four Council members.

Part II of the Constitution contained a Charter of Fundamental Rights. This laid down much more extensive rights than those contained in the European Convention on Human Rights, because, as well as containing civil and political rights, it contained social and economic rights.

Following the rejection of the European Constitution and a two year period of reflection, a Reform Treaty has been agreed in 2007 which adapts many of the planned reforms of the failed European Constitution. It aims to make the EU more democratic and more efficient. This treaty is expected to come into force in the summer of 2009.

Reading on the web

Access to the homepages of the European institutions can be obtained from the following website:

http://europa.eu/institutions/index_en.htm

European legislation is available at:

http://europa.eu.int/eur_lex/

Chapter summary

Introduction

The European Union currently has 27 members. It was established to create political unity within Europe and to prevent another world war.

The institutions of the European Union

There are four key institutions of the European Union: the Commission, the Council, the European Parliament and the European Court of Justice. The European Court of Justice has two separate functions: a judicial role where it decides cases of dispute and a supervisory role under Art. 234 of the Treaty of Rome.

Making European legislation

The Council, the Commission and the European Parliament all play a role in making European legislation. All legislation starts with a proposal from the Commission, though the Council enjoys the most power in the legislative process. Increasingly, the qualified majority system of voting is being used by the Council in agreeing new legislation.

Sources of European law

The different forms of European legislation are:

- treaties;
- regulations;
- directives; and
- decisions.

The impact of EU law on the UK

The impact of EU legislation on the UK is likely to increase in the future.

Question and answer guides

1. (a) Describe the role of any three institutions of the European Union.

Answer

The three institutions that will be considered are the European Commission, the European Parliament and the Council of Ministers, which all play key roles in the European Union. Looking first at the European Commission, this institution runs the day-to-day business of the European Union and has two main roles. First, it proposes new legislation and develops European policies and, secondly, it supervises the application of European legislation, including referring cases to the European Court of Justice. Commissioners from different Member States are required to represent the interests of the European Union rather than their home country. Each Commissioner is given a portfolio to look after a particular interest. The current UK Commissioner with responsibility for trade issues is Peter Mandelson, a former Labour member of Parliament.

The European Parliament does not propose, but has some involvement in the legislative process and provides a forum in which the legislation can be publicly debated. The Commission proposes issues to be debated by the Parliament which then returns them to the Commission for formal drafting. The European Parliament has a right to be consulted about legislation and in some cases has the power of co-decision, it has budgetary powers and can ask questions of the Council and the Commission. It can dismiss the Commission (which it did in 1999) and it can veto proposed new Commissioners.

Members of the European Parliament (MEPs) are directly elected by the citizens of Member States every five years and member seats are proportionate to their population. Most MEPs are affiliated to a political party and will vote along those lines; however, there are a considerable number of independent MEPs.

The Council of Ministers is at the apex of political power and control in the EU. It passes the new laws proposed by the Commission. It makes decisions on proposed policy and issues regulations and directives. Each Member State sends a minister representing them as the decision-maker to the Council meetings. This is often the Foreign Minister, but if a Council meeting is to be about dairy farming, for example, it may be more suitable for the Minister for Agriculture to attend. Each minister has a power of veto. If the meeting is one of the twice-yearly 'summit' meetings, the Heads of Government of each member state will attend. The permanent staffing of the Council is run by COREPER, the EU equivalent of the Civil Service.

(b) Explain the doctrine of the supremacy of Parliament, and consider two limitations to this doctrine.

Plan

- Parliament is the supreme law-maker.
- One sitting of Parliament cannot bind another.
- Judges can only interpret and apply parliamentary legislation, they cannot question its illegality. The unsuccessful challenge to the Hunting Act 2004 was based on the suggestion that the legislative process had not been correctly followed, so that the 2004 Act was not a genuine piece of parliamentary legislation. The content of the Hunting Act could not found a ruling that the Act was illegal, only the procedure used so that there was no genuine piece of legislation.
- European law provides a possible limitation on the supremacy of Parliament. Parliamentary legislation can be amended by delegated legislation to comply with European law. Increasingly, European law has direct effect in the UK.
- The Human Rights Act 1998 provides a second limitation on the supremacy of Parliament, though it is not entrenched like a Bill of Rights so that it could be repealed by a future Parliament passing ordinary legislation to this effect.

Group activity 1

Look at the website for the European Union:

http://europa.eu/index_en.htm

Carry out a search of the site on the subject of 'food safety'.

- Which European institutions are currently reviewing food safety?
- Identify one initiative from each of them on this subject.

This chapter discusses

- judicial and parliamentary law reform in practice;
- the impetus for law reform from pressure groups, judges, political parties, the civil service, treaty obligations, public opinion and media pressure;
- the different agencies that have been set up to consider the need for reform in areas referred to them by the government, including the Law Commission, Royal Commissions and public inquiries;
- the success of these agencies of law reform.

Introduction

An effective legal system cannot stand still. Both legal procedures and the law itself must adapt to social change if they are to retain the respect of at least most of society, without which they cannot survive. Many laws which were made even as short a time ago as the nineteenth century simply do not fit the way we see society today. Until the early part of the twentieth century, for example, married women were legally considered the property of their husbands, while, not much earlier, employees could be imprisoned for breaking their employment contracts.

Most legislation in this country stands until it is repealed – the fact that it may be completely out of date does not mean it technically ceases to apply. The offences of challenging to fight, eavesdropping and being a common scold, for example, which long ago dropped out of use, nevertheless remained on the statute book until they were abolished by the Criminal Law Act 1967. In practice, of course, many such provisions simply cease to be used, but where it becomes clear that the law may be out of step with social conditions, or simply ineffective, there is a range of ways of bringing about change.

Judicial activity

Case law can bring about some reform – one of the most notable recent examples was the decision in **R v R** (1991), in which the House of Lords declared that a husband who has sexual intercourse with his wife without her consent may be guilty of rape. Before this decision, the law on rape within marriage was based on an assertion by the eighteenth-century jurist Sir Matthew Hale, that 'by marrying a man, a woman consents to sexual intercourse with him, and may not retract that consent'. This position had been found offensive for many years before **R** *v* **R**. In 1976, Parliament considered it during a debate on the Sexual Offences Act, but decided not to make changes at that time, and it was not until 1991 that the Court of Appeal and then the House of Lords held that rape within marriage should be considered an offence.

Lord Keith stated that Hale's assertion reflected the status of women within marriage in his time, but since then both the status of women and the marriage relationship had completely changed. The modern view of husband and wife as equal partners meant that a wife could no longer be considered to have given irrevocable consent to sex with her husband; the common law was capable of evolving to reflect such changes in society, and it was the duty of the court to help it do so.

In practice, however, major reforms like this are rarely produced by the courts, and would not be adequate as the sole agency of reform. Norman Marsh's article 'Law Reform in the United Kingdom' (1971) puts forward a number of reasons for this.

First, as we saw in the chapter on case law, there is no systematic, state-funded process for bringing points of law in need of reform to the higher courts. The courts can deal with such points only as they arise in the cases before them, and this depends on the parties involved having sufficient finance, determination and interest to take their case up through the courts. Consequently, judge-made reform proceeds not on the basis of which areas of law need changes most, but on a haphazard presentation of cases.

Secondly, judges have to decide cases on the basis of the way the issues are presented to them by the parties concerned. They cannot commission research, or consult with interested bodies to find out the possible effects of a decision on individuals and organisations other than those in the case before them – yet their decision will apply to future cases.

Thirdly, judges have to recognise the doctrine of precedent, and for much of the time this prohibits any really radical reforms.

Marsh's fourth point is that reforming decisions by judges have the potential to be unjust to the losing party. Law reforms made by Parliament are prospective – they come into force on a specified date, and we are not usually expected to abide by them until after that date. Judicial decisions, on the other hand, are retrospective, affecting something that happened before the judges decided what the law was. The more reformatory such a decision is, the less the likelihood that the losing party could have abided by the law, even if they wanted to.

Finally, Marsh argues, judges are not elected, and therefore feel they should not make decisions which change the law in areas of great social or moral controversy. They themselves impose limits on their ability to make major changes and will often point out to Parliament the need for it to make reforms, as happened in the **Bland** case concerning the Hillsborough stadium disaster victim (see p. 368).

Reform by Parliament

The majority of law reform is therefore carried out by Parliament. It is done in four ways:

Repeal

Repeal of old and/or obsolete laws.

Creation

Creation of completely new law, or adaptation of existing provisions, to meet new needs. The creation of the offence of insider dealing (where company officials make money by using information gained by virtue of a privileged position) in the Companies Act 1980 was a response to public concern about 'sharp practice' in the City of London.

Consolidation

When a new statute is created, problems with it may become apparent over time, in which case further legislation may be enacted to amend it. Consolidation brings together successive statutes on a particular subject and puts them into one statute. For example, the legislation in relation to companies was consolidated in 1985.

Codification

Where a particular area of the law has developed over time to produce a large body of both case law and statute, a new statute may be created to bring together all the rules on that subject (case law and statute) in one place. That statute then becomes the starting point for cases concerning that area of the law, and case law, in time, builds up around it. The Criminal Attempts Act 1981 and the Police and Criminal Evidence Act 1984 are examples of codifying statutes. Codification is thought to be most suitable for areas of law where the principles are well worked out; areas that are still developing, such as tort, are less suitable for codifying.

These types of reform often happen together – the Public Order Act 1986, for example, created new public order offences designed to deal with specific problems of the time, such as football hooliganism, and at the same time, repealed out of date public order offences.

Some significant law reforms have come about as a result of Private Members' Bills (see p. 282) – an example is the Abortion Act 1967, which resulted from a Private Member's Bill put forward by David Steel.

Impetus for law reform

The inspiration for reform may come from a variety of sources, alone or in combination. As well as encouraging Parliament to consider particular issues in the first place, they may have an influence during the consultation stage of legislation.

Pressure groups

Groups concerned with particular subjects may press for law reform in those areas – examples include charities such as Shelter, Help the Aged and the Child Poverty Action Group; professional organisations such as the Law Society and the British Medical Association; business representatives such as the Confederation of British Industry. Justice is a pressure group specifically concerned with promoting law reform in general.

Task 19.1

The following organisations are examples of influential pressure groups:

The Campaign for Nuclear Disarmament: www.cnduk.org/
Greenpeace: www.greenpeace.org/international/
Shelter: www.shelter.org.uk/

Select the website of one of them and consider the ways in which they are trying to influence legal developments in this country.

Pressure groups use a variety of tactics, including lobbying MPs, gaining as much publicity as possible for their cause, organising petitions and encouraging people to write to their own MP and/or relevant ministers. Some groups are more effective than others: size obviously helps, but sheer persistence and a knack for grabbing headlines can be just as productive – the anti-porn campaigner Mary Whitehouse almost single-handedly pressurised the government into creating the Protection of Children Act 1978, which sought to prevent child pornography. The amount of power wielded by the members of a pressure group is also extremely important – organisations involved with big business tend to be particularly effective in influencing legislation, and there is a growing industry set up purely to help them lobby effectively, for a price. On the other hand, pressure groups made up of ordinary individuals can be very successful, particularly if the issue on which they are campaigning is one which stirs up strong emotion in the general public. A recent example was the Snowdrop Petition, organised after the shooting of 16 young children and their teacher in Dunblane, Scotland. Despite enormous opposition from shooting clubs, it managed to persuade the previous government to ban most types of handguns.

The judges

Sometimes the judges will explicitly observe in one of their judgments that the law is unsatisfactory and in need of reform by Parliament.

Political parties

Some of the most high-profile legislation is that passed in order to implement the government party's election manifesto, or its general ideology – examples include the privatisations of gas and water and the creation of the Poll Tax by the Conservative government which began in 1979.

The civil service

Although technically neutral, the civil service nevertheless has a great effect on legislation in general. It may not have party political goals, but various departments will have their own views as to what type of legislation enables them to achieve departmental goals most efficiently – which strategies might help the Home Office control the prison population, for example, or the Department of Health make the NHS more efficient. Ministers rely heavily on senior civil servants for advice and information on the issues of the day, and few would consistently turn down their suggestions.

Treaty obligations

The UK's obligations under the treaties establishing the European Union and the European Convention on Human Rights both influence changes in English law (see Chapter 18 on European law and p. 264 on the incorporation of the European Convention).

Public opinion and media pressure

sourcebook p. 202 →

As well as taking part in campaigns organised by pressure groups, members of the public make their feelings known by writing to their MPs, to ministers and to newspapers. This is most likely to lead to reform where the ruling party has a small majority. The media can also be a very powerful force for law reform, by highlighting issues of concern. In 1997, media pressure helped secure a judicial inquiry into the racially motivated killing of South London teenager Stephen Lawrence. The inquiry was authorised to look not only at the Lawrence case itself, but at the general issue of how racially motivated killings are investigated.

Public opinion and media pressure interact; the media often claim to reflect public opinion, but they can also whip it up. What appears to be a major epidemic of a particular crime may in fact be no more than a reflection of the fact that once one interesting example of it hits the news, newspapers and broadcasting organisations are more likely to report others. An example of this is the rash of stories during 1993 about parents going on holiday and leaving their children alone, which caught the headlines largely because of a popular film about just such a situation, *Home Alone*. Leaving children alone like this may have been common practice for years, or it may be something done by a tiny minority of parents, but the media's selection of stories gave the impression of a sudden epidemic of parental negligence. In 2000 there was a high-profile campaign by the *News of the World* to 'name and shame' paedophiles. The government subsequently introduced a limited reform of the law.

Quick quiz 19.2

1 Which court heard the final appeal in **R** v **R** (1991) and what is the *ratio decidendi* of this decision?

2 What are the four main ways in which Parliament can change the law?

3 Give three examples of pressure groups that seek to influence the development of the law.

4 What do you think of the campaign by the *News of the World* to name and shame paedophiles?

Agencies of law reform

Much law reform happens as a direct response to pressure from one or more of the above sources, but there are also a number of agencies set up to consider the need for reform in areas referred to them by the government. Often problems are referred to them as a result of the kind of pressures listed above – the Royal Commission on Criminal Justice 1993 was set up as a result of public concern and media pressure about high-profile miscarriages of justice, such as the 'Birmingham Six' and the 'Guildford Four'.

The Law Commission

Established in 1965 (along with another for Scotland), the Law Commission is a permanent body, comprising five people drawn from the judiciary, the legal profession and legal academics. In practice, the chairman tends to be a High Court judge, and the other four members to include a QC experienced in criminal law, a solicitor with experience of land law and equity, and two legal academics. They are assisted by legally qualified civil servants.

Under the Law Commission Act 1965 the Law Commission's task is to:

■ codify the law;
■ remove anomalies in the law;
■ repeal obsolete and unnecessary legislation;
■ consolidate the law;
■ simplify and modernise the law.

The Commission works on reform projects referred to it by the Lord Chancellor or a government department or on projects which the Commission itself has decided would be suitable for its consideration. At any one time the Commission will be engaged on between 20 and 30 projects of law reform.

A typical project will begin with a study of the area of law in question, and an attempt to identify its defects. Foreign legal systems will be examined to see how they deal with similar problems. The Commission normally publishes a consultation paper inviting comments on the subject. The consultation paper describes the present law and its shortcomings and sets out possible options for reform. The Commission's final recommendations are set out in a report which contains a draft Bill where legislation is proposed. It is then essentially for the government to decide whether it accepts the recommendations and to introduce any necessary Bill in Parliament.

Royal Commissions

These are set up to study particular areas of law reform, usually as a result of criticism and concern about the area concerned. They are made up of a wide cross-section

Figure 19.1 *News of the World*: its campaign to name and shame paedophiles

Source: *Remember When*, The Newspaper Archive. The *News of the World*, London, 23 July 2000. © News International Newspapers Limited, 23 July 2000.

of people: most have some expertise in the area concerned, but usually only a minority are legally qualified. The Commissions are supposed to be independent and non-political.

A Royal Commission can commission research, and also take submissions from interested parties. It produces a final report detailing its recommendations, which the government can then choose to act upon or not. Usually, a majority of proposals are acted upon, sometimes in amended form.

Important recent Royal Commissions include the 1981 Royal Commission on Criminal Procedure and the Royal Commission on Criminal Justice, which reported in 1993, and the Royal Commission on reform of the House of Lords which reported in 2000.

Public inquiries

Where a particular problem or incident is causing social concern, the government may set up a one-off, temporary committee to examine possible options for dealing with it. Major disasters, such as the Hillsborough football stadium disaster; the sinking of the ferry *Herald of Free Enterprise* and the Paddington railway disaster; events such as the Brixton riots during the 1980s; and advances in technology, especially medical technology (such as the ability to fertilise human eggs outside

Figure 19.2 **Victoria Climbie**
Source: © Rex Features Ltd.

the body and produce 'test-tube babies') may all be investigated by bodies set up especially for the job. In recent years, inquiries have been set up following the BSE crisis, the murder of Victoria Climbie (a young girl living away from her parents), and the conviction of the serial killer Harold Shipman. These inquiries usually comprise individuals who are independent of government, often with expertise in the particular area. Academics are frequent choices, as are judges – Lord Scarman headed the inquiry into the Brixton riots, and Lord Hutton (2004) headed the inquiry into the suicide of Dr David Kelly following the war in Iraq.

Public inquiries consult interested groups, and attempt to reach a consensus between them, conducting their investigation as far as possible in a non-political way. In the case of disasters and other events, they may try to discover the causes, as well as making recommendations on legislation to avoid a repeat.

Other temporary inquiries

From time to time, various government departments set up temporary projects to investigate specific areas of law. One of the most important recent examples is the inquiry by Lord Woolf into the Civil Justice System (p. 4).

Performance of the law reform bodies

The Law Commission

One of the principal tasks of the Commission at its inception was codification, and this programme has not on the whole been a success. The Commission's programme was ambitious: in 1965 it announced that it would begin codifying family, contract, landlord and tenant, and evidence law. Attempts in the first three were abandoned – family in 1970, contract in 1973 and landlord and tenant in 1978. Evidence was never begun.

Task 19.3

Visit the Law Commission's website at:

www.lawcom.gov.uk/

The work it undertakes is grouped together according to the area of law. Choose an area of law that you are currently studying or going to study. Find a report that has been prepared by the Law Commission in this field. At the end of the report you will find a summary of the Law Commission's proposals. Summarise three of its recommendations.

The Law Commission is particularly concerned with the government's failure to codify the criminal law. From 1968 to 1974 the Commission produced a series of working papers, but in 1980 announced that its shortage of resources would not allow it to continue, and appealed for help with the task. The Society of Public Teachers of Law responded, and set up a four-person committee which, by 1985, had produced a draft code. But this has never been legislated as law. In most countries criminal law is contained in a single code so that it is accessible to the people against whom it will be applied. The Commission has now embarked upon a programme to produce a series of draft Bills, based on the Code but incorporating appropriate law reform proposals, which will in themselves make substantial improvements in the law. If enacted, these Bills will form a criminal code. But at the moment there is no tangible sign of progress in implementation of any of their major reports dating back to 1993. Decisions of the courts continue to draw attention to defects in the substantive law in areas on which they have already reported. One ray of hope has been the passing of legislation consolidating the sentencing regime, and further impetus for codification has been given by the review of criminal procedure under Lord Justice Auld (2001). In the government's White Paper, *Criminal Justice: The Way Ahead* (2001), it stated that it did intend to codify the criminal law as part of its modernisation process.

Zander (1988) suggests the reasons for the failure are 'a mixture of conservatism and a realisation on the part of draftsmen, legislators and even judges that [codification] simply did not fit the English style of lawmaking'. The draftsmen were not keen on the idea that codes would have to be drawn up in a broader manner than was normal for traditional statutes. Legislators were doubtful of the concept of a huge Bill which would attempt to state the law in a vast area such as landlord and tenant. The judges objected to the vision promoted by Lord Scarman, the Commission's first chairman, of the code coming down like an iron curtain making all pre-code law irrelevant. As Zander explains, this appeared to the judges like 'throwing the baby out with the bath water – losing the priceless heritage of the past and wasting the fruits of legislation and litigation on numerous points which would still be relevant to interpret the new code'.

However, opinions are mixed on whether codification would prove to be of very great value even if it ever becomes possible. Supporters say it would provide accessibility, comprehensibility, consistency and certainty. A code allows people to see their rights and liabilities more clearly than a mixture of case law and separate statutes could, and should encourage judges and others who use it to look for and expect to find answers within it. Lord Hailsham has said that a good codification would save a great deal of judicial time and so reduce costs, and the academic Glanville Williams (1983) makes the point that criminal law is not like the law of procedure, meant for lawyers only, but is addressed to all classes of society, and so the greater accessibility and clarity of a code should be particularly welcomed in this area.

Critics say a very detailed codification could make the law too rigid, losing the flexibility of the common law. And if it were insufficiently detailed, as Zander (2004) points out, it would need to be interpreted by the courts, so creating a new body of case law around it, which would defeat the object of codification and make the law neither more accessible nor more certain. It may be that the Law Commission's failure to codify the law signifies a problem with codification, not with the Law Commission.

Instead of proceeding with large-scale codification, the Law Commission has chosen to clarify areas of law piece by piece, with the aim of eventual codification if possible. Family law, in particular, has been significantly reformed in this way, even if the results are, as Zander points out, a 'jumble of disconnected statutes rather than a spanking new code'.

As far as general law reform is concerned, as well as the major family law reforms, the Commission has radically changed contract law by recommending control of exclusion clauses which led to the passing of the Unfair Contract Terms Act 1977. Its report, *Criminal Law: Conspiracy and Criminal Law Reform* (1976), helped shape the Criminal Law Act 1977 and its working paper, *Offences Against Public Order* (1982), was instrumental in creating the Public Order Act 1986. Following its recommendations, the Computer Misuse Act 1990 introduced new criminal offences relating to the misuse of computers; and the Family Law Act 1996 changed the law on domestic violence and divorce.

In recent years, however, there has been a major problem with lack of implementation of Law Commission proposals. By 1999, 102 law reform reports had been implemented, which represented two-thirds of their final reports. There is a better chance of proposals from the Law Commission becoming legislation if the subject concerned comes within the remit of the Ministry of Justice; there is less chance if they concern other departments, particularly the Home Office. In any case, it has been pointed out that implementation of proposals is not the only benefit of a permanent law reform body. Stephen Cretney (1998), a legal academic who has been a Law Commissioner, suggests that one of its most important contributions has simply been getting law reform under discussion and examination, and drawing attention to the needs of various areas of law.

Royal Commissions

These have had mixed success. The 1978 Royal Commission on Civil Liability and Compensation for Personal Injury produced a report that won neither public nor government support, and few of its proposals were implemented.

The Royal Commission on Criminal Procedure had most of its recommendations implemented by the Police and Criminal Evidence Act 1984 (PACE), but subsequent criticisms of PACE mean this is less of a success than it appears. The Royal Commission stated that the aim behind its proposals was to secure a balance between the rights of individuals suspected of crime, and the need to bring guilty people to justice. PACE has, however, been criticised by the police as leaning too far towards suspects' rights, and by civil liberties campaigners as not leaning far enough.

Perhaps the most successful Royal Commission in recent years has been the Royal Commission on Assizes and Quarter Sessions, which reported in 1969. Its proposals for the reorganisation of criminal courts were speedily implemented.

As regards the 1993 Royal Commission on Criminal Justice, this has met with mixed results. Some of its recommendations were introduced in the Criminal Justice and Public Order Act 1994 and the Criminal Appeal Act 1995, which created the Criminal Cases Review Commission (see p. 98) in response to the Commission's criticism of the criminal appeals system. On the other hand, the government has ignored some of its proposals and has proceeded to introduce changes that the Royal Commission was specifically opposed to, for example the abolition of the right to silence.

Public inquiries and other temporary committees

These rely to a great extent on political will, and the best committees in the world may be ineffective if they propose changes that a government dislikes. Lord Scarman's investigation into the Brixton riots is seen as a particularly effective public inquiry, getting to the root of the problem by going out to ask the people involved what caused it (his Lordship took to the streets of Brixton and was seen on television chatting to residents and cuddling their babies). His proposals produced some of the steps towards police accountability in PACE. But the subsequent inquiry into the case of Stephen Lawrence shows that the progress made was not sufficient. The Law Lord, Lord Hutton, has headed the inquiry into the suicide of Dr David Kelly following the war in Iraq.

Governments can refuse to hold a public inquiry which they feel may prove politically embarrassing. The parents of four soldiers killed in Iraq are pushing for a public inquiry into whether the war in Iraq was illegal. The government has refused to establish such an inquiry and the families sought a judicial review of this decision, arguing that they have a right to a public inquiry under Art. 2 of the European Convention on Human Rights, which guarantees the right to life: **R (Gentle)** *v* **Prime Minister** (2006).

sourcebook p. 59 → The government has been concerned by the inefficiency and cost of recent public inquiries. For example, the inquiry into Bloody Sunday in Ireland took seven years and is reported to have cost £155 million. The Inquiries Act 2005 has now been passed. The stated aim of the government in passing this legislation was to modernise procedures, control costs and give more effective powers to those chairing the inquiries. Despite this, the legislation has been criticised and Amnesty International has claimed that any inquiries established under this legislation would be a 'sham' and urged judges to refuse appointments to them. It is

Figure 19.3 **Scene outside the Lawrence Inquiry, Elephant and Castle, London**
Source: © EMPICS. Photograph Tony Harris.

worried that the legislation fails to allow adequate public scrutiny and 'undermines the rule of law, the separation of powers and human rights protection'. The Act arguably gives too much power to the executive, as the executive will be able to decide whether or not to publish the final report of any inquiry, whether to exclude evidence if this is deemed 'in the public interest', and whether the inquiry or part of it will be held in public or private.

sourcebook p. 61 → The first inquiry to be set up under this legislation looked at allegations of state collusion in the murder of Patrick Finucane, who was an outspoken human rights lawyer in Northern Ireland. Amnesty International was concerned that this inquiry was ineffective because of the limitations of the Inquiries Act 2005.

Task 19.4

The Macpherson Report on the police investigation into the death of the black teenager Stephen Lawrence, along with the government's action plan in response to this report, is available on the Home Office website:

www.homeoffice.gov.uk

Carry out a search of this website and consider how effective you think this public inquiry has been in bringing about reforms to the English legal system.

Quick quiz 19.5

1 In what year was the Law Commission established?

2 How successful has the Law Commission been in its mission to codify the law?

3 Who chaired the public inquiry into the Brixton riots?

4 Has the work of the Law Commission led to the codification of the criminal law?

Problems with the law reform agencies

Lack of power

There is no obligation for government to consult the permanent law reform bodies, or to set up Royal Commissions or other committees when considering major law reforms. Mrs Thatcher set up no Royal Commissions during her terms of office, despite the fact that important and controversial legislation – such as that abolishing the GLC – was being passed.

Political difficulties

Governments also have no obligation to follow recommendations, and perfectly well-thought-out proposals may be rejected on the grounds that they do not fit in with a government's political position. An example was the recommendation of the Law Commission in 1978 that changes be made to the rule that interest is not payable on a contract debt unless the parties agreed otherwise. The idea was supported by the House of Lords in **President of India** *v* **La Pintada Compania Navigacion SA** (1984), but the government was persuaded not to implement the proposals after lobbying from the business community and consumer organisations.

Even where general suggestions for areas of new legislation are implemented, the detailed proposals may be radically altered. The recommendations of law reform agencies may act as justification for introducing new legislation, yet, as Zander (2004) points out, often when the Bill is published it becomes clear that the carefully constructed proposal put together by the law reform agency 'has been unstitched and a new and different package has been constructed'.

Lack of influence on results

Where proposals are implemented, ideas that are effective in themselves may be weakened if they are insufficiently funded when put into practice – a matter on which law reform bodies can have little or no influence. The 1981 Royal Commission on Criminal Procedure's recommendations were largely implemented in the Police and Criminal Evidence Act 1984, and one of them was that suspects questioned in a police station should have the right to free legal advice, leading to the setting up of the duty solicitor scheme. While the idea of the scheme was seen as a good one, underfunding has brought it close to collapse, and meant that in practice relatively small numbers of suspects actually get advice from qualified, experienced solicitors within a reasonable waiting time. This has clearly frustrated the aims of the Royal Commission's recommendation.

Too much compromise

Royal Commissions and temporary committees have the advantage of drawing members from wide backgrounds, with a good spread of experience and expertise. However, in some cases this can result in proposals that try too hard to represent a compromise. The result can be a lack of political support and little chance of implementation. It is generally agreed that this was the problem with the Pearson Report (1978), the report of the Royal Commission on Civil Liability and Compensation for Personal Injury.

Influence of the legal profession

Where temporary law reform committees have a high proportion of non-lawyers, the result can be more innovative, imaginative ideas than might come from legally trained people who, however open-minded, are within 'the system' and accustomed to seeing the problems in a particular framework. However, this benefit is heavily diluted by the fact that the strong influence of the legal profession on any type of reform can defeat such proposals even before they reach an official report.

An example was the suggestion of the Civil Justice Review in its consultation paper that the county courts and High Court might merge, with some High Court judges being stationed in the provinces to deal with the more complex cases there. Despite a warm welcome from consumer groups and the National Association of Citizens' Advice Bureaux, the proposals were effectively shot down by the outcry from senior judges, who were concerned that their status and way of life might be adversely affected, and the Bar, which was worried that it might lose too much work to solicitors. In the event the proposal was not included in the final report.

Waste of expertise

Royal Commissions and temporary committees are disbanded after producing their report, and take no part in the rest of the law-making process. This is in many ways a waste of the expertise they have built up.

Lack of ministerial involvement

There is no single ministry responsible for law reform so that often no minister makes it his or her priority.

Reading on the web

John Halliday has produced a report on the work of the Law Commission which has been published on the Law Commission's website:

www.homeoffice.gov.uk/documents/312280

The Law Commission's website is:

www.lawcom.gov.uk/

Chapter summary

The law needs to change to reflect the changes in society. Changes in the law can be made through the process of case law or by Parliament. The four ways in which Parliament can change the law are:

- repeal;
- creation;
- consolidation; and
- codification.

Impetus for law reform

The inspiration for reform may come from a variety of sources, including:

- pressure groups;
- political parties;
- the civil service;

■ treaty obligations; and
■ public opinion and media pressure.

Agencies of law reform

There are a number of agencies set up to consider the need for reform in areas referred to them by the government. These agencies are:

■ the Law Commission;
■ Royal Commissions;
■ public inquiries; and
■ other temporary inquiries.

The level of success of these agencies has varied considerably. Governments have no obligation to follow their recommendations. Some of the recommendations involve too many compromises, and where lawyers dominate the resulting reforms may be under-ambitious.

Question and answer guides

1. (a) Discuss three different sources of influence over Parliament when it is legislating.

Answer

Politicians need to be fully aware of public opinion because if the electorate is unhappy with their work they will not vote for them in the next election. MPs need to understand what the majority of the public want and think, so that the laws they formulate represent the will of the people. They hold local surgeries where they may be able to gauge local opinion, Tony Blair held many local focus groups and set up a website called the Big Conversation. Thus, in some respects, the three main influences on Parliament to be discussed here – the media, pressure groups and law reform agencies – are influential only because they help to keep MPs in tune with the mood of the general population.

Looking first at the media, national daily newspapers with adverse headlines demanding action about a current tragedy or situation, are difficult for politicians to ignore. There is a danger that a government will be hastened into action and fail to consult properly, as happened with the Dangerous Dogs Act 1991. The media can run high-profile campaigns for law reform such as the campaign for Sarah's law, looking for a reform of the way paedophiles are tracked in the community.

Newspapers are a powerful means of influencing peoples' view of the world and therefore influential in Parliament, but their ownership is concentrated in a few hands and newspapers can be used to push the viewpoint of the newspaper owner.

Pressure groups come in all shapes and sizes and have varying degrees of success. They can be broken down into four types: cause groups, protective groups, insider groups and outsider groups. Cause groups are those groups where members unite for a common cause like fathers4justice, the Royal Society for the Protection of Cruelty to Animals (RSPCA) and Greenpeace. Protective groups, such as trade unions, pomote the interests of their members. Insider groups lobby Parliament directly, while outsider groups promote their cause by direct action. The fox-hunting ban was a success story for the RSPCA and associated animal rights groups and resulted in a manifesto commitment to legislate which culminated in the Hunting Act 2004. The Obesity Awareness and Solutions Trust (TOAST) has announced that it is to close down following ten years promoting the issue of obesity awareness to government. MPs were lobbied by TOAST which culminated in a Select Committee's inquiry into obesity. This has now firmly placed obesity as one of the government's main health issues. Fathers4justice was a mixed success because, while it managed to put the position of fathers following separation on the political agenda, some of its stunts to achieve this were highly controversial. Trade unions are well established in the UK and have played an important role in protecting employees and developing their rights. The smoking ban can be seen as a success for the anti-smoking pressure groups, though ultimately it was introduced by those groups backing European law.

Official law reform agencies, such as the Law Commission, can be very influential over the work of Parliament. The Law Commission was set up in 1969, and it is the only permanent body identifying where law reform is necessary, putting forward suggestions for codification, consolidation and the repeal of obsolete laws. The Law Commission can initiate its own projects or is asked by the Lord Chancellor to look at specific areas. It carries out research on a topic, formulates proposals and then produces a report for consideration by others. It often publishes draft bills, which the government seldom adopts as much of the reform is technical and time consuming – there are no public votes to be won by acting on some of these proposals – so about 30 per cent of their work is shelved. Royal Commissions are set up in response to a specific event and work part time to investigate the subject. Each Royal Commission will have a different composition as they disband when their appointed task is done. The Runciman Commission was set up to look at the criminal justice system following a series of high-profile miscarriages of justice, including the Birmingham Six. This Commission was instrumental in the setting up of the Criminal Cases Review Commission which looks at convicted cases where all appeals have been exhausted but there is reasonable doubt as to guilt.

(b) Discuss one advantage of each of the three influences on parliament discussed in your answer to part (a).

Plan

- The media can respond immediately to social developments.
- Pressure groups can develop expertise in their field.
- The official agencies of law reform are effectively independent.

Group activity 1

Working in groups, find and read the Hunting Act 2004. This Act was the result of many years of protests by anti-hunting pressure groups, such as the League Against Cruel Sports and the Royal Society for the Prevention of Cruelty to Animals (RSPCA). The pro-hunting pressure group, the Countryside Alliance, ensured their point of view was not ignored. Investigate the campaigns for and against hunting and consider how the pressure groups tried to influence the work of Parliament on the subject. You may find the following sites helpful:

> http://www.opsi.gov.uk/acts/acts2004/20040037.htm
> http://banhunting.rspca.org.uk/servlet/Satellite?pagename=RSPCA/
> RSPCARedirect&pg=otherissues&marker=1&articleId=1181306037166
> www.ifaw.org/ifaw/general/default.aspx?oid=199695
> www.league.org.uk/content.asp?CategoryID=1511
> www.countryside-alliance.org.uk/blogsection/hunting-campaigns/

Visit **www.mylawchamber.co.uk/elliottocr** to access questions, quizzes and activities to test yourself on this chapter.

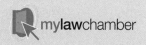

Appendix 1
ANSWERING EXAMINATION QUESTIONS

At the end of each chapter in this book, you will find detailed guidelines for answering exam questions on the topics covered. Many of the questions are taken from actual A-level past papers, but they are equally relevant for candidates of all law examinations, as these questions are typical of the type of questions that examiners ask in this field.

In this section, we aim to give some general guidelines for answering questions on the English legal system.

Citation of authorities

One of the most important requirements for answering questions on the law is that you must be able to back the points you make with authority, usually either a case or a statute. It is not good enough to state that the law is such and such, without stating the case or statute which says that that is the law. Some examiners are starting to suggest that the case name is not essential as long as you can remember and understand the general principle that the case laid down. However, such examiners remain in the minority and the reality is that even they are likely to give higher marks where the candidate has cited authorities; quite simply, it helps give the impression that you know your material thoroughly, rather than half-remembering something you heard once in class.

This means that you must be prepared to learn fairly long lists of cases by heart, which can be a daunting prospect. What you need to memorise is the name of the case, a brief description of the facts, and the legal principle which the case established. Once you have revised a topic well, you should find that a surprisingly high number of cases on that topic begin to stick in your mind anyway, but there will probably be some that you have trouble recalling. A good way to memorise these is to try to create a picture in your mind which links the facts, the name and the legal principle. For example, if you wanted to remember the contract law case of **Redgrave v Hurd**, you might picture the actress Vanessa Redgrave and the politician Douglas Hurd, in the situation described in the facts of the case, and imagine one of them telling the other the principle established in the case.

Knowing the names of cases makes you look more knowledgeable, and saves writing time in the exam, but if you do forget a name, referring briefly to the facts will identify it. It is not necessary to learn the dates of cases, though it is useful if you know whether it is a recent or an old case. Dates are usually required for statutes. Unless you are making a detailed comparison of the facts of a case and the facts of a problem question, in order to argue that the case should or could be distinguished, you should generally make only brief reference to facts, if at all – long descriptions of facts waste time and earn few marks.

When reading the 'Question and answer guides' sections at the end of each chapter in this book, bear in mind that for reasons of space, we have not highlighted every case which you should cite. The skeleton arguments outlined in those sections **must** be backed up with authority from cases and statute law.

When discussing the English legal system, as well as citing relevant cases and statutes, it is particularly important to cite relevant research and reports in the field being discussed. If there are important statistics in an area, being able to quote some of them will give your answers authority.

There is no right answer

In law exams, there is not usually a right or a wrong answer. What matters is that you show you know what type of issues you are being asked about. Essay questions are likely to ask you to 'discuss', 'criticise' or 'evaluate', and you simply need to produce a good range of factual and critical material in order to do this. The answer you produce might look completely different from your friend's but both answers could be worth 'A' grades.

Breadth and depth of content

Where a question seems to raise a number of different issues – as most do – you will achieve better marks by addressing all or most of these issues than by writing at great length on just one or two. By all means spend more time on issues which you know well, but be sure to at least mention other issues which you can see are relevant, even if you can only produce a paragraph or so about them.

Civil or criminal

In some cases, a question on the English legal system will require you to confine your answer to either the civil or criminal system. This may be stated in the question – for example, 'Discuss the system of civil appeals'. Alternatively, it may be something you are required to work out for yourself, as is often the case with problem questions. For example, a question might state:

> *Jane has been charged with criminal damage.*
> *(a) How may she obtain legal aid and advice? and*
> *(b) If convicted, to which courts may she appeal?*

This question only requires you to discuss the legal aid and advice available in criminal cases, and the criminal appeals system; giving details of civil legal aid and the civil appeals system will waste time and gain you no marks, as would bringing the criminal appeals system into the previous question. Equally, where a question does not limit itself to either civil or criminal legal systems, you will lose marks if you only discuss one.

Because of this danger, it is a good idea to make a point of asking yourself before you answer any legal system question whether it covers just the civil legal system, just the criminal, or both.

The structure of the question

If a question is specifically divided into parts, for example (a), (b) and (c), then stick to those divisions and do not merge your answer into one long piece of writing.

Law examinations tend to contain a mixture of essay questions and what are known as 'problem questions'. Tackling each of these questions involves slightly different skills, so we consider each in turn.

Essay questions

Answer the question asked

Over and over again, examiners complain that candidates do not answer the question they are asked – so if you can develop this skill, you will stand out from the crowd. You will get very few marks for simply writing all you know about a topic, with no attempt to address the issues raised in the question, but if you can adapt the material that you have learnt on the subject to take into account the particular emphasis given to it by the question, you will do well.

Even if you have memorised an essay which does raise the issues in the question (perhaps because those issues tend to be raised year after year), you must fit your material to the words of the question you are actually being asked. For example, suppose during your course you wrote an essay on the advantages and disadvantages of the jury system, and then in the exam you find yourself faced with the question 'Should juries be abolished?' The material in your coursework essay is ideally suited for the exam question, but if you begin the main part of your answer with the words 'The advantages of juries include . . .', or something similar, this is a dead giveaway to the examiner that you are merely writing down an essay you have memorised. It takes very little effort to change the words to 'Abolition of the jury system would ignore certain advantages that the current system has . . .', but it will create a much better impression, especially if you finish with a conclusion which, based on points you have made, states that abolition is a good or bad idea, the choice depending on the arguments you have made during your answer.

During your essay, you should keep referring to the words used in the question – if this seems to become repetitive, use synonyms for those words. This makes it clear to the examiner that you are keeping the question in mind as you work.

Plan your answer

Under pressure of time, it is tempting to start writing immediately, but five minutes spent planning each essay question is well worth spending – it may mean that you write less overall, but the quality of your answer will almost certainly be better. The plan need not be elaborate: just jot down everything you feel is relevant to the answer, including case names, and then organise the material into a logical order appropriate to the question asked. To put it in order, rather than wasting time copying it all out again, simply put a number next to each point according to which ones you intend to make first, second and so forth.

Provide analysis and fact

Very few essay questions require merely factual descriptions of what the law is; you will almost always be required to analyse the factual content in some way, usually highlighting any problems or gaps in the law, and suggesting possible reforms. If a question asks you to analyse whether lay magistrates should be replaced by professional judges, you should not write everything you know about magistrates and judges and finish with one sentence saying that magistrates should/should not be kept. Instead, you should select your relevant material and your whole answer should be targeted at answering whether or not magistrates should be kept.

Where a question uses the word 'critically', as in 'critically describe' or 'critically evaluate', the examiners are merely drawing your attention to the fact that your approach should be analytical and not merely descriptive; you are not obliged to criticise every provision you describe. Having said that, even if you do not agree with particular criticisms which you have read, you should still discuss them and say why you do not think they are valid; there is very little mileage in an essay that simply describes the law and says it is perfectly satisfactory.

Structure

However good your material, you will only gain really good marks if you structure it well. Making a plan for each answer will help in this, and you should also try to learn your material in a logical order – this will make it easier to remember as well. The exact construction of your essay will obviously depend on the question, but you should aim to have an introduction, then the main discussion, and a conclusion. Where a question is divided into two or more parts, you should reflect that structure in your answer.

A word about conclusions: it is not good enough just to repeat the question, turning it into a statement, for the conclusion. So, for example, if the question is 'Is the criminal justice system satisfactory?', a conclusion which simply states that the system is or is not satisfactory will gain you very little credit. Your conclusion will often summarise the arguments that you have developed during the course of your essay.

Problem questions

In problem questions, the exam paper will describe an imaginary situation, and then ask what the legal implications of the facts are – for example:

'Jane had suffered physical violence at the hands of her husband for many years. One day she lashes out and kills him. She is arrested by the police and later charged with murder. In which court will Jane be tried? If she is convicted, to what court may she appeal?'

Read the question thoroughly

The first priority is to read the question thoroughly, at least a couple of times. Never start writing until you have done this, as you may well get halfway through and discover that what is said at the end makes half of what you have written irrelevant – or at worst, that the question raises issues you have no knowledge of at all.

Answer the question asked

This means paying close attention to the words printed immediately after the situation is described. In the example given above, you are asked to advise about the courts and appeal procedure, so do not start discussing sentencing powers as this is not relevant to the particular question asked. Similarly, if a question asks you to advise one or other of the parties, make sure that you advise the right one – the realisation as you discuss the exam with your friends afterwards that you have advised the wrong party and thus rendered most of your answer irrelevant is not an experience you will enjoy.

Spot the issues

In answering a problem question in an examination you will often be short of time. One of the skills of doing well is spotting which issues are particularly relevant to the facts of the problem and spending most time on those, while skimming over more quickly those matters which are not really an issue on the facts, but which you clearly need to mention.

Apply the law to the facts

What a problem question requires you to do is to spot the issues raised by the situation, and to consider the law as it applies to those facts. It is not enough simply to describe the law without applying it to the facts. So in the example given above it is not enough to write about the appeal procedure in general for civil and criminal cases; you must apply the rules of criminal appeal to the particular case of Jane. She has committed an indictable offence that would have been tried by the Crown Court, so you are primarily concerned with appeals from the Crown Court to the Court of Appeal. Nor should you start your answer by copying out all the facts. This is a complete waste of time, and will gain you no marks.

Unlike essay questions, problem questions are not usually seeking a critical analysis of the law. If you have time, it may be worth making the point that a particular area of the law you are discussing is problematic, and briefly stating why, but if you are addressing all the issues raised in the problem you are unlikely to have much time for this. What the examiner is looking for is essentially an understanding of the law and an ability to apply it to the particular facts given.

Use authority

As always, you must back up your points with authority from case or statute law.

Structure

The introduction and conclusion are much less important for problem questions than for essay questions. Your introduction can be limited to pointing out the issues raised by the question, or, where you are asked to 'advise' a person mentioned in the problem, what outcome that person will be looking for. You can also say in what order you intend to deal with the issues. Your conclusion might simply summarise the conclusions reached during the main part of the answer, for example that Jane will be tried in the Crown Court and her main route of appeal will be to the Court of Appeal.

There is no set order in which the main part of the answer must be discussed. Sometimes it will be appropriate to deal with the problem chronologically, in which case it will usually be a matter of looking at the question line by line, while in other cases it may be appropriate to group particular issues together. Problem questions on the English legal system are often broken down into clear parts – a, b, c and so on – so the answer can be broken down into the same parts. Thus with the example about Jane, the question was clearly broken into two parts, and so your question should deal with first the trial court and then with the issue of appeal.

Whichever order you choose, try to deal with one issue at a time – for example, finish talking about the trial court before looking at the issue of appeal. Jumping backwards and forwards gives the impression that you have not thought about your answer. If you work through your material in a structured way, you are also less likely to leave anything out.

What makes a good answer?

In order to achieve the highest grades, the student must demonstrate that they have fully met the three assessment objectives of the exam board. These are published by the examination board on their website.

AO1 Demonstrate knowledge and understanding

Demonstrate knowledge and understanding of legal rules and principles by selecting and explaining relevant information and illustrating with examples and citation.

For example, in Chapter 1 we gave a sample answer for the question 'Briefly explain the three track system of civil justice'. To satisfy the first assessment objective, students needed to demonstrate 'knowledge and understanding' of the legal rules and principles on the subject. This could be achieved by providing a clear analysis of the small claims track, the fast track and the multi-track. In doing so you are required to provide 'relevant information' and illustrate with examples. To achieve this you could illustrate how the fast track works by giving a typical timetable for a case. The requirement of 'citation' could be catered for by referring to John Baldwin's research on the small claims track. Frequently, you would satisfy the requirement of citation by referring to specific cases on the subject.

AO2 Analysis, evaluation and application

Analyse legal material, issues and situations, and evaluate and apply the appropriate legal rules and principles.

When answering the question on the three tracks of the civil justice system mentioned above, you would satisfy this assessment criteria by referring to the Access to Justice Act 1999 and the Civil Procedure Rules. This is the process of analysing 'legal material'. By weighing up the strengths and weaknesses of the three track system you are 'evaluating' these rules and principles.

AO3 Communication and presentation

Present a logical and coherent argument and communicate relevant material in a clear and effective manner using appropriate legal terminology.

Write in a structured way, with your text broken down into paragraphs. A quick essay plan before you start will help you organise your material logically. Always use the correct legal terminology and case names if you know them and ensure that your argument flows. If a question relates to advantages and disadvantages you should deal with advantages together, then the disadvantages. Finally, conclude with your view which should be easily substantiated by your preceding argument.

Exam question terminology

1 **Describe:** This means 'tell me about', be descriptive. It is important to restrict your answer to relevant points and not just write everything you know about the whole subject.

2 **Outline:** This means provide a brief description of the major points on the subject. Be careful to balance the amount of time you have in the exam with the amount of marks the question is allocated. Do not spend half the exam answering a question worth only five marks where the examiner has expressly asked you to only 'outline' the topic.

3 **Explain:** This question requires you to go into more depth on a subject than if you had been asked simply to 'describe' it. Your answer might explain why the law has developed in a certain way, thus more than a mere description is being required and the advantages and disadvantages of the system could fall within the explanation.

4 **Discuss or Comment:** This requires you to present arguments for and against a proposal and, usually, to come to a conclusion. Your conclusion should follow logically from your arguments already detailed.

5 **Criticise:** This primarily means present the case against a proposition, though you could mention some advantages as counter-arguments to these criticisms. You could include possible alternatives to the current legal arrangements.

Appendix 2
A GUIDE TO LAW REPORTS AND CASE REFERENCES

We have seen that much of the law is contained in cases decided before the courts. It is therefore important that a written record is kept of the decisions of the courts. Lawyers and students of law need to be able to find these written records.

The law reports

Over 2,000 cases are published in law reports each year. The most respected series of law reports is called *The Law Reports*, because before publication the report of each case included in the series is checked for accuracy by the judge who tried it. It is this series that should be cited before a court in preference to any other. The series is divided into several sub-series depending on the court which heard the case, as follows:

- **Appeal Cases** (decisions of the Court of Appeal, the House of Lords and the Privy Council).
- **Chancery Division** (decisions of the Chancery Division of the High Court and their appeals to the Court of Appeal).
- **Family Division** (decisions of the Family Division of the High Court and their appeals to the Court of Appeal).
- **Queen's Bench** (decisions of the Queen's Bench Division of the High Court and their appeals to the Court of Appeal).

Neutral citation

In 2001 a form of neutral citation was introduced in the Court of Appeal and Administrative Court. This form of citation was introduced to facilitate reference to cases reported on the Internet and in CD-ROMs. Unlike reports in books, these reports do not have fixed page numbers and volumes. A unique number is now given to each approved judgment and the paragraphs in each judgment are numbered. The three forms of the neutral citation are as follows:

- Civil Division of the Court of Appeal: [2000] EWCA Civ 1, 2, 3, etc.
- Criminal Division of the Court of Appeal: [2000] EWCA Crim 1, 2, 3, etc.
- Administrative Court: [2000] EWHC Admin 1, 2, 3, etc.

The letters 'EW' stand for England and Wales. For example, if **Brown** *v* **Smith** is the fifth numbered judgment of 2002 in the Civil Division of the Court of Appeal, it would be cited: **Brown** *v* **Smith** [2002] EWCA Civ 5. If you wished to refer to the fourth paragraph of the judgment, the correct citation is: [2002] EWCA Civ 5 at [4].

Case reference

Each case is given a reference(s) to explain exactly where it can be found in a law report(s). Such a reference can be used to go and find and read the case in a law library which stocks the relevant law report. This is important, as a textbook can only provide a summary of the case and has no legal status in itself; it is the actual case which contains the law.

The reference consists of a series of letters and numbers that follow the case name. The pattern of this reference varies depending on the law report being referred to. The usual format is to follow the name of the case by:

- **A year.** Where the date reference tells you the year in which the case was decided, the date is normally enclosed in round brackets. If the date is the year in which the case is reported, it is given in square brackets. The most common law reports tend to use square brackets.
- **A volume number.** Not all law reports have a volume number, sometimes they simply identify their volumes by year.
- **The law report abbreviation.** Each series of law reports has an abbreviation for their title so that the whole name does not need to be written out in full.

The main law reports and their abbreviations are as follows:

All England Law Reports	All ER
Appeal Cases	AC
Chancery Division	Ch D
Criminal Appeal Reports	Cr App R
Family Division	Fam
King's Bench	KB
Queen's Bench Division	QB
Weekly Law Reports	WLR

- **A page number.** This is the page at which the report of the case commences.
- **Neutral citation.** Where a case has been decided after 2001, the neutral citation for decisions of the Court of Appeal and Administrative Court will appear in front of the law report citation.

Examples of case references

Cozens *v* **Brutus** [1973] AC 854
The case was reported in the Appeal Cases law report in 1973 at p. 854.

DPP *v* **Hawkins** [1988] 1 WLR 1166
The case was reported in the first volume of the Weekly Law Report of 1988 at p. 1166.

R *v* **Angel** (1968) 52 Cr App R 280
The case was reported in the fifty-second volume of the Criminal Appeal Reports at p. 280.

Brown *v* **Smith** [2002] EWCA Civ 5, [2002] QB 432, [2002] 3 All ER 21
The case was the fifth decision to be decided in 2002 by the Civil Division of the Court of Appeal. It was reported in the Queen's Bench law report in 2002 at p. 432 and in the third volume of the All England Law Report in 2002 at p. 21.

Select bibliography

Abel, R. (1988) *The Legal Profession in England and Wales*, Oxford: Basil Blackwell.

Abel-Smith, B., Zander, M. and Brooke, R. (1973) *Legal Problems and the Citizen*, London: Heinemann-Educational.

Advice Services Alliance (2004) *The Independent Review of the Community Legal Service. The Advice Services Alliance's response to the Department of Constitutional Affairs' consultation on the recommendations made by Matrix Research and Consultancy*, London: ASA.

Alternative Dispute Resolution – A Discussion Paper (1999), London: Lord Chancellor's Department.

Anti-Social Behaviour Orders – Analysis of the first six years (2004), London: National Association of Probation Officers.

Aquinas, St T. (1942) *Summa Theologica*, London: Burns Oates & Washbourne.

Atiyah, P. S. (1979) *The Rise and Fall of Freedom of Contract*, Oxford: Clarendon Press.

Audit Commission (1996) *Streetwise: Effective Police Patrol*, London: HMSO.

—— (1997) *Misspent Youth: Young People and Crime*, London: Audit Commission Publications.

—— (2003) *Victims and Witnesses*, London: Audit Commission Publications.

—— (2004) *Youth Justice*, London: Audit Commission Publications.

Auld, Sir R. (2001) *Review of the Criminal Courts*, London: HMSO.

Austin, J. (1954) *The Province of Jurisprudence Determined*, London: Weidenfeld & Nicolson.

Bailey, S. and Gunn, M. (2000) *Smith and Bailey on the Modern English Legal System* (4th edn), London: Sweet & Maxwell.

Baldwin, J. (1992) *The Role of Legal Representatives at the Police Station* (Royal Commission on Criminal Justice Research Study No. 2), London: HMSO.

—— (1997) *Small Claims in County Courts in England and Wales: The Bargain Basement of Civil Justice?* Oxford: Clarendon Press.

—— (1992) *Video Taping Police Interviews with Suspects: An Evaluation*, London: Home Office.

—— (2002) *Lay and Judicial Perspectives on the Expansion of the Small Claims Regime*, London: Lord Chancellor's Department.

—— (2003) *Evaluating the Effectiveness of Enforcement Procedures in Undefended Claims in the Civil Courts*, London: Lord Chancellor's Department.

Baldwin, J. and McConville, M. (1979) *Jury Trials*, Oxford: Clarendon Press.

Baldwin, J. and Moloney, T. (1992) *Supervision of police investigations in serious criminal cases* (Royal Commission on Criminal Justice Research Study No. 4), London: HMSO.

Barton, A. (2001) 'Medical litigation: who benefits?', 322 *British Medical Journal* 1189.

Bell, J. and Engle, Sir G. (eds.) (1995) *Statutory Interpretation*, London: Butterworths.

Bennion, F. A. R. (2007) 'Executive estoppel: **Pepper** *v* **Hart** revisited', *Public Law* 1.

—— (1999) 'A naked usurpation?' 149 NLJ 421.

—— (1990) *Statutory Interpretation*, London: Butterworths.

Blom-Cooper, L. (1972) *Final Appeal: A Study of the House of Lords in its Judicial Capacity*, Oxford: Clarendon Press.

Bond, R. A. and Lemon, N. F. (1979) 'Changes in Magistrates: Attitudes During the First Year on the Bench', in Farrington, D. P. *et al.* (eds.) (1979) *Psychology, Law and Legal Processes*, London: Macmillan.

Booth, A. (2002) 'Direct effect', *Solicitors Journal* 924.

Bottoms, A. E. and Preston, R. H. (eds.) (1980) *The Coming Penal Crisis: A Criminological and Theoretical Exploration*, Edinburgh: Scottish Academic Press.

Bowling, B. and Ross, J. (2006) 'The serious organised crime agency – should we be afraid', *Criminal Law Review* 1019.

Bowman, Sir J. (1997) *Review of the Court of Appeal (Civil Division)*, London: Lord Chancellor's Department.

Boyron, S. (2006) 'The rise of mediation in administrative law disputes: Experiences from England, France and Germany', *Public Law* 230.

Brazier, R. (1998) *Constitutional Reform*, Oxford: Oxford University Press.

Bridges, L. *et al.* (2007) *Evaluation of the Public Defender Service in England and Wales*, London: TSO.

Bridges, L. and Choongh, S. (1998) *Improving Police Station Legal Advice: The Impact of the Accreditation Scheme for Police Station Legal Advisers*, London: Law Society's Research and Planning Unit: Legal Aid Board.

Brown, D. (1998) *Offending While on Bail*, Home Office, Report No. 72, London: Home Office.

Brown, D. and Neal, D. (1988) 'Show Trials: The Media and the Gang of Twelve', in Findlay, M. and Duff, P. (eds.) (1988) *The Jury under Attack*, London: Butterworths.

Brown, D. *et al.* (1992) *Changing the Code: Police Detention Under the Revised PACE Codes of Practice*, Home Office Research Study No. 129, London: HMSO.

Brownlee, I. (2004) 'The statutory charging scheme in England and Wales: towards a unified prosecution system', *Criminal Law Review* 896.

Burney, E. (1979) *Magistrates, Court and Community*, London: Hutchinson.

Campbell, S. (2002) *A review of anti-social behaviour orders*, Home Office Research Study No. 236, London: Home Office.

Carlen, P. (1983) *Women's Imprisonment: A Study in Social Control*, London: Routledge.

Carter, Lord (2006) *Legal aid: a market-based approach to reform*, Department for Constitutional Affairs: London.

Carter, P. (2003) *Managing Offenders, Reducing Crime*, London: Strategy Unit, Home Office.

Chalmers, J., Duff, P. and Leverick, F. (2007) 'Victim impact statements: can work, do work (for those who bother to make them)', *Criminal Law Review* 360.

Citizens' Advice Bureau (2004) *Geography of Advice*, London: Citizens' Advice Bureau.

—— (2005) *No win, no fee, no chance*, London: Citizens' Advice Bureau.

Consumer Council (1970) *Justice Out of Reach: A Case for Small Claims Courts: A Consumer Council Study*, London: HMSO.

Cotton, J. and Povey, D. (2004) *Police Complaints and Discipline, April 2002–March 2003*, London: Home Office.

Cretney, S. (1998) *Law, Law Reform and the Family*, Oxford: Clarendon Press.

Criminal Justice: the Way Ahead (2001) Cm 5074, London: Home Office.

Cross, Sir R. (1995) *Statutory Interpretation*, London: Butterworths.

Cutting Crime – Delivering Justice: Strategic Plan for Criminal Justice 2004–08 (2004) Cm 6288, London: Home Office.

Darbyshire, P. (1991) 'The lamp that shows that freedom lives – is it worth the candle?', *Criminal Law Review* 740.

De Tocqueville, A. (2000) *Democracy is America* (George Lawrence, trans.; J. P. Mayer, ed.) New York: Perennial Classics.

—— (1999) 'A comment on the powers of magistrates' clerks', *Criminal Law Review* 377.

Denning, A. (1982) *What Next in the Law?* London: Butterworths.

—— (1952) 'The need for a new equity' (1952) 5 Current Legal Problems, 1.

Dennis, I. (2006) 'Convicting the guilty: outcomes, process and the Court of Appeal', *Criminal Law Review* 955.

Department for Constitutional Affairs (2004) *The Independent Review of the Community Legal Service*, London: DCA.

—— (2004) *Transforming Public Services: Complaints, Redress and Tribunals*, London: Stationery Office.

—— (2005) *Supporting magistrates courts to provide justice*, Cm. 6681, London: TSO.

—— (2004) *Broadcasting Courts*, CP 28/04, London: DCA.

—— (2006) *Delivering simple, speeds, summary justice*, 37/06, London: DCA.

Department for Trade and Industry (2004) *Fairness for All: A New Commission for Equality and Human Rights*, Cm 6185, London: Stationery Office.

Devlin, P. (1956) *Trial by Jury*, London: Stevens.

—— (1965) *The Enforcement of Morals*, Oxford: Oxford University Press.

—— (1979) *The Judge*, Oxford: Oxford University Press.

Dicey, A. (1982) *Introduction to the Study of the Law of the Constitution*, Indianapolis: Liberty Classics.

Dickens, L. (1985) *Dismissed: A Study of Unfair Dismissal and the Industrial System*, Oxford: Blackwell.

Director General of Fair Trading (2001) *Competition in professions*, OFT 328, London: OFT.

Dodgson, K. *et al.* (2001) *Electronic monitoring of released prisoners: an Evaluation of the Home Detention Curfew Scheme*, London: Home Office.

Dow, J. and Lapuerta, C. (2005) *The benefits of multiple ownership models* available on the website of the former Department for Constitutional Affairs at http://www.dca.gov.uk/legalsys/dow-lapuerta.pdf

Durkheim, E. (1983) *Durkheim and the Law*, Oxford: Robertson.

Duster, T. (1970) *The Legislation of Morality*, New York: Free Press.

Dworkin, R. (1977) *Taking Rights Seriously*, London: Duckworth.

—— (1978) *Political judges and the rule of Law* (1978) Proceedings of the British Academy 259.

—— (1986) *Law's Empire*, London: Fontana Press.

Edwards, I. (2002) 'The Place of Victims' Preferences in the Sentencing of "Their" Offenders', *Criminal Law Review* 689.

Ellis, T. and Hedderman, C. (1996) *Enforcing Community Sentences: Supervisors' Perspectives on Ensuring Compliance and Dealing with Breach*, London: Home Office.

Enright, S. (1993) 'Cost effective criminal justice', 143 *New Law Journal* 1023.

Epstein, H. (2003) 'The liberalisation of claim financing', 153 *New Law Journal* 153.

Evans, Sir A. (2003) 'Forget ADR – think A or D', *Civil Justice Quarterly* 230.

Evans, R. (1993) *The Conduct of Police Interviews with Juveniles*, London: HMSO.

Fenton, A. and Dabell, F. (2007) 'Time for change (1)', 157 *New Law Journal* 848.

—— (2007) 'Time for change (2)', 157 *New Law Journal* 964.

Findlay, M. (2001) 'Juror Comprehension and complexity: strategies to enhance understanding' 41 *British Journal of Criminology* 56.

Flood-Page, C. and Mackie, A. (1998) *Sentencing During the Nineties*, London: Home Office Research and Statistics Directorate.

Freeman, M. D. A. (1981) 'The Jury on Trial', 34 *Current Legal Problems* 65.

Fuller, L. (1969) *The Morality of Law*, London: Yale University Press.

Galanter, M. (1984) *The emergence of the judge as a mediator in civil cases*, Madison: University of Wisconsin.

Genn, H. (1982) *Meeting Legal Needs?: An Evaluation of a Scheme for Personal Injury Victims*, Oxford: S.S.R.C. Centre for Socio-Legal Studies.

—— (1987) *Hard Bargaining: Out of Court Settlement in Personal Injury Actions*, Oxford: Clarendon Press.

—— (1998) *The Central London County Court Pilot Mediation Scheme: Evaluation Report*, London: Lord Chancellor's Department.

—— (2002) *Court-based ADR Initiatives for Non-Family civil disputes: the Commercial Court and the Court of Appeal*, London: Lord Chancellor's Department.

Genn, H. and Genn, Y. (1989) *The Effect of Representation at Tribunals*, London: Lord Chancellor's Department.

Goriely, T. and Gysta, P. (2001) *Breaking the Code: The Impact of Legal Aid Reforms on General Civil Litigation*, London: Institute of Advanced Legal Studies.

Green, P. (ed.) (1996) *Drug Couriers: A New Perspective*, London: Quartet.

Griffith, J. A. G. (1997) *The Politics of the Judiciary*, London: Fontana Press.

Grout, Paul A. (2005) *The Clementi Report: Potential Risks of External Ownership and Regulatory Responses – A Report to the Department of Constitutional Affairs*, London: Department for Constitutional Affairs.

Gudjonsson, G. H. (1992) *The Psychology of Interrogations, Confessions and Testimony*, Chichester: Wiley.

Hale, Sir M. (1979) *The History of the Common Law of England*, Chicago: University of Chicago Press.

Halliday, J. (2001) *Making Punishment Work, Report of the Review of the Sentencing Framework for England and Wales*, London: Home Office.

Hart, H. L. A. (1963) *Law, Liberty and Morality*, Oxford: Oxford University Press.

—— (1994) *The Concept of Law*, Oxford: Clarendon Press.

Hayek, F. (1982) *Law, Legislation and Liberty: A New Statement of the Liberal Principles of Justice and Political Economy*, London: Routledge.

Hedderman, C. and Hough, M. (1994) *Does the Criminal Justice System Treat Men and Women Differently?* London: Home Office Research and Planning Unit.

Hedderman, C. and Moxon, D. (1992) *Magistrates' Court or Crown Court? Mode of Trial Decisions and Sentencing*, London: HMSO.

Herbert, A. (2003) 'Mode of trial and magistrates' sentencing powers: will increased powers inevitably lead to a reduction in the committal rate?', *Criminal Law Review* 314.

HM Chief Inspector of Prisons (1997) *Women in Prison: A Thematic Review*, London: Home Office.

HM Inspectorate (1999) *Police Integrity: Securing and Maintaining Public Confidence*, London: Home Office Communication Directorate.

Hohfeld, W. N. and Cook, W. W. (1919) *Fundamental Legal Concepts as Applied in Judicial Reasoning*, London: Greenwood Press.

Holland, L. and Spencer, L. (1992) *Without Prejudice? Sex Equality at the Bar and in the Judiciary*, London: Bar Council.

Home Office (2003) *Statistics on Women and the Criminal Justice System*, London: Home Office.

—— (2004) *Are Special Measures Working? Evidence from surveys of vulnerable and intimidated witnesses*, Home Office Research Study 283, London: Home Office.

—— (2004) *One Step Ahead: A 21st Century Strategy to Defeat Organised Crime*, London: Stationery Office.

—— (2005) *Exclusion or Deportation from the UK on Non-conducive Grounds*, London: Home Office.

—— (2004) *Modernising Police Powers to meet Community Needs*, London: Home Office.

—— (2007) *Asset Recovers Action Plan*, London: Home Office.

—— (2007) *Modernising Police Powers: Review of the Police and Criminal Evidence Act 1984*, London: Home Office.

—— (2003) *Statisticson Race and the Criminal Justice System*, London: Home Office.

—— (2006) *Making Sentencing Clearer*, London: Home Office.

—— (1990) *Crime, justice and protecting the public*, Cm 965, London: HMSO.

Home Office Research Development and Statistics Directorate (2000) *Jury Excusal and Deferral* (Research Findings No. 102).

Honess, T., Charman, E. and Levi, M. (2003) 'Factual and Effective Recall of Pretrial Publicity: Their Relative Influence on Juror Reasoning and Verdict in a Simulated Fraud Trial' [2003] Journal of Applied Social Psychology Volume 33 Issue 7, 1404.

Hood, R., Shute, S. and Seemungal, F. (2003) *Ethnic Minorities in the Criminal Courts: perceptions of fairness and equality of treatment*, London: Lord Chancellor's Department.

Horowitz, I. and Fosterlee, L. (2001) 'The effects of note-taking and trial transcript access on mock jury decisions in a complex civil trial' 25 *Law and Human Behaviour* 373.

Hucklesby, A. (2004) 'Not necessarily a trip to the police station: the introduction of street bail', *Criminal Law Review* 803.

Hutton, Lord, J. B. (2004) *Report of the Inquiry into the Circumstances Surrounding the Death of Dr David Kelly C.M.G.*, London: Stationery Office.

Idriss, M. (2004) 'Police perceptions of race relations in the West Midlands', *Criminal Law Review* 814.

Ingman, T. (1987) *English Legal Process*, London: Blackstone Press.

Jackson, R. M. (1989) *The Machinery of Justice in England*, Cambridge: Cambridge University Press.

Johnson, N. (2005) 'The training framework review – what's all the fuss about?', 155 *New Law Journal* 357.

Joseph, M. (1981) *The Conveyancing Fraud*, London: Woolwich.

—— (1985) *Lawyers Can Seriously Damage Your Health*, London: Michael Joseph.

Kakalik, J. and others (1996) *An Evaluation of Judicial Case Management under the Civil Justice Reform Act*, California: Rand Corporation.

Kairys, D. (1998) *The Politics of Law: A Progressive Critique*, New York: Basic Books.

Kelsen, H. (1949) *General Theory of Law and State*, Cambridge, Mass: Harvard University Press.

Kennedy, H. (1992) *Eve was Framed: Women and British Justice*, London: Chatto.

King, M. and May, C. (1985) *Black Magistrates: A Study of Selection and Appointment*, London: Cobden Trust.

Law Commission (1976) *Criminal Law: Report on Conspiracy and Criminal Law Forum*, London: HMSO.

—— (1982) *Offences Against Public Order*, London: HMSO.

—— (1999) *Bail and the Human Rights Act 1998* (Report No. 157), London: HMSO.

Laws, J. (1998) 'The limitations of human rights', *Public Law* 254.

Lee, S. (1986) *Law and Morals*, Oxford: Oxford University Press.

Leigh, L. and Zedner, L. (1992) *A Report on the Administration of Criminal Justice in the Pretrial Phase in London, France and Germany*, London: HMSO.

Leng, R. (1993) *The Right to Silence in Police Interrogation* (Royal Commission on Criminal Justice Research Study No. 10), London: HMSO.

Lester, A. (1984) 'Fundamental Rights: The United Kingdom Isolated?' (1984) Pub. L. 46.

Levi, M. (1988) 'The Role of the Jury in Complex Cases' in Findlay, M. and Duff, P. (eds.) (1988) *The Jury under Attack*, London: Butterworths.

—— (1992) *The Investigation, Prosecution and Trial of Serious Fraud*, London: HMSO.

Lidstone, K. (1984) *Magisterial Review of the Pre-Trial Criminal Process: A Research Report*, Sheffield: University of Sheffield Centre for Criminological and Socio-Legal Studies.

Lightman, J. (2003) 'The Civil Justice System and legal profession – the challenges ahead', *Civil Justice Quarterly* 235.

Llewellyn, K. (1962) *Jurisprudence: Realism in Theory and Practice*, Chicago: University of Chicago Press.

Lloyd-Bostock, S. (2007) 'The Jubilee line jurors: does their experience strengthen the argument for judge-only trial in long and complex fraud cases', *Criminal Law Review* 255.

Locke, J. (1967) *Two Treatises of Government*, London: Cambridge University Press.

Lord Chancellor's Department (2000) *The House of Lords: Completing the Reform*, CM 5291, London: TSO.

—— (1998) *Determining Mode of Trial in Either Way Cases*, London: Lord Chancellor's Department.

—— (2002) *Further Findings: A Continuing Evaluation of the Civil Justice Reforms*, London: Lord Chancellor's Department.

—— (2003) *Delivering Value for Money in the Criminal Defence Service*, Consultation Paper, London: Lord Chancellor's Department.

Macpherson Report (1999) Cm 4262-I, London: HMSO.

Maine, Sir H. (1917) *Ancient Law*, London: Dent.

Mair, G. and May, C. (1997) *Offenders on Probation* (Home Office Research Study No. 167), London: HMSO.

Making Simple CFAs a Reality (2004), London: Department for Constitutional Affairs.

Malleson, K. (1993) *A Review of the Appeal Process* (Royal Commission on Criminal Justice Research Series No. 17), London: HMSO.

Malleson, K. and Roberts, S. (2002) 'Streamlining and Clarifying the Appellate Process', *Criminal Law Review* 272.

Mansfield, M. (1993) *Presumed Guilty: The British Legal System Exposed*, London: Heinemann.

Markus, K. (1992) 'The Politics of Legal Aid' in *The Critical Lawyer's Handbook*, London: Pluto Press.

Martinson, R. (1974) 'What Works? Questions and Answers About Prison Reform The Public Interest', 35: 22–54.

Marsh, N. (1971) 'Law reform in the United Kingdom: A new institutional approach', 13 *William and Mary Law Review* 263.

Marx, K. (1933) *Capital*, London: Dent.

Matthews, R., Hancock, L. and Briggs, D. (2004) *Jurors' Perceptions, Understanding Confidence and Satisfaction in the Jury Systems: A Study in Six Courts*, London: Home Office.

Mayhew, L. and Reiss, A. (1969) 'The social organisation of legal contacts' [1969] 34 American Soc. Rev. 309.

McCabe, S. and Purves, R. (1972) *The Jury at Work: A Study of a Series of Jury Trials in which the Defendant was Acquitted*, Oxford: Blackwell.

McConville, M. (1992) 'Videotaping Interrogations: Police Behaviour On and Off Camera', *Criminal Law Review* 532.

McConville, M. and Baldwin, J. (1977) *Negotiated Justice: Pressures to Plead Guilty*, Oxford: Martin Robertson.

—— (1981) *Courts, Prosecution and Conviction*, Oxford: Oxford University Press.

McConville, M. and Hodgson, J. (1993) *Custodial Legal Advice and the Right to Silence* (Royal Commission on Criminal Justice Research Study No. 16), London: HMSO.

McConville, M., Sanders, A. and Leng, P. (1993) *The Case for the Prosecution: Police Suspects and the Construction of Criminality*, London: Routledge.

Mendelle, P. (2005) 'No detention please, we're British?', 155 *New Law Journal* 77.

Mill, J. S. (1859) *On Liberty*, London: J. W. Parker.

Millar, J., Bland, N. and Quinton, P. (2000) *The Impact of Stop and Search on Crime and the Community*, Police Research Series Paper 127, London: Home Office.

—— (2000) *Upping the PACE? An Evaluation of the Recommendations of the Stephen Lawrence Inquiry on Stop and Search*, Police Research Series Paper 128, London: Home Office.

Modernising Justice (1997) Cm 4155, London: Home Office.

Montesquieu, C. (1989) *The Spirit of the Laws*, Cambridge: Cambridge University Press.

Moore, R. (2003) 'The use of financial penalties and the amounts imposed: The need for a new approach', *Criminal Law Review* 13.

Moore, R. (2004) 'The methods for enforcing financial penalties: the need for a multidimensional approach', *Criminal Law Review* 728.

Moorhead, R. *et al.*, (2001) *Quality and Cost: Final Report on the Contracting of Civil, Non-family Advice and Assistance*, London: TSO.

Moorhead, R. and Cape, E. (2005) *Demand Induced Supply? Identifying Cost Drivers in Criminal Defence Work*, London: Legal Services Commission.

Morgan, R. and Russell, N. (2000) *The Judiciary in the Magistrates' Courts* (Home Office RDS Occasional Paper No. 66), London: Home Office.

Moxon, D. (1985) *Managing Criminal Justice: A Collection of Papers*, London: HMSO.

Moxon, D. and Crisp, D. (1994) *Case Screening by the Crown Prosecution Service: How and Why Cases are Terminated*, London: HMSO.

Mullins, C. (1990) *Error of Judgement: The Truth About the Birmingham Bombings*, Dublin: Poolbeg Press.

Narey, M. (1997) *Review of Delay in the Criminal Justice System*, London: Home Office.

National Audit Office (2005) *Facing Justice: Tackling Defendants Non-attendance at Court* (HC 1162), London: TSO.

—— (1999) *Criminal Justice Working Together*, London: Stationery Office.

—— (2003) *Community Legal Service: The Introduction of Contracting*, HC 89, 2002–03, London: HMSO.

National Association of Citizens Advice Bureaux (1995) *Barriers to Justice: CAB Client's Experience of Legal Services*, London: NACAB.

—— (1999) *A Balancing Act: Surviving the Risk Society*, London: NACAB.

—— (2006) *CPS: effective use of magistrates' court hearings*: London: Stationery Office.

New Zealand Law Commission (2001) *Juries in Criminal Trials*, Report 69, Wellington.

Nobles, R. (2005) 'The Criminal Cases Review Commission: establishing a workable relationship with the Court of Appeal', *Criminal Law Review* 173.

No More Excuses – A New Approach to Tackling Youth Crime in England and Wales (1998), London: Home Office.

Norwich Union (2004) *A modern compensation system: moving from concept to reality*, Norwich: Norwich Union.

Nozick, R. (1975) *Anarchy, State, and Utopia*, Oxford: Blackwell.

Nuttall, C., Goldblatt, P. and Lewis, C. (1998) *Reducing Offending: An Assessment of Research Evidence on Ways of Dealing with Offending Behaviour* (Home Office Research Study No. 187), London: Home Office.

Olivercrona, K. (1971) *Law as Fact*, London: Stevens.

Ormerod, D. (2003) 'ECHR and the Exclusion of Evidence: Trial Remedies for Article 8 Breaches?', *Criminal Law Review* 61.

Ormerod, D. and Roberts, A. (2003) 'The Police Reform Act 2002 – Increasing Centralisation, Maintaining Confidence and Contracting Out Crime Control', *Criminal Law Review* 141.

Owers, A. (1995) 'Not Completely Appealing', 145 *New Law Journal* 353.

Packer, H. (1968) *The Limits of the Criminal Sanction*, Stanford, California: Stanford University Press.

Pannick, D. (1987) *Judges*, Oxford: Oxford University Press.

Parliamentary Penal Affairs Groys (1999) *Changing Offending Behaviour – Some Things Work*, London: Parliament.

Partington, M. (2004) 'Alternative Dispute Resolution: Recent Developments, Future Challenges', *Civil Justice Quarterly* 99.

Paterson, A. (1982) *The Law Lords*, London: Macmillan.

Peach, Sir L. (1999) *Appointment Processes of Judges and Queen's Counsel in England and Wales*, London: HMSO.

Philips, C. (1981) *The Royal Commission on Criminal Procedure*, Cmnd 8092, London: HMSO.

Pickles, J. (1988) *Straight from the Bench*, London: Coronet.

Pleasence, P. (2004) *Causes of action: civil law and social justice*, London: HMSO.

Plotnikoff, J. and Wilson, R. (1993) *Information and Advice for Prisoners about Grounds for Appeal and the Appeal Process* (Royal Commission on Criminal Justice Research Study No. 18), London: HMSO.

Pound, R. (1968) *Social Control Through Law*, Hamden: Archon Books.

Quinton, P., Bland, N. and Miller, J. (2000) *Police Stops, Decision-making and Practice*, Police Research Series Paper 130, London: Home Office.

Quirk, H. (2006) 'The significance of culture in criminal procedure reform: why the revised disclosure scheme cannot work', 10 *International Journal of Evidence and Proof* 42.

Race and the Criminal Justice System: an overview to the complete statistics 2003–2004 (2005) London: Criminal Justice System Race Unit.

Raine, J. and Walker, C. (2002) *The Impact of the Courts and the Administration of Justice of the Human Rights Act 1998*, London: Lord Chancellor's Department, Research Secretariat.

Ramsbotham, Sir D. (1997) *Women in Prison*, London: Home Office.

Rawls, J. (1971) *A Theory of Justice*, Oxford: Oxford University Press.

—— (1972) *Political Liberalism, John Dewey Essays in Philosophy*, New York: Columbia University Press.

Renton, D. (1975) *The Preparation of Legislation*, London: HMSO.

Restorative justice: helping to meet local need (2004), London: Office for Criminal Justice Reform.

Review of the Crown Prosecution Service (The Glidewell Report) (1998) Cm 3960, London: HMSO.

Robertson, G. (1993) *Freedom, The Individual and The Law*, London: Penguin.

Royal Commission on Criminal Justice Report (1993), Cm 2263, London: HMSO.

Royal Commission for the Reform of the House of Lords, Report of the (2000) *A House for the Future*, Cm 4534, London: HMSO.

Runciman, G. (1993) *Report of the Royal Commission on Criminal Justice*, London: HMSO.

Ryan, E. (2007) 'The unmet need: focus on the future', 157 *New Law Journal* 134.

Sanders, A., Hoyle, C., Morgan, R. and Cape, E. (2001) 'Victim Impact Statements: Don't Work, Can't Work', *Criminal Law Review* 447.

Sanders, A. (1993) 'Controlling the Discretion of the Individual Officer', in Reiner, R. and Spencer, S. (eds.) *Accountable Policing*, London: Institute for Public Policy Research.

Sanders, A. and Bridge, L. (1982) 'Access to Legal Advice', in Walker, C. and Starmer, K. (eds.) *Justice in Error*, London: Blackstone Press.

Sanders, A. *et al.* (1989) *Advice and Assistance at Police Stations and the 24 hour Duty Solicitor Scheme*, London: Lord Chancellor's Department.

Scarman, L. (1982) *The Scarman Report: The Brixton Disorders, 10–12 April, 1981*, London: Penguin Books.

Schur, E. (1965) *Crimes Without Victims: Deviant Behaviour and Public Policy, Abortion, Homosexuality, Drug Addiction*, New York: Prentice-Hall.

Sherman, L. and Strang, H. (2007) *Restorative Justice: The Evidence*, London: The Smith Institute.

Skryme, Sir T. (1979) *The Changing Image of the Magistracy* (2nd edn, 1983), London: Macmillan.

Smith and Bailey: see Bailey, S. and Gunn, M. (2002) *Smith and Bailey on the Modern English Legal System* (2nd edn), London: Sweet & Maxwell.

Smith, D. and Gray, J. (1983) *Police and People in London* (The Policy Studies Institute), Aldershot: Gower.

Smith, J. C. and Hogan, B. (2002) *Criminal Law*, London: Butterworths.

Smith, R. *et al.* (2007) *Poverty and Disadvantage among Prisoners' Families*, London: Joseph Rowntree Foundation.

Spencer, J. R. (2006) 'Does our present criminal appeal system make sense?', *Criminal Law Review* 677.

Stern, V. (1987) *Bricks of Shame: Britain's Prisons*, London: Penguin.

Steyn, J. (2001) '**Pepper** *v* **Hart**: A Re-examination', *Oxford Journal of Legal Studies* 59.

Summers, R. (1992) *Essays on the Nature of Law and Legal Reasoning*, Berlin: Duncker & Humblot.

Supperstone, M., Stilitz, D. and Sheldon, C. (2006) 'ADR and Public Law', *Public Law* 299.

Tain, P. (2003) 'Master of the game?', *Solicitors Journal* 192.

Tata, C. *et al.* (2004) 'Does mode of delivery make a difference to criminal case outcomes and clients' satisfaction? The public defence solicitor experiment', *Criminal Law Review* 120.

Taylor, R. (1997) *Cautions, Court Proceedings and Sentencing in England and Wales 1996*, London: Home Office.

Thomas, D. (1970) *Principles of Sentencing: The Sentencing Policy of the Court of Appeal Criminal Division*, London: Heinemann.

—— (2004) 'The Criminal Justice Act 2003: Custodial sentences', *Criminal Law Review* 702.

Tonry, M. (1996) *Sentencing Matters*, Oxford: Oxford University Press.

Twining, W. and Miers, D. (1991) *How To Do Things With Rules*, London: Weidenfeld & Nicolson.

Vennard, J. (1985) 'The Outcome of Contested Trials', in Moxon, D. (ed.) *Managing Criminal Justice*, London: HMSO.

Vennard, J. and Riley, D. (1988a) 'The use of peremptory challenge and stand by of jurors and their relationships with trial outcome', *Criminal Law Review* 723.

—— (1988b) *Triable Either Way Cases: Crown Court or Magistrates' Court?* London: HMSO.

Vogt, G. and Wadham, J. (2003) *Deaths in custody: redress and remedies*, London: Liberty.

Wade, Sir W. (2000) 'Horizons of horizontability', 116 *Law Quarterly Review* 217.

Wakeham, Lord (2000) *A House for the Future*, Cm 4534, London: HMSO.

Waldron, J. (1989) *The Law*, London: Routledge.

Warnock, M. (1986) *Morality and the Law*, Cardiff: University College Cardiff.

Weber, M. (1979) *Economy and Society*, Berkeley: University of California Press.

White, P. and Power, I. (1998) *Revised Projections of Long Term Trends in the Prison Population to 2005*, London: Home Office.

White, P. and Woodbridge, J. (1998) *The Prison Population in 1997*, London: Home Office.

White, R. (1973) 'Lawyers and the Enforcement of Rights', in Morris, P., White, R. and Lewis, P. (eds.) *Social Needs and Legal Action*, Oxford: Martin Robertson.

Whittaker, C. and Mackie, A. (1997) *Enforcing Financial Penalties*, London: Home Office.

Williams, G. (1983) *Textbook of Criminal Law*, London: Stevens and Sons.

Willis, J. (1938) 'Statutory interpretation in a nutshell', 16 *Canadian Bar Review* 13.

Windlesham, Lord (2005) 'The Constitutional Reform Act 2005: Ministers, judges and constitutional change, Part 1', *Public Law* 806.

Wolfenden, J. (1957) 'Report of the Committee on Homosexual Offences and Prostitution', Cmnd 2471, London: HMSO.

Women in Prison: A Thematic Review (1997), London: Home Office.

Woodhead, Sir P. (1998) *The Prison Ombudsman's Annual Report*, London: Home Office.

Woodhouse, D. (2007) 'The Constitutional Reform Act 2005 – defending judicial independence the English way', 5(1) *International Journal of Constitutional Law* 153.

Wooler, S. (2006) *Review of the Investigation and Criminal Proceedings Relating to the Jubilee Line Cases*, London: H.M. Crown Prosecution Service Inspectorate.

Woolf, Lord Justice H. (1995) *Access to Justice: Interim Report to the Lord Chancellor on the Civil Justice System in England and Wales*, London: Lord Chancellor's Department.

—— (1996) *Access to Justice*, London: Lord Chancellor's Department.

Yarrow, S. (1997) *The Price of Success: Lawyers, Clients and Conditional Fees*, London: Policy Studies Institute.

Young, J. (1971) *The Drugtakers: The Social Meaning of Drug Use*, London: Paladin.

Young, S. (2005) 'Clementi: in practice', 155 *New Law Journal* 45.

Your Right to Know (1997) Cm 3818, London: HMSO.

Zander, M. (1988) *A Matter of Justice*, Oxford: Oxford University Press.

—— (1998) 'The Government's plans on civil justice', 61 *Modern Law Review* 382.

—— (1999) *The Law-Making Process*, London: Butterworths.

—— (2000) 'The complaining juror', 150 *New Law Journal* 723.

—— (2001a) 'Should the legal profession be shaking in its boots?', 151 *New Law Journal* 369.

—— (2001b) 'A question of trust', *Solicitors Journal* 1100.

—— (2005) 'The Prevention of Terrorism Act 2005', 155 *New Law Journal* 438.

—— (2006) 'Mission Impossible', 156 *New Law Journal* 618.

—— (2007) 'Carter's wake (1)', 157 *New Law Journal* 872.

—— (2007) 'Carter's wake (2)', 157 *New Law Journal* 912.

—— (2007) 'Full speed ahead?', 157 *New Law Journal* 992.

—— (2007) 'Change of PACE', 157 *New Law Journal* 504.

Zander, M. and Henderson, P. (1993) *Crown Court Study*, London: HMSO.

Glossary

Absolute discharge When a court has found a person guilty it can order an *absolute discharge*. This will be done where the court believes that in the circumstances it is unnecessary to punish the person. It effectively means that no action is taken at all against the individual.

Actus reus Comprises all the elements of a criminal offence other than the state of mind of the defendant.

Administrative law The body of law which deals with the rights and duties of the state and the limits of its powers over individuals.

ADR An abbreviation for 'alternative dispute resolution'. It refers to methods of resolving disputes outside the traditional court forum.

Adversarial system A legal system which puts considerable emphasis on a public trial where the parties are able to present evidence orally and the judge merely plays the role of an arbiter. The adversarial system is frequently contrasted with an inquisitorial system.

Advisory, Conciliation and Arbitration Service (ACAS) This body mediates in many industrial disputes and unfair dismissal cases.

Advocates General These assist the judges in the European Court of Justice. They produce opinions on the cases assigned to them, indicating the issues raised and suggesting conclusions. Their opinions do not bind the judges but are frequently followed in practice.

Alternative dispute resolution (ADR) Methods of resolving disputes outside the traditional court forum.

Anti-social behaviour order Section 1 of the Crime and Disorder Act 1998 provides that an anti-social behaviour order (ASBO) can be made against a person aged 10 or over who has acted in an anti-social manner and is likely to do so again. Anti-social behaviour is behaviour that is likely to cause harassment, alarm or distress to someone not in the same household. While the ASBO is obtained using civil procedures, breach of the ASBO can give rise to the criminal sanctions of a fine or imprisonment.

Appropriate adult An adult who accompanies the young offender in the police station. They may be any responsible adult, including the young person's parent or a social worker.

Arbitrators Individuals who hear arbitration cases. They may be lawyers or experts in the subject of the dispute.

Arraignment The process whereby the accused is called to the Bar of the court to plead guilty or not guilty to the charges against him or her.

Bail Bail may be granted to a person accused of an offence, convicted or under arrest. When a person is granted bail it means that they are released under a duty to attend a court or police station at a given time.

Bar Council   The governing body for barristers. It acts as a kind of trade union, safeguarding the interests of barristers, and also as a watchdog, regulating barristers' training and activities.

BarDIRECT   A scheme under which individuals and organisations, such as police forces and insurers, may be approved by the Bar Council to instruct barristers directly.

Bench   A term used to describe the judge or judges (including magistrates) who sit and hear a case.

Bill of Rights   A statement of the basic rights which a citizen can expect to enjoy.

Binding over to be of good behaviour   This order can be made against any person who has breached the peace. People who are bound over have to put up a sum of money and/or find someone else to do so; this sum will be forfeited if the undertaking is broken. The order usually lasts for a year.

Bye-laws   A form of delegated legislation made by local authorities, public and nationalised bodies.

Cab rank rule   Under the cab rank rule, barristers must accept any case which falls within their claimed area of specialisation and for which a reasonable fee is offered, unless they have a prior engagement.

Case management   The court, and in particular the judge, is the active manager of the litigation.

Case stated   Under this procedure, a person who was a party to a case before the magistrates (or the Crown Court when it is hearing an appeal from the magistrates) may question the decision of the court on the ground that there was an error of law or the court had acted outside its jurisdiction. The party asks the court to state a case for the opinion of the High Court on the question of law or jurisdiction.

Caution   1. A warning to an accused person administered on arrest or before police questioning. Since the abolition, by the Criminal Justice and Public Order Act 1994, of the right to silence, the correct wording is: 'You do not have to say anything. But it may harm your defence if you do not mention when questioned something which you later rely on in court. Anything you do say may be given in evidence.'
   2. A formal warning given to an offender about what he or she has done, designed to make him or her see that he or she has done wrong and deter him or her from further offending. This process is used instead of proceeding with the prosecution.

Caution-plus   Sir Robin Auld has recommended that a system of *caution-plus* should be introduced. This would allow the prosecutor, with the consent of the offender, to impose a caution combined with a condition as to their future conduct where a minor offence is alleged to have been committed. Offenders would be brought before the court if they breached one of the conditions.

Certiorari   An order quashing an *ultra vires* decision.

Chambers   The offices of a barrister.

Claimant   The party who issues legal proceedings.

Class action   A claimant or small group of claimants bring an action for damages on behalf of a whole class of claimants.

Committal proceedings An initial hearing in the magistrates' courts for triable either-way offences. They are designed to allow the magistrates to check that there is sufficient evidence to proceed to a full Crown Court trial and to filter out weak cases.

Community sentence This means a sentence of one or more community orders.

Conditional fee agreement A lawyer agrees to take no fee or a reduced fee if he or she loses a case, and raises the fee by an agreed percentage if it is won, up to a maximum of double the usual fee.

Constitution A set of rules and customs which detail a country's system of government; in most cases it will be a written document but in some countries, including Britain, the constitution cannot be found written down in one document and is known as an unwritten constitution.

Contingency fee A fee payable to a lawyer (who has taken on a case on a 'no win, no fee' basis) in the event of him or her winning the case.

Convention 1. A long-established tradition which tends to be followed, although it does not have the force of law.
 2. A treaty with a foreign power.

Conveyancing The legal process of transferring an interest in land.

Corporation aggregate This term covers groups of people with a single legal personality (e.g. a company, university or local authority).

Corporation sole This is a device which makes it possible to continue the official capacity of an individual beyond their lifetime or tenure of office; e.g. the Crown is a corporation sole; its legal personality continues while individual monarchs come and go.

Council on Tribunals A body that was established following the 1957 Franks Report. It exercises an advisory role over the tribunal system. It has 10 to 15 members appointed by the Lord Chancellor.

Counsel's opinion A barrister's advice.

CPS An abbreviation for 'Crown Prosecution Service'. This institution brings criminal prosecutions on behalf of the state.

Cracked trial A case in which public money and administration is wasted because, once the court room is booked and the parties ready to proceed with a full trial, the defendant pleads guilty, leaving no time to arrange for another case to slot into the court timetable.

Criminal Defence Service This has replaced the old system of criminal legal aid. Through the Legal Services Commission, the Criminal Defence Service provides direct funding for the provision of criminal legal services, employs public defenders and pays for duty solicitor schemes.

Crown Prosecution Service (CPS) This institution brings criminal prosecutions on behalf of the state.

Curfew Home detention curfews were introduced by the Crime and Disorder Act 1998. Released prisoners under a curfew are required to remain at a certain address at set times, during which period they will be subjected to electronic monitoring.

Custody officer The police officer who has responsibility for the welfare of any individual being held in detention in the police station. One of the ways he or she does this is by maintaining a custody record.

Custody plus   Under a system of custody plus, an offender spends a maximum of three months in custody, and is then released and subjected to a minimum six months' post-release supervision in the community. A court can attach specific requirements to the sentence, based upon those available under a community sentence.

Custom   'Such usage as has obtained the force of law' (**Tanistry Case**, 1608).

Deferred sentence   A court is allowed to delay passing a sentence for up to six months after conviction.

Delay defeats equities   Where a claimant takes an unreasonably long time to bring an action, equitable remedies will not be available.

Directives   A form of European legislation discussed on p. 331.

Disclosure of documents   The procedure whereby one party to an action provides the other party with a list of documents relating to the action which are or have been in his or her possession. The other party can then ask to see some or all of the documents.

Divisional Court   This is also known as the Queen's Bench Division and is a Division of the High Court. The major part of its work is handling those contract and tort cases which are unsuitable for the county courts. Its judges also hear certain criminal appeals and applications for judicial review.

Double jeopardy   In the past once a person had been tried and acquitted they could not be retried for the same offence, under the principle of double jeopardy. The application of this principle has been significantly reduced by the Criminal Justice Act 2003.

Draft Bill   A proposed piece of legislation.

Duty solicitors   Solicitors working under the duty solicitor schemes. They are available to give free legal advice at police stations and magistrates' courts.

Either-way cases   Criminal cases that can be tried either in the magistrates' court or in the Crown Court.

***Ejusdem generis* rule**   General words which follow specific ones are taken to include only things of the same kind.

Enabling Act   An Act of Parliament which grants the power to make delegated legislation.

Equity   In law it is a term which applies to a specific set of legal principles which were developed by the Chancery Court and add to those provided in the common law.

Executive   The administrative arm of the state.

Expert witness   A person who is not a party to legal proceedings, but who provides expert evidence to the court.

Expressio unius est exclusio alterius   Express mention of one thing implies the exclusion of another.

Freemasonry   A secret society with an all-male membership. Among its stated aims is the mutual advancement of its members.

Habeas corpus   This is an ancient remedy which allows people detained to challenge the legality of their detention and, if successful, to get themselves quickly released.

Hereditary peers   These are members of the British aristocracy who inherit their title.

He who comes to equity must come with clean hands   This means that a claimant who has been in the wrong in some way will not be granted an equitable remedy.

He who seeks equity must do equity   Anyone who seeks equitable relief must be prepared to act fairly towards his or her opponent.

Indictable offences   These are the more serious offences, such as rape and murder. They can only be heard by the Crown Court. The indictment is a formal document containing the alleged offences against the accused, supported by brief facts.

Inquisitorial system   A legal system where the judge plays a dominant role in collecting evidence before the trial. The final trial is often just to rubber-stamp the investigating judge's findings.

Intermediate recidivist   An offender in his or her late twenties or early thirties with a criminal record dating back to childhood.

Judicial review   The courts undertake a review of the process that has been followed in making a decision and can make sure that the public authority had the power to make this decision.

Jury vetting   This consists of checking that the potential juror does not hold 'extremist' views which some feel would make them unsuitable for hearing a case. It is done by checking police, Special Branch and security service records.

Justice of the Peace   An alternative name for lay magistrates.

Law centres   Offices which offer a free, non-means-tested legal service to people who live or work in their area.

Law Commission   A government body that considers possible reforms of the law.

Law Officers   They are the Attorney-General and the Solicitor-General.

Law Society   The solicitors' professional body.

Lawyer   This is a general term which covers both branches of the legal profession, namely barristers and solicitors, as well as many people with a legal qualification.

Leap-frog procedure   This is the procedure provided for in the Administration of Justice Act 1969, whereby an appeal can go directly from the High Court to the House of Lords, missing out the Court of Appeal.

Legal executive   A member of the Institute of Legal Executives, who frequently carries out legal work within a firm of solicitors or as an in-house lawyer.

Limited liability partnerships   These were created in 2001. Solicitors can choose to form a limited liability partnership. Under this type of partnership a partner's liability is limited to negligence for which he or she was personally responsible.

Lord Chancellor   A government minister who used to be responsible for the Lord Chancellor's Department.

Lord Chief Justice   He or she presides over the Criminal Division of the Court of Appeal.

Mandamus   An order requiring a particular thing to be done.

Master of the Rolls   He or she presides over the Civil Division of the Court of Appeal.

McKenzie friend   A litigant in person may take with him to the court or tribunal someone to advise him (a McKenzie friend), but that person may not usually address the court.

Means test   This looks at the financial position of the applicant for state funding.

Mediation   This is an alternative method of dispute resolution. A mediator is appointed to help the parties to a dispute reach an agreement which each considers acceptable.

Mens rea   Traditionally refers to the state of mind of the person committing the crime.

Natural law   A kind of higher law, to which we can turn for a basic moral code. Some, such as St Thomas Aquinas, see this higher law as coming from God, others see it simply as the basis of human society.

Obiter dicta   This is Latin and can be translated as 'things said by the way'. All the parts of the judgment which do not form part of the *ratio decidendi* of the case are called *obiter dicta*. This part of the judgment is merely persuasive and not binding.

Orders in Council   A form of delegated legislation made by government in times of emergency. They are approved by the Privy Council and signed by the Queen.

Parenting order   A court order designed to help and support parents (or guardians) in addressing their child's anti-social behaviour.

Parliament   Consists of the House of Commons, the House of Lords and the monarch.

Per incuriam   Where a previous decision has been made in ignorance of a relevant law it is said to have been made *per incuriam*.

Pilot schemes   These are established to test in selected areas the impact of reforms that could subsequently be introduced more widely.

Plaintiff   This is the old term used to describe the person who issued legal proceedings. Following reforms introduced to civil litigation in 1999, the plaintiff is now known as the claimant.

Plea bargaining   This is the name given to negotiations between the prosecution and defence lawyers over the outcome of a case; e.g. where a defendant is choosing to plead not guilty, the prosecution may offer to reduce the charge to a similar offence with a smaller maximum sentence in return for the defendant pleading guilty to that offence.

Practice direction   An official announcement by the court laying down rules as to how it should function.

Pre-action protocol   A code of conduct for pre-trial proceedings.

Prohibition   An order prohibiting a body from acting unlawfully in the future; e.g. it can prohibit an inferior court or tribunal from starting or continuing proceedings which are, or threaten to be, outside their jurisdiction, or in breach of natural justice.

Public Bills   Proposals for a piece of legislation that have been prepared by the Cabinet.

Public defenders   Defence lawyers who are employed by the Legal Services Commission. They are based in regional offices, can provide the same services as lawyers in private practice and have to compete for work.

Puisne judges   High Court judges are also known as puisne judges (pronounced puny) meaning junior judges.

Pupillage   A one-year apprenticeship in which pupils assist a qualified barrister, who is known as their pupil master.

Queen's Bench Division   A Division of the High Court. The major part of its work is handling those contract and tort cases which are unsuitable for the county courts. Its judges also hear certain criminal appeals and applications for judicial review.

Queen's Counsel   Senior members of the barrister profession.

Ratio decidendi   This is Latin and can be translated as the 'reason for deciding'. The *ratio decidendi* of a judgment is the legal reasons on which the decision is based.

Remand   Detention prior to a conviction or sentencing where bail has been refused.

Restorative justice   Offenders are required to provide a remedy to their victims or the community at large.

Retribution   Retribution is concerned with recognising that the criminal has done something wrong and with taking revenge on behalf of both the victim and society as a whole.

Rights of audience   The rights to carry out advocacy in front of a court.

Royal Assent   A procedure under which the monarch consents to the passing of legislation. It transforms a Bill into an Act of Parliament.

Royal Commission   These are established to study a particular area of law reform, usually as a result of criticism and concern about the area involved.

Secret soundings   A process which involves civil servants in the Lord Chancellor's Department gathering information about potential candidates for judicial office over a period of time by making informal inquiries from leading barristers and judges.

Small claims track   This is a procedure used by the county courts to deal with claims under £5,000.

Solicitor advocates   Solicitors who have successfully completed the additional training required in order to exercise their rights of audience before the higher courts.

Sovereignty of Parliament   This has traditionally meant that the law which Parliament makes takes precedence over that from any other source, but this principle has been qualified by membership of the European Union.

Stand by   As members of the jury panel are called and before they are sworn in, the prosecution may ask for them to *stand by*, without giving any reasons for this. They will then not be able to sit on the jury.

Stare decisis   This is Latin and can be translated as 'let the decision stand'. Under this principle, once a decision has been made on how the law applies to a particular set of facts, similar facts in later cases should be treated in the same way.

Statutory charge   Where a person has received state funding for civil proceedings, if the costs recovered from the other party and the contributions made by the state-funded party do not cover the amount paid by the state, the difference can be recovered from the damages awarded by the court (subject to certain restrictions in matrimonial cases). Where the statutory charge applies, the state funding is more like a loan.

Stereotype   A presumption as to the characteristics of a group of people.

Stipendiary magistrates   These judges are now known as 'district judges (magistrates' court)'. They are professional judges who sit in the magistrates' court.

Summary offences   These are the most minor crimes and are only triable summarily in the magistrates' courts. 'Summary' refers to the process of ordering the defendant to attend court by summons, a written order usually delivered by post, which is the most frequent procedure adopted in the magistrates' court.

Tariff system   The tariff sentencing system is based on treating like cases alike: people with similar backgrounds who commit similar offences in similar circumstances should receive similar sentences.

Ultra vires   This is Latin and can be translated as 'beyond the powers'. It refers to the situation where a public authority has overstepped their powers.

Veto   A power to block a decision.

Wednesbury principle   This principle, which was laid down in **Associated Picture Houses Ltd *v* Wednesbury Corporation**, is that a decision will be held to be outside a public body's power if it is so unreasonable that no reasonable public body could have reached it.

Woolf Report   The official name of the Woolf Report is *Access to Justice*, which was published in 1996. It is the report of the review of the civil courts which was chaired by Lord Woolf and was the basis for the reforms to the civil justice system that were introduced in 1999.

Youth court   Young offenders are usually tried in youth courts (formerly called juvenile courts), which are a branch of the magistrates' court. Youth courts must sit in a separate court room, where no ordinary court proceedings have been held for at least one hour. Strict restrictions are imposed as to who may attend the sittings of the court.

Zero tolerance   A concept that was developed in the US during Ronald Reagan's time in office; it has come to mean that the law will be strictly enforced in order to reduce crime.

Answers to exercises

Chapter 1 The civil courts

Quick quiz 1.1

1 The burden of proof is usually on the claimant who must prove his/her case on the balance of probabilities.
2 The Courts and Legal Services Act 1990.
3 *Access to Justice*.
4 Queen's Bench Division, Family Division, Chancery Division.

Quick quiz 1.2

1 They priaritise preparation for a settlement.
2 26 April 1999.
3 The overriding objective is that the Civil Procedure Rules should enable the courts to deal with cases justly.
4 Yes. See r. 1.1(2) of the Civil Procedure Rules, discussed on p. 5.

Task 1.3

1 Cases for a claim worth between £3,000 and £5,000.
2 Cases for a claim worth more than £50,000.

Quick quiz 1.4

1 A claimant.
2 A claim form.
3 The county court.
4 Compliance with a pre-action protocol is not compulsory, but if a party unreasonably refuses to comply, then this can be taken into account when the court makes orders for costs.
5 The judge in court.

Know your terms 1.5

1 The *Queen's Bench Division* is a Division of the High Court. The major part of its work is handling those contract and tort cases which are unsuitable for the county courts. Its judges also hear certain criminal appeals and applications for judicial review.
2 The official name of the Woolf Report is *Access to Justice*, which was published in 1996. It is the report of the review of the civil courts which was chaired by Lord Woolf and was the basis for the reforms to the civil justice system that were introduced in 1999.
3 See p. 8.
4 See p. 8.

Know your terms 1.6

1 See p. 12.
2 See p. 10.
3 Under the disclosure procedures, the parties are required to disclose the documents on which they intend to rely and also the documents which go against their case.
4 See p. 12.

Task 1.7

1 Access to justice.
2 There is no fixed answer to this question.
3 An interim report is a report which is published before the final report, and contains the provisional proposals which, following consultation, may be changed in the final report.
4 No, the government has adopted most of Lord Woolf's proposals.

Quick quiz 1.9

1 Small claims track, fast track and multi-track.
2 The small claims track.
3 See p. 18.
4 Case management tended to increase costs.

Chapter 2 Civil appeals

Quick quiz 2.1

1 Either the court that made the disputed decision, or the appellate court itself.
2 Three.
3 The Civil Division of the Court of Appeal.
4 The Court of Appeal does not hold a full rehearing of the case.

Chapter 3 Alternative methods of dispute resolution

Know your terms 3.1

1 An *adversarial process* places an emphasis on a public trial where the parties are able to present evidence and question the evidence of the other parties. The judge plays only a limited role in the trial proceedings. This type of procedure is frequently contrasted with an inquisitorial system.
2 *Arbitrators* hear arbitration cases. They may be lawyers or experts in the subject of the dispute.
3 *ADR* stands for 'alternative methods of dispute resolution'.
4 *ACAS* stands for 'Advisory, Conciliation and Arbitration Service'. This body mediates in many industrial disputes and unfair dismissal cases.

Quick quiz 3.2

1 The Advisory, Conciliation and Arbitration Service (ACAS).
2 The Family Law Act 1996.
3 The Association of British Travel Agents (ABTA).
4 The Arbitration Act 1996.

Chapter 4 The police

Quick quiz 4.1

1 The Human Rights Act 1998.
2 Article 6.
3 The successful appeal of the Birmingham Six.
4 Lord Runciman.

Quick quiz 4.2

1 Police and Criminal Evidence Act 1984.
2 Criminal Justice and Public Order Act 1994.
3 They do not form part of the law and breach of these codes cannot be the ground for a
   legal action, but can give rise to disciplinary procedures.
4 The Home Office.

Quick quiz 4.3

1 Section 1 of PACE.
2 Code of Practice A.
3 See pp. 58–59.
4 When a member of the public detains a person suspected of committing a crime.

Chapter 5 Criminal courts

Task 5.1

Type of offence	Trial court
Summary	Magistrates' court
Triable either way	Magistrates' court or Crown Court
Indictable offence	Crown Court

Task 5.2

1 A motoring offence.
2 There is no fixed answer to this question.
3 46 per cent.

Chapter 6 Criminal appeals

Task 6.1

1 The House of Lords.
2 The Criminal Division.
3 Decrease.
4 The House of Lords' workload had remained the same until 2001 when it increased
   slightly. This increase has levelled out in recent years.

Quick quiz 6.2

1 The High Court.
2 The House of Lords.
3 1 per cent.
4 New evidence can be admitted if the Court of Appeal thinks it 'necessary or expedient in the interests of justice': Criminal Appeal Act 1968, s. 23(1).

Task 6.3

1 A stakeholder in this context is anyone with an interest in the service provided by the CCRC, with includes lawyers and convicts, and ultimately includes all members of the public.
2 The backlog in undecided cases.
3 An increase in the number of cases being referred to it and problems with recruiting staff.

Know your terms 6.4

1 See p. 31.
2 The *Divisional Court* is also known as the Queen's Bench Division and is discussed at p. 4.
3 See p. 94.
4 See p. 92.

Quick quiz 6.5

1 1995.
2 Where the court thinks the conviction is unsafe.
3 See p. 92.
4 The High Court.

Chapter 7 Principles of sentencing

Quick quiz 7.1

1 Punishment, reduction of crime, reform and rehabilitation, protection of the public and reparation.
2 Criminals often act on impulse.
3 See p. 105.
4 Yes. The research *Restorative Justice: the Evidence* (2007) found that the victim's symptoms of post traumatic stress disorder are reduced, partly because meeting their offender demystifies the offence.

Chapter 8 Court sentencing powers

Task 8.1

1 Some parents felt that they had been forced to become unpaid jailers.
2 No.
3 The aim should be to make a real impact on crime figures and reoffending rates.

Quick quiz 8.2

1 The judge.
2 Life imprisonment.
3 See p. 113.
4 Their licence can be revoked and they can be recalled to prison.

Quick quiz 8.3

1 See pp. 118–121.
2 £36,000.
3 75,000.
4 More.

Know your terms 8.5

1 *Retribution* is concerned with recognising that the criminal has done something wrong and with taking revenge on behalf of both the victim and society as a whole.
2 When a court has found a person guilty it can order an *absolute discharge*. This will be done where the court believes that in the circumstances it is unnecessary to punish the person. It effectively means that no action is taken at all against the individual.
3 Anti-social behaviour orders are provided for in s. 1 of the Crime and Disorder Act 1998. They are civil orders issued by a court to protect the public from behaviour that causes harassment, alarm and distress.
4 Where a person is discriminated against because of their sex.

Chapter 9 The judiciary

Know your terms 9.1

1 The process of *secret soundings* involved civil servants in the Lord Chancellor's Department gathering information about potential candidates for judicial office over a period of time by making informal inquiries from leading barristers and judges.
2 A judge in the House of Lords.
3 The *Master of the Rolls* presides over the Civil Division of the Court of Appeal.
4 The *Lord Chief Justice* presides over the Criminal Division of the Court of Appeal.

Task 9.2

1 No.
2 Horse hair.
3 No.

Quick quiz 9.3

1 The Criminal Division of the Court of Appeal.
2 The body responsible for administering the judicial appointments process.
3 The Judicial Studies Board.
4 The doctrine of the separation of powers was first put forward by the eighteenth-century French political theorist, Montesquieu. This doctrine states that the only way to safeguard individual liberties is to ensure that the power of the state is divided between three

separate and independent arms: the judiciary, the legislature and the executive. The idea is that each arm of the state should operate independently, so that each one is checked and balanced by the other two and none becomes all-powerful.

Quick quiz 9.4

1 Dismissal, discipline, resignation, retirement and removal.
2 The French political theorist, Montesquieu.
3 66.
4 No.

Know your terms 9.5

1 The *executive* is the administrative arm of the state.
2 *Freemasonry* is a secret society with an all-male membership. Among its stated aims is the mutual advancement of its members.
3 The *Law Society* is the solicitors' professional body.
4 A *stereotype* is a presumption as to the characteristics of a group of people.

Chapter 10 The legal profession

Know your terms 10.1

1 The *Law Society* is the governing body of the solicitor profession.
2 *Conveyancing* is the legal process of transferring an interest in land.
3 *Rights of audience* are the rights to carry out advocacy in front of a court.
4 *Solicitor advocates* are solicitors who have successfully completed the additional training required in order to exercise their rights of audience before the higher courts.

Quick quiz 10.2

1 98,000.
2 They automatically acquire full rights of audience on becoming qualified, though they are only able to exercise these rights on completion of the necessary additional training.
3 98 per cent.
4 Legal Complaints Service.

Task 10.3

1 The Office of Fair Trading has suggested that the rank of QC inflates the prices of barristers' services. The Bar Council argue that it is an important quality mark which directs the clients to experienced, specialist lawyers as required.

Know your terms 10.4

1 *Limited liability partnerships* were created in 2001. Solicitors can choose to form a limited liability partnership. Under this type of partnership a partner's liability is limited to negligence for which he or she was personally responsible.
2 The *Bar Council* is the governing body for barristers. It acts as a kind of trade union, safeguarding the interests of barristers.

3 *Pupillage* is a one-year apprenticeship in which pupils assist a qualified barrister, who is known as their pupil master.

4 *Queen's Counsel* are senior members of the barrister profession.

Task 10.6

1 The person who uses the legal services.

2 Competition can ensure that professional fees are not higher than they need to be and that the professional rules do not unnecessarily inhibit efficiency.

3 Standards, integrity and concern for the client.

4 In trying to achieve a minor goal, something very valuable may be lost.

Chapter 11 Magistrates

Quick quiz 11.1

1 The Lord Chancellor appoints lay magistrates in the name of the Crown.

2 The Local Advisory Committees interview candidates for the lay magistracy and make recommendations to the Lord Chancellor as to who should be appointed.

3 An applicant must be under 65 and live within 15 miles of the commission area for which he or she is appointed.

4 The Judicial Appointments Commission.

Know your terms 11.2

1 *Stipendiary magistrates* are now known as 'district judges (magistrates' court)'. They are professional judges who sit in the magistrates' court.

2 The term *Justice of the Peace* is an alternative name for lay magistrates.

3 *The Bench* is the term used to describe the judge or judges (including magistrates) who sit and hear a case.

4 *Royal Commissions* are established to study a particular area of law reform, usually as a result of criticism and concern about the area concerned. They are discussed on p. 344.

Quick quiz 11.4

1 See p. 191.

2 Three.

3 The primary function of the justices' clerk is to advise the lay magistrates on law and procedure. They are not supposed to take any part in the actual decision of the Bench.

4 See p. 195.

Chapter 12 The jury

Quick quiz 12.1

1 No.

2 18–70.

3 Yes – see the case of **R v Abdroikov** (2005).

4 No, a majority verdict is now possible.

Quick quiz 12.2

1 See p. 205.
2 Where a jury has been reduced to 10, then a majority of nine votes is required. For a full jury a majority of 10 is required.
3 No.
4 You could have cited **R v Kronlid** (1996) or **R v Ponting** (1985).

Task 12.3

1 Yes.
2 No.

Quick quiz 12.4

1 On the ground that the jury's decision had been perverse.
2 The matter has not yet been considered by the European Court of Human Rights, but Sir Robin Auld thought that the Convention right was probably not violated.
3 A trial in a magistrates' court.
4 No.

Know your terms 12.5

1 *Jury vetting* consists of checking that the potential juror does not hold 'extremist' views which some feel would make him/her unsuitable for hearing a case. It is done by checking police, Special Branch and security service records.
2 As members of the jury panel are called and before they are sworn in, the prosecution may ask for them to *stand by*, without giving any reasons for this. They will then not be able to sit on the jury.
3 A summary offence is an offence that can only be tried in the magistrates' court.
4 Jury nobbling occurs when inappropriate pressure is put on a juror to reach a verdict regardless of the evidence.

Chapter 13 Paying for legal services

Quick quiz 13.1

1 April 2000.
2 The Legal Services Commission.
3 The Fundery code sets out the criteria and procedures to be used when deciding whether a particular case should be funded.
4 The five categories are:
  ■ Legal Help.
  ■ Legal Representation.
  ■ Help at Court.
  ■ Approved Family Help.
  ■ Family Mediation.

Know your terms 13.2

1 See p. 229.
2 A *means test* looks at the financial position of the applicant for state funding.

3 The *Criminal Defence Service* has replaced the old system of criminal legal aid. Through the Legal Services Commission, the Criminal Defence Service provides direct funding for the provision of criminal legal services, employs public defenders and pays for duty solicitor schemes.

4 *Public defenders* are defence lawyers who are employed by the Legal Services Commission. They are based in regional offices, can provide the same services as lawyers in private practice and have to compete for work.

Task 13.4

1 A person being detained in a police station is in a very vulnerable position and access to a free lawyer aims to prevent miscarriages of justice. However, a minority of people detained in the police station are rich enough to pay for the services of a lawyer.

2 There might, for example, be cases which are particularly serious or where the detainee is particularly vulnerable (perhaps due to their age or disability) that make it particularly important that they see a lawyer.

3 Some defendants who turned up at court without a lawyer would have to represent themselves. They might not be able to express themselves clearly.

4 It may cause delay. Hearings may need to be postponed until a defendant has found a lawyer.

5 The number is likely to increase.

Quick quiz 13.5

1 See p. 237.

2 See p. 238.

3 The research found that many people felt that the legal system had given them a second-rate service. The research criticised the apparent lack of commitment and poor communication of some solicitors. There were still not enough solicitors and advisers specialising in areas like social security, housing, disability, discrimination, employment and immigration law.

4 An area where appropriate state funded legal advice services are not available.

Know your terms 13.6

1 *Duty solicitors* work under the duty solicitor schemes. They are solicitors who are available to give free legal advice at police stations and magistrates' courts.

2 *Pilot schemes* are established to test in selected areas the impact of reforms that could subsequently be introduced more widely.

3 *Law centres* offer a free, non-means-tested legal service to people who live or work in their area.

4 Under a *conditional fee agreement* a lawyer can agree to take no fee or a reduced fee if he or she loses a case and to raise the fee by an agreed percentage if he/she wins, up to a maximum of double the usual fee.

Chapter 14 Judicial precedent

Know your terms 14.1

1 *Stare decisis*: this is Latin and can be translated as 'let the decision stand'. Under this principle, once a decision has been made on how the law applies to a particular set of facts, similar facts in later cases should be treated in the same way.

2 *Ratio decidendi*: this is Latin and can be translated as the 'reason for deciding'. The *ratio decidendi* of a judgment is the legal reason on which the decision is based.

3 *Obiter dicta*: this is Latin and can be translated as 'things said by the way'. All the parts of the judgment which do not form part of the *ratio decidendi* of the case are called *obiter dicta*.

Task 14.2

The judges in **Re Pinochet** were Lord Browne-Wilkinson, Lord Goff, Lord Nolan, Lord Hope and Lord Hutton.

Quick quiz 14.3

1 Case law, Acts of Parliament, delegated legislation and legislation of the European Union.
2 1966.
3 Where the previous decision was made in ignorance of a relevant law; there are two previous conflicting decisions; there is a later, conflicting House of Lords' decision; and a proposition of law was assumed to exist by an earlier court and was not subject to argument or consideration by that court.
4 The High Court.
5 When a decision of a lower court is overruled, the outcome of the decision remains the same. When it is reversed, the decision of the lower court is changed.
6 William Blackstone.

Task 14.4

1 In this context 'retrospectively' refers to the fact that judgments can have an effect on matters that occurred prior to the date that the decision was given.
2 See the first paragraph of the Practice Statement.
3 See the second paragraph of the Practice Statement.
4 See the third paragraph of the Practice Statement.

Chapter 15 Acts of Parliament

Task 15.2

A prohibition order prohibits a person from entering a place specified in the order for a maximum period of two years.

The explanatory notes state at paragraph 26 that:

'This Part of the Act provides for the extension of electronic monitoring. It creates a new disposal – an exclusion order – which can be used as a free-standing sentence or as a requirement of a community penalty. This order will require an offender to stay away from a certain place or places at certain times. Such monitoring is aimed at offenders who present a particular danger or nuisance to a particular victim or particular victims.'

Quick quiz 15.3

1 Green Paper.
2 Public Bill drafted.
3 First reading in the House of Commons.

4 Second reading in the House of Commons.
5 Committee stage in the House of Commons.
6 Report stage.
7 Third reading.
8 House of Lords considers the Public Bill.
9 Royal Assent.

Know your terms 15.4

1 *Hereditary peers* are members of the British aristocracy who inherit their title.
2 *Royal Assent* is when the monarch consents to the passing of legislation, transforming a Bill into an Act of Parliament.
3 *Public Bills* are proposals for a piece of legislation that have been prepared by the Cabinet.

Task 15.5

1 It prohibits the use of torture by the state.
2 The former leader of the Conservative Party.
3 They do not have the power to strike down Acts of Parliament, but can only declare an Act to be incompatible with the European Convention.

Chapter 16 Delegated legislation

Task 16.1

1 The Data Protection Act 1998 (Commencement) Order 2000 brought the 1998 Act into Force. The power to make the Order was granted by ss. 67(2) and 75(3) of the Data Protection Act 1998.
2 The main provisions of the Data Protection Act 1998 came into force on 1 March 2000.

Know your terms 16.2

1 In a *judicial review* hearing the courts undertake a review of the process that has been followed in making a decision and can make sure that the public authority had the power to make this decision.
2 The term *ultra vires* is Latin and can be translated as 'beyond the powers'. It refers to the situation where a public authority has overstepped its powers.
3 *Bye-laws* are a form of delegated legislation made by local authorities, public and nationalised bodies.
4 *Orders in Council* are a form of delegated legislation made by government in times of emergency. They are approved by the Privy Council and signed by the Queen.
5 An *enabling Act* is an Act of Parliament which grants the power to make delegated legislation.

Quick quiz 16.3

1 Statutory instruments, bye-laws and Orders in Council.
2 You could mention any of the following: insufficient parliamentary time, speed, technicality of the subject matter, need for local knowledge, flexibility and future needs.

3 Under the affirmative resolution procedure delegated legislation is laid before one or both Houses of Parliament and becomes law only if a motion approving it is passed within a specified time.

4 Procedural *ultra vires*, substantive *ultra vires* and unreasonableness.

Chapter 17 Statutory interpretation

Quick quiz 17.1

Any of the following cases could have been mentioned:

Literal rule	See **Whiteley** *v* **Chapell** (1868) and **Fisher** *v* **Bell** (1961) on p. 308
Golden rule	See **R** *v* **Allen** (1872), **Adler** *v* **George** (1964) and **Inco Europe Ltd** *v* **First Choice Distribution** (2000) on p. 309
Mischief rule	See **Smith** *v* **Hughes** (1960) and **Elliott** *v* **Grey** (1960) on p. 310

Quick quiz 17.2

1 The literal rule, the golden rule and the mischief rule.

2 The statute itself, rules of language and presumptions.

3 You could mention any of the following: the historical setting, dictionaries and text books, explanatory notes, reports that preceded the legislation, the Human Rights Act 1998 and *Hansard*.

4 The House of Lords ruled that *Hansard* could be consulted in order to determine the intention of Parliament when interpreting statutes.

Chapter 18 European law

Quick quiz 18.2

1 27.

2 The Commission, the Council, the European Parliament and the European Court of Justice.

3 This is discussed on p. 328.

4 Unanimity, simple majority and qualified majority. This is discussed on p. 330.

Know your terms 18.3

1 The *Advocates General* assist the judges in the European Court of Justice. They produce opinions on the cases assigned to them, indicating the issues raised and suggesting conclusions. These do not bind the judges but are frequently followed in practice.

2 A *veto* is a power to block a decision. The European Parliament has a power of veto over the appointment of the Commission as a whole.

3 The *European Commission* is discussed on p. 326.

4 *Directives* are a form of European legislation discussed on p. 332.

Chapter 19 Law reform

Quick quiz 19.2

1 The case went to the House of Lords. The *ratio decidendi* of a case is the legal principle on which the decision was based. In this case the *ratio decidendi* was that a man could be criminally liable for the offence of rape where the victim was his wife.
2 Repeal, creation, consolidation and codification.
3 There are various pressure groups which you could have given as examples. Some examples are given in the text at p. 342.
4 There is no right or wrong answer here. One of the reasons the government was opposed to the campaign was that known paedophiles were likely to move and hide their new addresses making them a greater danger to children as their movements could not be monitored by the police and social services.

Quick quiz 19.5

1 1965.
2 This is discussed on pp. 347–349.
3 Lord Scarman.
4 No.

Index